After Apartheid

After Apartheid

Reinventing South Africa?

Edited by Ian Shapiro and Kahreen Tebeau

University of Virginia Press

CHARLOTTESVILLE AND LONDON

University of Virginia Press
© 2011 by the Rector and Visitors of the University of Virginia
All rights reserved
Printed in the United States of America on acid-free paper

First published 2011

First paperback edition published 2012

ISBN 978-0-8139-2827-2 (paper)

9 8 7 6 5 4 3 2 1

The Library of Congress has cataloged the hardcover edition as follows:
Library of Congress Cataloging-in-Publication Data

After apartheid / reinventing South Africa? / edited by Ian Shapiro and Kahreen Tebeau.
    p.   cm.
  Includes bibliographical references and index.
  ISBN 978-0-8139-3097-8 (cloth: alk. paper) — ISBN 978-0-8139-3101-2 (ebook)
  1. Post-apartheid era—South Africa. 2. Democracy—South Africa. 3. South
Africa—Politics and government—1994– 4. South Africa—Social conditions—1994–
5. South Africa—Economic conditions—1991–   I. Shapiro, Ian. II. Tebeau, Kahreen,
1977–
  DT1971.A34 2011
  968.06—dc22

                                                                    2011006943

Contents

After Apartheid

Introduction

Ian Shapiro and Kahreen Tebeau

The new South Africa is a teenager. It seems only yesterday it was a miraculous young life, an infant bubbling with promise. How could one overstate the hope and enthusiasm that accompanied its improbable birth? Millions throughout the country and around the world cheered as long lines of first-time voters queued patiently for hours over those three days in late April 1994 to legitimate the peaceful transition from apartheid and select their first democratic government. The process has now been repeated in enough national, regional, and local elections that it has come to seem routine, yet it was a dream that many South Africans still living today never believed would come true.

South Africa's fourth national election, held in April 2009, was both a striking affirmation of the nascent democratic regime and a remarkable consolidation by the African National Congress (ANC) of its power. True, the ANC's 65.9 percent share of the vote was four percentage points less than it had won five years earlier. The decline cost the party thirty-three seats in Parliament, leaving it with 264 seats—three short of the two-thirds majority required unilaterally to change the constitution. The opposition Democratic Alliance (DA), led by Cape Town mayor Hellen Zille, won 16.7 percent of the vote and gained seventeen seats for a total of sixty-seven—its strongest showing ever. The DA also took control of the Western Cape provincial government, which had the important effect of curtailing the ANC's regional power.

Significant as these developments were, the larger story of the 2009 election was that South Africa's nascent political institutions had weathered their most serious constitutional crisis to date, and the ANC had survived the most internally threatening leadership crisis in its history. The dynamics by which these developments took place were less than prepossessing, but this scarcely differentiated South African politics from what we have witnessed in other struggling democracies, such as Mexico or Iraq, not to mention in such established democracies as Britain or the United States in recent decades.

Although less commented upon than the leadership struggle within the ANC, South Africa's successful navigation of a potentially destabilizing constitutional crisis between 2007 and 2009 is perhaps the more consequential development. Attending to what did not happen—to the dog that did not bark—does not typically commend itself to our attention. Yet it is worth reflecting on what was avoided in the run-up to the 2009 election. In mid-2005, supporters of President Thabo Mbeki began floating trial balloons about the possibility of changing the constitution to enable him to run for a third term as president. Initially he refused to rule out the possibility, but by early 2006 enough ANC bigwigs had weighed in against the idea that he was forced to back down.[1] During the same period, Mbeki's long-simmering conflict with his deputy president, Jacob Zuma, came to a head. Zuma was a populist who had built an independent base of support in COSATU, the trade union movement, and the left-leaning ANC Youth League. Zuma had long been a thorn in Mbeki's side, and when the opportunity presented itself, owing to a series of rape and corruption allegations, Mbeki seized the opportunity and fired Zuma in June 2005.[2]

But Mbeki broke a primal rule: if you're going to shoot an elephant, you'd better be sure to kill it. Zuma was acquitted of some of the charges, in some cases based only on technicalities, and succeeded by various legal maneuverings in getting the others postponed and ultimately dropped.[3] He mounted a challenge to Mbeki's leadership, provoking Mbeki to seek an additional term as leader of the ANC—even though he could not be president of the country for a third term. Zuma prevailed at a raucous ANC National Conference in Polokwane in December 2007, creating the anomaly that the country's president was no longer the leader of his political party. The potential for this situation to precipitate a major political crisis was manifest in South Africa's quasi-parliamentary system, in which the president is elected by, and relies on the continued confidence of, Parliament. Mbeki became increasingly isolated as his supporters were replaced in key ANC structures by Zuma's people. Mbeki resigned the presidency in September 2008 after being "recalled" by the ANC's National Executive Committee, following a court finding (that would later be reversed) of improper interference in

Zuma's corruption prosecution. The remaining charges against Zuma were dropped as a result of the alleged procedural improprieties, but he could not easily become president immediately because he was not a member of Parliament. Mbeki was replaced by the moderate deputy president, Kgalema Motlanthe, until Zuma could be installed in the presidency following the April 2009 elections.

At first blush, that a man with Zuma's checkered past has become president of South Africa might not seem to be a cause for celebration. But it is worth remembering that his election occurred at the same time as the last vestiges of democratic process were being dismantled by Robert Mugabe not very far to the north. President Mbeki scarcely distinguished himself by conspicuously refusing to deploy South Africa's soft power to try to tip the scales against Mugabe's power grab and attendant destruction of civil liberties in Zimbabwe, but it is notable how scrupulously procedural propriety was observed at home. No major player even hinted at overstepping the boundaries of his constitutional authority in the delicate power transitions from Mbeki to Motlanthe, and from Motlanthe to Zuma. Political opponents were not arrested. Press freedom was not curtailed. The April elections, marked by a high 77 percent turnout, were quickly declared to be free and fair by South Africa's Independent Electoral Commission and by international observers—still a comparative rarity in contemporary Africa.[4] No doubt this orderly transfer of power owed a good deal to the precedent set by Nelson Mandela in choosing to relinquish the presidency in 1999, but it is notable nonetheless that the potential for a major political crisis was averted.

This is to say nothing of the shakeup within the ANC. That a Zulu lacking any formal education could rise to the top of a political movement and party whose top leadership had long been in the control of Xhosa elites was remarkable enough. True, the ANC has large Zulu constituencies (even in Zulu-dominated KwaZulu Natal it has always polled at least 40 percent of the vote), and Zuma has impeccable credentials, given his history in Umkhonto we Sizwe (the military wing of the ANC) and the ten years he served in prison with Mandela on Robben Island. But others with comparable credentials and constituencies had been successfully outmaneuvered by Mbeki in the past, most notably Cyril Ramaphosa, the founder of the National Union of Mineworkers and secretary general of the ANC, and Tokyo Sexwale, former Gauteng premier, both of whom Mbeki edged aside when he succeeded Mandela in 1999.

It took considerable skill for Zuma to create a coalition powerful enough to displace the entrenched leadership. He had cultivated strong support

from COSATU and the ANC Youth League, both of which had had significant conflict with Mbeki. From time to time there had been speculation that
either group might precipitate splintering within the ANC, and perhaps
even the formation of a labor or populist breakaway party. But no one anticipated what actually happened: that these groups would sponsor what was
in effect Zuma's hostile takeover of the ANC itself.

The splinter group that actually materialized was no less improbable.
Mbeki loyalists, led by former defense minister and party chairman Mosiuoa
"Terror" Lekota, stormed out of the ANC in December 2008 and formed a
new party, the Congress of the People (COPE). The ANC split drew intense
media attention and was widely welcomed by South Africa's opposition parties. For a while it seemed that COPE might become a significant force, but
it was stymied from the outset by its lack of any real alternative to the ANC's
program, and it soon succumbed to internal squabbling. In February 2009
Lekota was unhorsed from COPE's leadership and replaced by a political
novice, a Methodist bishop named Mvume Dandala. In the April elections
COPE polled a disappointing 7.4 percent—less than half the DA's vote, and
considerably less than had been anticipated by the media.[5] This gave COPE
a mere thirty seats in Parliament. The only consolation COPE could glean
from the results was that it was the second largest party in four provincial
legislatures and had outdone the once formidable Inkatha Freedom Party,
the ethnic Zulu party, in the national election. (Inkatha polled less than
5 percent of the national vote, winning a mere eighteen seats, largely as a result of inroads made by Zuma's ANC into its voter base.) The big winner was
clearly the ANC, which had survived an internal earthquake without any
discernible damage to its national political hegemony.

It is conventional for political scientists to withhold the judgment that
a democracy has been consolidated until the governing party has twice lost
an election and peacefully handed over power.[6] By that stringent test the
United States was not a democracy until 1840, Japan and India have not
been democracies until very recently, and the jury remains out on many of
the newly democratizing countries that have emerged in Latin America and
the former communist world since 1989. Had the schism within the ANC
precipitated a more serious challenger than COPE, South Africa in its second
postapartheid decade might have begun to experience the kind of competitive politics that is needed for the democratic consolidation characterized by
alternation in government. As things have turned out, while there are elements of meaningful democratic competition, particularly in comparison
with much of the rest of Africa, the new South Africa remains a teenager.

Adolescent South African democracy has certainly brought its disappointments. Poverty and inequality, at some of the highest levels in the world, were not diminished under Mandela's or Mbeki's governments. The economy did not grow fast enough to put a dent in one of the world's highest unemployment rates. The staggering unemployment has in turn fueled ugly xenophobia, resulting in deadly eruptions against refugees and migrant workers from Zimbabwe and Mozambique. Rates of violent crime, particularly murder and rape, remain gruesomely high by both global and historical South African standards.[7] The HIV/AIDS pandemic has been shockingly mishandled at the highest levels of government. Infection rates continue to be overwhelming. Local infrastructure and service delivery have, in many respects, failed badly. The power grid is stretched beyond capacity. Black empowerment has accelerated the growth of an incipient black middle class and a tiny group of black million- and billionaires, yet it is widely derided for legion inefficiencies and ineffectiveness. Despite Zuma's populist background, rhetoric, and constituencies, it is doubtful that much of this will change under his leadership. The global financial crisis that erupted in late 2008 has made it unsurprising that Zuma's first order of business would be to reassure investors and financial markets that there would be no major policy changes. His cautious, not to say conservative, cabinet choices underscored that message.[8]

Yet things could certainly be worse. The country could have undergone any number of horrific transformations that have not occurred: toward brutal authoritarianism, economic disintegration, extended racial violence, civil war, or some combination of these. The situation in neighboring Zimbabwe is but one sobering reminder. There are many others: Algeria, Nigeria, Eritrea, and Somalia, to name a few. The potential for a catastrophically bad outcome in South Africa, particularly given the uncertainty that characterized the 1990–94 transition, should not be discounted. Many of the tens of thousands of white South Africans who fled in the face of the looming change anticipated dreadful developments that have not, as of yet, materialized. The government, though free of any meaningful electoral threat from a political opposition, by and large adheres to the constitution (and a very progressive one to boot). People go about their lives without fear of repression or political violence. Overall, the military and the police recognize their subordination to civilian political leaders. They have not become major contestants for political influence or power, as has often been the case in other African countries, as well as in South Africa itself under the Vorster and Botha regimes. The economy, at least prior to the 2008–9 global recession, was stable and steadily, if slowly, growing. Corruption, though present, is being highlighted and targeted. These achievements are not inconsiderable for a government that was a reinvented liberation movement less than two decades earlier.

Is this cause for optimism? In the early years after the transition the ANC government mirrored developments in former settler colonies such as Zimbabwe, Namibia, and Kenya. Like South Africa, both Namibia and Zimbabwe transitioned to independence under exceedingly popular parties that had functioned as the main liberation movements against predecessor white supremacist regimes. Kenya's Kenya African National Union (KANU) party had few ties with the Mau Mau resistance movement, even though party leaders eagerly posed as pro-Mau Mau sympathizers once they took power. In all of these countries the early years of independence were marked by relative economic stability and adherence to the rule of law, with particular emphasis on respect for property rights. Even Zimbabwe was hailed as a uniquely successful African story and a model of land reform by global institutions, including the World Bank.[9]

Given the similarities between the early years of these postliberation governments and South Africa's experience under the ANC, their later trajectories are bound to give us pause. Will South Africa's future trajectory under the ANC mirror those of Zimbabwe and Kenya, where the rise of opposition movements either from within the established parties or from opposition parties marked the full-scale plunge into more repressive politics and bad economic governance? People often cite the rise of the Movement for Democratic Change (MDC) in 1999 as the critical point in Zimbabwe, but the challenge by the Zimbabwe African People's Union (ZAPU) in the mid-1980s provoked an exceedingly violent response from Mugabe that saw the massive slaughter of people in ZAPU's stronghold in Matabeleland. In Kenya, the transition to multiparty democracy in 1992 was preceded in the late 1960s by repression against Oginga Odinga's Kenya People's Union (KPU), which had posed a serious challenge to KANU.

Our examination of the crisis associated with the transition from Mbeki to Motlanthe and then to Zuma is encouraging. Unlike ZANU-PF and KANU, the ANC showed a willingness not to use its popular support to stifle democracy and further consolidate its power. Unlike in Kenya, where the secession of Oginga Odinga from KANU to form the KPU sparked an authoritarian response from KANU (including the banning of the party and imprisonment of its leaders), COPE has been able to operate fairly freely in South Africa. The ANC has not tried to shift the country to an official one-party state, as KANU did in 1982. Moreover, Mbeki's rejection—however grudging—of the temptation to change the constitution to allow for a third term, along with Mandela's earlier willingness to step aside after one term, are hopeful signs. They reveal a party that has so far avoided the phenomenon of presidents with unlimited mandates that came to mark politics in Kenya and Zimbabwe.

Present and likely future challenges are daunting, to be sure, but they stand in need of realistic appraisal in light of successes and failures to date. That is what the contributors to this volume seek to provide. In the realms of politics, economics, health, the rule of law, language, literature, and the media, our contributors assess the changes to date with an eye to emerging challenges. These are the major policy areas that any government must confront and, as a middle-income developing country, South Africa must face them in an international context over which it has little—if any—control.

Being a price-taker in the global economy scarcely distinguishes South Africa from the rest of the continent, so the question arises whether South Africa's national liberation movement-turned-government reveals anything new about the art of government in Africa. Was the Mandela-Mbeki era merely another example of newly democratizing states, to be assessed with the conventional wisdom of political science, or did something new and innovative emerge from this experience of governing a complex and divided society with the limited resources of the postapartheid state?

Many of the essays that follow reflect serious pessimism, but it is worth emphasizing that there are few cases in which a nationalist liberation movement, originally aimed at overthrowing an oppressive regime (rather than at governance), has managed to move so far in the direction of democracy and comparatively good government as has the ANC. As well as the failed fledgling democracies already mentioned (Chad and the Congo could be added to the list), there have been many cases in which nationalist movements that aimed to overthrow the colonial order gave way directly to decades of authoritarianism. Morocco, Tunisia, Gabon, the Central African Republic, Mali, and Ivory Coast are all cases in point. Considered in comparative perspective, South Africa's progress toward democratic consolidation is remarkable. A teenager, perhaps, but a teenager in a region of unruly toddlers.

To the extent that South Africa's success to date has depended on contingencies of restraint in leadership, it is difficult to extrapolate optimism into the future. Whether or not present and future leaders will turn out be restrained when such restraint is needed will depend, in substantial part, on the personal character of Zuma and his successors in circumstances that cannot be foreseen. In any case it would be imprudent to load too much in the way of expectations on contingencies of leadership. As James Madison warned his contemporaries two centuries before the South African transition, it is unwise to count much on enlightened leadership in politics, because "enlightened statesmen will not always be at the helm."[10]

But there are perhaps less ephemeral reasons to think that the ANC took the reins of power better prepared to govern in 1994 than has typically been the case in postcolonial Africa and that the country the ANC inherited made the task more manageable than was the case elsewhere on the subcontinent. For one thing, most other anticolonial movements had fairly short histories, leaving them ill-prepared to govern. The ANC had existed for decades and had developed functioning organizational structures both at home and abroad. That, together with the comparatively ordered pace of the transition, meant that it had considerably more time to develop a coherent plan of action and functioning institutions in order to step in and govern once apartheid crumbled. Moreover, the transition itself was more carefully "pacted" than was the case with most other decolonizations, providing for amnesty and National Party participation as a junior partner in the new government. This provided a high degree of predictability and continuity, which surely helped with international investors as well as local players who might be tempted to defect.[11]

Second, despite the history of apartheid and immense inherited inequality, South Africa and the ANC leadership have enjoyed substantial advantages over many of the continent's postindependence ex-colonies. The postapartheid state is high capacity in a number of respects: richer, more urbanized, with long-functioning institutions. Even with its significant shortfalls in local service delivery, South Africa's infrastructure and energy consumption are substantially superior to the rest of sub-Saharan Africa's.[12]

A third factor concerns the quantity and continuity of human capital. Whites have lived in South Africa since the seventeenth century, and at almost 4.3 million they represent more than 9.5 percent of the population.[13] Unlike Algeria's settlers, who decamped on decolonization, creating serious economic upheaval, the greater part of South Africa's white community has stayed—in defiance of predictions to the contrary. This means that despite the challenges posed by affirmative action (not least white resentment), the new South Africa has inherited a sizable skilled community by most measures, which bodes well for the future. There is always the possibility that they will leave, but it seems a plausible conjecture that the 20 percent who have left since the transition are those for whom the impulse to go was strongest and the costs of exit lowest.[14]

Considering human capital more broadly, South Africa has been comparatively well endowed since independence, and this has continued into the postapartheid era. In 1965, secondary school enrollments were three times higher in South African than elsewhere in the region. Attainment rates were also higher in South Africa in this period for both secondary and tertiary education. The average years of schooling for the population over age twenty-five was three times higher in South Africa than in the region. Moreover, whereas tertiary education of women was negligible across the region, it stood at about 6 percent in South Africa.[15]

In 1995 the South African population was still notably better educated than that of sub-Saharan Africa. Gross enrollment ratios in secondary education in South Africa were about four times the average for the region, and twice that in neighboring Zimbabwe. The gap in tertiary education was even larger: in South Africa six people enrolled in tertiary education for every person who did so in the region. Attainment rates were double those elsewhere in Sub-Saharan Africa. Not surprisingly, public spending on education was also much higher in South Africa. In 1995 it spent about 6.8 percent of its GNP on education—double that of the average sub-Saharan African country.[16] This meant that the ANC was handed the best-educated workforce in the region, if not on the entire African continent. These relative advantages should be kept in mind as we explore the achievements and challenges of the early postapartheid decades.

PART I: POLITICS AND THE MACROECONOMY

In our opening essay, Jeremy Seekings points to a clear failure on the part of the government to significantly redress the extreme levels of poverty and inequality in South Africa, but he also suggests avenues by which progress can be made in the future. He starts by sifting through a veritable mountain of conflicting studies and data, concluding that both poverty and inequality actually worsened in the first five years after apartheid. He attributes the causes of continuing high levels of poverty and inequality to various factors. An economic growth path that discourages job creation for the low-skilled has contributed to the extremely high unemployment rates. This, coupled with a low-quality educational system for the poor, perpetuates poverty and inequality—though this is somewhat mitigated by a remarkably redistributive social welfare system. He argues that only by changing labor market policy to reduce the cost of labor or by expanding the social welfare net can poverty and inequality be significantly reduced.

In the next essay, Anthony Butler takes a critical look at the evolving set of policies known under the umbrella term of black economic empowerment (BEE). He explains that although BEE could have taken many forms, including the nationalized socialism called for by the South African Communist Party, BEE has been limited in practice to transfers of shares in businesses to black entrepreneurs and preferential state procurement policies favoring businesses scoring high on the BEE "scorecard." In response to criticisms that the initial phase of BEE empowered only a tiny elite minority of blacks, the government unveiled "broad-based black economic empowerment" (BBBEE) in 2003. The problem with both BEE and BBBEE, Butler points out, is that black businesspeople lack capital, and therefore the very ambitious goal of transferring 25 percent ownership of the private economy to black people is not realizable under any short- to medium-term time horizon. In addition to the general infeasibility of its own targets, BEE has been plagued by a number of other defects. Because of the shortage of black capital, BEE deals are often achieved through costly and risky financing schemes, leaving them vulnerable to economic downturns, such as those emerging in 2008 and 2009. The sustainability of BEE deals is therefore a cause for concern. The heavy regulatory burden BEE places on individual companies could also discourage much-needed foreign direct investment in South Africa, as well as damage the competitiveness of domestic enterprises in the world market. Perhaps even more troubling, BEE, as with any policy located at the nexus of business and politics, creates fertile ground for state patronage and corruption. Finally, and more fundamentally, it is debatable whether those black businesspeople owning shares in BEE companies are in fact empowered at all, or whether they serve as "fronts" for what continues in practice to be white-dominated business. Butler offers a glimmer of hope for the future of BEE, though, suggesting that "as BEE becomes a more established aspect of conventional business practice, the greatest potential threats it poses will be reduced."

In the next essay, Robert Mattes asks to what extent the ANC has managed to foster various forms of democratic legitimacy since 1994. The particular forms he looks at include a shared sense of national identity, irrespective of skin color or ethnic background; a sense of the inherent (as opposed to instrumental) value of the democratic regime, as well as the moral authority of its bureaucratic institutions; and finally a commitment on the part of citizens to active democratic participation. Avid democrats do not simply come into being because a country undergoes a democratic transition; they must be forged. In this endeavor, Mattes argues, the ANC has been only partially successful. A widespread identification with a common "South Africanness" has flourished, but support for the democratic regime is still relatively lukewarm and is also, surprisingly, much lower than in many other African countries. The perceived legitimacy of state institutions is also lower than one might have hoped, in part because of the ANC's drive to instill political hegemony within these institutions at the expense of their bureaucratic autonomy. Finally, South Africans' political engagement and participation rank abysmally low, both absolutely and when compared with their African counterparts'. Engagement at the local government level has been increasing, but Mattes argues that at the national level, fundamental institutions, such as the electoral system, need to be changed to foster deeper citizen participation in, and legitimacy of, the democratic system.

In looking at the role of business during and after the transition, Theuns Eloff in the next essay finds reasons for optimism. He documents how business, through a loose organization called the Consultative Business Movement, provided significant support and facilitation for the peace process and transition, and continues, in the form of the National Business Initiative, to play a positive role in socioeconomic development. Several impediments to an ideal business environment still exist, including a shortage of skilled labor, heavy regulatory burdens, and crime, but Eloff insists that it is as much in the interest of business as it is in the interest of wider society to tackle these obstacles together, through public-private partnerships. Despite the amplitude of the problems that need to be addressed to increase growth and employment, Eloff is hopeful that the South African economy will continue to grow, and that business, along with its proactive role, will continue to grow along with it.

Concluding the section on politics and the macroeconomy, Janine Aron offers a synoptic look at the major achievements in South Africa's macroeconomic policy governance and performance since 1994, and the remaining obstacles to increasing economic growth. Fiscal policy—or policies relating to taxation and government expenditure—has been a resounding success. Revenues have increased, even as the overall tax burden has been lowered, and spending has been prudently redirected toward much-needed social services, such as education, welfare, and health care. The budget deficit and overall debt have also been significantly reduced. Monetary policy has also seen major improvements since the ANC government took office in 1994, particularly with the advent of inflation targeting in 2000. This has contributed to increased monetary policy credibility and transparency and has resulted in lower levels of inflation, lower real interest rates, and reduced currency volatility. These achievements have contributed to an overall success story in terms of South African economic growth. Like Seekings and Eloff, Aron argues that there remains considerable room for improvement, especially in developing a higher-quality educational system to alleviate the acute skills shortage. But Aron is confident that South Africa will continue into the next decade to reap the benefits of this new macroeconomic policy framework.

PART II: HEALTH AND SOCIAL WELFARE

In the opening essay of this section, Nicoli Nattrass explores the causes and consequences of President Mbeki's AIDS denialism. In a country that now has one of the highest HIV prevalence rates in the world, it is shocking that the head of government and state would actively try to prevent the use of antiretrovirals—which have been proven effective in the fight against HIV/AIDS—yet this is exactly what Mbeki and his health minister did throughout his presidency. Why? Nattrass explores various possible explanations, ranging from an anticolonial distrust of Western science to Mbeki's peculiar personality traits, his revolutionary background, and finally cold hard capitalist economics, yet she finds none of these explanations entirely satisfactory. Whatever the reasons for Mbeki's denialism, it has led to the loss of hundreds of thousands of lives. It has also undermined the scientific governance of medicine in South Africa. Nattrass notes that this problem remains a central challenge, but is pessimistic as to whether it will be addressed adequately under the Zuma government.

The AIDS debate in South Africa takes place against the backdrop of a robust panoply of social and economic rights that have been enshrined in the constitution. What these guarantees have meant on the ground is taken up by Lauren Paremoer and Courtney Jung in the following essay. The ANC, which commands a huge majority—if no longer a supermajority—in Parliament, faces little meaningful electoral opposition to its policies. Democratic scholars largely concur that opposition is necessary for ensuring a healthy democracy, particularly by ensuring government accountability. Paremoer and Jung argue, though, that the government can still be, and has been, held accountable, not by an opposition party in Parliament but rather by civil society through the courts. Socioeconomic rights, such as the rights to housing and health care, have provided individual citizens and civil society organizations the basis for challenging the government when it fails to deliver on these rights. The authors examine three court cases, all of which were heard before the Constitutional Court, to illuminate how the existence of socio-economic rights has expanded the sphere for public deliberation of policy and government accountability. Paremoer and Jung argue that these court cases facilitate public deliberation by producing public information, in the form of testimony, affidavits, and evidence. They also increase government accountability by requiring the government publicly to justify its policies in terms of its constitutional obligations. And when the government has not provided adequate justification, such as in the Treatment Action Campaign (TAC) case involving the government's failure to provide nevirapine for the prevention of mother-to-child transmission of HIV, the Court has brought judgment against the government and ordered it to change its policy.

Paremoer and Jung argue that using the Court as a site of opposition is especially effective when it is coupled with other political strategies, as the TAC case also demonstrates. Thus, although the future of formal oppositional politics in South Africa looks bleak, at least in the short term, the protection of social and economic rights in the constitution may provide an alternative, and potentially potent, avenue by which to promote the deliberation and accountability necessary to a healthy democracy. Their discussion leads naturally to a larger consideration of legality and the rule of law, the subject of the essays in part III.

PART III: THE RULE OF LAW

In the opening essay of this section, David Dyzenhaus inquires into the extent to which the rule of law has been established in postapartheid South Africa. He assures us that the new South Africa has made an explicit commitment to the supremacy of the constitution and the rule of law, yet he argues that this is not what differentiates it from the old apartheid order. Indeed, the old regime also recognized the supremacy of the constitution and upheld the ideal of legality in its functioning. What differentiates the new order from the old, Dyzenhaus explains, is that the apartheid regime upheld only a procedural conception of legality—in other words, actions by government officials had to be backed up by a warrant in law. However, heinous acts were made legal under this system because the officials carrying them out were authorized by Parliament. In contrast, the new regime is bound not only by this procedural conception of legality but also by a substantive conception, which requires that the rights and liberties ensconced in the constitution, as well as common law principles such as reasonableness, must also be protected. The content of the law matters. Officials of the new South

Africa may not trample someone's liberties simply because they have been authorized by Parliament to do so.

Dyzenhaus welcomes this departure from the old apartheid days, but warns that it is not enough. The Constitutional Court—South Africa's court of final appeal on all constitutional matters—must also be vigilant in defending its own independence. Here Dyzenhaus notes that there have been troubling examples of the ANC government attempting to sidestep, ignore, or completely defy the Court. Whether South Africa degenerates into a "prerogative state," in which officials act in a legally uncontrolled and unaccountable manner, or whether it will continue to uphold either or both conceptions of legality will depend on this vigilance.

In the next essay, Marianne Camerer explores the controversy of corruption surrounding the new South African president, Jacob Zuma, and deploys novel data to assess the degree to which institutional mechanisms are in place to combat and prevent corruption, and to evaluate whether these mechanisms are functioning in practice. On paper, South Africa boasts an impressive array of anticorruption legislation, as well as extensive oversight and enforcement agencies. Its central anticorruption law is considered even by international standards to be comprehensive. In practice, the law functions fairly effectively, earning South Africa an overall "moderate" rating from the international NGO Global Integrity, which measures the existence and effectiveness of anticorruption mechanisms in forty-three countries around the world.

But Camerer notes that there are important exceptions to this overall positive picture, most notably those laws dealing with whistle-blower protection and public access to information. Whistle-blowers, despite being explicitly protected by law, are often harassed or dismissed. And although there are channels for citizens to request access to government records, too often these requests are ignored. Additionally, some tools are notably absent from South Africa's anticorruption legislation, the most important being a law regulating post–public-sector employment, as well as laws regulating the disclosure of private funding for political parties. It is not difficult to see how corruption could pose a risk in either of these contexts.

Despite its anticorruption reform efforts, South Africa has not been spared several high-profile corruption scandals, including the infamous arms deal and Travelgate scandals. To strengthen the system's ability to prevent these abuses, Camerer urges reforms relating to the disclosure and regulation of political party funding, as well as a strengthened Parliament, which can more effectively oversee the executive. Unfortunately, there is little sign of the necessary political will to implement these reforms, leaving us with a decidedly mixed picture of anticorruption efforts in South Africa.

Lungisile Ntsebeza in the following essay deals with another major aspect of the law in South Africa: the right to property and its relation to land reform. During the colonial era, nearly 90 percent of the land in South Africa was taken from indigenous Africans and settled by white farmers. The dawn of democracy in 1994 brought high hopes for many of an extensive land reform program that would redistribute the land from white farmers back to blacks. In 1994 the ANC adopted the World Bank's recommendation that 30 percent of the land be transferred within the first five years of democracy. After five years, only a paltry 1 percent had been transferred from white to black ownership, and after fifteen years only 5 percent had been transferred.

Ntsebeza tries to understand the causes of this general land reform failure. He argues that the entrenchment of private property rights in the constitution is the most important obstacle to a successful land reform program in South Africa. True, the constitution also permits the government to expropriate property for the public interest—a provision that could and has been used for land reform purposes—but Ntsebeza argues that this clause is inadequate as the foundation for land reform. For one thing, it clearly sits uneasily beside the clause protecting private property rights, and thus is open to legal challenge. For another, expropriation is permitted, but only when accompanied by "agreed" compensation or, failing agreement, by compensation that is determined by a court of law to be "just and equitable." The ANC government opted for the former avenue of "agreed" compensation, adopting a "willing buyer, willing seller" principle. Unfortunately, as Ntsebeza points out, most potential sellers are not willing, and they are especially unwilling at the prices that would be necessary if the government were to effect large-scale land reform. In 2005 the Department of Land Affairs resolved to abandon the willing buyer, willing seller rule, yet the pace of land reform has not increased. The government seems as unwilling as ever to expropriate land. One reason identified by Ntsebeza is the difficulty of determining what is "just and equitable" compensation. If the formula continues to be based primarily on the market, land reform will still proceed too slowly. Ntsebeza contends that the protection of property rights as currently enshrined in the constitution needs to be reconsidered, and that civil society—particularly those most affected by land dispossession—must organize and actively struggle for their interests if the land question is ever to be settled equitably.

PART IV: LANGUAGE AND THE MEDIA

In a country such as South Africa, where social categories are so starkly defined in racial terms, the language question is often overlooked. In the opening essay of this section, Neville Alexander highlights the social, economic, and political importance of language, and hence of language policy, in the new South Africa. Alexander makes a powerful case for the importance of a mother tongue–based education. South Africa has eleven official languages, including not only the languages of the former colonial powers, English and Afrikaans, but also nine indigenous African languages. It also has an extraordinarily progressive set of constitutional provisions designed to elevate the status and use of indigenous African languages. These provisions might lead one to assume that no more needs to be done in terms of language policy. Alexander argues, however, that although these legislated provisions were great cause for excitement among advocates of indigenous language at the time of the transition, language policy has in practice been a disappointment.

The de facto official language in the formal economy, as well as in public education and government bureaucracy, continues to be English. A notable exception to this is the continued use of Afrikaans by the Afrikaner minority in both education and the economy and by many of South Africa's three million Cape Coloureds. Indigenous African languages continue to be marginalized and excluded from the public domain, much as they were during the apartheid era. The troubling result is that many indigenous African language speakers are taught in languages over which they have little command, causing them to underperform in school and leaving them ill-equipped with the requisite language or educational competence to enter the formal economy. In sum, the current language policy not only disempowers black South Africans, the majority of whose mother tongue is an indigenous African language. It also constrains the development of a truly democratic society and productive economy. Alexander urges further research into and implementation of mother tongue–based education, as well as the recognition and development of the market value of indigenous African languages.

In the final essay of the book, Guy Berger guides us through the complex developments surrounding control over the media in postapartheid South Africa. He acknowledges that aspirations for a nonracial and pluralistic media have largely been fulfilled. Yet the ANC government has persistently increased its involvement and control over communications policymaking while simultaneously stifling participatory input from civil society.

While these trends have in part reflected a sincere desire to steer communications for "transformational" reasons, such as toward the deepening of nonracialism, democracy, and development, there are also clear examples of government using communications policy for politically self-serving ends.

The problem, Berger argues, lies in government's commitment to an inherently contradictory approach of "managed liberalization" of the communications arena, whereby it seeks both to unleash market forces and at the same time to steer them in the interests of "transformation" and the ANC's political self-interest. The result has been pluralistic contestation of a wide range of communication policy matters, yet one that is primarily elite driven. Berger foresees continued elite contestation over communications policy in the coming decade, as well as technological and market dynamics diminishing the role of government—for better or worse.

The overall picture is mixed. When we look back at what many feared at the time of the transition, South Africa today has made great strides. Yet when we look forward, daunting problems still face South Africa, just as they did in 1994. It is this duality—the tension between how far South Africa has progressed versus how far it still must go—that renders possible a certain guarded optimism. It is possible that the next decade will also defy today's reasonable fears. For this to happen, though, the existing problems and obstacles must be identified and well understood. As with any teenager, this will take understanding, patience, and a good deal of hard work—not to mention luck.

NOTES

1. See "S.A.'s Mbeki Rules Out Third Term," *BBC News Online,* 6 February 2006, http://news.bbc.co.uk/2/hi/africa/4684752.stm (accessed 25 May 2009).

2. See "South African Leader Sacks Deputy," *BBC News Online,* 14 June 2005, http://news.bbc.co.uk/2/hi/africa/4092064.stm (accessed 25 May 2009).

3. See "Timeline: Zuma's Legal Problems," *BBC News Online,* 6 April 2009, http://news.bbc.co.uk/2/hi/africa/7153378.stm (accessed 25 May 2009).

4. See "IEC Declares Election Free and Fair," 28 April 2009, http://www.sa goodnews.co.za/politics/iec_declares_election_free_and_fair.html (accessed 28 May 2009), and "South African Election Free and Fair—African Union," *Harare Tribune,* 25 April 2009, http://www.hararetribune.com/world/southern-africa/629-south -africa-election-free-and-fair-african-union.html (accessed 28 May 2009).

5. See, e.g., Nkepile Mabuse, "S. African Vote Tests ANC's Grip on Power," *CNN.Com,* 21 April 2009, http://edition.cnn.com/2009/WORLD/africa/04/21/south africa.elections/index.html (accessed 29 May 2009), which cited polls predicting that COPE would win 15 percent.

6. See Shapiro (2003, 78–103).

7. According to the United Nations' Office on Drugs and Crime, South Africa's intentional homicide rate in 2004 was the highest in Africa and one of the highest in the world. See United Nations' Office on Drugs and Crime, "International Homicide Statistics," http://data.un.org/Data.aspx?d=UNODC&f=tableCode%3A1 #UNODC (accessed 17 November 2009).

8. See "Zuma's Cabinet: Press Reaction," *BBC News Online,* 11 May 2009, http://news.bbc.co.uk/2/hi/africa/8043791.stm (accessed 27 October 2009).

9. See Moyo (1986, 165-66) and de Villiers (2003, 5).

10. See Hamilton, *The Federalist,* 10 (2009, 50).

11. See Jung, Lust, and Shapiro (2010).

12. See "World Development Indicators," World Bank, http://ddp-ext.world bank.org/ext/DDPQQ/member.do?method=getMembers&userid=1&queryId=135 (accessed 28 October 2009).

13. *Digital Census Atlas,* 2001 South African Census, http://www.statssa.gov.za/census2001/digiAtlas/index.html (accessed 27 October 2009).

14. Between 1995 and 2006, South Africa's white population fell by about 841,000 or a fifth. See "Fears over White Exodus," *BBC News Online,* 6 October 2006, http://news.bbc.co.uk/2/hi/africa/5412892.stm (accessed 28 October 2009).

15. See World Bank 2000.

16. Ibid.

BIBLIOGRAPHY

de Villiers, Bertus. 2003. *Land Reform: Issues and Challenges.* Johannesburg: Konrad Adenauer Foundation.

Hamilton, Alexander. 2009. *The Federalist* no. 10. In Alexander Hamilton, James Madison, and John Jay, *The Federalist Papers,* ed. Ian Shapiro. New Haven, CT: Yale University Press.

Jung, Courtney, Ellen Lust, and Ian Shapiro. 2005. "Problems and Prospects for Democratic Settlements: South Africa as a Model for the Middle East and Northern Ireland?" In *The Real World of Democratic Theory,* ed. Ian Shapiro, 80–142. Princeton, NJ: Princeton University Press.

Moyo, Sam. 1986. "The Land Question." In *Zimbabwe: The Political Economy of Transition 1980-1986,* ed. Ibbo Mandaza, 165–66. Dakar: Codesria.

Shapiro, Ian. 2003. *The State of Democratic Theory.* Princeton, NJ: Princeton University Press.

World Bank, Task Force on Higher Education and Society. 2000. *Higher Education in Developing Countries: Peril and Promise.* Washington, DC: World Bank.

PART I

Politics and the Macroeconomy

Poverty and Inequality in South Africa, 1994–2007

Jeremy Seekings

The first three governments led by the African National Congress (ANC) after 1994 had only modest success in tackling the challenges of poverty and inequality they inherited from the apartheid era. While the expansion of the welfare state has mitigated income poverty, especially in the early 2000s, the economy has continued to grow along a path that is unfriendly to the poor. This situation has resulted from the retention of key elements of the "distributional regime" of the apartheid period, in particular policies that favored capital- and skill-intensive growth despite chronic unemployment.

Democratic South Africa inherited income poverty that was low by the standards of the rest of Africa. The proportion of the South African population with incomes below the equivalent of U.S. $1 per day (adjusted for local purchasing power) was about 24 percent, compared to about 50 percent in countries such as Kenya and Senegal and 85 percent in Zambia. But income poverty in South Africa was much higher than in other *middle*-income countries. The comparable poverty rates in Chile, Mexico, and Indonesia were about 15 percent, and in Jamaica, Malaysia, and Tunisia they were about 5 percent. Only Brazil matched South Africa (United Nations Development Programme [UNDP] 1999, table 4). Income poverty was strikingly visible in South Africa because it coexisted with great affluence against a backdrop of high inequality, and also because this inequality correlated with race. Even though some African people had enjoyed rapid upward income and class mobility in the last years of apartheid, the formerly disfranchised African majority was, for the most part, poor, while the small white minority that had held power was conspicuously rich.

Apartheid perpetuated income poverty and exacerbated income inequality in very obvious ways. African people were dispossessed of most of their land, faced restricted opportunities for employment or self-employment, were limited to low-quality public education and health care, and were physically confined to impoverished parts of the countryside or cities. At the same time, the white minority benefited from discriminatory public policies. It was hardly surprising that South Africa competed with Brazil and a handful of other countries for the indignity of having the most unequal distribution of income. Poverty did not occur alongside affluence because segregation kept the rich and poor apart, but they certainly coexisted in the same country (see Wilson and Ramphele 1989; Seekings and Nattrass 2005). Observers from all parts of the political spectrum turned to crudely dualistic descriptions of this reality, distinguishing between the "first" and "third world" parts of the country or analyzing the political economy in terms of "internal colonialism" or "colonialism of a special type."

Democratization was therefore accompanied by high hopes that income poverty and inequality would be reduced. The poor were to be enfranchised, the pro-poor and pro-black ANC would be elected to office, and public policies and private practices would be deracialized. The ANC promised "a better life for all" in its 1994 election campaign. Its election manifesto—the Reconstruction and Development Programme (RDP)—promised that "attacking poverty and deprivation" would be "the first priority of the democratic government." The RDP would empower the poor to seize opportunities "to develop to their full potential" and "to sustain themselves through productive activity," with the state ensuring improved access to social security, public education, and other services. All South Africans should enjoy "a decent living standard and economic security" (ANC 1994, 15, 16, 79).

The ANC-led government that was elected in 1994 immediately adopted a highly modernist approach to the challenges of development. The apartheid state never collected data on poverty among African people, but even before the 1994 election the ANC joined with the World Bank and the University of Cape Town to conduct South Africa's first countrywide income and expenditure survey. After taking office, the ANC-led government immediately transformed the parastatal statistics agency (renamed Statistics South Africa) and invested heavily in the collection of statistics on poverty, first through the October Household Surveys (OHSs) and Income and Expenditure Surveys (IESs) and later through the General Household Surveys (GHSs); it also collected data on labor market issues (through dedicated Labour Force Surveys, or LFSs). A major study of poverty and inequality was commissioned in 1995–96. A range of public policies were reoriented around "developmental" concerns.

Socioeconomic rights were also included in the 1996 constitution. Section 27 specifies that "(1) Everyone has the right to have access to (a) health care services . . . ; (b) sufficient food and water; and (c) social security, including, if they are unable to support themselves and their dependents, appropriate social assistance. (2) The state must take reasonable legislative and other measures, within its available resources, to achieve the progressive realization of each of these rights." Section 28 stipulates specific rights for children, and section 29 establishes rights to education. These and other rights are said to be based on the "democratic values of human dignity, equality and freedom" (sec. 7, para. 2). The Constitutional Court has stated that realizing socioeconomic rights is necessary if citizens are to enjoy the other rights enshrined in the constitution and if South Africa is to become a society based on the above values.

The ANC and the government were quick to claim they had made progress. In the 1999 elections the ANC campaigned on the general theme that South Africa was "changing," although this change needed to be "speeded up" (Lodge 1999). In 2003, in an assessment anticipating ten years of democratic government, the government acknowledged that poverty had grown, but implied that this was more than offset by redistributive measures (South Africa 2003). In the 2004 elections, the ANC claimed that it had laid the "foundation for a better life," including two million new jobs and expanded public services. It called on citizens to vote for it "so that together we can do more to achieve a Better Life for All." Its election manifesto, entitled *A People's Contract to Create Work and Fight Poverty,* emphasized the creation of "a more caring society" and a "radical" reduction in unemployment and poverty (ANC 2004). The following year, a senior ANC member (and billionaire), Cyril Ramaphosa, was quoted as saying that new data showed that South Africans had "never had it so good" (South African Advertising Research Foundation n.d.). In May 2006, President Mbeki himself told Parliament that "between 1994 and 2004, the real incomes of the poorest 20 percent of our population increased by 30 percent" (Mbeki 2006). More detail was provided in a "discussion document" on macrosocial trends in South Africa. "The proportion of people with low (poverty) income increased marginally during the period 1993 to 2000," the government conceded, but recent research "shows that there has been a marked decline in poverty since 2000, from approximately 18,5 million poor people to approximately 15,4 million poor people in 2004" (South Africa 2006a, 12). These general claims were repeated in the 2007 *Mid-Term Review:* the poverty headcount (i.e., the number of people with incomes below a poverty line) and poverty gap (i.e., the aggregate deficit of poor people's incomes below the poverty line) were both lower in 2006 than they had been in 1993–94 (South Africa 2007c, 21–24). (Note that both the poverty headcount and gap can be expressed in terms of either absolute numbers, i.e., millions of people or billions of rands, or relative to the total population or national income.) In the 2009 general elections, the ANC claimed to have "pushed back the frontiers of poverty," citing the provision of basic services, housing, social assistance, and job creation—but without making any specific claims about trends in income poverty, and at the same time acknowledging that "much more needs to be done" (ANC 2009).

This positive representation of progress contrasts with the negative assessments made by a long series of unashamedly leftist scholars. The ubiquitous journalist John Pilger, for example, proclaims that "apartheid did not die" (Pilger 2006). Affluent spaces in the new South Africa might be populated by black people wearing matching Gucci sunglasses and suits alongside still privileged white people, Pilger claims, but the lives of the poor were unchanged, to the extent that the poor—or "poors," as they are sometimes called (Desai 2002)—have risen up in protest, in the streets and through "new" social movements. The alleged persistence or even deepening of poverty is widely attributed to the ANC-led government's supposed embrace of "neoliberal" policies.

THE RISE AND FALL OF INCOME POVERTY

Discerning what really happened to income poverty and inequality is difficult even without its politically explosive implications. Despite—or rather, to some extent, because of—the growth of data in postapartheid South Africa, there is no consensus on trends. Obvious and not so obvious flaws in the data mean that the data have to be "decontaminated" (Bhorat and Kanbur 2006, 3), and this requires complex assumptions and methodological innovations (see Seekings 2006b).

There is, nonetheless, broad academic consensus that income poverty worsened in the late 1990s, although precise findings vary according to the specific data used and the assumptions made in the analysis. The poverty headcount grew both in absolute numbers and as a proportion of the total population, and the poverty gap widened also. Hoogeveen and Özler, for example, found that the number of people with incomes below U.S. $1 per day grew by approximately 1.8 million between 1995 and 2000, and the number living on less than $2 per day by 2.3 million (2006, 87; see also Meth and Dias 2004; Leibbrandt et al. 2005, 2006). This academic consensus was contrary to most of the claims made by the ANC and government but consistent with the criticisms made by Pilger and others. Even the government later conceded that income poverty had risen in the late 1990s (e.g., South Africa 2006a).

The overall growth rate of the South African economy sped up somewhat in the early 2000s, fuelling hopes that poverty might decline. Van der Berg et al., using an innovative methodology that they themselves describe as "not uncontroversial," found that there had been "a noticeable decline in poverty" after 2000, and especially after 2002 (van der Berg et al. 2006, 23). Their finding held for a variety of measures of income poverty—although, they noted at one point, "we may be at risk of overestimating the progress that has been made" (ibid, 29). In a detailed riposte, Meth (2006a) argued that van der Berg-et al. underestimated substantially the numbers of people in poverty. Meth conceded that the proportion and number of poor people might have declined in the early 2000s, but by much less than van der Berg et al. claimed.

The poverty rate is undoubtedly sensitive to quite small changes in income flows (whether through employment or through government-provided social assistance). There are many poor people just below (as well as just above) any of the widely used poverty lines, and it does not require large income flows to raise them out of poverty. Bhorat (2003a) calculated that the poverty gap in 1995 was only R13 billion, using a poverty line of R293 per person per month. This amounted to 10 percent of government spending at the time, meaning that the government could eliminate income poverty entirely if it increased its expenditures by just 10 percent and allocated all of the additional funds to perfectly targeted transfers to the poor. There is widespread consensus that the decline in poverty in the early 2000s—whatever its magnitude—resulted primarily from the substantial increase in the government's real expenditure on well-targeted social assistance programs.

The precise change in income poverty in the early 2000s remains unclear, however. Because many people have incomes close to the poverty line and because there is such pronounced inequality between rich and poor, even small methodological differences can have large effects on *measured* poverty rates. Van der Berg et al. and Meth reach very different findings because they responded differently to the fundamental deficiency in the existing data on incomes in South Africa, namely, a growing problem of underreporting of incomes. Surveys and censuses fail to collect complete or credible information on some households (in the sample, in the case of surveys) and fail to collect any data on others. Overall, the incomes recorded by the censuses and surveys fall far short of the national income derived from the national accounts. Because underreporting appears to be changing over time, it is necessary to distinguish between real changes in incomes over time and changing levels of reporting. This is especially complicated insofar as wealthier people especially have become less and less willing to report their incomes (Seekings,Nattrass, and Leibbrandt 2004).

One solution is to impute missing or questionable data (Ardington et al. 2005; Leibbrandt et al. 2006). Van der Berg et al. (2006) employed an entirely different methodology. Their model building entails three stages. First, they accept the veracity of national accounts data on the overall growth of national income, disregarding entirely the apparent trend in census and (most) survey data. Second, they use data from national accounts and other, nonsurvey sources to calculate *inter*racial income distribution, that is, the shares of national income accruing to white, Indian, coloured, and African people. They find that African people's share of total income rose sharply after 2002, faster even than their share of the population. In the third stage of their methodology, van der Berg et al. use data from the All Media and Products Survey (AMPS), collected for the advertising and marketing industry, on *intra*racial income distribution. Crucially, the AMPS data suggest that intraracial income inequality within the African population peaked in 2000 and declined thereafter (although overall inequality rose steadily throughout the period). The combination of declining intra-African inequality and a rising African income share produces the result that poor (African) people fared especially well. Poor African people got a larger share (relative to non-poor African people) of a growing African share of the total pie (relative to non-African people).

Each stage in the methodology of van der Berg et al. is open to challenge. As Meth wrote, "it is not obvious why the magnitude of adjustments resulting from such a procedure should bear any resemblance to the size of actual under-reporting errors by income or expenditure class (which, all agree, are likely to plague any survey instrument)" (2006a, 10). The accuracy of the findings of van der Berg et al. depends on the accuracy of their data on interracial and intra-African distributions. This accuracy remains to be demonstrated. One would have more confidence in their findings if they showed why AMPS data on intra-African income distribution, collected for the advertising and marketing industry, suffers from fewer flaws than the data collected in dedicated surveys by Statistics South Africa. Meth (2006a) tried to identify what assumptions would need to be made about Statistics South Africa survey data to produce the kind of results obtained by van der Berg et al. using other sources and methodologies. He concludes that the estimates of van der Berg et al. require assumptions about underreporting that are beyond the bounds of plausibility.

A major concern with any survey is the difficulty of interviewing rich households. This has major implications for the interracial distribution of income, as it was (on average) harder to collect information from (richer) white South Africans than from (poorer) African South Africans. The standard response to this problem was to reweight data by race (or by race and province) (see Seekings et al. 2004; Hoogeveen and Özler 2006). This implies that nonresponse within the reweighted categories was random. Nonrandom nonresponse within the reweighted categories might have major implications for any analysis that requires data on distribution. Van der Berg et al. (2006) agreed that the African "middle class" has experienced dramatic growth. If AMPS data underestimated the growth of prosperity among rich African people, then van der Berg et al. would have overestimated the benefits of growth that accrue to poor African people. Small underestimates in the size or prosperity of richer Africans meant proportionately large overestimates in the incomes of poor Africans, and this is especially significant insofar as even small sums can raise many people above the poverty line.

While these concerns mean that the findings of van der Berg et al. on the magnitude of the decline in poverty should be viewed with caution, the general trend does seem to have been corroborated by a preliminary analysis of data from the 2005–6 IES by Bhorat and van der Westhuizen (2008). Bhorat and van der Westhuizen found that the proportion of South Africans living in poverty fell from about 31 percent in 1995 to about 23 percent in 2005, using a low poverty line, while the poverty gap shrank from 12 percent to 7 percent of national income. When a higher poverty line was used, the poverty rate fell less dramatically, from about 52 percent to about 48 percent, while the poverty gap fell from 26 percent to 21 percent. With either a low or a high poverty line, therefore, income poverty seems to have fallen across this period. A different source of data provides further broad corroboration for the argument of van der Berg et al. The GHSs ask respondents whether, "in the past twelve months," any adult or child in the respondent's household had gone "hungry because there wasn't enough food." Respondents had to choose between five response options: "never," "seldom," "sometimes," "often," and "always." Responses in households with children indicate clearly that reported child hunger declined over quite a short period

Table 1.1   Frequency of childhood hunger in South African households, 2002–7 (percent)

	Never	Seldom	Sometimes	Often	Always
2002	69.2	7.1	17	4.5	2.2
2003	69.9	5.2	17.8	4.3	2.7
2004	73.9	5.1	15.8	3.1	2
2005	76.8	4.7	13.7	2.6	2.1
2006	84	2.9	10.7	1.5	1
2007	85	2.75	10.2	1.24	0.8

Source: General Household Surveys (GHS), 2002–7.

of time: the combined proportions of respondents living in households in-cluding children who said that a child went hungry "seldom," "sometimes," "often," or "always" fell from more than 30 percent in 2002 to about 15 per-cent in 2007 (table 1.1). Reported hunger among adults declined similarly.

Although the quality of the data requires some caution, it is very likely that weak employment growth and, more important, a sharp increase in pro-poor public expenditure on social assistance programs did lead to a re-duction in income poverty in the early 2000s. Trends in the late 1990s might have corroborated the criticisms of Pilger and others, but trends in the early 2000s almost certainly contradict them.

HIGH (AND WORSENING) INEQUALITY

Income inequality worsened after 1994, including in the early 2000s. This trend has been found by studies using a variety of data sets and stands in contrast to the picture of stable levels of overall income inequality in the final decades of apartheid. Leibbrandt's calculations using the 1995 and 2000 IESs showed that the Gini coefficient—a widely used measure of in-equality, which can vary in value from an egalitarian 0 to an inegalitarian 1—for household per capita income rose by about five percentage points over five years, from 0.65 to 0.7 (Seekings, Nattrass, and Leibbrandt 2004). The Gini coefficient for expenditure rose, but by less (Hoogeveen and Özler 2006, 60). Leibbrandt et al. (2006, 101) compared data from the 1996 and 2001 Population Censuses and also found that the Gini coefficient rose by five percentage points, from 0.68 to 0.73. Simkins (2004) corroborates both the IES and census findings. Even van der Berg et al. (2006) found that their model of income distribution indicated rising income inequality between 1994 and 2004.

The Gini coefficient might not be the most appropriate measure of income distribution in the South African case, as it is reportedly less sensitive to changes at either end of the income distribution and more sensitive to changes in the middle. South Africa's rich are unusually rich and South Africa's poor are exceptionally poor, even relative to other unequal societies. If the poor are getting relatively poorer, therefore, the Gini coefficient shows less change than alternative measures of distribution, such as the mean logarithmic deviation (Hoogeveen and Özler 2006, 72). There are also, as I have already suggested, grounds for suspecting that the weights used in survey and census data do not pay adequate attention to the (probably worsening) problem of low response rates among rich, and therefore necessarily upwardly mobile, African households. This would lead to an underestimate of the growth of both intra-African and overall income inequality.

In 1998, Mbeki famously described South Africa as a "two-nation" society: "One of these nations is white, relatively prosperous, regardless of gender or geographic dispersal. . . . The second and larger nation . . . is black and poor, with the worst-affected being women in the rural areas, the black rural population in general, and the disabled." These two "nations" were distinguished by unequal access to infrastructure of all kinds, and unequal access to opportunities.[1] In a detailed analysis of the changing nature of inequality in South Africa in the second half of the twentieth century, Nattrass and I argue that the basis of inequality had shifted from race to class long before 1998 (Seekings and Nattrass 2005). Apartheid served to transform the state-imposed privileges of being white into the advantages of class that were rewarded by markets, ensuring that the white elite became a middle class whose continued privileges no longer depended on active racial discrimination by the state. This shift meant that the state could dismantle policies of racial discrimination without undermining white privilege. This in turn meant that growing numbers of black South Africans could be upwardly mobile into the middle classes. Privilege no longer correlated with race, as suggested by Mbeki's use of the "two nations" analogy.

The Theil index is a measure of inequality that allows for overall inequality to be decomposed into within-group and between-group components. Applied to South African racial categories, this decomposition distinguishes the shares of inequality arising from interracial as opposed to intraracial differences. Whiteford and Van Seventer (2000), using census data on incomes, showed that the between-race share declined from 62 percent in 1975 to 42 percent in 1991, and to 33 percent in 1996, while the within-race share rose commensurately, from 38 percent to 58 percent to 67 percent. A series of studies found that this trend continued after 1996 (see Seekings, Nattrass, and Leibbrandt et al. 2004; Bhorat, Naidoo, and van der Westhuizen 2006; Hoogeveen and Özler 2006; Leibbrandt et al. 2006). Van der Berg et al. (2006) found that the Gini coefficient for incomes was higher in 2006 (0.685) than in 1993 (0.672). Within-race inequality contributed 39 percent of total inequality in 1993, but 60 percent in 2006, using the Theil-T index.[2] The removal of racial constraints allowed the accelerated upward mobility of some African people and the consequent deepening of class differences within the African population. Upward mobility by some African people was reflected in the changing racial composition of the top or rich income deciles (Seekings, Nattrass, and Leibbrandt 2004; Leibbrandt et al. 2006; van der Berg et al. 2006). By the 2000s, many rich people were not "white," even if almost all white people were still rich.

HUMAN DEVELOPMENT, AIDS, AND LIFE EXPECTANCY

Income poverty is just one measure of welfare. The Human Development Index (HDI) is a broader measure, developed by the United Nations Development Programme (UNDP), and reported in the UNDP's annual *Human Development Report*. Table 1.2 shows the absolute HDI for South Africa together with South Africa's ranking relative to other countries.[3] The HDI in South Africa rose steadily in the last years of apartheid, as it did in most other countries. It peaked around 1995, then declined steadily until 2004. The HDI rose slightly between 2004 and 2005, probably due primarily to rising GDP per capita. Nonetheless, South Africa's ranking declined from 90th in the world in 1994 to 125th in 2006. This dramatic decline in South Africa (and other countries in East and Southern Africa) is almost unique in recent global history. The HDI comprises three components: an "educational attainment index," constructed out of adult literacy rates and gross school enrollment rates; a "life expectancy index," derived from data on life expectancy at birth; and an index of GDP per capita, taking into account purchasing power. The UNDP selected these variables for the HDI because they are readily measured and together provide a good indication of the reality of social and economic well-being in a country or region. The rapid decline in South Africa's absolute and relative HDI is entirely due to the rapid decline in life expectancy. In 2003, for example, South Africa ranked 52nd in the world in terms of GDP per capita (taking into account purchasing power), 78th on the composite education index, but 150th on life expectancy. The

Table 1.2 Human Development Index (HDI) for South Africa, 1994–2006

	HDI	Global rank
1994	0.73	90
1995	0.7326	89
1996	0.7309	unavailable
1997	0.7268	101
1998	0.7193	103
1999	0.7085	94
2000	0.6954	107
2001	0.6871	111
2002	0.6774	119
2003	0.6675	120
2004	0.653	121
2005	0.674	121
2006	0.67	125

Sources: *South Africa Human Development Report 2003* (table 24, 281–82); United Nations Development Programme, *Human Development Report,* various years.

reason why life expectancy has declined is AIDS, which has rolled back the gains of decades of development in Southern Africa (see Nattrass 2002). By 2010, AIDS was expected to have reduced life expectancy at birth in South Africa by twenty years. Without AIDS, it would have been sixty-eight years; with AIDS it will be forty-eight, perhaps even less.

The combination of poverty and AIDS has dire consequences for infant and child mortality. In Brazil, both the infant and child mortality rates are about twenty deaths per one thousand births. In South Africa, the rates are fifty-six per one thousand and sixty-nine per one thousand, respectively. HIV is reported to be a factor in about four out of every five deaths among children less than five years old.[4]

Life expectancy should be a far more important component of studies of income poverty and inequality than is currently the case, because of both changes in average life expectancy over time and inequalities in life expectancy across society. Studies of income poverty and inequality are rightly concerned with an individual's or household's income over time: chronic poverty is very different from transitory poverty, in terms of both the experience for the people concerned and the implications for policy design. But long lives are clearly preferred to short ones. The tardiness of the South African government in providing treatment for the AIDS sick and in using antiretroviral drugs to slow the spread of the pandemic (Nattrass 2007) constitutes a massive indictment of postapartheid policy.

CAUSES OF POVERTY AND INEQUALITY: UNEMPLOYMENT AND EDUCATION

Poverty in postapartheid South Africa is rooted in deagrarianization and unemployment. South Africa's poor are not landholding peasants, supplementing subsistence production with occasional sales of agricultural produce, casual employment, or remittances from migrant labor. South Africa's peasantry was slowly destroyed in the course of the twentieth century (Seekings and Nattrass 2005, chaps. 3 and 6). Forced removals from large commercial farms, overcrowding in the "homelands" or "Bantustans," low-quality schooling, poor links to urban and industrial labor markets, and the growing capital intensity of production in most economic sectors have resulted in the growth of unemployment among unskilled workers and mass poverty among them and their dependents. Large-scale open unemployment seems to have replaced underemployment in the 1970s, then grew steadily through the 1980s and early 1990s (ibid., chap. 5). Surveys conducted around 1994 suggested that the unemployment rate was less than 20 percent, when a strict or narrow definition of unemployment (including only active job seekers) was used, and about 30 percent when a broad or expanded definition was used (including people who want employment but are not looking for it in supposedly "active" ways). Unemployment rates rose steadily under post-1994 ANC governments, at least until 2002. Figure 1.1 shows unemployment using the narrow and broad definitions; the 1993 data come from the 1993 PSLSD survey, the 1994–99 data from OHSs, and the 2000–2007 data from the LFSs conducted in September of each year. Unemployment peaked in early 2003 at 31.2 percent (by the narrow or strict definition) or 42.5 percent (using the broad or expanded definition).[5] By the early 2000s, more than four million people were unemployed by the narrow definition and about eight million were unemployed by the broad definition. Unemployment rates dropped marginally from 2002–3, but they remain higher than they were in 1994 and are higher than anywhere else in the world (for which there are data) except Iraq and some of South Africa's immediate neighbors in Southern Africa.[6]

The coincidence of steady (if low) economic growth, rising unemployment rates, and apparently stagnant employment growth led many commentators to describe the South African economic experience in terms of "jobless growth." Given that trade liberalization contributed to job losses in unionized sectors, COSATU—the Congress of South African Trade Unions—

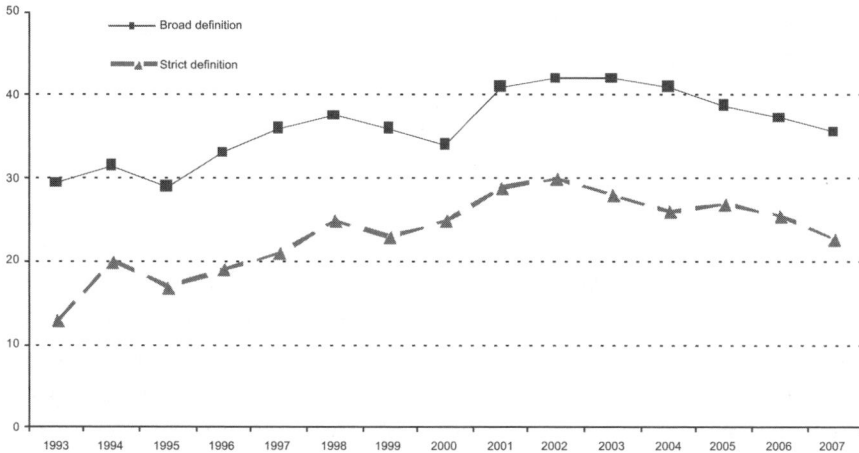

Figure 1.1   Unemployment in South Africa, 1993–2007 (percentage of labor force)

joined the chorus of critics of the government, whose policies were said to have produced a "jobs bloodbath." Such claims were disputed by Bhorat. Using data from post-1993 household surveys (the OHS and LFS), he argued that total employment rose, with as many as two million net new jobs created between 1995 and 2003–4 (Bhorat 2003b; Bhorat and Oosthuizen 2006; Oosthuizen 2006). Casale, Muller, and Posel (2005) showed that about one-third of this employment growth was due to changes in measurement (with a more inclusive definition of self-employment). The actual new "jobs" divided almost equally between the survivalist (i.e., very low-income) informal sector and the formal sector. This is why rising employment did not lead to a drastic reduction in poverty but rather resulted in a growing number of "working poor." By 2003, almost one-third of working South Africans reported earnings that were lower than the statutory minimum wage for a domestic worker. Overall, it is clear, recent economic growth has not been markedly more pro-poor than growth in previous decades.

The effects of unemployment on poverty are accentuated by the growth of an "underclass" of people who suffer systematic disadvantage in the labor market, with the result that they face no real possibility of escaping poverty (Seekings and Nattrass 2005, chap. 8). For many unemployed people, poverty is transitory, ending when they find employment. But others lack the skills (including language skills), credentials, and (especially) the connections (i.e., social capital) that are crucial to securing employment. These others make up the underclass. Probably the most important form of social capital is having family or friends who have jobs and are able to help someone find employment. It is therefore especially worrying that the number and proportion of the unemployed living in "workerless" households—households where no one is in wage employment—have risen. The number (and proportion) of unemployed people living in workerless households, using the broad definition of unemployment, rose from 1.8 million (42 percent) in 1995 to four million (49 percent) in 2004 (Oosthuizen 2006, 47), dropping marginally thereafter (according to LFS data). In the mid-1990s, most of this underclass of workerless households was located in the former Bantustans. Rural-to-urban migration has resulted in some relocation of poverty to town (Bhorat and Kanbur 2006, 4). By late 2007, however, only one in four unemployed people in workerless households were living in any of the country's metropolitan areas (according to LFS data).

Education is a second immediate cause of income poverty and inequality. Lam (1999) showed that most of South Africa's very high inequality in income distribution could be explained in terms of differential rates of return to education and unequal grade attainment. Although the bulk of the population has already left school, the education and skills of new entrants into the labor force are of great importance in shaping the ways that inequalities evolve over time. In 2006, the official pass rate on the matriculation (or grade twelve) school-leaving examination was 66.5 percent. In the early 2000s, pass rates rose sharply, but a large part of the increase was because the matriculation examination became less demanding. Even though the 2006 examination was probably easier than examinations a decade earlier, the pass rates in key subjects remained very low (Taylor 2007). More alarmingly, surveys show that only a minority (about 40 percent) of each age cohort successfully completes grade twelve (and some respondents might say they have completed grade twelve even if they did not actually pass the matriculation examination). The median grade attainment among young people in their mid-twenties, that is, at an age when as many have taken matriculation examinations as will ever do so, is grade eleven, and almost one in three young people have attained grade ten or less (according to 2005 GHS).

More worryingly still, it is very unclear what skills are associated with any particular level of grade attainment, including even matriculation. Only 5 percent of the half-million candidates who took their matriculation examination in 2006 passed mathematics at the higher grade. Only one in four of the students who *passed* matriculation examinations passed mathematics at *either* the higher *or* the standard grade (Taylor 2007). Data from the Cape

Area Panel Study show there is a very weak correlation between the grade in which students are enrolled and their scores on numeracy and literacy tests. Many students are promoted into higher grades without having mastered basic numeracy and literacy. The results are shown in cross-national research on skills. In the 2003 round of the Trends in International Mathematics and Science Study (TIMSS), South African grade eight students performed worse on both science and mathematics tests than their counterparts in every other country that participated, including Egypt, Botswana, and Ghana. Indeed, the seventy-fifth percentile in South Africa achieved about the same score as the twenty-fifth percentile in Botswana (Reddy 2006). Other cross-national studies provide a similarly worrying and unambiguous message: South Africa performs poorly in comparison even with some of its much poorer neighbors. In the 2000 round of SACMEQ, South African grade six students performed worse in reading and mathematics than their counterparts in Mozambique, Botwana, Swaziland, Tanzania, and elsewhere (van der Berg 2005b; Taylor 2006).

The reasons are clear. Most South African schools provide a very low quality of education. In some cases, the quality is clearly constrained by inadequate conditions. But in most cases the redistribution of public resources from schools in rich neighborhoods to schools in poor neighborhoods schools (as shown by van der Berg and colleagues) has removed the most glaring inequalities in conditions. What remains are inequalities in family background—which South Africa shares with many other countries in the global South—and inequalities in the classroom that result from differences in the quality of teaching and the level of student discipline (both of which are probably affected by the quality of school management). The restructuring of the school curriculum after 1994 has certainly not improved the quality of education and may in fact have exacerbated inequalities, because teachers in schools in poor neighborhoods often lack the skills or motivation to apply the new curriculum.

Despite considerable expenditure on public education—amounting to about 7 percent of GDP—most young South Africans leave school and enter the labor market with limited skills. They are not equipped for semiskilled or especially skilled employment. Given that the economy continues to restructure around skilled employment, there is a serious mismatch between the supply and demand for labor. This fuels unemployment among the unskilled and low earnings among those unskilled workers who are lucky enough to find jobs.

PRO-POOR SOCIAL INTERVENTIONS

The decline in income poverty in the early 2000s appears to be due primarily to the expansion of social assistance, that is, tax-financed, noncontributory programs providing for the elderly, the disabled, and poor parents with young children. The three ANC-led governments in office from 1994 to 2009 made no substantive changes to the basic design of the public welfare system, and the real value of the major grants was much the same in 2007 as in 1994. But the second and third ANC-led governments (i.e., in Thabo Mbeki's two terms as president) presided over a substantial increase in total expenditure on social assistance to a rapidly growing number of poor people. Expenditure on social assistance almost doubled, from about 2 percent of GDP in 2000 to about 3.5 percent in 2006 and 2007 (see fig. 1.2).[7] Figure 1.3 disaggregates the growth in numbers of beneficiaries between the major programs. There was little change in the number or pattern of beneficiaries until 2000. Thereafter there was an extraordinary explosion in the number of beneficiaries, but this was almost entirely due to the growth of child support grants being paid out. The child support grant, although modest in value, very quickly reached ten times the number of children reached by its predecessor, the state maintenance grant. By April 2009, about seven million child support grants were paid monthly, compared with just 230,000 child allowances under the state maintenance grants during the peak year of 1998. Figure 1.3 also shows the slow but significant rise in disability grants. There has been less change in the pattern of actual expenditures because the child support grant is so modest in value compared with the other grants. Nonetheless, in 2003–4, for the first time, old-age pensions counted for less

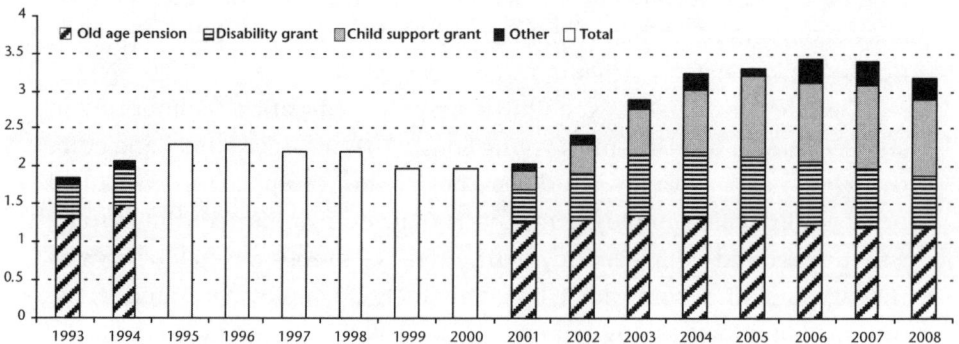

Figure 1.2   South African social assistance program expenditure as percentage of GDP, 1993–2008

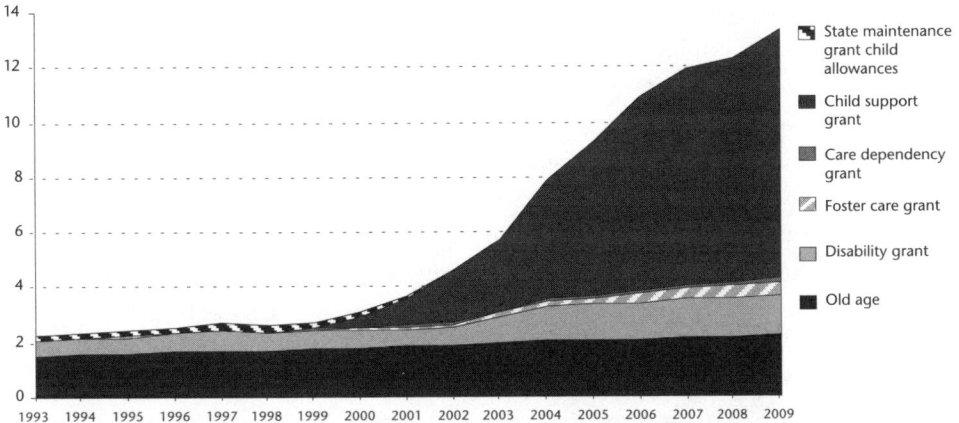

Figure 1.3   Numbers of social assistance beneficiaries in South Africa by program, 1993–2009 (millions)

than one-half of all social assistance. These social assistance programs had a major effect on poverty because they were well targeted to the poor (van der Berg 2001, 2005a, 2006a, 2009). Almost 60 percent of social assistance expenditure went to households in the poorest income quintile. About 30 percent was shared between households in the second and third income quintiles, and households in the richest two income quintiles received just 10 percent. Well-targeted cash transfers amounting to about 3.5 percent of GDP inevitably had a major effect on poverty rates.

Other areas of government social expenditure were also progressive. Van der Berg applied standard analysis of fiscal incidence to government spending on education, health, and housing (where the benefits are in kind, in the form of free or subsidized education, health care, and housing), as well as social assistance (entailing cash transfers). Van der Berg (2001) estimated that 33 percent of total social spending in 1997 went to the poorest household income quintile, compared with just 8 percent for the richest household income quintile. This was marginally more pro-poor than in 1993, when 31 percent went to the poorest quintile and 12 percent to the richest. Because total spending had increased, however, the slightly higher share of the poor meant a substantial increase in real spending on them. Van der Berg subsequently (2005a, 2009) repeated his earlier analysis using data from the 1995, 2000, and 2005–6 IESs, showing that the share of social spending on the poorest income quintile rose marginally between these dates. When social spending in kind (such as public education and health care), social spending as cash (primarily social assistance), and taxation are considered, the Gini coefficient for the distribution of "income" in South Africa was reduced by fourteen percentage points in 1995, eighteen percentage points in 2000, and twenty-two percentage points in 2005–6 (van der Berg 2009, 24).

The problem with fiscal incidence analysis is that it apportions government spending among different sections of the population without assessment of the actual value of this spending to the poor (see van der Berg 2005a, 39–43). Government spending in South Africa is pro-poor primarily in the sense that the government pays salaries to teachers working in schools in poor neighborhoods and to doctors and nurses in public clinics and hospitals. Health spending might be an effective means of assisting the poor, but it is far from clear what benefit the poor actually receive from the considerable funds spent on teachers' salaries. It is clear that schools in rural areas, and many urban areas, provide a very poor education, and that there is at most a weak relationship between spending on schools and the actual quality of education. Indeed, pro-poor spending on education might be viewed more accurately as pro-teacher spending, not pro-poor spending (Seekings 2004).

There was also a dramatic improvement in access to water, electricity, and housing (Bhorat, Naidoo, and van der Westhuizen 2006; Leibbrandt et al. 2006). The number of households with electric connections doubled between 1993 and 2004, and the number with telephones rose almost threefold (through the spread of cell phones, not fixed land lines). Access to water and sanitation improved, as did access to formal housing (in terms of the number of households in formal housing, but not in terms of the proportion of the total number of households). Critics charged that many poor households have been disconnected from the new services or evicted from their new homes because they have been unable to pay (McDonald 2002). But a careful study of water services concluded that the number of people affected by cutoffs because of nonpayment is very much lower than critics claimed (Hemson and Owusu-Amponah 2006).

The area of service delivery in which the state was most obviously and consequentially negligent was health, especially AIDS-related health care and the provision of antiretroviral drugs. By stalling the rollout of antiretroviral drugs and failing to organize government publicity around the threat of HIV/AIDS, the government failed to prevent the explosion of ill health and death among people who were still young (Nattrass 2007). Life expectancy, as we have seen, plummeted. While rich people could get antiretroviral drugs, if necessary through private medical aid schemes, the poor suffered, lost incomes, and died young. There can surely be nothing as fundamental to inequality as this.

THE UNCHANGING DISTRIBUTIONAL REGIME
AND GROWTH PATH

The disappointing progress in reducing poverty (and inequality) was not due to the lack of pro-poor social assistance. Nor was it due to the evident lack of land reform, because even when land was redistributed, it had only limited effects on poverty reduction. Economic growth was not the culprit. Although GDP per capita was stagnant in the late 1990s, it grew steadily from 2000 (until the onset of recession at the end of 2008). Real gross national income per capita rose by about one-fourth between 1994 and 2007, which might have been expected to have had a dramatic effect on poverty (although faster growth would, of course, have been better). Continuing poverty and inequality were, rather, the product of the overall economic growth path, which continued to be capital- and skill-intensive. Growth may not have been entirely "jobless," but the benefits were concentrated on the better skilled and already employed. Continued adherence to the growth path of the apartheid period inevitably resulted in persistent unemployment, especially among the less skilled, and hence continuing poverty.

Inegalitarian patterns of economic growth were encouraged by the global economic environment, but South African government policies also played an important part. Crucially, policies and institutions regulating wages and working conditions discouraged low-wage job creation and hence kept the economy on an inegalitarian growth path. The postapartheid government announced with great fanfare the introduction of "new" labor legislation: a Labour Relations Act in 1995, the Basic Conditions of Employment Act of 1997, the 1998 Employment Equity Act, and the Skill Development Act of 1999. Notwithstanding their claimed novelty, this legislation essentially took the existing legislation that had been introduced to protect unionized, skilled, and semiskilled white workers in the 1920s and extended it to protect unionized, skilled, and semiskilled workers of all racial groups in the 1990s. This deracialization was clearly just, in many senses. But in deracializing the legislation that formerly protected the privileges of an elite of (white) workers, the postapartheid state extended rather than dismantled a system of privilege that entailed benefits for labor market "insiders." Workers in formal employment were now all "insiders," while the unemployed, casual workers, and informally employed remained "outsiders." Policies and institutions that affected wage determination and working conditions also served to promote a capital-intensive, and relatively jobless, growth path, insofar as they pushed up labor costs, especially among unskilled workers, and provided incentives to employers to substitute capital for labor and skilled for unskilled labor.

Labor market policy had negative effects on the demand for unskilled labor in two major ways. First, industrial relations procedures resulted in very high costs to employers of dismissing labor. By one estimate, it cost business 1 percent of GDP to dismiss workers each year, and three times the number of workdays were lost through dismissal procedures than through work stoppages. Some of the labor lawyers responsible for drafting the relevant labor legislation spoke out against the gap between what they intended and what ensued.[8] Second, wages were negotiated in centralized, sector-based Bargaining Councils, which are dominated by the large, more capital-intensive employers together with the trade unions, which have a common interest in setting wages at high levels to eliminate competition from small, less capitalized, and less organized employers.

The precise extent to which labor market policies serve to advantage employed insiders at the expense of unemployed outsiders remains unclear. Much of the evidence and argument presented in defense of current labor market policies was much less decisive than their champions suggested. But neither was the evidence that labor market policies restricted job creation conclusive. The argument against labor market policies essentially rested on the absence of any alternative explanation of why profit-seeking South African employers did not choose to invest in labor-intensive production techniques that entailed large-scale employment of unskilled labor but instead invested again and again in capital-intensive production that entailed modest employment of skilled or semiskilled labor. If wages or hidden labor costs (such as the costs of dismissal) were not high in South Africa, or if the labor market was really as flexible as some pro-union researchers claimed, then why was there not more employment of cheap, unskilled labor? Ironically, even those researchers who defend existing union-friendly labor market policies concur on the need for wage subsidies (e.g., Pollin et al. 2006), which implies that they accept that wage rates are a disincentive to job creation.

The government itself slowly shifted toward accepting the need for labor market reform. The 1996 Growth, Employment, and Redistribution (GEAR) macroeconomic strategy envisaged minor relaxation of the very labor market policies that the Department of Labour was in the process of legislating. In 1999, the government initiated a review of labor legislation, but only very minor reforms were implemented. In the same year, the Minister of Labour introduced very minor changes to the regulations affecting small businesses employing less than ten workers. In mid-2005, ANC leaders finally declared their intention of tackling the sacred cow of labor market policy. A discussion document, tabled at a major ANC conference in 2005, proposed excluding small employers from some regulatory requirements and from the sectoral wage deals negotiated between large employers and unions. Such reforms of labor market policy were strongly opposed by the ANC's powerful allies COSATU and the South African Communist Party (SACP), which lobbied strongly against them at the conference and secured a final resolution that left labor market reform off the immediate agenda.[9] The election of Jacob Zuma as president of the ANC at the ANC's conference at Polokwane in December 2007, with very energetic support from COSATU and the SACP, marked the death of plans to reform significantly the country's labor market policies. Indeed, the post-Polokwane ANC's unambiguous commitment to "decent work" and increased real wages generally indicated that the economy would be moving down a higher-wage growth path with almost no likelihood of low-wage job creation outside of tax-funded public works programs.

PROSPECTS FOR REDUCING POVERTY AND INEQUALITY

The global recession in 2008–9 dispelled optimism about South Africa's prospective economic growth. Whereas the ANC-led government had envisaged accelerated growth, the economy actually contracted, despite massive investments in infrastructure in preparation for the 2010 football World Cup. Even had it remained steady, however, economic growth per se would have entailed little reduction in poverty or inequality. It is very unlikely that job creation would have matched even the flow of new entrants into the labor force, so that the unemployment rate would (at best) have fallen slowly. The ANC's 2004 election promises to halve unemployment and poverty rates by 2014, or its 2009 promises to provide more and "decent" jobs, were simply not achievable within the policy framework to which the ANC seems committed (Meth 2006b). Indeed, given that most of the net "new jobs" created in the early 2000s entailed precisely the kind of low-wage work that COSATU considered "indecent," even the modest job creation of the early 2000s was at risk, and there was a real prospect of unemployment growing even after recovery from recession.

The limits of government policy can be identified with respect to both the aborted policy framework adopted by the third ANC-led government (led by Mbeki) in the mid-2000s and the alternative policies put forward by the fourth ANC-led government (led by Zuma), elected into office in 2009.

Both sets of policies recognized that economic growth was necessary but not sufficient for poverty reduction: To have a significant effect on poverty, the benefits of growth must be "shared." This ambition was reflected in the title of the strategy developed in 2005 and launched in early 2006, under the leadership of the then deputy president (Phumzile Mlambo-Ngcuka, who left the ANC for the breakaway Congress of the People in 2009). The *Accelerated and Shared Growth Initiative for South Africa* (ASGISA) document envisaged achieving the ANC's 2004 election goals of halving poverty and unemployment rates through increasing the economic growth rate (to 6 percent per annum) and sharing growth, primarily through absorbing more labor into the "mainstream economy." Key elements of the plan included increased public investment in infrastructure, accelerated skills development, and reducing the regulatory burden on small and medium-sized businesses (South Africa 2006c).

These policies could not suffice to generate shared growth. ASGISA emphasized primarily skills development, in another reiteration of the skills-led growth strategy that the ANC has followed since the early 1990s. There was no discussion in the ASGISA document of the effects of wage levels. Any jobs created under ASGISA were likely to be high-skill, high-wage jobs, and therefore unlikely to make much of a dent in unemployment or to result in the benefits of growth being shared with the poor. A related problem is identified in the first report on progress under ASGISA. In this report, the government notes that poverty is concentrated in the former Bantustans, where there is no likelihood of significant formal employment creation. Poverty reduction therefore requires either massive migration out of those areas to the towns, where formal jobs could be created, or targeted public works programs in the former Bantustans, or expanding grants or employment subsidies for working-age unemployed adults (South Africa 2007a, 28). ASGISA promised to share growth primarily through upgrading the skills of a small number of people. The strategy was essentially skills led and depended on a newly skilled workforce being sufficiently competitive on a global level that the economy would boom, creating more opportunities. If there was no such boom, then the benefits of growth would be concentrated in the more skilled and productive sections of the labor force. In the absence of a significant level of low-wage job creation, shared growth would depend on the continued expansion of the welfare state.

At the ANC's Polokwane conference in late 2007, the coalition headed by then president Mbeki was overthrown by a rival coalition headed by Jacob Zuma. COSATU and the SACP, as mentioned, were powerful players in the

Zuma coalition. The new ANC leadership, and especially COSATU and the SACP, denounced what they called "the 1996 class project" of the Mbeki era, referring to the supposed class interests behind the GEAR macroeconomic strategy. The new ANC policies would, they proclaimed, entail a deepened commitment to "decent work" through intensified regulation of casual, informal, and outsourced employment. The government would implement more aggressively and comprehensively minimum wage setting in all sectors. The post-Polokwane approach notionally emphasized education and skills development, along the lines of ASGISA, but its primary emphasis was on the expansion of regulation, directly through its regulatory mechanisms and indirectly through government procurement policies.

Whereas ASGISA envisaged a process whereby a more skilled and productive workforce would be globally competitive and attract investment and hence overall job creation, the post-Polokwane approach emphasized state-led growth and redistribution. The state would expand its "developmental" capacity—although it was unclear what this would entail beyond protecting and nurturing selected industries through raised tariffs, public expenditure, and reducing interest rates. More clearly, public expenditure would rise across the board: on public sector wages and salaries, on public investment (especially in infrastructure), on public education and health care systems (with discussion of a national health insurance system), and on a "massive program" of employment on public works, wage subsidies, and expanded social assistance (through raising the age limit for child support grants and introducing provision for selected categories of unemployed people).

Neither the macroeconomic nor the institutional nor the political viability of such a program of public expenditure was self-evident. It is unlikely that the South African state has the capacity to expand greatly the number of people employed on public works programs, or to introduce a system of wage subsidies sufficiently fast and effectively to make any impact on unemployment. It was also implausible that the state could readily and effectively play the role of a developmental state. It was—and is—therefore likely that the post-Polokwane approach would entail much the same economic growth path as its predecessors, with benefits concentrated among the skilled and already employed, with few (and perhaps even fewer) opportunities for the unskilled and unemployed.

In this context of an entrenched and poor-unfriendly economic growth path, significant poverty reduction is likely to require a further expansion of the welfare state, that is, redistribution through the budget. In the mid-2000s, senior ANC and government leaders were generally ambivalent about, if not hostile to, cash transfers, even as they resorted to cash transfers to contain or reduce poverty. Government ministers and officials were slow to take pride in the system of social assistance, often denouncing rising expenditure on "handouts," which (they asserted) led to a culture of "dependency" and "entitlement." The government was said to be spending "too much" on social assistance, and the move to a "welfare state" was to be resisted (South Africa 2006b; ANC 2007). The National Treasury's proposals to expand the contributory welfare system (South Africa 2007b) were driven in part by a concern to reduce expenditures on noncontributory social assistance programs.

Indeed, some of the impetus behind the expansion of the welfare state came from the courts, interpreting the constitutional commitment to income security. In 2004, the Constitutional Court ordered the state to desist from discrimination against noncitizens who had permanent residence in South Africa. In 2006, cases were brought against the state challenging the exclusion of men ages sixty to sixty-four from the old-age pension (on the basis that women of the same age were eligible) and the age limit of fourteen years on the child support grant. Required to justify the shape of the welfare state, the state defended the status quo on the grounds that it was targeting its scarce resources toward those groups who were most "disadvantaged" or most "vulnerable." While the state's normative framework was defensible, its empirical case was flawed (Seekings 2008), and in 2008 the government conceded on the old-age pension issue. At Polokwane, the ANC endorsed the goal of raising the age limit for the child support grant to eighteen, although the following year the new Zuma administration seemed in no hurry to implement this new, higher age limit. Although the state can limit the overall size of the welfare state through allowing the real value of benefits to decline, the parametric reform of social assistance through incremental extensions of existing programs would serve to plug some of the holes in the safety net and reduce poverty levels.

If the welfare state is to be extended in ways that reduce poverty without providing significant disincentives to people to provide for themselves, then it should probably extend child support grants to children ages fourteen and fifteen (i.e., ages when children are required to attend school) and consider reducing the pension age for men and women to below sixty. Men and women without skills, above the age of fifty years, and living in rural areas are unlikely to find employment again. Removing them from the labor force would have few costs other than the direct costs of the cash transfers themselves. Indeed, this would also have the political benefit to the state of reducing the unemployment rate as well as the poverty rate. If the means test for the noncontributory old-age pension was abolished, as the National Treasury proposed (South Africa 2007b), then reducing the age of eligibility would not serve as a disincentive either to work (for the minority who have a real option) or to save for one's retirement. These expansions of the welfare state would bring the total cost of social assistance to over 5 percent of GDP, and the total number of grants paid monthly would rise to about fifteen million. The net additional costs would be lower if the real value of the old-age pension was allowed to decline, which could be defended in an environment of expanding coverage, or if the age of eligibility was reduced only in rural areas. Poverty would be reduced substantially.

A more radical suggestion is to introduce a minimum or basic income grant (BIG). In 2002, the government-appointed Committee of Inquiry into a Comprehensive System of Social Security for South Africa (the Taylor Committee) recommended the introduction of a BIG of R100 per month, to be phased in on condition that administrative costs could be contained (South Africa 2002; see also Seekings 2002; Standing and Samson 2003). The government dismissed the proposal, with its powerful spokesperson, Joel Netshitenzhe, telling the media that the government has a rather different "philosophy." Able-bodied adults should not receive "handouts," but should be helped to "enjoy the opportunity, the dignity and the rewards of work" (*Sunday Times,* 28 July 2002; see also Matisonn and Seekings 2003; Makino 2004; Meth 2004). But the BIG continues to have significant backers in the churches and, especially, the trade union movement. Trade unions have a material interest in (as well as an ideological commitment to) socializing the cost of providing for the poor, even though few of their own members are poor themselves (Matisonn and Seekings 2003). But, while trade unions and their allies can keep the idea of a BIG on the agenda within the ANC, they are very unlikely to be either keen or strong enough to overcome the opposition of powerful members of the ANC. If their pressure did intensify, the government could almost certainly defuse it by reducing the age of eligibility for the old-age pension, which would be a well-targeted and less costly intervention. It was revealing that a BIG was omitted from the otherwise "generous" 2009 election manifesto of the ANC and the agenda of the new Zuma administration.

The ANC-led government continued to emphasize public works programs to reduce poverty among the working-age adult population. Public works programs provide cash incomes, but only for those who are able to work and only in areas where work is provided. In South Africa, trade unions hold sufficient political power to prevent public works programs paying very low wages, which has the effect of limiting the number of jobs that can be provided within any given budget, and possibly has disruptive effects on existing opportunities to earn a modest income (Seekings 2006a).

Just as trade union power limits the space for reform of labor market policies and for low-wage public works programs, so it also constrains reform of public education. The power of the South African Democratic Teachers' Union (SADTU) makes it difficult for the state to introduce reforms that reward good teachers and ensure that bad teachers either improve their teaching or leave the profession (Seekings 2004).

This discussion of the prospects for policy reform assumes that there are no fundamental changes in South Africa's political system. This seems a reasonable assumption. "New" social movements might have emerged around specific grievances (Ballard et al. 2006), but it is difficult to imagine any mass mobilization around social grants, job creation, or the quality of public schooling. Nor is there any immediate prospect of an intensification of partisan competition for the votes of the poor. Insofar as voters grow more dissatisfied with the ANC, this is likely to lead to a process of overall dealignment (from all parties) rather than one of realignment (with an alternative party). Overall, the prospects for sustainable, pro-poor policy reform do not seem to be very good.

NOTES

1. *Hansard,* House of Assembly, 29 May 1998, col. 3,378.

2. Bhorat and van der Westhuizen (2008), in their preliminary analysis of the 2005–6 IES, found contrary evidence.

3. These data are compiled from successive issues of the UNDP *Human Development Report* and *South African Human Development Report.*

4. Data from UNICEF (http://www.unicef.org/infobycountry/southafrica_statistics.html).

5. The LFS uses a rotating panel, which raises questions about attrition. If people who lose jobs or are new entrants into the labor force are more likely to attrit than people in steady employment, or if unemployed people are less likely than working people to be included in the new part of each panel, then there is likely to be a tendency both to underestimate unemployment and to overestimate any downward trend.

6. In 2008 the twice-yearly LFS was replaced by a new quarterly LFS. The expanded unemployment rate dropped dramatically, in part because of changes in the definition.

7. Figures 1.2 and 1.3 are based on data from the *Budget Review* and *Inter-*

governmental Fiscal Review, published by the National Treasury. The slight decline in spending as a percentage of GDP in 2006 reflected in part the growth spurt of GDP.

8. *Financial Mail,* 18 February 2005, 34–35; 4 March 2005, 26.

9. *Financial Mail,* 1 July 2005, 18–20.

BIBLIOGRAPHY

African National Congress (ANC). 1994. *The Reconstruction and Development Programme.* Election manifesto. Johannesburg: ANC.

———. 2004. *A People's Contract to Create Work and Fight Poverty.* 2004 election manifesto. Johannesburg: ANC.

———. 2007. "Social Transformation." African National Congress Policy Discussion Document. http\\www.anc.org.za.

———. 2009. *Working Together We Can Do More.* Election manifesto. Johannesburg: ANC.

Ardington, Cally, David Lam, Murray Leibbrandt, and Matthew Welch. 2005. "The Sensitivity of Estimates of Post-Apartheid Changes in South African Poverty and Inequality to Key Data Imputations." CSSR Working Paper no. 106, Centre for Social Science Research, University of Cape Town.

Ballard, Richard, Adam Habib, Imraan Valodia, and Elke Zuern. 2006. "Introduction: From Anti-Apartheid to Post-Apartheid Social Movements." In *Voices of Protest: Social Movements in Post-Apartheid South Africa,* ed. Richard Ballard, Adam Habib, and Imraan Valodia, 1–22. Peitermaritzburg: University of KwaZulu-Natal Press.

Bhorat, Haroon. 2003a. "A Universal Income Grant for South Africa: An Empirical Assessment". In *A Basic Income Grant for South Africa,* ed. Guy Standing and Michael Samson, 77–101. Cape Town: University of Cape Town Press.

———. 2003b. "The Post-Apartheid Challenge: Labour Demand Trends in the South African Labour Market, 1995–1999." DPRU Working Paper no. 03/82, Development Policy Research Unit, University of Cape Town.

Bhorat, Haroon, and Ravi Kanbur. 2006. "Poverty and Well-being in Post-Apartheid South Africa." In *Poverty and Policy in Post-Apartheid South Africa,* ed. Haroon Bhorat and Ravi Kanbur, 1–17. Pretoria: HSRC Press.

Bhorat, Haroon, Pranushka Naidoo, and Carlene van der Westhuizen. 2006. "Shifts in Non-Income Welfare in South Africa, 1993–2004." DPRU Working Paper no. 06/108, Development Policy Research Unit, University of Cape Town.

Bhorat, Haroon, and Morné Oosthuizen 2006. "Evolution of the Labour Market: 1995–2002." In *Poverty and Policy in Post-Apartheid South Africa,* ed. Haroon Bhorat and Ravi Kanbur, 143–200. Pretoria: HSRC Press.

Bhorat, Haroon, and Carlene van der Westhuizen. 2008. "Economic Growth, Poverty and Inequality in South Africa: The First Decade of Democracy." Unpublished manuscript, Development Policy Research Unit, University of Cape Town.

Casale, Daniele, Colette Muller, and Dorrit Posel. 2005. "'Two Million Net New

Jobs': A Reconsideration of the Rise in Employment in South Africa, 1995–2003." DPRU Working Paper no. 05/97, Development Policy Research Unit, University of Cape Town.

Desai, Ashwin. 2002. *We Are the Poors: Community Struggles in Post-Apartheid South Africa*. New York: Monthly Review Press.

Hemson, David, and Kwame Owusu-Amponah. 2006. "The 'Vexed Question': Interruptions, Cut-offs and Water Services in South Africa." In *South African Social Attitudes: Changing Times, Diverse Voices*, ed. Udesh Pillay, Benjamin Roberts, and Stephen Rule, 150–75. Pretoria: HSRC Press.

Hoogeveen, Johannes, and Berk Özler 2006. "Poverty and Inequality in Post-apartheid South Africa." In *Poverty and Policy in Post-Apartheid South Africa*, ed. Haroon Bhorat and Ravi Kanbur, 59–94. Pretoria: HSRC Press.

Lam, David 1999. "Generating Extreme Inequality: Schooling, Earnings and Intergenerational Transmission of Human Capital in South Africa and Brazil." Research Report no. 99–439, Population Studies Center at the Institute for Social Research, University of Michigan, Ann Arbor.

Leibbrandt, Murray, James Levinsohn, and Justin McCrary. 2005. "Incomes in South Africa since the fall of Apartheid." Unpublished manuscript, School of Economics, University of Cape Town.

Leibbrandt, Murray, Laura Poswell, Pranushka Naidoo, and Matthew Welch. 2006. "Measuring Recent Changes in South African Inequality and Poverty Using 1996 and 2001 Census Data." In *Poverty and Policy in Post-Apartheid South Africa*, ed. Haroon Bhorat and Ravi Kanbur, 95–142. Pretoria: HSRC Press.

Lodge, Tom. 1999. "The African National Congress." In *Election '99 South Africa: From Mandela to Mbeki*, ed. Andrew Reynolds, 64–87. London: James Currey.

Makino, Kumiko. 2004. "Social Security Policy Reform in Post-Apartheid South Africa: A Focus on the Basic Income Grant." Centre for Civil Society Research Report no. 11, University of KwaZulu-Natal, Durban.

Matisonn, Heidi, and Jeremy Seekings. 2003. "Welfare in Wonderland? The Politics of the Basic Income Grant in South Africa. 1996–2002." In *The Basic Income Grant in South Africa*, ed. Guy Standing and Michael Samson, 56–76. Cape Town: University of Cape Town Press.

Mbeki, Thabo. 2006. "Address of the President of South Africa, Thabo Mbeki, at a Joint Sitting of the Houses of Parliament on the Occasion of the 10th Anniversary of the Adoption of the Constitution of the Republic of South Africa." Cape Town, 8 May. www.parliament.gov.za.

McDonald, David. 2002. "The Bell Tolls for Thee: Cost Recovery. Cutoffs, and the Affordability of Municipal Services in South Africa." In *Cost Recovery and the Crisis of Service Delivery*, ed. David McDonald and John Pape, 161–82. Pretoria: HSRC Press.

Meth, Charles. 2004. "Ideology and Social Policy: 'Handouts' and the Spectre of 'Dependency.'" *Transformation* 56: 1–30.

———. 2006a. "What Was the Poverty Headcount in 2004 and How Does It Compare to Recent Estimates by van der Berg et al?" Unpublished manuscript, School of Development Studies, University of Kwa-Zulu Natal, 18 May.

———. 2006b. "Half-Measures Revisited: The ANC's Unemployment and Poverty Reduction Goals." In *Poverty and Policy in Post-Apartheid South Africa,* ed. Haroon Bhorat and Ravi Kanbur, 366–458. Pretoria: HSRC Press.

Meth, Charles, and Rosa Dias. 2004. "Increases in Poverty in South Africa, 1999–2002." *Development Southern Africa* 211: 59–85.

Nattrass, Nicoli. 2002. "AIDS and Human Security in Southern Africa." *Social Dynamics* 28, no. 1: 1–19.

———. 2007. *Mortal Combat: AIDS Denialism and the Struggle for Anti-retrovirals in South Africa.* Pietermaritzburg: University of KwaZulu-Natal Press.

Oosthuizen, Morné. 2006. "The Post-Apartheid Labour Market: 1995–2004." DPRU Working Paper no. 06/103, Development Policy Research Unit, University of Cape Town.

Pilger, John. 2006. *Freedom Next Time.* London: Bantam.

Pollin, Robert, Gerald Epstein, James Heintz, and Leonce Ndikumana. 2006. *An Employment-Targeted Economic Programme for South Africa.* Brasilia: UNDP International Poverty Centre.

Reddy, Vijay. 2006. *Mathematics and Science Achievement at South African Schools in TIMSS 2003.* Pretoria: HSRC Press.

South African Advertising Research Foundation. n.d. "Big Improvement in South Africans' Living Standards Post 1994." Press release, South African Advertising Research Foundation, Johannesburg.

Seekings, Jeremy, ed. 2002. *Welfare Reform in South Africa.* Special issue. *Social Dynamics* 28, no. 2.

———. 2004. "Trade Unions: Social Policy and Class Compromise in Post-apartheid South Africa." *Review of African Political Economy* 100: 299–312.

———. 2006a. "Employment Guarantee or Minimum Income? Workfare or Welfare in Developing Countries." *International Journal of the Environment, Workplace and Employment* 2, no. 1: 44–68.

———. 2006b. "Facts, Myths and Controversies: The Measurement and Analysis of Poverty and Inequality after Apartheid." Paper presented at a TIPS/DPRU conference, Johannesburg, 18–20 October.

———. 2008. "Deserving Individuals and Groups: The Post-Apartheid State's Justification of the Shape of South Africa's System of Social Assistance." *Transformation* 68: 28–52.

Seekings, Jeremy, and Nicoli Nattrass. 2005. *Race, Class and Inequality in South Africa.* New Haven, CT: Yale University Press.

Seekings, Jeremy, Nicoli Nattrass, and Murray Leibbrandt. 2004. "Income Inequality after Apartheid." CSSR Working Paper no. 75, Centre for Social Science Research, University of Cape Town.

Simkins, Charles. 2004. "What Happened to the Distribution of Income in South Africa between 1995 and 2001?" Unpublished manuscript.

South Africa. 2002. *Report of the Committee of Inquiry into a Comprehensive System of Social Security for South Africa. Pretoria.* Pretoria: Department of Social Development.

———. 2003. *Towards a Ten Year Review.* Pretoria: Policy Co-ordination and Advisory Services, the Presidency.

———. 2006a. *A Nation in the Making: A Discussion Document on Macro-Social Trends in South Africa.* Pretoria: Policy Co-ordination and Advisory Services, the Presidency.

———. 2006b. *Strategic Plan 2006/7–2009/10.* Pretoria RP 22/2006. Pretoria: Department of Social Development.

———. 2006c. "Accelerated and Shared Growth Initiative—South Africa: A Summary." Pretoria: The Presidency. http://www.info.gov.za/asgisa.

———. 2007a. *AsgiSA: Annual Report. 2006.* Pretoria: The Presidency. http://www.info.gov.za/asgisa.

———. 2007b. *Social Security and Retirement Reform: Second Discussion Document.* Pretoria: National Treasury.

———. 2007c. *Mid-Term Review.* Pretoria: The Presidency.

Standing, Guy, and Michael Samson, eds. 2003. *A Basic Income Grant for South Africa.* Cape Town: University of Cape Town Press.

Taylor, Nick. 2007. "How Should We Think About the 2006 Matric Results?" http://www.jet.org.za.

———. 2006. "Equity, Efficiency and the Development of South African Schools." Unpublished manuscript.

United Nations Development Programme. 1999. *Human Development Report 1999.* Geneva: United Nations Development Programme.

———. 2003. *South African Human Development Report.* Cape Town: Oxford University Press for the UNDP.

van der Berg, Servaas. 2001. "Redistribution through the Budget: Public Expenditure Incidence in South Africa, 1993–1997." *Social Dynamics* 27, no. 1: 140–64.

———. 2005a. "Fiscal Expenditure Incidence in South Africa, 1995 and 2000." Report for the National Treasury, Pretoria.

———. 2005b. "Apartheid's Enduring Legacy: Inequalities in Education." Paper presented at the Oxford University/University of Stellenbosch conference, "South African Economic Policy under Democracy," Stellenbosch, 27–28 October.

———. 2006a. "Public Spending and the Poor since the Transition to Democracy." In *Poverty and Policy in Post-Apartheid South Africa,* ed. Haroon Bhorat and Ravi Kanbur, 201–31. Pretoria: HSRC Press.

———. 2006b. "How Effective Are Poor Schools? Poverty and Educational Outcomes in South Africa." Stellenbosch Economic Working Paper no. 06/06, University of Stellenbosch.

———. 2009. "Fiscal Incidence of Social Spending in South Africa." Stellenbosch Economic Working Paper no. 10/09, University of Stellenbosch.

van der Berg, Servaas, Ronelle Burger, Rulof Burger, Megan Louw, and Derek Yu.

2006. "Trends in Poverty and Inequality since the Political Transition." DPRU Working Paper no. 06/104, Development Policy Research Unit, University of Cape Town.

van der Berg, Servaas, Megan Louw, and Derek Yu. 2008. "Post-transition Poverty Trends Based on an Alternative Data Source." *South African Journal of Economics* 76, no. 1: 58–76.

Whiteford, Andrew, and Dirk Van Seventer. 2000. "Understanding Contemporary Household Inequality in South Africa." *Studies in Economics and Econometrics* 24, no. 3: 7–30.

Wilson, Francis, and Mamphela Ramphele. 1989. *Uprooting Poverty: The South African Challenge.* Cape Town: David Philip.

Black Economic Empowerment since 1994
Diverse Hopes and Differentially Fulfilled Aspirations

Anthony Butler

The fuller participation of black South Africans in the formal economy has been a central aspiration of African National Congress (ANC) policymakers since 1994. The government's current "broad-based black economic empowerment" (BBBEE) strategy is a response to the widely criticized elite enrichment that purportedly marked the first phase of black economic empowerment (BEE). BBBEE aims to increase the ownership, management, and control of businesses by black citizens, and especially by women. It also seeks to support the emergence of new skills and small businesses, to make finance more readily accessible to black entrepreneurs, and to use "preferential procurement" by the state and its agencies to spread empowerment across the private economy.

Empowerment has been highly controversial. Former president Thabo Mbeki's brother Moeletsi Mbeki (quoted in Reed 2003) has described BEE as an attempt by white oligarchs to buy black members into their club. One head of the South African Chamber of Business (Wakeford 2004) summed up BEE as "crony capitalism, fronting, enrichment and debt-burdened deals."

This essay investigates the diverse hopes that have arisen around BEE and explores the degree to which they have been variously fulfilled. The first part of the essay offers a periodization of BEE aspirations. It addresses the pre-1994 attempts of the National Party (NP) government to build a black middle class, and the parallel initiatives of big business in the late apartheid period. It goes on to explore the strategies of the South African Communist Party (SACP), in particular its wish to ensure that nationalist rule would not simply change the racial composition of exploitative elites, and the avowed goal of policymakers around Thabo Mbeki to create a "patriotic bourgeoisie." The essay then traces the changing conceptions of BEE across the Mandela and Mbeki governments, explaining how the current "broad-based" policy emerged and setting out some of its potential implications. Finally, it investigates the role BEE played in the downfall of Thabo Mbeki, the creation of the breakaway party, the Congress of the People (COPE), and the rise of Jacob Zuma to the state presidency in April 2009.

THE HISTORICAL ORIGINS OF EMPOWERMENT POLICY

Broad-based BEE is only one part of government's wider strategy to deracialize public institutions, provide employment and social benefits to the poor, accelerate land reform, and improve public service delivery. The spatial dimension of apartheid policy, prohibitions against asset accumulation, and the systematic undermining of human capital through "Bantu education" created deep-seated racial disadvantage. As politician and businessman Cyril Ramaphosa (2004, 74) has emphasized, empowerment initiatives must be broad, given the pervasiveness of the centuries-old economic disempowerment they are intended to redress. Although this essay focuses on the cluster of initiatives specifically designated as BEE, it is important to remember that empowerment cannot be understood or evaluated in isolation from these wider challenges and interventions.

Black Empowerment under the National Party

Afrikaner economic empowerment has influenced many ANC intellectuals. Afrikaners' long march toward equality with English speakers began in the 1920s, when organized farmers pressed successfully for tariff protection, state research support, and direct subsidies (O'Meara 1983). After the NP's 1948 election win, Afrikaner nationalists exploited affirmative procurement, reserved state contracts, and employment creation in the parastatals. They built up ethnic insurance companies and banks, and transformed their language and educational institutions into instruments of collective progress. As Thabo Mbeki's imprisoned father observed, Afrikaners were determined to establish "business enterprises which were to be the main pillars around which in the future large concentrations of Afrikaner enterprise were to take shape" (Mbeki 1991, 23).

While it seems strange to talk about empowerment in the context of the post-1948 NP governments, black empowerment also originated directly in efforts to bolster the viability of the systems of segregation and Bantu self-government. After 1948 the NP introduced a variety of new laws designed to further disempower black South Africans in the economy. The Native Laws Amendment Act of 1952 narrowed the defined group of black people with the right of permanent residence in towns. Meanwhile, the 1953 Bantu Education Act sought to provide black South Africans with nothing more than the meager skills necessary to work in the homelands or to function in menial or laboring jobs. It dramatically undermined science and mathematics teaching and interrupted the funding of the mission schools that had been centers of black educational excellence. The 1959 Extension of University Education Act prohibited black students from attending white universities, and mandated separate tertiary institutions for different population groups.

Africans were provided with specific new opportunities that were designed to deepen racial segregation by building a black professional and business class to service black populations and by bolstering the homelands provided for by the Promotion of Bantu Self-Government Act. Such aspirations were legislated in the 1951 Bantu Building Workers Act and the Bantu Investment Corporation (BIC) Act. The BIC, however, granted only a modest number of loans to Africans for the development of small-scale businesses in transport, retailing, cafes, butcheries, brickworks, and furniture manufacture, totaling perhaps R2.5 million by the middle of the 1960s (Bunting 1986). By contrast, some R300 million was invested in the white so-called "border industries" on the edges of Bantustans between 1960 and 1965, incentivizing Africans to look to their "homelands" (or rather to the white people on the outskirts of them) for economic opportunities.

Moribund black business policy was unexpectedly energized by the political upheavals of 1976. In the aftermath of the Soweto uprising, government recapitalized the BIC and increased homeland development subsidies, a policy buttressed by white business initiatives such as the Urban Foundation and the Small Business Development Corporation. Both the NP and its liberation movement enemies saw a black middle class as a bulwark against black radicalism and political unrest (Iheduru 2004, 4–5).

Red-Tinged Dreams

During the 1980s, the exiled ANC failed to develop a coherent policy for postapartheid BEE, but two emphases did emerge. The first was nationalization of haphazardly selected "commanding heights" of the economy, such as major resources groups, heavy industries, and financial institutions. This aspiration to public ownership was largely undeveloped in policy terms, and there were no real attempts to map out the practical obstacles to such a nationalization program or to the purposes it could practically realize.

In 1990, a newly released Nelson Mandela declared in favor of nationalization in his speech from Cape Town's city hall. However, when he received Anglo American chairman Gavin Relly and his assistant Michael Spicer at his Soweto home soon afterward, the men did not even raise the issue for discussion. One of the throng of reporters asked Relly, "Are you anxious about nationalisation?" Relly responded, "Nationalisation will be subject to the test of time and circumstance" (Spicer 2006). His confidence was based on Anglo Americans' careful intelligence gathering and bridge building with the liberation movement. Relly's September 1985 journey to Lusaka, in defiance of the instructions of P. W. Botha and Harry Oppenheimer, had already persuaded him that O. R. Tambo, Thabo Mbeki, Mac Maharaj, and Pallo Jordan were patriotic moderates (Frankel 2006). Relly also understood that nationalization was an immense practical task, requiring carefully planned administrative and legislative programs. He returned confident that the ANC's leading economic thinkers, such as Thabo Mbeki, had no practical strategy for turning the idea of state ownership into a credible program of nationalization (Spicer 2006).

The collapse of the USSR later discouraged even committed proponents of nationalization. Essop Pahad, a leading figure in the SACP at the time, remarked that "the extent of the intervention must be determined by a whole lot of factors of which we are not even in control and on which we do not have information" (Pahad 1990). Communist intellectual Jeremy Cronin later (1991) observed that "if you take away from Anglo American a whole lot of the economy, and then give it over to a bunch of bureaucrats, the democratization process, working power, is not being advanced necessarily at all by that."

The second aspect of liberation movement business policy was elaborated by communist intellectuals. At the 1969 ANC conference, communists introduced into the ANC's *Strategy and Tactics* document the demand that "our nationalism must not be confused with the classical drive by an elitist group among the oppressed people to gain ascendancy so that they can replace the oppressor in the exploitation of the masses" (ANC 1969).

The SACP's long-range goal was "international socialism," but its immediate objective was a national liberation that would not preclude the later realization of such socialism. Joe Slovo (1988) identified "the real question" as how to achieve the "intermediate" stage of national liberation without "blocking the route onwards to the next destination." SACP intellectuals' concerns evidently stemmed from postcolonial liberation movements' inability elsewhere to avoid parasitic dependency on state resources and the suppression of erstwhile trade union and communist allies.

Established Business Aspirations after 1976

As the vague but anticapitalist ANC economic stance was translated into policy proposals in the early 1990s, options were shaped by three aspects of the transition. First, the unraveling of the Soviet economic model created a crisis of intellectual confidence among communist parties. Second, the New Right policy revolutions of Reagan's America and Thatcher's Britain helped to launch the "Washington consensus": economic liberalization, privatization, reduced barriers to trade, and fiscal conservatism were suddenly the order of the day. Third, established white business was convinced that sustainable growth in the 1990s would depend on rapid reentry into international capital markets. It would also demand the enhanced competitiveness of South African businesses that had stagnated behind tariff walls and sanctions.

Gelb (2005, 369) describes the result as an "implicit bargain" between the ANC and big business that preceded the political transition (see also Beall, Gelb, and Hassim 2005). The liberation movement accepted orthodox fiscal policy, macroeconomic stability, and the dismantling of barriers to the movement of goods and money across South Africa's borders. Mandela even agreed to participate in meetings with the so-called Brenthurst Group, an informal panel of the half-dozen most powerful businessmen in South Africa. Meanwhile, business appeared to accept the need for "capital reform" to open ownership and management of South African businesses to black citizens.

The aspirations of established businesspeople, however, had a complex history of their own. The white business community had been deeply shaken by the events of June 1976 and was determined to cement black political stability. A memorandum from the Transvaal Chamber of Industries to the prime minister five weeks after the uprisings began captured this new sense of urgency: "The thought most basic to our submission is the need to ensure a stable, contented urbanized black community in our metropolitan areas." In the view of the chamber, "the mature family-oriented urban black already places the stability of his household uppermost, and is more interested in his pay-packet than in politics. Our prime point of departure should be that this 'middle class' is not weakened by frustration and indignity" (Transvaal Chamber of Industries 1976).

The most significant response from business was the establishment of the ameliorative and developmental Urban Foundation, initially spurred by Irene and Clive Menell of the Anglovaal dynasty. Irene Menell (2006) was fired up by the uprising to "mobilize resources, existing resources, which were simply going to waste, and use them to address practical problems," her inspiration being the New Detroit project from late 1960s Michigan. In July 1976 the Menells and others hatched a plan to hijack an Anglo American "do-gooders" conference and sell their idea to Harry Frederick Oppenheimer and Anton Rupert, the self-made giant of Afrikaner business (Menell 2006). Both men partly embraced the Menells' idea that high levels of poverty and limited social provision in peri-urban townships were ameliorable causes of social unrest. They agreed to convene a "businessmen's conference on the quality of life of urban communities" in place of a scheduled urban housing conference in Johannesburg's Carlton Hotel, on 29 and 30 November 1976.

The highlight of the event was Rupert's closing speech. "Storm clouds," he cautioned, were gathering both around the corner and over the horizon. "This," he sternly warned, "is how Knossos, the rich and civilized capital of ancient Crete, fell in a night to the invading Mycenaeans! . . . This is how Rome fell to the Barbarians!" (quoted in Domisse 2005, 238). In practical terms, Rupert observed, "We cannot survive unless we have a free market economy, a stable black middle class with the necessary security of tenure, personal security and a feeling of hope for betterment in the heart of all our peoples."

The way forward, he concluded, was "to establish an urban development foundation to accommodate and coordinate, on an ongoing basis, the private sector's endeavors at improving the quality of life in the urban black townships . . . to encourage and assist as a catalyst the transformation of South Africa's urban black communities into stable, essentially middle-class societies subscribing to the values of a free enterprise society and having a vested interest in their own survival" (Domisse 2005, 238–41). These ideas were met with acclaim, and the Urban Foundation was born. Within five years the foundation was receiving funds from more than 150 businesses.

Lipton (1988, 2007) has observed that such interventions must be understood as part of a complex relationship between capitalism and apartheid (see also Butler 1998, 30–53). Business is not homogenous, and the interests and intentions of companies change greatly over time. Many businesses certainly benefited in the early decades of segregation and apartheid from access to cheap and controlled labor. However, as the economy developed, some sectors began to require a skilled and permanent workforce, needs that militated directly against the apartheid policies of Bantu education and influx control. Moreover, apartheid constrained the size of the domestic consumer goods and services markets and undermined the export performance of many companies. Over time, there was a growing convergence of the interests of business in favor of reform, and hence increasingly concerted pressure by some business organizations to have apartheid modified or brought to an end (Lipton 2007, 294–97).

Predictably, it was Anglo American businesses that took the lead in the 1980s. The Urban Foundation survived, perhaps enjoying protected status as Harry Oppenheimer's creation. However, it was clear that business needed a new mechanism to engage with domestic struggle activists. After a number of meetings with the United Democratic Front leadership arranged secretly under the auspices of Anglo American subsidiaries between 1986 and 1988 (Butler 2008, 274–77), the Consultative Business Movement (CBM) was created in 1988 to formalize interactions between business and the domestic wing of the struggle.

CBM leaders such as Neil Chapman and Murray Hofmeyr came from Anglo subsidiaries. Anglo therefore adopted a three-pronged approach: it took a conservative position by means of the South Africa Foundation, which campaigned against international sanctions; it played a developmental role using the Urban Foundation; and now it assumed a more reformist demeanor by quietly controlling the activities of the CBM.

This consultative process was significant in that issues fundamental to the future of the society were raised and discussed. Intense debate over the racial inequalities of ownership in the South African economy in these forums allowed participants to develop the beginnings of what was later to become BEE policy. Moreover, in the relationships that were built up between activists and businesspeople, networks were established that would later crystallize into empowerment business relationships. As a result of these engagements, it is arguable that the "economic transition" was moving ahead of the political transition.

Empowerment under Mandela

Post-1994 government began as a "government of national unity" in which emphasis was given to confidence building in economic policy. Continuity was signaled by Reserve Bank governor Chris Stals remaining in office and the key post of finance minister remaining out of ANC hands. To the degree that BEE policy was articulated at all, it took the form of employment equity policy, the first stages of deracializing the state, efforts to take control of parastatal and regulatory institutions, and the nurturing of small and medium-sized business. BEE across the wider private sector was left to voluntary initiatives and networks, and the private economy remained for many ANC members a hostile realm responsible for an "investment strike" and "malicious acts of capital flight" (ANC 2000, sec. C). Nevertheless, ANC rhetoric concealed diverse approaches to private business; as Mandela (1990) observed, the ANC is a coalition in which some members "support free enterprise, others socialism. Some are conservatives, others are liberals. We are united solely by our determination to oppose racial oppression."

A National Empowerment Fund was created to channel privatization proceeds into emerging business, and public sector procurement protocols obliged suppliers to develop empowerment strategies. New agencies in the department of Trade and Industry provided management skills and finance for emerging black businesses. This "developmental" approach to BEE through the fostering of small and medium-sized businesses was often perceived as too limited by ANC activists.

At the ANC's 1997 Mafeking conference the ANC amended its *Strategy and Tactics* document to reflect new thinking that the black middle class and black bourgeoisie—and not merely the working class—were significant factors in the movement's "national democratic revolution." Government had recently adopted the controversial Growth, Employment and Redistribution (GEAR) program. Perceived by activists as a "neoliberal" policy foisted on the liberation movement by international capital, GEAR was responsible for a futile political backlash against economic orthodoxy.

Meanwhile, the voluntary process of black empowerment was cruelly undermined (Ramaphosa 2004, 73–78). Deals had been financed using "special-purpose vehicles" (SPVs) established to allow purchase of equity in an established target company. SPVs used shares as collateral against loans, and the 1998 emerging market crisis saw the banks wind most of them up. The unsustainable financial structuring of BEE deals resulted in black ownership on the Johannesburg Stock Exchange falling in 1998 from 7 percent of market capitalization to perhaps 2.2 percent (Beall, Gelb, and Hassim 2005, 693).

While voluntary empowerment was signally failing to produce a sustainable increase in black ownership, the "deployment" of ANC cadres to business accelerated. Black businesspeople began to press for a strategy less dependent on the questionable good faith of white business. Incoming president Thabo Mbeki's more radical rhetoric suggested that more meaningful progress would be made after 1999.

Mbeki's Patriotic Black Bourgeoisie

Thabo Mbeki (1994, 2) had argued in a well-known exile essay that "non-racialism in politics has to be accompanied by non-racialism in the economy." By the time he became state president, he was associated with the more specific argument that "we must strive to create and strengthen a black capitalist class" (Mbeki 1999). His position owed something to the lessons of Afrikaner empowerment, but he also drew on Malaysian experience. The United Malays' National Organization's historic program to transfer equity from minority ethnic Chinese to the majority Malays set twenty-year targets for the transfer of 30 percent of major enterprises (Daniel, Southall, and Lutchman 2005, xx). Like Afrikaner leaders, Mahathir bin Mohamed, Malaysian prime minister from 1981 to 2003, insisted that stakes in privatized state assets should not be given as "handouts" to the poor but rather should be directed toward those capable of retaining and building on them—already wealthy Bumiputera (sons of the soil).

The purported triumph of Malaysian empowerment is tarnished by the Malay elite's rent-seeking behavior and its continuing dependence on government favors. Mahathir himself has lamented the Bumiputera policy's creation of empowerment speculators trading in state contracts and licenses (Cargill 2005). Despite its practical drawbacks, Mbeki's strategy remains politically compelling. The central case for creating a black bourgeoisie turns on the need to build effective communications between business and politics. A black elite can open up reasonably honest lines of communication between politicians and businesspeople and nurture the confidence on which long-term investment is based in what has been a society of mutual distrust.

Sectoral Charters and the BEE Commission

The empowerment process followed two distinct paths during Mbeki's first term. Negotiations around "sectoral charters" got under way, initially in the petroleum and liquid fuels industry, then in mining and financial services, and ultimately across much of the economy. The charter process brought together stakeholders from business, labor, and government to agree on transformation objectives for a given sector, defined in terms of black ownership, employment equity, training and capacity building, business development, and a host of others (Iheduru 2004). The process was haphazard and uneven, and created a patchwork of potentially competing definitions and jurisdictions.

Empowerment was reinvigorated by a second approach, initiated in the 2001 report of the so-called Black Economic Empowerment Commission (BEECom), compiled under the chairmanship of ANC leftist-turned-businessman Cyril Ramaphosa. The commission, first mooted at the Black Management Forum's November 1997 conference, had a quasi-official status that allowed it to "think the unthinkable." It proposed an investment-for-growth accord, the creation of a national procurement agency, and the appropriation of public sector pension funds. At BEECom's intellectual heart, however, was a compelling rationale for "broad-based" empowerment, rooted in the report's understanding of the broad-based character of historical black disempowerment.

BEECom inspired the Broad Based Black Economic Empowerment Act of 2003, which combined a range of empowerment measures. Its key instrument is a "balanced scorecard" that measures every enterprise against wide-ranging criteria. The key fields of assessment, each accounting for around a fifth of the total points, are ownership, management control and employment equity, skills development, preferential procurement, and enterprise development and corporate social investment. Every element of the scorecard is clarified by "codes of good practice" dealing with employment equity, skills, procurement, enterprise development, the status of transformation charters, and a framework for BEE rating agencies. The already gazetted codes are binding on all state and public entities and are applied in all decisions involving procurement, licensing, concessions, public-private partnerships, and the sale of state-owned assets. No private company can escape the codes, moreover, because the requirements of the procurement component cascade down public sector supply chains.

The "generic scorecard" may appear to complement the various sectoral "transformation charters" already negotiated or under negotiation. Its effect, however, will be to leave charters dead in the water because they are either redundant through duplication or cannot pass the test of "substantial compatibility" with the generic codes that allows them to be legally enforceable.

CENTRAL CONCERNS SURROUNDING BEE

Fears about the overall thrust of empowerment policy relate to its over-all feasibility, its direct economic costs, the character of the "empowerment state" it might produce, its implications for ANC unity, and the shadow of uncertainty that it casts over the country's future.

Overall Limitations

For observers who believe there is no such thing as a free lunch, BEE is largely a mirage. The overall ownership targets for BEE suggest that a quarter of the private economy should be owned by black South Africans within a decade. Despite frenetic activity, we have so far seen something of the order of R200 billion committed to empowerment deals. Yet private sector assets total around R5 trillion (R5,000 billion). It remains quite unclear how this massive scaling up can occur, especially given the continuing shortage of black capital.

Banks that have reentered the BEE lending market refuse to carry signifi-cant risks. Vendor companies increasingly "facilitate" transactions, provid-ing loan guarantees, price discounts, or internal vendor financing at below-market rates. This is in effect a subsidy from established business to BEE investors (Cargill 2005, 23). Some established businesses quietly complain they are becoming underwriters responsible for excessive costs and assum-ing investment and interest-rate risk. These burdens raise the investment hurdle and so reduce overall investment in the economy.

Many black partners continue to buy high-risk equity while the finan-cial structuring of their debt leaves them vulnerable to economic downturn. The current generation of transactions, in short, may prove almost as un-sustainable as its predecessors. Deals continue to depend heavily on the ap-preciation of target companies' share prices. Even on the most optimistic as-sumptions, BEE companies face escalating debt-service requirements across the terms of their debt, with company earnings usually insufficient to cover interest and capital repayments (Cargill 2005, 23–25). Even "net equity" is merely "paper wealth," in that lock-in provisions have hitherto prevented the sale of the shares in order to protect BEE credentials against dilution. Such lock-ins, whether formal or otherwise, expose the fundamental ten-sion between vendors' desire to maintain high black shareholding levels and empowerment shareholders' yearning to realize value from their invest-ments (Jack 2005, 30).

In the difficult economic climate that emerged in 2008 and 2009, a large number of empowerment deals became vulnerable to failure. Some BEE companies—those most dependent on dividend income—have already failed or have been obliged to secure costly short-term funding to see them through the recession. During this downturn, however, much more risk is being shouldered by established companies, because they cannot permit the dilution of BEE status that would follow from the collapse of their empowerment partners (Temkin 2009).

Even when more favorable conditions return, only a part of the hoped-for ownership revolution will be realized, and ownership shifts may have less impact than often assumed on the distribution of economic power across the society. Even an unencumbered 25 percent shareholding may not in fact confer real power over the activities of a company, because minority shareholders have few formal legal rights and cannot compel action from an executive board.

Direct Economic and Business Costs

Business often argues that current BEE models are far too costly. It is difficult to see how the overall potential impact of BEE on economic growth could be calculated. Nevertheless, government's 6 percent growth target has already been obstructed by an inadequate savings rate. The transfer of shareholdings to black South Africans may eventually tie up as much as R450 billion of resources (Cargill 2005, 25). There is an evident tension with government's overall medium-term project to identify and reduce impediments to accelerated growth.

The ownership scorecard may create a swathe of dysfunctional empowerment partnerships. Jack (2005, 29) observes that "operational partnerships" with existing black industry experts will comprise a smaller proportion of deals as empowerment accelerates. Many deals will be "broad-based" partnerships such as development trusts or employee share schemes, which lack an economic rationale and are administratively costly. There will also be a growing prevalence of "influence-based" partnerships, usually operating through diversified investment holding companies whose key asset is political influence.

BEE will also discourage some of the foreign investment that might otherwise compensate for the savings shortfall. International investors cannot confidently predict that ten years hence empowerment obligations will not be renewed or even dramatically intensified. Domestic and foreign businesses alike are presumably not reassured by unwillingness in government to debate the very idea of "BEE costs." Meanwhile, BEE success stories like Eskom and Telkom have become associated with escalating administered prices and abused monopoly powers.

BEE may also result in an explosion of "fronting." Black managers will be employed but discouraged from participating in the operations of the business. Wakeford (2004) observes that fronting is likely to migrate down the supply chain to small and medium-sized companies, where it will be harder to detect, because "fat and underperforming" big business will try to hide its own poor ownership, skills, and employment equity performance by boosting empowerment procurement ratings.

Numerous lesser controversies surround broad-based empowerment: the legal status of the scorecard has been problematic because it conflicts with earlier preferential procurement legislation; enterprise development is poorly understood by business; the concerns of foreign and small businesses, although catered to, remain serious; corporate social investment is expensive and its beneficiaries often see no returns; "trusts" are being abused to circumvent the law and exploit black partners; and verification agencies seem unable to solve the problem of false empowerment self-assessments by business. In general, established white business complains that broad-based BEE is altogether too intrusive and places a heavy regulatory burden on business; emerging black business argues that limited ambition, exploitation, and fronting have made a mockery of the intentions behind the supposed BEE revolution.

The Empowerment State

There has been concern, in particular on the left of the tripartite alliance—the historic alliance of the ANC with the SACP and the Congress of South African Trade Unions—about the character of the emerging empowerment state (Cronin 2005). Such a state might become the slave of narrow interests rather than the "developmental state" that government has recently championed. BEE requirements can disguise the growth of patronage relationships between officials and entrepreneurs. They could ultimately lead every business to believe it needs a state patron to land government contracts or to secure licenses.

Industrial policy could become a life support system for politically well-connected companies. Given a drastic shortage of empowerment finance, public sector and parastatal pension funds might be drained in support of risky investments. Government departments might increasingly act at the behest of individuals rather than in the national interest. Intelligence systems and diplomatic capital might be put at the disposal of companies with high-risk foreign investments simply because of their close relationships with ministers or officials. Major infrastructure investments—in power generation and transmission, nuclear energy, or new-generation rail systems—might be still more often secured by golf-course handshakes rather than by social and economic cost-benefit calculations. The key financial beneficiaries will continue to be established businesses, but with politically connected black empowerment partners receiving a cut in return for their political influence.

Along the way, regulatory institutions, individual regulators, and peripheral institutions such as the public broadcaster may become casualties in battles between well-connected empowerment groups. In sectors such as oil and armaments, where scale, technical complexity, and secrecy make media and parliamentary oversight difficult, BEE vehicles have allegedly been instruments for massive personal enrichment. Media houses and the public broadcaster have been used to attack business rivals and to destroy the careers of scrupulous officials and regulators. "Revolving-door" problems have also arisen, with no effective confidentiality requirements or cooling-off periods constraining departing government officials. There are also widespread conflicts of interest between officials' roles as public servants and their external directorships.

The ANC and Private Capital

Critics in addition have become concerned about the implications of empowerment for the integrity and stability of the ANC. Capitalism evidently structurally limits the ability of black owners and managers to act in the interests of the oppressed. However, there is little to prevent influence moving in the opposite direction. Highlighting deals involving Manne Dipico, Popo Molefe, and Valli Moosa, one journalist memorably asked if the ANC might not already be "mortgaged to private capital" (Msomi 2005). Procurement scandals have meanwhile raised the specter of alleged "retro-kickbacks" to party funds. And one broad-based empowerment scheme, Batho Bonke, run by politician-entrepreneur and presidential aspirant Tokyo Sexwale, enriched thousands of prominent South Africans, sometimes to the tune of millions of rands.

Empowerment vehicles have been implicated in the alleged abuse of preferential procurement to bring kickbacks to party funds, and in the purported interference of business in the presidential succession process. BEE mechanisms can also cloak spreading patronage and corruption. SACP intellectuals worry that South Africa is following the road of some other postcolonial states in which liberation movement elites have thrown off colonial oppression only to become parasitic looters of state resources themselves.

SACP deputy general secretary Jeremy Cronin (2005) observes that "political tensions within the state and ANC leadership are 'resolved' (i.e. managed) by allowing some to be 'deployed' into the private sector. However, the converse of this is that the leading financial and mining conglomerates are increasingly reaching into the state and the upper echelons of the ANC and its Leagues—actively backing (betting on) different factions and personalities, and seeking to influence electoral outcomes and presidential succession."

ANC secretary general Kgalema Motlanthe (2005) has argued that "the central challenge facing the ANC is to address the problems that arise from our cadres' susceptibility to moral decay occasioned by the struggle for the control of and access to resources." Such challenges are not caused by BBBEE, but empowerment vehicles can be used as masks behind which patronage and corruption can spread. Any legal and regulatory framework can be exploited for private gain. However, more successful state controls over officials' conflicts of interest, and more effective ANC initiatives to police the activity of its own cadres, are prerequisites for containing the growth of patronage. It remains an open question whether a liberation movement already changed by its interaction with economic power will be able to steer empowerment in a benign direction.

BEE AND THE FALL OF THABO MBEKI

The emerging black business class engendered by BEE played an important role in the massive internal upheavals in the ANC after 2005. The central dynamic of these internal conflicts concerned the efforts of Thabo Mbeki's incumbent faction of the ANC to establish longer-term control of the movement and the state. These efforts came to a head in 2007, when Mbeki allowed his name to go forward for a third term as ANC president. His victory at the December 2007 ANC National Conference in Polokwane would have left him well placed to determine who should succeed him as state president. His factional allies—many of them "empowered" black businesspeople—would have become, at the very least, the new powers behind the throne.

The rise of Mbeki's antagonist Jacob Zuma had complex causes, some of which concerned the allocation of business opportunities in the modern ANC. Regional dimensions to the conflict emerged, with the tripartite alliance and provincial black businesses in KwaZulu-Natal presenting a uniquely cohesive platform for Zuma's campaign. Discontent with the perceived hold on national power and wealth exercised by prominent families from the Eastern Cape establishment, however, was a far wider phenomenon. Across the ANC, discontented businesspeople were willing to back Zuma in the hope that he might end supposed injustices in the allocation of empowerment opportunities and tenders.

Many of Mbeki's most vehement opponents in provincial ANC structures had been sidelined by the ruling national faction as a result of their manipulations of provincial finances. Some popular provincial leaders were marginalized for grotesque innovations in financial mismanagement and for creating vast patronage-based systems of factional enrichment that undermined provinces' capacity to deliver public services. Zuma's complaint of victimization was echoed by numerous others, who hoped to ride on his coattails after Polokwane.

The rise of Zuma was also fuelled by branch-level discontent about the monopolization of patronage opportunities by incumbents and by the general high-handedness that characterized an administration seemingly oriented toward external business opportunities.

Zuma's victory at Polokwane was followed by a wave of instability across the ANC, in which officeholders were "recalled" and Mbeki "loyalists" were purged. This process culminated in the recall of Mbeki from the state presidency in September 2008 and his interim replacement by ANC deputy president Kgalema Motlanthe. The recall precipitated the creation of a breakaway party that eventually came to be known as the Congress of the People. Although it presented itself as a party of clean government, with its primary objective the protection of constitutional government, COPE was evidently funded—and in most respects controlled—by members of the business establishment closely associated with Mbeki.

The vulnerability of those associated with former ANC president Thabo Mbeki quickly became apparent. Bulelani Ngcuka, centrally implicated in the alleged "plot" unjustly to prosecute Zuma, was ejected from a consortium chasing a R7.5 billion BEE deal. His business partners apparently concluded that his ties to Mbeki would count against them in the Zuma era—a presumption strongly fuelled by the comments of incoming ANC treasurer general Mathews Phosa. Fellow members of the consortium, however, were also perceived to be Mbeki men, and the deal was quickly put on ice.

Jeff Radebe and other ANC leaders held a major meeting with black businesspeople and professionals in Sandton in December 2008 at which the ANC's continued support for BEE and employment equity was reiterated, and a sympathetic ear was offered to businesspeople suffering from anxiety about what a new order might bring. In early 2009, Zuma himself launched a new Confederation of Black Business Organisations in recognition of this group's importance. COPE was meanwhile shooting itself in the foot as a result of inconsistent policy proposals from its leader Mosiuoa Lekota and others, suggesting that amendments to preferential procurement and employment equity policy might be desirable.

The influence of black business on the ANC continued into the election campaign. A realistic estimate of ANC spending across the campaign as a whole would be in the region of half a billion rands. Official party funding accounted for little more than R50 million, and the movement was rumored to have secured funds from foreign political parties, but open and hidden corporate donations clearly accounted for the overwhelming bulk of the movement's war chest. An ANC Progressive Business Forum was launched to milk businesses in exchange for access to policymakers, promising places on trade delegations, "ongoing dialogue" with national policymakers, and the chance to "share your aspirations and concerns" (ANC 2009).

ANC leaders attended numerous fund-raising breakfasts, dinners, and galas aimed at winning access to the deep pockets of black (and white) business. A Gauteng-based organization, Friends of the ANC, sometimes charged R20,000 for a seat at a gala dinner table, and spent the money on high-profile interventions such as a branded helicopter that allowed Zuma to campaign in rural areas. The growing confidence in the post-Polokwane and pre-election period of hitherto little-known black business actors suggested that a vigorous circulation of elites was under way, and rising figures evidently expected their influence in internal ANC politics and empowerment business dealings would continue to grow.

CONCLUSIONS: THE POTENTIAL COSTS OF UNCERTAINTY

Empowerment in some form remains a political and moral imperative, but the hope of most policymakers is that the current character of BEE will mature rapidly into something less politicized and more productively stable. Black entrepreneurs will look to exercise their newfound freedom to make deals and established businesses will seek out the skills and connections that black partners can bring. Businesses of all kinds, however, will also hunger for access to government contracts and to the ear of powerful decision makers.

A widely shared aspiration for BEE over the next decade is that it will progress so rapidly that the selective political manipulation of business opportunities by particular ANC leaders will begin to become less feasible. Although there is little reason to believe that such hopes will be realized in the immediate future, some current costs and dangers of BEE may conceivably decline. Once all established businesses are "empowered" by black directors, the ground rules for open competition for government business and for a more pluralist politics of policy influence may be easier to establish. A successful BEE policy that encourages more intense interaction between black business, established capital, and the state might also establish clearer rules to manage such relationships. By so doing it will create a more transparent and plural politics of competing interests.

Whether such aspirations will be realized in the future also depends on two sites of policymaking: the ANC and the public service. Conflicts of interest should not be allowed to continue between individuals' roles as public servants and their positions as directors of private companies that conduct business with the state. But it remains unclear whether government knows how to limit the proliferation of such relationships, to enforce a strict policy on revolving doors, or to curtail family and social network patronage. Equally important, the ANC may be unable to prevent the mutation of the party's own provincial and national offices into trading sites in which procurement and policy influence can be exchanged for party funds. A subcommittee of the ANC's National Executive Committee has stalemated for more than two years over proposals to introduce new rules of conduct to prevent such abuses.

Beyond these key sets of concerns about the future of BEE there lies a final and usually unspoken worry. The first voluntary phase of empowerment failed to produce a sustainable increase in black ownership and control. Black entrepreneurs remain vulnerable to recently deteriorating economic conditions. If the current generation of transactions collapses, a wider range of broad-based beneficiaries, an indebted new middle class, and politically well-connected empowerment partners will be implicated. The resulting political turbulence might generate a counterreaction against voluntary and business-friendly empowerment and mark the beginning of a more damaging and direct era of intervention. Uncertainty about the future of BEE is already undermining the business confidence that is a prerequisite for realizing government's pressing economic and developmental objectives.

NOTE

Parts of this essay appeared in a different form in *Business Day* (Johannesburg), 12 June 2006.

BIBLIOGRAPHY

African National Congress (ANC). 1969. *Strategy and Tactics of the African National Congress.* Johannesburg: ANC, May.

———. 2000. "Tasks of the National Democratic Revolution and the Mobilization of the Motive Forces." *Umrabulo* 8 (May).

———. 2009. "Progressive Business Forum." ANC. http://www.anc.org.za/pbf/index .php?include=benefits.html.

Beall, Jo, Stephen Gelb, and Shireen Hassim. 2005. "Fragile Stability." *Journal of Southern African Studies* 31, no. 4: 681–700.

Bunting, Brian. 1986. *Rise of the South African Reich.* London: International Defence and Aid Fund for South Africa.

Butler, Anthony. 1998. *Democracy and Apartheid: Political Theory, Comparative Politics and the Modern South African State.* New York: Macmillan.

———. 2008. *Cyril Ramaphosa.* Oxford: James Currey.

Cargill, Jenny. 2005. "Black Corporate Ownership: Complex Codes Can Impede Change." In *Conflict and Governance: Economic Transformation Audit 2005,* ed. Sue Brown, 21–27. Cape Town: Institute for Justice and Reconciliation.

Cronin, Jeremy. 1991. Interview by Padraig O'Malley, 26 August. Heart of Hope, University of the Western Cape. http://www.omalley.co.za/.

———. 2005. "The People Shall Govern." Communist University of Johannesburg, 5 November. http://amadlandawonye.wikispaces.com/2005-11-05,+Cronin, +The+People+Shall+Govern (accessed 21 March 2006).

Daniel, John, Roger Southall, and Jessica Lutchman. 2005. "President Mbeki's Second Term: Opening the Golden Door?" In *State of the Nation: South Africa 2004–2005,* ed. Roger Southall, John Daniel, and Jessica Lutchman, xix–xliii. Cape Town: HSRC Press.

Domisse, Ebbe. 2005. *Anton Rupert: A Biography.* Cape Town: Tafelberg.

Frankel, Sidney. 2006. Interview by Anthony Butler. Cape Town, 31 October.

Gelb, Stephen. 2005. "An Overview of the South African Economy." In *State of the Nation: South Africa 2004–2005,* ed. Roger Southall, John Daniel, and Jessica Lutchman, 367–400. Cape Town: HSRC Press.

Iheduru, O. C. 2004. "Black Economic Power and Nation-building in Post-apartheid South Africa." *Journal of Modern African Studies* 42, no. 1: 1–30.

Jack, Vuyo. 2005. "Empowerment Partnerships." *New Agenda* 20: 27–31.

Lipton, Merle. 1988. "Capitalism and Apartheid." In *South Africa in Question,* ed. John Lonsdale, 52–63. London: James Currey.

——. 2007. "The Role of Business under Apartheid." In *History Making and Present Day Politics: The Meaning of Collective Memory in South Africa,* ed. Hans Erik Stolten, 292–305. Uppsala: Nordiska Afrikainstitutet.

Mandela, Nelson. 1990. Interview. *Washington Post,* 26 June.

Mbeki, Govan, 1991. *Learning from Robben Island: The Prison Writings of Govan Mbeki.* London: James Currey.

Mbeki, Thabo. 1994. "This Seed Must Grow into a Tree." In *Black Business Pioneers,* ed. Thami Mazwai. New York: Houghton-Mifflin, Black Enterprise.

——. 1999. Speech to the Black Management Forum, Kempton Park, South Africa, November 20.

O'Meara, Dan. 1983. *Volkskapitalism: Class, Capital and Control in the Development of Afrikaner Nationalism.* Cambridge: Cambridge University Press.

Menell, Irene. 2006. Interview by Anthony Butler. Parktown, Johannesburg, 26 October.

Motlanthe, Kgalema. 2005. *ANC Secretary General's Organizational Report.* Johannesburg: ANC National General Council, June.

Msomi, T. 2005. "ANC Mortgaged to Private Capital." *City Press,* 27 November.

Pahad, Essop. 1990. Interview by Padraig O'Malley. 24 August.

Ramaphosa, Cyril. 2004. "Black Empowerment: Myths and Realities." In *South Africa at 10,* ed. F. Sicre, 72–84. Cape Town: Human and Rousseau.

Reed, John. 2003. "South Africa's 'Cappuccino Effect': Will Economic Empowerment Do More Than Create a Sprinkling of Black Tycoons?" *Financial Times,* 5 November, 11.

Slovo, Joe. 1988. *The South African Working Class and the National Democratic Revolution.* Umsebenzi Discussion Pamphlet, South African Communist Party, Johannesburg.

Spicer, Michael. I 2006. Interview by Anthony Butler. Parktown, Johannesburg, 24 October.

Temkin, Sanchia. 2009. "Leveraged BEE Deals at Risk, But 'Not Write-offs.'" *Business Day,* 4 August, 18.

Transvaal Chamber of Industries. 1976. Memorandum from the Transvaal Chamber of Industries to the Prime Minister of the Republic of South Africa. 29 July. DISA Online Archive.

Wakeford, Kevin. 2004. "Empowerment Must Be an Investment, Not a Cost." *Business Day,* 9 September, 9.

Forging Democrats

A Partial Success Story?

Robert Mattes

To describe the African National Congress (ANC) as an ambitious political movement is a massive understatement. Presented with a highly fractured society characterized by high levels of disempowerment, inequality, and destitution, the ANC set out in 1994 to forge unity around a new national identity and a common constitutional dispensation. It proposed to provide dignity and freedom to the previously oppressed through economic empowerment, but also by providing political rights and liberties and by enabling people to participate in political and economic decision making. It sought to end minority control and privilege, politically through the introduction of representative majoritarian democratic institutions and the transformation of the public service, and economically through affirmative action and black economic empowerment. And finally, it sought to eliminate widespread poverty through redistributive taxation and public spending to provide public services (such as education, health care, water, sewerage, housing, and welfare grants) and job opportunities. In other words, as it prepared to take political power in the early 1990s, the ultimate goal of the ANC was nothing less than the total transformation of South African society, reshaping a breathtaking cross section of political, economic, and social life.[1]

Such a transformation, however, was dependent on the development of a strong, effective, and competent state capable of overcoming the legacies of apartheid and carrying out this long list of intended duties and responsibilities. It was also dependent—at least in the eyes of the ANC—on redressing the relationship between the citizen and the larger political system to create a common popular pride in, loyalty to, and engagement with the new democratic South Africa, and thus to endow the state and the larger political system with the legitimacy or normative authority with which to effect these massive changes.[2]

If this is an accurate, if simplified, portrayal of the ANC's goals, what has actually happened in the ensuing fifteen years since the advent of democracy? To assess this question, I use data about public attitudes taken largely from successive surveys of nationally representative samples of South Africans conducted initially by the Institute for Democracy in South Africa (IDASA) in 1995, 1997, and 1998, and later by the Afrobarometer (a larger continent-wide consortium in which IDASA is a core partner) in 2000, 2002, 2004, 2006, and 2008.[3] While the earlier IDASA surveys focused only on South Africa, the Afrobarometer is a comparative cross-national survey of public attitudes in sub-Saharan Africa conducted in now twenty countries in West Africa (Benin, Burkina Faso, Cabo Verde, Ghana, Liberia, Mali, Nigeria, and Senegal), East Africa (Kenya, Madagascar, Tanzania, and Uganda), and southern Africa (Botswana, Lesotho, Malawi, Mozambique, Namibia, South Africa, Zambia, and Zimbabwe).[4] To bring these data to bear on the question at hand, I use a conceptual framework developed by political scientists to organize and classify citizens' attitudes toward the political system, but one that also has direct relevance to the way the ANC thought about its tasks as it attempted to revise the relationship between the rulers and the ruled (Almond and Verba 1962; Easton 1965; Norris 1999).

LEGITIMACY AND DEMOCRATIC GOVERNANCE

In any state, the popular acceptance of territorial boundaries and political rules, decisions, duties, and obligations is based ultimately on a sense of legitimacy rather than coercion (Easton 1965). Governments cannot make every decision based on consensus, and they cannot take a vote on every single decision they face. Almost all decisions will be opposed by minorities, and sometimes even by majorities. A widespread sense of legitimacy (or the belief that decisions ought to be obeyed because political leaders have the authority or the right to make those decisions) enables states to obtain compliance and cooperation from citizens, business, and civil society, even if they disagree with those decisions (Tyler 1990, 27–28). Legitimacy, therefore, constitutes a form of "diffuse" support for a political system that, according to political scientist David Easton (1965), does not have to be earned but inheres in the rules and institutions of the political system rather than in the current occupants of those institutions or their policies. It constitutes a "reserve of support that enables a system to weather the many storms when outputs cannot be balanced off against input demands. It is a kind of support that a system does not have to buy with more or less direct benefits" (273). Legitimacy, it is said, "endows" official rules and decisions "with moral oughtness" (Eldridge 1977, 8).

But the South Africa of the early 1990s was not just any state. To achieve its ambitious goals, the ANC needed to generate loyalty not only to a set of reformed state institutions but also to what for most citizens was an entirely new political community, with new borders and new rules. And it needed to foster citizen engagement with and participation in an entirely new range of duties, obligations, and procedures. It was thus necessary to forge several different types of legitimacy.

First of all, if democracy means "rule by the people," some basic consensus on "who are the people" was essential (Rustow 1970; Gellner 1983). In a historically divided society like South Africa, it was necessary to create a widespread sense of *national legitimacy* in which virtually all citizens accepted both the borders and the identity of the national political community, as well as expressed some sense of solidarity with if not pride in that community. Similarly, a new constitutional architecture of freedom, rights, and democratic rules of decision making would not long endure without endorsement by all relevant elites and by a substantial majority of the population who saw democracy as the best form of government for South Africa. Thus, developing *democratic legitimacy* meant creating the belief that, in Juan Linz and Alfred Stepan's (1996) memorable turn of phrase, democracy was "the only game in town" (see also Diamond 1998). Third, in a country where so few people had ever enjoyed the right to influence the decisions of their leaders in any meaningful way, elections and representative institutions would soon become a hollowed-out and fragile shell without the development of a widespread belief in the *legitimacy of democratic citizenship*. Such a legitimacy would produce citizens who not only regularly voted but also regularly communicated their preferences and needs to elected leaders and officials, monitored their performance, refrained from political violence, and defended democracy if it were under threat.[5] And of course, creating an effective and authoritative state meant developing a sense of *institutional legitimacy* of the new state based on its occupants' perceived right to make binding decisions and the lack of any alternative set of structures or institutions to which people owed their loyalties.

THE ANC'S THEORY OF GOVERNANCE AND LEGITIMACY

The ANC's collective thinking about its task in redressing the connection between citizens and the new democratic state paralleled in many ways the framework I have just laid out (though there were also some important differences). However, before I proceed to investigate this in detail, I want to address a possible objection to such a narrow focus on the ANC to the exclusion of other political parties, movements, or structures. Such an objection would flow from the assertion that South Africa's new political system was a grand compromise that reflected a wide mix of ideological and partisan preferences. Indeed, the ANC certainly made some important concessions from its initial bargaining positions that were of lasting consequence, such as an electoral system based on proportional representation, provincial governments with constitutionally defined powers, and the security of private property. But it is important to remember that the custodians of the ancien regime, the National Party (NP), failed to obtain most of its key constitutional demands.[6] And while the 1993 interim constitution did contain a number of other, temporary ANC concessions, they were of no lasting consequence because they were either ignored in practice once the ANC won the 1994 election or were eliminated from the final 1996 constitution by the ANC-dominated Constitutional Assembly.[7] Indeed, the ANC's original concession on proportional representation soon ceased to be a concession at all once it came to embrace that electoral system and defended it vigorously against any suggestions for electoral reform. Thus, what ultimately resulted from six long years of constitution making was a relatively majoritarian and very centralized system with few "veto players" (Tsebelis 2002)—a system that basically enabled the majority party to do what it wanted with few effective checks.

But regardless of the formal power it harnessed through constitutional negotiations and the 1994 election victory, the ANC believed that if was to achieve its goals and the new democratic order was to endure, deepen, and prosper, it would have to take a series of explicit steps to engineer a sense of patriotism and widespread popular attachment to the "new South Africa," a general popular commitment to democratic rules, an extensive trust in and respect for the institutions embedded within that regime, and an engaged, "participatory" citizenship. While the ANC may never have put it in so many words, the task it set for itself was one of creating legitimacy—or a "sense of moral oughtness" (Eldridge 1977) around the territorial and symbolic identity of the new South Africa, the democratic regime, the range of political institutions embedded within that regime, and its vision of participatory citizenship. Consistent with Easton's arguments, the ANC implicitly accepted that no political system can long survive simply through constant coercion or through regular quid pro quo exchanges of material payouts for "specific" or instrumental popular support. Rather, it needed to build the new dispensation on a more enduring, diffuse sense of intrinsic support that would not have to be constantly earned through the delivery of political and economic goods. Such support would ultimately manifest itself negatively, in citizens refraining from emigration, insurrection, protest, boycotts, or stay-aways, and positively, through regular political participation, tax payment, and law abidance. This was nothing less than a task of winning hearts and minds over to the new political order.

At the level of *political community,* the ANC was explicitly and actively concerned with a project of nation building. In reaction to the apartheid divisions of the populace into four population groups along racial lines and the subdivision of black South Africans into nine separate ethnic homelands, the ANC endeavored to create a single citizenship within a unitary territorial entity that would generate a feeling of national unity and a common loyalty to the new state (Johns and Davis 1991, 303). Moreover, it consistently saw this project as essentially one of attitudinal conversion to a new national identity, or what it variously called in its official documents a "shared sense of South Africanness" (ANC 1992), a "broad South Africanism" (ANC n.d.-c), or "the over-arching identity of being South African" (ANC 1997a).

Yet the ANC's vision of attitudinal conversion did not require the destruction of existing subnational identities. Rather, it recognized the vast cultural, religious, and linguistic diversity of South African society and often went out of its way to assert that it would work to protect cultures and give equal status to eleven different national languages (including the European languages of English and Afrikaans) (Johns and Davis 1991, 303). This new overarching national identity was to be achieved through common citizenship, equal rights, and the avoidance of ethnically defined federalism, through the state's active promotion of symbols such as a new national flag, place names, holidays, coats of arms, and national medals through the national news media and in the schools, as well as by aiding the development of museums, heritage sites, and arts (ANC 1992, 2002b).

ANC thinking on the subject of nation building was not without internal tensions, however. Even while it saw nation building fundamentally as a function of attitude change, many in the party equated it with socioeconomic change, or at least saw attitudinal change as a consequence of changes in material conditions. In the very same 1992 policy document that saw the party declare its basic objective "to encourage the flourishing of the feeling that South Africa belongs to all who live in it, [and] to promote a common loyalty to and pride in the country," it also flatly stated, "We cannot have a nation if half the people live in darkness, half in light" (ANC 1992, parts 1, 6). Indeed, the party's 1994 election platform document, the *Reconstruction and Development Programme* (RDP), saw nation building as part and parcel of a common development effort aimed at eliminating first and third world divides (ANC 1994a, parts 1.3.5–6). Many saw the RDP as a "starting point" that would "create the material basis for nation building. As long as our people are divided by a wide social and economic gap, which is reflected in racial, geographical and gender terms, nation building will be difficult to achieve" (ANC 2002b, part 162). This line of thinking was perhaps best illustrated in then deputy president Thabo Mbeki's 1999 speech to Parliament in which he argued that "nation building is the construction of the reality and the sense of common nationhood which would result from the abolition of disparities in the quality of life among South Africans based on the racial, gender and geographic inequalities we all inherited from the past."

ANC thinking on nation building was also marked by tension over how to define that nation. The ANC was committed to the tenet, first articulated in its 1955 Freedom Charter, that "South Africa belongs to all who live in it" (Johns and Davis 1991, 81), yet some party thinkers questioned the usefulness of the "Rainbow Nation" imagery first advanced by Bishop Desmond Tutu and Nelson Mandela and called instead for "a continuing battle to assert African hegemony in the context of a multicultural and nonracial society," arguing that all parts of the rainbow should form "a new African nation" (ANC n.d.-c, part 7). In this sense, nation building was seen in a quite different light, as a task of "building an African nation on the southern tip of the continent" (ANC 1997a; ANC 2002b, part 5).

In terms of the new *political regime,* the commitment to at least some form of democratic government had been a principal theme of ANC thinking for at least forty years, as articulated in the famous if vague phrase of the Freedom Charter, "the people shall govern" (Johns and Davis 1991, 8). The onset of constitutional negotiations in 1991, however, forced the ANC to specify and sharpen this commitment to mean a popularly based, elected government that is accountable and accessible, but also reflects the will of the majority (ANC 1991). That said, the ANC pursued a particular variant of democracy. After years of ascriptively defined minority rule, it understandably emphasized designing a government that reflected the "will of the majority" rather than ways to protect minority rights or ensure minority influence. Its notion of "the majority" was static and monolithic (rather than fluid and cyclical), and its idea of "the people" was collective and monolithic (rather than a collection of disparate individual interests). Thus, it justified its conversion to proportional representation rules for electing the National Assembly on the grounds that it would create a legislature that was "representative of the people as a whole" (ANC 1991) rather than one with clear links to geographic constituencies. And it entered constitutional negotiations with a strong suspicion of mechanisms that might give influence to political minorities such as supermajority thresholds for constitutional amendments, federalism, or proportional representation in the executive cabinet. Indeed, it saw the process of democratization as not simply achieving a free and fair founding election and producing a popularly elected government but as a much larger process of systematically eliminating minority control and privilege (ANC 1994a, part 1.3.7).

The ANC's quest to deliver democracy was made even more daunting by its conception of democracy, which consistently combined political and civil rights with notions of economic democracy (Johns and Davis 1991, 8). As a 1997 party document declared, "Democracy and development are intertwined and one cannot be separated from the other" (ANC 1997a). ANC officials and documents often spoke of "democratizing the economy" or "democratizing society." Thus, the political equality enshrined in the constitution, protected by the courts, and manifested in the 1994 election was only a first step toward what the ANC conceived of as democracy. It called on the national and provincial legislatures, following the founding elections, to "establish legislation and programmes which ensure substantive equality rather than formal equality" (ANC 1994a, part 5.4.1). Thus, supplying democracy not only entailed free and fair elections, civil liberties, and political rights but also material equality and economic emancipation.

Yet while the ANC devoted a significant degree of its official thought to transforming public attitudes to achieve the goal of nation building and legitimate the idea of the new South African political community, there is little evidence that it saw the necessity of taking proactive steps to legitimate the idea of a democratic South Africa. To the extent that it did think about it, the ANC understood what political scientists refer to as democratic consolidation as the absence of counterrevolutionary forces.[8] On the one hand, this lack of consideration implies that the party's thinkers simply assumed that people naturally preferred democracy as a political regime. On the other hand, at least some ANC leaders did worry that democracy could easily lose mass support if the democratically elected government failed to deliver economic goods. Nelson Mandela, for example, justified the party's massive RDP by arguing that "Democracy will have little content, and indeed, will be short lived if we cannot address our socio-economic problems with an expanding and growing economy" (ANC 1994a, preface). Or as a 1997 discussion document put it, "No political democracy can survive and flourish if the mass of our people remain in poverty, without land, without tangible prospects for a better life" (ANC 1997b, part 1.2.7). Thus, if only by default, the party did have some basic awareness of the issue of democratic legitimacy, but saw it turning sharply on the issue of economic delivery. Where Easton saw diffuse support as the bedrock of political stability, the ANC tried to build democratic legitimacy through the generation of specific support based on the delivery of economic goods.

As noted at the outset of this essay, almost all of the ANC's goals depended on the aggressive use of state institutions to remedy the country's political, social, and economic inequalities by delivering social and economic goods (Johns and Davis 1991, 9). While it was eager to take control of the reins of the relatively effective and powerful state machinery built by the NP, it also feared that it was full of politically recalcitrant bureaucrats, and realized that it was bloated and either had never been present or did not work in many parts of the country. Immediately after coming to power, the ANC began to decry the problems it faced in merging and integrating fourteen different ministries or departments across each policy area,[9] and complained that many rural areas simply had no administration (ANC 1994c). Within a year after coming to power, the party despaired at the lack of capacity and the level of incompetence it found in the security forces, and complained of "rear guard resistance" from old-guard bureaucrats (ANC 1995). As recently as 2002, party officials still found it necessary to call for improved "human resource capacity," grumbling about continuing challenges to coordinating policy across national, provincial, and local governments, as well as about the quality of available information with which to monitor policy impact (ANC 2002c). As a discussion document summed it up, "We need a state that knows what it should be doing, how to do it and to do it well" (ANC 2002c, part 45).

Yet in parallel with the process of building an effective and efficient state, the ANC also quickly realized the necessity of creating a legitimate state. Two years before it came to power, the ANC worried only about rebuilding public trust in the security forces.[10] But within months of taking office, it realized that it faced a far more widespread crisis of popular compliance with a wide range of government agencies, declaring that "we now have to deal with a mass constituency in which there is not always a strong tradition of paying for services, and the like," pointing to emerging problems of middle-class compliance such as white-collar crime, tax evasion, and illegal currency exports (ANC 1994c).

The ANC believed that effective state building, especially at local levels, was vital to the generation of institutional legitimacy. Initially it believed that this would require a public campaign in which the government went "out to the people to talk, clarify, and explain, and to answer questions" (ANC 1994b, parts 2.7.3, 2.7.8). Yet its desire to build an effective state was accompanied by a desire to transform the occupants of the state. It aimed to replace the overwhelmingly white, NP-appointed bureaucracy and make the public service physically representative of the population through affirmative action, coupled to be sure with training and advancing officials from previously disadvantaged backgrounds, as well as the retraining of old-guard officials (ANC 1992).

Its desire to build an effective state was also accompanied by a desire to maintain political control over that state. Even as it was just beginning to emphasize the need to develop skills and expertise in the public service, the party awakened to the fact that ANC appointees were developing new institutional loyalties. Strategists worried that the party was now "spread across a whole set of institutions," and complained that ANC ministers and deputy ministers were beginning to view the world from the "narrow perspective of their ministries, at the expense of a broader ANC outlook." They pointed to growing strains between national and provincial ANC executives, as well as to different approaches taken by ANC parliamentary study groups, ANC-led parliamentary committees, and ANC ministers.

Recognizing that "We are, therefore, now confronted with the additional challenge of maintaining and deepening a common ANC strategic sense of purpose across this very wide spread" (ANC 1994c), the ANC's response was, and has been, to try to impose tight party discipline across the state bureaucracy. It declared that "the constitutional structures of the ANC must assume an overall political, strategic primacy over the legislative and governmental institutions in which we are located" (ANC n.d.-b), reminded elected legislators that they "should continue to be seen as ANC cadres deployed in the various legislatures," and reaffirmed that they remained subject to the party's discipline and policies regardless of their new positions (ANC 1994c). Indeed, the difficulty of achieving representation, effectiveness, *and* partisan accountability was manifested in the fact that eight years after assuming office, the party still complained about the difficulty of building a public service that was representative and effective yet "politically accountable" (ANC 2002c, part 12).

Finally, at the level of the individual citizen, the ANC set for itself the goal of generating a high level of public participation, which it saw as one of the defining elements of democratic citizenship. The preferred method by which it intended to do this was largely through creating various channels and forums for participation. "The democratic order we envision," declared the party's 1994 RDP manifesto, "must foster a wide range of institutions of participatory democracy in partnership with civil society on the basis of informed and empowered citizens . . . and facilitate direct democracy" (ANC 1994a, part 5.2.6). "Democracy is more than electing representatives to power once every few years. It means enabling people, especially women, to participate in decision making at all levels of their lives" (ANC n.d.-a, part 4).

Yet the ANC's approach to participatory citizenship has revolved around a particular conception of the methods by which citizens should participate in political and economic decisions. In general, it has tried to effect a form of political participation that is mobilized by organized groups, channeled through extralegislative, often corporatist institutions, and ultimately aimed at generating consent for government policy. While it recognized that "there should be a clear right of access to the parliamentary legislative procedures to allow inputs from interested parties" (ANC 1994a, part 5.4.2), the ANC devoted remarkably little attention to the question of how to bring this about. Instead, the party fixed its attention on developing mechanisms of participatory and direct democracy, including "referenda where appropriate," but also "new forms of popular activism and governance" (ANC n.d.-b), including "people's forums," "negotiating forums," "local development committees," "community policing forums," "participatory local government budgeting," and "workplace forums" (ANC 1994a, part 5.2.6; n.d.-a, part 4; n.d.-b). These mechanisms also included corporatist-style "sectoral" or "multi-partite policy forums," which represented "the major role players in different sectors" at local, provincial, and national levels and would "promote efficient and effective participation of civil society in decision-making" (ANC 1994a, parts 5.13.7–8).

Thus, the purpose of encouraging public participation was as much one of mobilizing consent for state policies as it was of creating opportunities for people to influence, change, or even oppose public policy. Public participation forums, party thinkers argued, "constitute important opportunities for organs of civil society to participate in and influence policy making. Similarly they provide the democratic government with an important mechanism for broad consultation on policy matters" (ANC 1994a, part 5.13.8). To the ANC, "The rationale for a more participatory form of democracy is part of creating vehicles for dialogue between governments and people and is grounded in the view that where people are not involved in the decisions that affect their lives, social policies and political interventions are likely to fail" (ANC 2002c, part 59).

The ANC believed that government had an important role to play in mobilizing political participation. At the local level, the ANC "tasked" its municipal leaders "with the responsibility to generate mass participation in local government" (ANC 2002c, part 41). Nationally, the ANC argued that government had a responsibility to provide civil society organizations with "capacity building assistance": "They need to be assisted (and sometimes restructured) to improve their effectiveness, representivity and accountability" (ANC 1994a, part 5.13.8). "The democratic state therefore has a responsibility to ensure that this independent and non-governmental sector has the necessary strength to play its role in the ensuring that the people themselves, and in their own interest, become conscious activists for development and social transformation" (ANC 1996, sec. 4.11.6).

WHITHER LEGITIMACY?

To what extent has the ANC's vision of a new relationship between citizens and the political system actually been realized? Has a common national identity around the new South Africa emerged? Is democracy now widely seen to be the normatively preferred political regime? Are the country's new political institutions endowed with the right to make binding decisions? And have South Africans become more engaged and active in the affairs of government?

Political Community

To what extent have large, or increasing, proportions of South Africans come to accept the goals of "nation building" and embrace what the ANC called a "shared sense of South Africanness" or a "broad South Africanism"? To measure this, I turned to a series of survey items designed to measure personal national identity.[11] At least three initial observations can made about the data. First, against many expectations, responses to these question items demonstrate very high levels of national identity. Since 1995, between eight and nine out of ten respondents have regularly declared to interviewers that they were "proud to be called a South African," that "being South African" was "a very important part" of how they saw themselves, and that they wanted their children to "think of themselves as South African" (fig. 3.1). Second, these high levels of personal national identity were evident as early as 1995, only a year after the first nationwide election. Third, there has been a small but relatively consistent and statistically significant reduction in support from these items over the past decade, dropping from approximately 90 percent in 1998 to just over 80 percent in 2008.

One reason why the national identity measured by these indicators has been so high might be that different respondents have had different things in mind when they thought about being South African: white South Africans (and to a lesser extent Indian and coloured respondents), for example, might be thinking of the "old" South Africa rather than the new, inclusive South Africa. To check this possibility, I turned to a separate set of indicators that measure a more inclusive sense of identity beyond one's personal connection with the country. These items also demonstrate high levels of agreement, though at slightly lower rates of endorsement than the items on personal national identity, but they also show signs of slow erosion. Between three quarters (in 2008) and nine in ten (in 1998) of respondents have agreed over the past twelve years that people should see themselves as "South Africans first, and stop thinking of themselves in terms of the group they belong

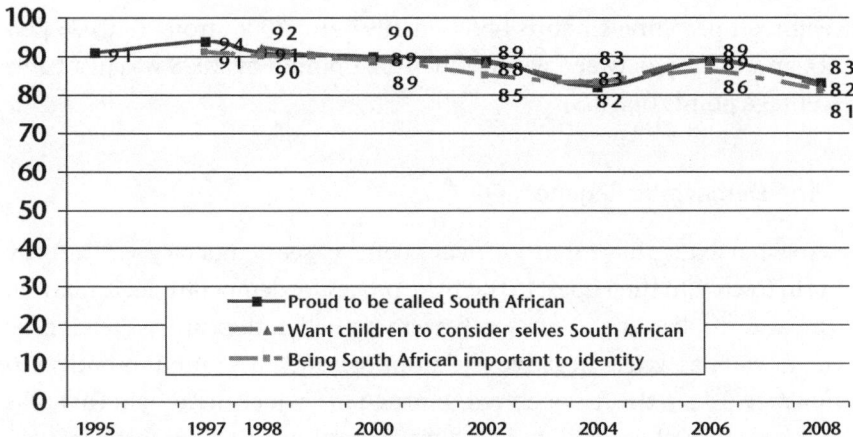

Figure 3.1   South Africans' views of personal national identity, 1995–2008 (percent)

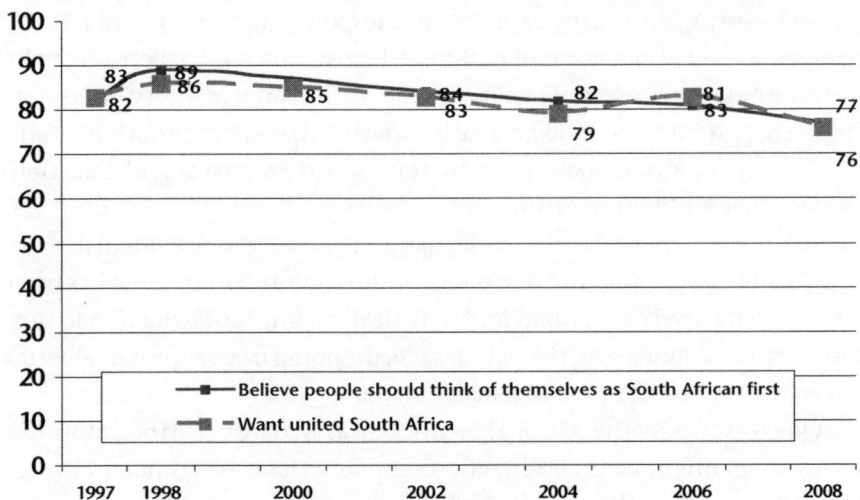

Figure 3.2   South Africans' views of inclusive national identity, 1997–2008 (percent)

to," and have agreed that it is "desirable to create one united South African nation out of all the different groups who live in this country" (fig. 3.2).[12] But even more telling trends appear once we disaggregate these figures by race. The result reveals that there were sharp racial differences in responses to these items in 1995, with white endorsement of the desirability of a common nation a full thirty percentage points lower than blacks' endorsement. But in contrast to arguments that the Mbeki government alienated whites and worsened intergroup relations with its "two nations" focus on issues of race and identity (Johnson 2009), the proportion of white respondents who think that a united South Africa is desirable actually *increased* steadily by eighteen percentage points between 1997 and 2006 (from 58 to 76 percent), and the gap between white and black opinion by 2008 was just three percentage points (fig. 3.3).

The Democratic Regime

To what extent have South Africans come to see democracy as "the only game in town"? In their quest to track the process of democratic legitimation, IDASA and Afrobarometer surveys have measured both positive preferences for democracy as well as negative rejections of nondemocratic alternatives to democracy. To tap the first element, I turned to a widely used item that asks respondents whether democracy is always preferable to other forms of government.[13] The results demonstrate that the proportion of South Africans

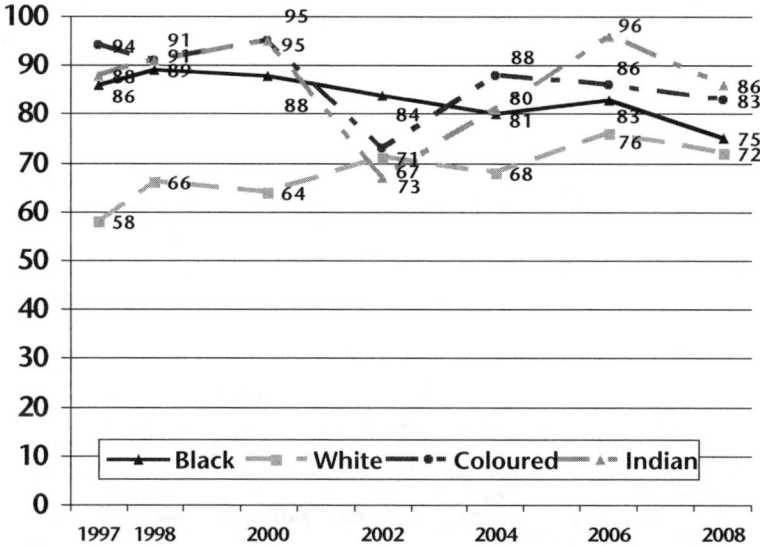

Figure 3.3　South Africans who want a unified nation, by race, 1997–2008 (percent)

(67 percent) who said in 2008 that "democracy is always preferable to other forms of government" was just marginally higher than the response to the same question in 1998 (63 percent), the first year in which it was measured. To obtain a longer time series of positive preferences for democracy, I used a different item that began by stating "sometimes democracy does not work," and then asked respondents whether under such a situation democracy was still always best, or whether they would prefer a strong, unelected leader.[14] While responses to this question indicate a slight, statistically significant increase in the proportions who said that "democracy is always best," from 47 percent in 1995 to 55 percent in 2003,[15] they confirm the broader picture provided by the first item: there has been little or no substantively meaningful increase in support for democracy across the South African population (fig. 3.4). Moreover, according to the 2008 Afrobarometer results, the two-thirds who support democracy ranks South Africa in the bottom half of the twenty African countries included in that survey, substantially lower than the 80 percent or more registered in Botswana, Zambia, Cabo Verde, and Benin (not shown).

To tap the second dimension of democratic legitimacy, the Afrobarometer has asked people since 2000 whether they would approve or disapprove if the country were ruled by an unelected strong man or by the military, if only one political party were allowed to stand for office, or if the country re-

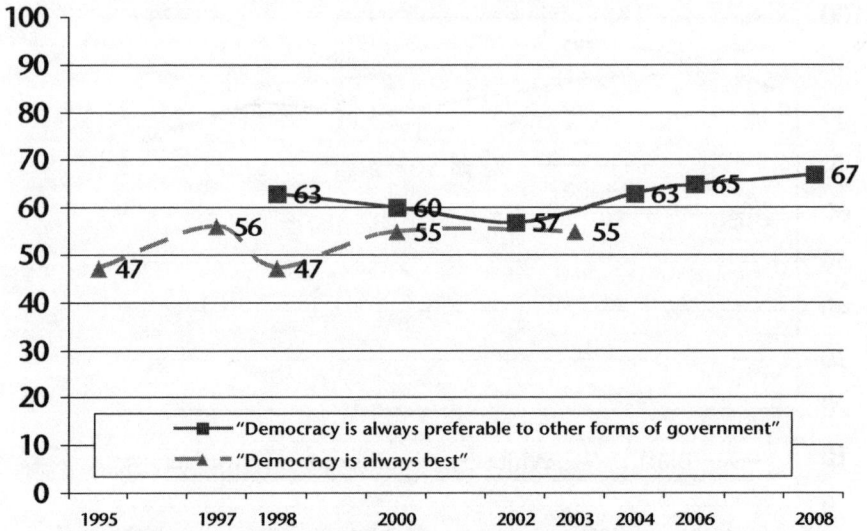

Figure 3.4   Public support for democracy in South Africa, 1995–2008 (percentage who agreed with each statement)

turned to apartheid rule.[16] The time-series data indicate that the proportion who reject a return to apartheid fluctuated significantly over the past eight years, but in 2008 stood just about where it started (from 65 percent in 2000 to 63 percent in 2008). While rejection of one-party rule increased by seven percentage points (from 56 to 63 percent) over the same period, rejection of military and strongman forms of rule actually decreased slightly, standing at 67 percent and 63 percent respectively in 2008 (fig. 3.5). As with support for democracy, South Africans' rejection of nondemocratic alternatives lags considerably behind that of many other African states. For example, while 63 percent of South Africans oppose "a strong president who does not have to bother with elections or parliament," nine in ten respondents rejected this option in Botswana, Zambia, Kenya, Tanzania, and Botswana. In fact, in only one country, Mozambique, is opposition to presidential dictatorship lower than in South Africa (not shown).

Because this time series begins only in 2000, I turned to a different indicator to obtain a longer picture of public attitudes to nondemocratic rule. It is an admittedly loaded question that is intended to force people to choose between democracy and an effective, efficient authoritarian government that delivers a range of valued goods.[17] When put this way, just three in ten (29 percent) of South Africans said in 2008 that they were "unwilling" to "give up regular elections and live under" a "non-elected government or

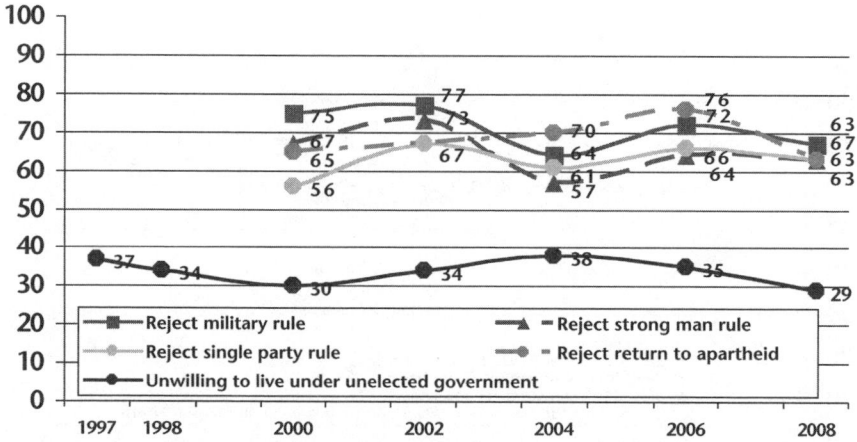

Figure 3.5 South Africans' views of authoritarian government, 1997–2008 (percent)

leader" who "could impose law and order, and deliver houses and jobs," which is the lowest-level measure since the question was first asked in 1997 (fig. 3.5).

State Institutions

To what extent have South Africans come to grant their new political institutions the right to make binding decisions? To measure the popular legitimacy of South Africa's state institutions, I used a set of questions that assess peoples' sense of the "normative authority" of the law, the constitution, and key state enforcement institutions.[18] On the positive side, in 2006 eight out of ten South Africans agreed that people should "obey the government in power no matter who you voted for" (80 percent) and that "it is better to find lawful solutions to problems even if it takes longer" (77 percent). However, agreement around these broad norms declines once respondents are presented with more specific items. In 2008, seven in ten (68 percent) agreed that "The Courts have the right to make decisions that people always have to abide by," and two-thirds (64 percent) said that the police "always have the right to make people obey the law." A still smaller 58 percent felt that the South African Revenue Service "always has the right to make people pay taxes." And given the substantial efforts that the government has made to publicize the constitution, including an extensive program of public input into the Constitutional Assembly, it is surprising that public affection for the constitution, which should be the source of all legitimacy, was rela-

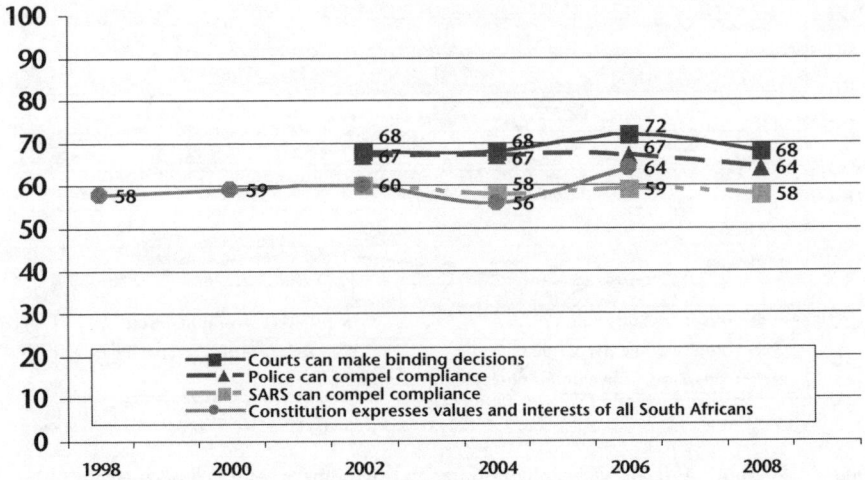

Figure 3.6   South Africans' views of constitutional and state legitimacy, 1998–2008 (percentage who agree)

tively low: just two-thirds (64 percent) in 2006 agreed that it "expresses the values and hopes of all South Africans" (fig. 3.6).

Not only do these results imply that significant minorities either reject or are indifferent to the legitimacy of South Africa's constitution and key law enforcement agencies, figure 3.6 demonstrates that there has been little, if any, substantive increase in legitimacy over the past few years. Moreover, South Africans accord the law and their institutions lower levels of legitimacy than citizens of other African states accord their own institutions. For example, while eight in ten South Africans agree that one should obey the government in power and three-quarters favor finding legal solutions to problems, the 2006 results for Ghana were 95 percent and 91 percent, respectively. And the expressed legitimacy of law enforcement institutions in South Africa places it near the bottom of the league table of twenty African countries in 2008 (not shown).

Political Participation

Finally, to what extent have South Africans come to engage with and participate in their political system? Things began on an encouraging note with a massive voter turnout for the founding 1994 election, estimated conservatively at 86 percent of the voting-age population (the estimate is due to the lack of a voters' roll). While turnout dropped to 71 percent in 1999, most South African analysts interpreted this as a natural "regression to the mean,"

given the liberation nature of the first election and the subsequent introduction of voter registration, and concluded that citizen participation was
still quite healthy. Yet turnout continued to plummet in 2004, dropping to
56 percent, a decline of thirty percentage points since 1994. While turnout
increased in 2009 to 59 percent, it is still far lower than where comparative
evidence suggests it ought to be. All other things held equal, a country using
South Africa's form of electoral system (proportional representation) ought
to have turnout levels around 70 percent; a country at South Africa's age of
democracy in 2004 should have had a turnout level around 69 percent, and
a country with South Africa's level of economic development should have
produced a turnout of approximately 64 percent (Norris 2003).

Moreover, the available evidence demonstrates that several other forms
of campaign participation drastically declined over the first ten years (we do
not yet have comparable data for the 2009 elections). The proportions who
said they were "interested" or "very interested" in the campaign dropped
from 64 percent in 1999 to 48 percent in 2004.[19] Where 44 percent reported
having attended an election rally in the 1994 campaign, 19 percent made
a contribution to a political party, and 11 percent performed some kind of
work for a political party, the figures had dropped to 23 percent, 3 percent,
and 5 percent, respectively, by 2004 (fig. 3.7).[20]

Declines in campaign participation have not, however, been caused by
any decline in South Africans' overall levels of "cognitive engagement" in
politics (Dalton 1988). Rather, South Africans' interest in politics and their

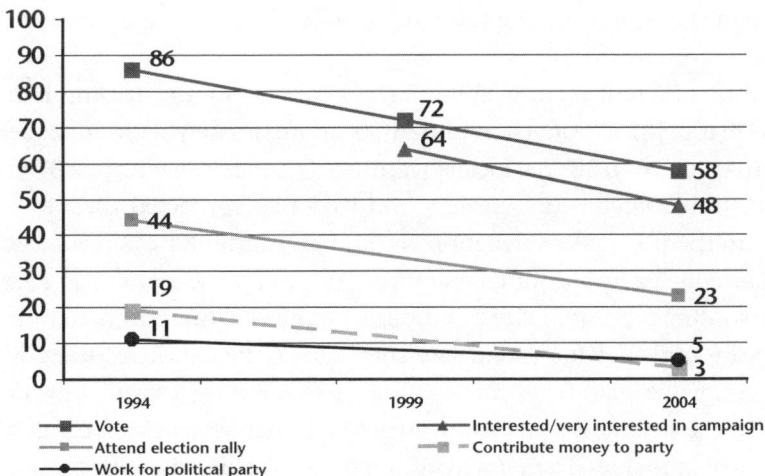

Figure 3.7 Campaign participation in South Africa in the 1994, 1999, and 2004 elections
(percentage of eligible voters)

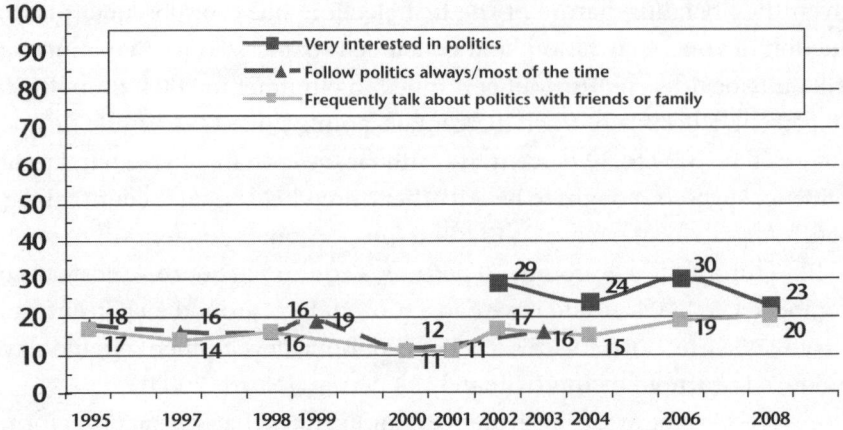

Figure 3.8   South Africans' interest in politics, 1995–2008 (percent)

rates of political discussion have been at relatively low levels since 1995 (fig. 3.8).[21] On average, between 15 and 20 percent of South Africans have told pollsters since 1995 that they regularly "follow politics," and anywhere between 11 and 20 percent have said that they "frequently" discuss politics and public affairs with friends and neighbors. In a more recent question, 23 to 30 percent said they were "very interested" in politics and public affairs between 2002 and 2008. Not only have these levels remained stagnant, but Afrobarometer data show that South Africans' levels of cognitive engagement fall in the bottom third of the eighteen countries surveyed in 2008, even though they consume the highest levels of news from television and newspapers (not shown).

A slightly different picture emerges from data on South Africans' contact with their political leaders. In mid-2000, approximately six months before South Africa's transitional local governments came to an end, just 3 percent told Afrobarometer interviewers that they had contacted their local councilor in the previous twelve months, and an additional 1 percent said they had attended a local council meeting.[22] While a subsequent change in question wording prevents a direct comparison, the next Afrobarometer survey in 2002 found that 16 percent said they had contacted their local government councilor.[23] However, our confidence in inferring a steady upward trend since the installation of South Africa's present system of local government (which included a majority of single-member wards, with proportional "top-up" seats) is reinforced by the fact that citizen-councilor interactions continued to increase over the next three surveys even as the question

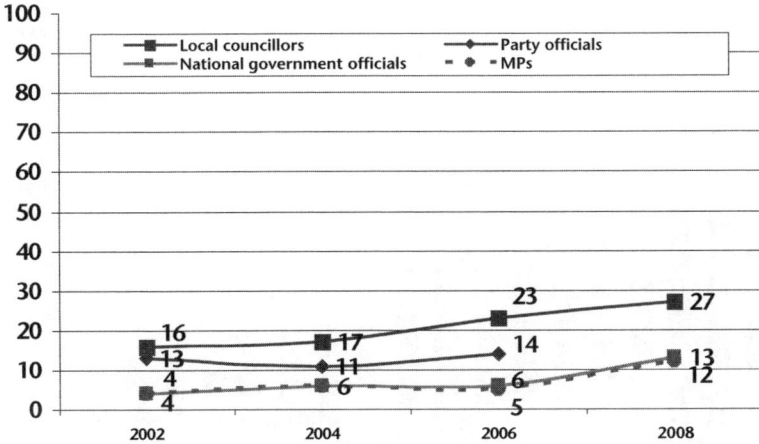

Figure 3.9   South Africans who have had contact with political leaders, 2002–8 (percent)

format remained the same, reaching 27 percent in 2008 (fig. 3.9). Yet even though citizen contact with elected local representatives has been increasing, South Africans' rates of contact are still far lower than in several other African countries, such as Botswana, Ghana, Kenya, or Uganda (not shown).

In contrast, contact with members of Parliament, who are all elected from national or provincial lists, has stood at 4–6 percent over the past several years. Although it doubled to 12 percent in the November 2008 survey, this increase probably reflected campaign activity ahead of the upcoming 2009 election. Rates of contact with MPs still fall in the bottom half of Afrobarometer countries surveyed in 2009.

Furthermore, South Africans have yet to grasp one of the basic elements of the representative process. The last round of Afrobarometer surveys included a question that asked respondents: "Who should be responsible for making sure that, once elected," local councilors and members of Parliament "do their jobs"? Most people assigned this responsibility either to the president (29 percent for MPs and 17 percent for councilors), to the legislative chamber (30 percent said Parliament had the main responsibility for holding MPs accountable, and 35 percent said local councils should do the same with their councilors), or to the political party (19 percent for MPs and 14 percent for councilors). Only one in ten and one in five respondents saw the voters as responsible for holding MPs (11 percent) or elected councilors (14 percent) accountable. Yet respondents in far less-developed countries were far more likely to possess a sense of agency in the representative process. In Malawi and Madagascar, more than seven in ten felt that this was the

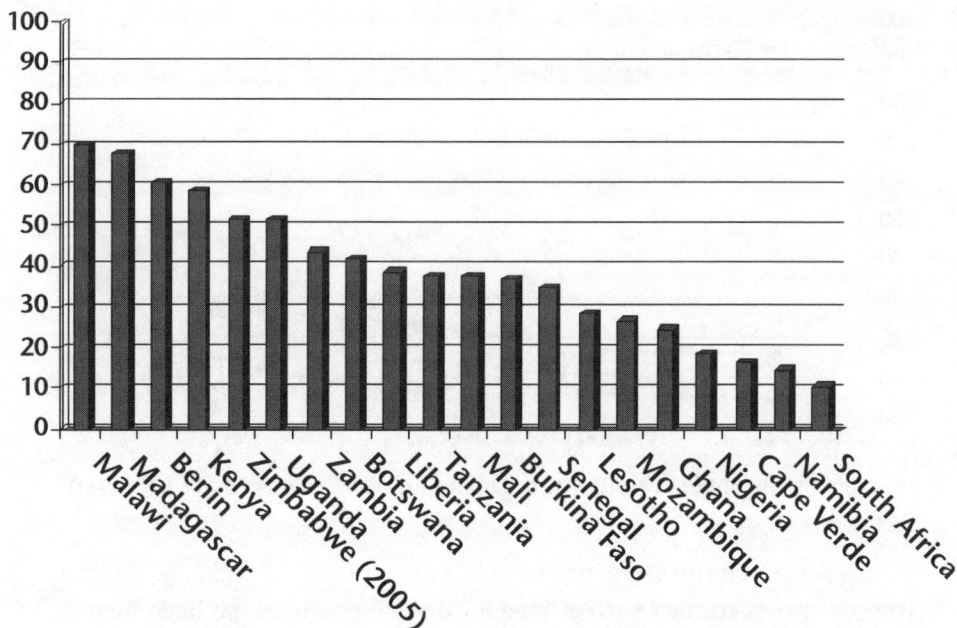

Figure 3.10   Percentage of Africans who consider voters responsible for holding MPs accountable, by country, 2008

primary responsibility of the voters, as did more than half in Benin, Kenya, and Uganda (fig. 3.10).

Consistent with the recorded increases in direct engagement with local government, citizen initiative with respect to local issues has increased somewhat. While 30 percent of all respondents told interviewers in 2000 that they had "got together with others to raise an important issue," the figure stood at 38 percent in 2008. While the proportions who said they "had attended a community meeting" at least once in the previous year has fluctuated, the 2008 result was identical to the 2000 findings. And since 2000, an average of one in four respondents indicated they had attended a protest or demonstration (which in South Africa has overwhelmingly tended to revolve around local issues), decreasing somewhat to 19 percent in 2008 (fig. 3.11).[24]

Again, however, civic participation in South Africa falls near the bottom of the twenty African countries surveyed by Afrobarometer in 2009. In sharp contrast, South Africans' rates of protest participation are the *highest* recorded across all countries (not shown). Thus, despite a raft of institutional devices designed to facilitate public participation in local government, South Africans have not rushed to take part. Rather, a slow learning process seems

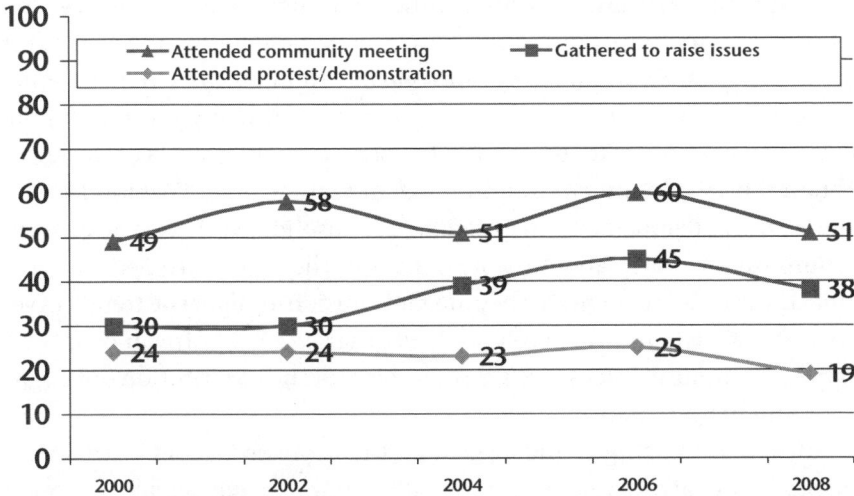

Figure 3.11 South Africans' community participation (percentage that did each at least once in the preceding year)

to be under way in which citizens are gradually grasping what they can and cannot achieve by way of influencing their elected representatives within the limits imposed by South Africa's constitutional dispensation.

DISCUSSION

Fifteen years into South Africa's new democratic political dispensation, the available evidence suggests that the "new South African" remains a decidedly incomplete democratic animal. Against most expectations, South Africans do endow their new political community with a great deal of legitimacy. They accept and embrace the new, inclusive South Africa, see it as a source of personal pride and affirmation, want to pass that identity on to their children, and are willing to subordinate their group identity to it.[25] Yet there is little evidence of change. With the exception of the sharp, and surprising, increase in white support for a "rainbow," "united South Africa," virtually all of these trend lines are relatively flat, if not decreasing. In other words, South Africans probably exhibited strong levels of personal national identity before any serious political program of officially sponsored nation building had even begun.

But while a basic consensus on the identity of a people supposed to govern itself may be a precondition for democracy in a historically divided society like South Africa, it is clearly not sufficient. Nine in ten people are proud of being South African, but only around six in ten prefer democracy, and between five and seven in ten reject nondemocratic forms of government for South Africa. These majorities are solid but far lower than in many other young African democracies. Moreover, there are few if any meaningful upward trends in aggregate support for democracy. By the criteria of the legitimation school of democratization (Linz and Lipset 1996; Diamond 1998), South Africa's democracy remains far from consolidated. The same generalizations can be drawn about the legitimacy of the new South African state: while these levels seem high, they are far from consensual, the trend curves are relatively flat, and the levels are lower than in other African countries. Significant minorities lack any sign of respect for the constitution or key law enforcement agencies.

Most discouragingly, and against all the expressed hopes of the ANC, the new political order has failed to build a culture of participatory citizenship. South Africans' cognitive engagement with politics has stagnated at relatively low levels, and voter turnout plummeted by thirty percentage points between 1994 and 2004, recovering only slightly in 2009. Rates of contact with MPs are extremely low (with a possibly momentary spike in 2008), though contact with local councilors and citizen initiative in community affairs have been increasing. Nonetheless, South Africans have the highest rates of protest of all twenty Afrobarometer countries.

A conclusive explanation for these attitudes and trends lies far beyond the scope of this essay. However, I conclude by identifying a small set of key factors that merit a central focus in any attempt to understand South Africa's new political culture. First, it is quite likely that South Africa's levels of national identity were and have remained high because, in contrast to those multicultural societies that attempted to suppress ethnicity and impose an artificial transformational identity, but then broke apart on liberalization or democratization (such as the Soviet Union, Yugoslavia, and Czechoslovakia), apartheid tried to impose ethnic and racial identities and deny the "South Africanness" of the majority of its citizens. Moreover, as Heribert Adam (1994, 38, 41) has pointed out, whereas distinct nationalities were largely located in distinct territories in those countries, imposed apartheid group memberships spanned languages and religions. Social groups were geographically interspersed, and there was a significant degree of economic interdependence among groups.[26]

Second, it is also likely that South Africans' support for democracy is weak because of the way they have been taught to understand democracy. As outlined earlier in this essay, the ANC has historically embraced a largely substantive, socioeconomic view of democracy and aggressively sold this conception to its followers. Unsurprisingly, Afrobarometer data demonstrate that South Africans are the most likely citizens in Africa to say that economic aspects such as "jobs for everyone," "equal education," and "basic necessities like shelter, food and water for everyone" are "essential" aspects of democracy, while simultaneously denying that political aspects such as "complete freedom for anyone to criticize the government," "regular elections," and "at least two political parties competing with each other" are essential. Yet it is a procedural, not a substantive, understanding that helps build a diffuse, intrinsic type of commitment to democracy in Africa (Bratton, Mattes, and Gyimah-Boadi 2004; Mattes and Bratton 2007).

Third, the modest levels of legitimacy of the law and state institutions can most likely be traced, at least in part, to the legacy of apartheid. Because the law was used as the prime agent of apartheid discrimination and oppression, the NP delegitimated the law in the eyes of black South Africans (Gibson and Gouws 1997). But it can also be traced in part to the political thinking of the ANC. As discussed earlier, the party developed a strong commitment to building institutional competence and effectiveness through massive (re)training in law enforcement, economic planning, and delivery. Ultimately, however, effective institutionalization requires not only skills but a degree of institutional autonomy, perspective, and loyalty (Polsby 1968; Simon 1976; March and Olsen 1989). But the development of such autonomy has constantly collided with the ANC's pursuit of "hegemony" and the consequent attempt to maintain political control over its "deployed" membership in the civil service and in national, provincial, and local legislatures (Giliomee, Myburgh, and Schlemmer 2001). With the exception of the courts, every time an important institution's attempt to assert autonomy in pursuit of its institutional mandate has brought it into conflict with the ANC—the Health Commission, Parliament's Standing Committee on Public Accounts, the Scorpions, and most recently the National Directorate of Public Prosecutions—the ANC has responded by emasculating or even simply eliminating that institution.

Finally, South Africa's low levels of political participation are quite likely a reflection of both the ANC's electoral dominance and the set of institutional choices made during constitutional negotiations. Cross-national evidence demonstrates that voter turnout in countries where the winning party consistently wins more than 60 percent of the vote have particularly low levels of voter turnout, averaging 57 percent, almost exactly the level to which South Africa's voter turnout has fallen (Norris 2003).

South Africa's institutional matrix has simply too few "veto players," or institutions of countervailing power with which to check the hegemonic aspirations of the ANC or fracture that party electorally. The list proportional representation (PR) form of electoral system appears to have had especially negative effects. Cross-national analysis across eighteen African countries demonstrates that, even after controlling for a wide range of social-structural variables, cultural values, and performance evaluations, people who live in countries that use list PR are less informed about politics, less likely to interact with elected leaders, less likely to express critical views about political performance, and less likely to demand democracy (Mattes and Shenga 2007; Mattes, Mozaffar, and Barkan 2007). Combined with a parliamentary system, extremely weak federalism, a history of strong party discipline, and the electoral dominance of the ANC, list PR removes any incentives for elected representatives to seek out and learn about citizen views because they might conflict with the signals sent by party bosses. And it simultaneously removes any incentives for people to contact those same representatives because they know they will ultimately have to toe the party line.

This situation in turn leads us back to the thinking of the ANC. As detailed above, the ANC has historically made a conceptual distinction between, and expressed preference for, "participatory" democracy over "representative" democracy. It based its assumptions about the development of widespread popular support for democracy on a hard-headed view of human nature, rooted in classic Marxist materialist thought, and concluded that citizens had to be motivated by economic incentives to pay their taxes and support the democratic system. Yet it based its assumptions about public participation on a decidedly wooly, wholly romantic view of human nature, rooted apparently in Rousseauian thought, and concluded that citizens have a natural predisposition and innate desire to participate in community affairs. Thus, it saw its main task as one of designing a wide range of participation forums through which people could participate ("Build it, and they will come," in the words of the Hollywood movie *Field of Dreams*) rather than one of designing institutions that would provide incentives to participate.

If this analysis is accurate, the data reviewed in this essay clearly suggest three main areas on which reformers need to focus their attention if South Africa is to increase the democratic content of its political culture and thus consolidate and deepen its democracy. First, there needs to be renewed attention to a sustained program of civic education, both for adults and in the schools, that teaches people to see institutions as authoritative and to value democracy intrinsically rather than instrumentally. Second, the country's electoral system needs to be reformed as a matter of urgency to include at least some element of constituency representation to establish direct linkages between citizens and elected officials.

Yet electoral reform will be extremely difficult given the interests of the ANC leadership in maintaining the present rules because these rules facilitate leaders' dominance over their elected officials, civil servants, and the rank and file. Ultimately, what may matter most is a change in the way the ANC thinks about democracy. To the extent that it is concerned with the endurance and deepening of democracy, the ANC needs to concentrate less on the delivery of economic goods (which is ephemeral and unpredictable) and more on the delivery of political goods, such as the rule of law, accountability and responsiveness, and the institutional reforms necessary to encourage greater participation in politics.

Whether or not the ANC is poised to make such a conceptual leap may depend on the nature of the dynamics that led to the party's unprecedented vote at its 2008 Polokwane conference to deny President Thabo Mbeki a third term as party president. If the vote was based fundamentally on a principled rejection of Mbeki's attempt to retain ultimate control through a hand-picked successor as state president or on his record of centralizing power and abusing state institutions to neutralize political challengers, then there are legitimate grounds to believe that the internal party split has led the party rank and file to develop a new appreciation for the rule of law, accountability, and the dangers of unchecked political power. If, however, Mbeki's democratic shortcomings merely provided a convenient excuse for those whose real objection was to his economic policies, it is likely that the party's approach to procedures and institutions will continue to be governed by political expedience, and the legitimacy of the South Africa's new political dispensation will remain incomplete.

NOTES

The initial research for the larger project from which this essay is drawn was supported by a Reagan-Fascell Democracy Fellowship from the National Endowment for Democracy and a Focus Area Grant from the South African National Research Foundation. I thank Joseph Tucker and Andrew Brooks of the NED and Amanda Lucey of the University of Cape Town for their able research assistance in the preparation of the longitudinal database on which this article is based. I also thank the following people for their helpful comments during earlier presentations of these arguments: Richard Rose, Roland Rich, Shaheen Mozaffar, Michael McFaul, Peter Lewis, Hoon Jaung, Steve Finkel, Larry Diamond, Marianne Camerer, Michael Bratton, Jeremy Seekings, and Kahreen Tebeau.

1. The scope of these ambitions can be traced to several different sources. First, it can be partially attributed to the equally breathtaking and nearly totalitarian nature of the apartheid regime that the ANC was trying to displace, which itself had attempted to control a wide range of human behavior, from politics to economics to social and even sexual interaction. Second, it partially had its roots in the hubris that accumulates in an organization that emerged victorious after dedicating eighty years of its existence to defeating white minority rule in South Africa. Third, it can also be traced to its own political thought, based in Marxism and Marxist understandings of historical determinism. And fourth, part of this ambition can be traced to the apparent example of the significant material advances enjoyed by white Afrikaners as a result of vigorous state intervention and assistance between 1948 and 1990, and the relatively effective state left behind by the National Party.

2. I take the notion of legitimacy as normative authority from James Gibson (2006).

3. The IDASA surveys cited in this chapter were supported through grants from the United States Agency for International Development (USAID), the United States Institute of Peace (USIP), the Southern African Migration Project (SAMP), and Irish Aid. The 2000–2006 South Africa Afrobarometer surveys were supported by grants from USAID, and the 2008 survey was supported collectively by the core donors of the Afrobarometer: the Swedish International Development Agency (SIDA), the Royal Dutch Ministry of Foreign Affairs (RDMFA/DANIDA), the UK Department for International Development (DFID), as well as CIDA and USAID.

4. All South African surveys have used personal interviews conducted in the language of the respondent's choice, with questionnaires translated into all relevant languages through "double-blind" methods. All surveys have used random, clustered, stratified, and proportionate area probability samples, thus producing estimates representative of the national public to within at least plus or minus two percentage points.

5. The standard distinction between attitudes toward the political community, political regime, political institutions, and political incumbents and attitudes toward the self as a political actor emanate from Almond and Verba (1962) and Norris (1999).

6. The NP had wanted the final constitution to be written by the Convention for a Democratic South Africa, or CODESA, a nonelected body equally representing nineteen different political organizations of vastly varying size and legitimacy, a collective and revolving presidency, a proportional cabinet that made decisions by consensus (effectively allowing minority party vetoes), and overrepresentation of minor parties in the upper legislative chamber. And once it conceded that CODESA

would write only an interim constitution, it demanded legislative supermajorities of 70 percent (and even 75 percent on fundamental rights) to ratify or amend the final constitution. None of these demands came to fruition.

7. For example, the ANC agreed to a Government of National Unity based on a proportional cabinet in which all parties with 10 percent of the vote were represented and all parties with 20 percent of the vote were able to appoint a deputy president, and which would operate in the spirit of consensus. But after just two years of operation, NP members realized that the ANC had little intention of consulting them on anything of real importance, and also saw that the Constitutional Assembly was ready to scrap the entire idea, and thus walked out. With regard to federalism, the interim document gave some significant exclusive and concurrent powers to the federal provinces, including writing their own constitutions. But the ANC never exercised any of these powers in the provinces it controlled, and the Constitutional Assembly removed virtually every meaningful exclusive provincial power from the final constitution. In terms of local government, the interim constitution provided a large number of relatively small local government units, with a two-tiered system in metropolitan areas and overrepresentation of white voters on most councils (though for historical reasons, black areas were effectively overrepresented in the Western Cape Province). But the two-tiered system of metropolitan municipal government was abandoned in the final constitution in favor of "megacities" run by executive mayors, and the total number of local governments was severely reduced, thus increasing the size and decreasing the accountability of local government.

8. The ANC's National Executive Committee had concluded by 1999 that the strategic environment was characterized by a "consolidated legitimacy of the democratic order, marginalizing any forces that had intentions of strategic violent counter-revolution" (cited in ANC 2002a, part 1).

9. This refers to the ministries of the ten Bantustan governments, and the three "own affairs" ministries and one national ministry of the tricameral system.

10. "The South African security institutions themselves developed a racist, closed, secretive, undemocratic structure, lacking legitimacy in the eyes of the people. The process of democratization will not be complete without addressing this problem" (ANC 1992, part Q.1).

11. "Please tell me whether you agree, neither agree nor disagree, or disagree with these statements:

- It makes you proud to be called a South African.
- You would want your children to think of themselves as South African.
- Being South African is a very important part of how you see yourself."

12. "Please tell me whether you agree, neither agree nor disagree, or disagree with these statements:

- People should realize we are South Africans first, and stop thinking of themselves in terms of the group they belong to.
- It is *desirable* to create one united South African nation out of all the different groups who live in this country."

13. "Which of these three statements is closest to your own opinion? A. Democracy is preferable to any other form of government; B. In certain situations, a non-democratic government can be preferable; C. To people like me, it doesn't matter what form of government we have."

14. "Sometimes democracy does not work. When this happens, some people say that we need a strong leader who does not have to bother with elections. Others say that even when things don't work, democracy is always best. What do you think? With which statement do you agree most: A. Need strong leader; B. Democracy is always best."

15. The 2003 result comes from a *Washington Post*/Henry Kaiser Foundation survey.

16. "Some people say that we would be better off if we had a different system of government. Would you approve or disapprove of:

- Military rule?
- One-party rule?
- One-man rule?
- We returned to the system of rule we had under apartheid?"

17. "If a non-elected government or leader could impose law and order, and deliver houses and jobs, how willing or unwilling would you be to give up regular elections and live under such a government?"

18. "Which of the following statements is closest to your view? Choose Statement A or Statement B?

- A: It is important to obey the government in power no matter who you voted for.
  B. It is not necessary to obey the laws of a government that I did not vote for.
- A: It is better to find lawful solutions to problems even if it takes longer.
  B: It is sometimes better to ignore the law and solve problems immediately using other means."

"For each of the following statements, please tell me whether you disagree or agree?

- Our constitution expresses the values and hopes of the South African people.
- The courts have the right to make decisions that people always have to abide by.

- The police always have the right to make people obey the law.
- The tax department always has the right to make people pay taxes."

19. In 1999, IDASA's Opinion 99 survey, conducted with the South African Broadcasting Corporation and the Electoral Institute of South Africa, asked: "Some people don't pay too much attention to political campaigns. How about you? Would you say that you are: A. Very interested, B. Somewhat interested, C. Not Interested." In 2004, the University of Cape Town/Comparative National Elections Project Post Election Survey asked respondents: "Could you please tell me to what extent you were interested in following this election campaign? A. Very interested, B. Somewhat interested, C. Not very interested, D. Not interested at all."

20. The 1994 IDASA South African National Post Election Survey asked respondents: "During the campaign, did you: Go to a mass rally or a speech made by a candidate? Do any work for a political party (e.g. canvass for votes)? Make contributions to a political party?" The 2004 University of Cape Town/Comparative National Elections Project South African National Post-Election Survey asked respondents: "Did you attend any party meetings or rallies during the election campaign? Did you work for any party or candidate during the election campaign? Did you contribute money to a party or candidate during the campaign?"

21. The construct of cognitive engagement is measured with two items:

- "How interested would you say you are in public affairs?
- When you get together with your friends or family, would you say you discuss political matters?"

22. "In the past year, have you contacted a government or political party official about some important problem or to give them your views?"
    If the person said yes, he or she was then asked, "What type of official was it?"

23. "During the past year, how often have you contacted any of the following persons about some important problem or to give them your views?" Respondents were then read a list of leaders. While the previous question may have underestimated levels of participation, since the respondent had to recall whether and which types of officials he or she had contacted, this question may overestimate it by making it seem more socially desirable to say that one had made contact.

24. "Here is a list of actions that people sometimes take as citizens. For each of these, please tell me whether you, personally, have done any of these things during the past year. If not, would you do this if you had the chance?

- Attended a community meeting?
- Got together with others to raise an important issue?
- Attended a protest or demonstration march?"

25. The single, recent anecdotal observation that for me confirmed reams of data on this issue occurred in October 2007, when the crowd of fifty-odd white

South Africans I had joined to watch South Africa play in the Rugby World Cup sprang to their feet prior to the game and belted out "N'kosi Sikeleli" ("God Bless [Africa]," a Xhosa song and part of the joint national anthem since 1994).

26. To be sure, none of this should be taken to suggest that national legitimation necessarily leads to greater levels of social civility. A strong sense of identification between people and the overarching political community does not necessarily make them any more likely to trust their fellow citizens, treat them equally, or tolerate their political differences, all of which remain major problems in South Africa (Gibson and Gouws 2003; Gibson 2004; Foster 2007).

BIBLIOGRAPHY

Adam, Heribert. 1994. "Nationalism, Nation-building and Non-racialism." In *Democratic Nation-building in South Africa,* ed. Ian Liebenberg and Nic Rhoodie, 37–51. Pretoria: HSRC Press.

African National Congress (ANC). 1991. *Constitutional Principles for a Democratic South Africa.* Marshalltown, South Africa: ANC, April.

———. 1992. *Ready to Govern: ANC Policy Guidelines for a Democratic South Africa Adopted at the National Conference.* Marshalltown, South Africa: ANC, 28–31 May.

———. 1994a. *The Reconstruction and Development Programme: A Policy Framework.* Marshalltown, South Africa: ANC.

———. 1994b. *RDP White Paper: Discussion Document.* Marshalltown, South Africa: ANC, September.

———. 1994c. *State of Organization: From Resistance to Reconstruction and Nation-building.* Marshalltown, South Africa: ANC, 17–21 December.

———. 1995. *One Year of Government of National Unity: African National Congress Discussion Document.* Marshalltown, South Africa: ANC, 13 October.

———. 1996. *The State and Social Transformation: Discussion Document.* Marshalltown: ANC, November.

———. 1997a. *All Power to the People! Building on the Foundation for a Better Life. Draft Strategy and Tactics of the African National Congress.* Marshalltown, South Africa: ANC, July.

———. 1997b. *The National Question in Post-'94 South Africa: A Discussion Paper in Preparation for the 50th National Conference of the ANC.* Marshalltown, South Africa: ANC, August.

———. 2002a. *The Balance of Forces,* no. 16. Marshalltown, South Africa: ANC, August.

———. 2002b. *Social Transformation: Fighting Poverty and Building a Better Life,* no. 16. Marshalltown, South Africa: ANC, August.

———. 2002c. *Transforming the State and Governance,* no. 16. Marshalltown, South Africa: ANC, August.

———. n.d.-a. *A Basic Guide to the Reconstruction and Development Programme.* Marshalltown: ANC.

————. n.d.-b. *The Character of the ANC.* Marshalltown, South Africa: ANC.

————. n.d.-c. *Nation-Formation and Nation Building: The National Question in South Africa.* Marshalltown, South Africa: ANC.

————. n.d.-d. *Organizational Democracy and Discipline in the Movement.* Marshalltown, South Africa: ANC.

Almond, Gabriel, and Sydney Verba. 1962. *The Civic Culture: Political Attitudes and Democracy in Five Nations.* Boston: Little, Brown and Co.

Bratton, Michael. 1998. "Second Elections in Africa." *Journal of Democracy* 9, no. 3: 51–66.

Bratton, Michael, Robert Mattes, and E. Gyimah-Boadi. 2004. *Public Opinion, Democracy and Market Reform in Africa.* Cambridge: Cambridge University Press.

Dalton, Russell. 1988. *Citizen Politics in Western Democracies: Public Opinion and Political Parties in the United States, Great Britain, West Germany and France.* Chatham, NJ: Chatham House.

Diamond, Larry. 1998. *Developing Democracy.* Baltimore: Johns Hopkins University Press.

Easton, David. 1965. *A Systems Analysis of Political Life.* Chicago: University of Chicago Press.

Eldridge, Albert. 1977. "Introduction: On Legislatures in Plural Societies." In *Legislatures in Plural Societies: The Search for Cohesion in National Development,* ed. Albert Eldridge. Durham, NC: Duke University Press.

Foster, Donald. 2007. "Social Change and Contact: Macro-political Considerations." Paper presented at the Centre for Social Science Research Seminar, University of Cape Town.

Gellner, Ernst. 1983. *Nations and Nationalism.* Oxford: Basil Blackwell.

Gibson, James. 2004. *Overcoming Apartheid: Can Truth Reconcile a Divided Nation?* New York: Russell Sage Foundation.

————. 2006. "The Evolving Legitimacy of the South African Constitutional Court." Paper presented at the Centre for Social Science Research Seminar, University of Cape Town.

Gibson, James, and Amanda Gouws. 1997. "Support for the Rule of Law in the Emerging South African Democracy." *International Social Science Journal* 152: 173–91.

————. 2003. *Overcoming Intolerance in South Africa.* Cambridge: Cambridge University Press.

Giliomee, Hermann, James Myburgh and Lawrence Schlemmer. 2001. "Dominant Party Rule, Opposition Parties and Minorities in South Africa." *Democratization* 8, no. 1 (Spring): 161–82.

Johns, Sheridan, and R. Hunt Davis Jr. 1991. *Mandela, Tambo and the African National Congress: The Struggle against Apartheid, 1948–1990: A Documentary Source.* New York: Oxford University Press.

Johnson, R. W. 2009. *South Africa's Brave New World: The Beloved Country since the End of Apartheid.* London: Allen Lane.

Linz, Juan, and Alfred Stepan. 1996. *Problems of Democratic Transition and Consolidation: Southern Europe, South America and Post Communist Europe.* Baltimore: Johns Hopkins University Press.

March, James, and Johan Olsen. 1989. *Rediscovering Institutions: The Organizational Basis of Politics.* New York: Free Press.

Mattes, Robert, and Michael Bratton. 2007. "Learning about Democracy: Awareness, Performance and Experience." *American Journal of Political Science* 51, no. 5 (January): 192–217.

Mattes, Robert, Shaheen Mozaffar, and Joel Barkan. 2007. "The 'Dumbing Down' Effect? The Impact of Electoral Systems Design on Democratic Citizenship in Africa." Paper presented at the Konrad Adenauer Stiftung and Electoral Institute of Southern Africa Conference on Electoral Systems and Accountability: Options for South Africa. Cape Town, South Africa, 28 August.

Mattes, Robert, and Carlos Shenga. 2007. "Uncritical 'Citizenship' in a 'Low-Information' Society: Mozambicans in Comparative Perspective." Afrobarometer Working Paper no. 91. East Lansing, MI, Cape Town, Accra: Afrobarometer. www.afrobarometer.org.

Norris, Pippa. 1999. "Introduction: The Growth of Critical Citizens?" In *Critical Citizens: Global Support for Democratic Governance.* Oxford: Oxford University Press.

———. 2003. *Democratic Phoenix: Political Activism Worldwide.* Cambridge: Cambridge University Press.

Polsby, Nelson. 1968. "The Institutionalization of the U.S. House of Representatives." *American Political Science Review* 62, no. 1 (March): 144–68.

Rustow, Dankwart. 1970. "Transitions to Democracy: Toward a Dynamic Model." *Comparative Politics* 2 (April): 337–63.

Simon, Herbert. 1976. *Administrative Behavior.* New York: Free Press.

Tsebelis, George. 2002. *Veto-Players: How Political Institutions Work.* Princeton, NJ: Princeton University Press.

Tyler, Tom. 1990. *Why People Obey the Law.* Chicago: University of Chicago Press.

The Business Community after Apartheid and Beyond

An Analysis of Business's Engagement in the Second Decade of Democracy

Theuns Eloff

The subprime mortgage lending crisis that emerged in the United States during 2007 created the worst economic crisis in the world in 2008, and the first economic recession in South Africa in seventeen years in 2009. The recession was formally announced by Statistics South Africa during the same month, April 2009, that President Zuma was sworn in as the third president of a democratic South Africa. Despite all the good political intentions of the Zuma presidency, the economy will be his greatest challenge, linked to his relationship to business in general, while his political allies sing leftist and labor power songs.

In 1997 the African National Congress (ANC) acknowledged that "the business community in South Africa was not in the past, any more than it is now, a monolith. It consisted of many different firms operating in several sectors, numerous individuals at various levels of decision-making and a number of business organizations" (ANC 1997).

Precisely because it is so difficult to treat business as a homogeneous entity, this essay seeks rather to investigate what business has done collectively, through its mandated and jointly established organizations, and to identify trends. As a subtheme, the issue of aspirations versus reality is raised.

It is important to remember that at the beginning of the transition to democracy, different groups of South Africans had vastly different expectations. The disadvantaged majority expected freedom, peace and security, human rights, jobs, proper education, houses, electricity, water, and land—and this list is not exhaustive. Business as a collective shared some of these desires but specifically expected a peaceful transition, a stable environment conducive to doing business, economic growth and wealth creation, safety and security, and human rights.

To evaluate the engagement of the South African business community in the new South Africa in the second decade of democracy, it is necessary to trace briefly business's steps in the last years of apartheid and the transition years, or roughly the years 1990–2004.

A HISTORICAL OVERVIEW OF BUSINESS'S ENGAGEMENT SINCE THE SIXTIES

Surviving alongside Apartheid (1960–70)

Like most business communities in the world, business under apartheid initially adopted a "survive with the regime" attitude. "The business of business is business, and leave the politics to the politicians," was the general attitude.

It is an incontrovertible fact that (white) business benefited from apartheid. The benefit came especially from the (artificial and temporary) stability brought about by apartheid in the sixties and early seventies, with GDP growth at almost 6 percent.

In hindsight, though, it is also clear that apartheid had huge costs for business, especially in terms of the modern triple bottom line—economic, social, and environmental. In addition, the lack of skilled human resources (because most of the population was excluded from the full benefits of the educational system or the economy) is costing business (and the country) dearly today (Gumede 2005).

The Eighties and Early Nineties: Engaging with and Challenging Apartheid (The Consultative Business Movement)

During the mid-eighties, the "business of business is business" attitude was first challenged by business leaders who made contact with the liberation movements (e.g., in Lusaka and Dakar). However, they also engaged the National Party (NP) government (e.g., P. W. Botha's Carlton Conference in 1981). The ANC stated that it "welcomes and acknowledges the fact that business broke ranks with the Botha regime in this way, and believes that it contributed to creating a climate within the privileged minority community more receptive to genuine, inclusive negotiation. At the same time, we feel obliged to point out that in the mid-1980s this break was not yet absolute" (ANC 1997).

Some business-based and business-sponsored organizations criticized apartheid policies publicly (e.g., the Urban Foundation), while others worked as facilitators for change. Among these were the Consultative Business Movement, or CBM (Eloff 1999b). CBM was launched in early 1989 as a direct response to the challenge of a peaceful transition from apartheid to a democratic South Africa (CBM 1988). It was spearheaded by a group of forty senior business leaders and formed after consultation with a wide spectrum of stakeholders.

Although not a formal representative organ of business, and not seeing a direct role for itself in negotiations, CBM did, however, based on certain principles for a future constitutional dispensation, believe that it (and individual business leaders) could perform a crucial catalyst role. This was done by lobbying the parties, popularizing and defining a values-driven negotiations process, stating support for the guidelines to the process of negotiations, intervening incisively on issues relating to business interests, and influencing other business organizations and politicians along the process to ensure a stable and effective political-economic solution (CBM 1997).

It is important to note that the broader business community at this stage still had not fully embraced a role in the transition. Slabbert (1992) points out that the private sector politically endorsed F. W. de Klerk's initiatives in the early nineties enthusiastically, but economically adopted a "wait-and-see attitude to the business consequences of the transition."

By 1990 CBM's leadership, however, had accepted that it was necessary to address inequalities of the past and that when restructured, damage to the economy needed to be averted in the national and self-interest. In addition, CBM influenced and informed business, community organizations, and others about one another's viewpoints, increased awareness among business colleagues about the present political-economic issues, and promoted in-house sensitization and transformation within companies (CBM 1997).

It is clear that a significant section of the business leadership had, before the peace process started a year later, and before the multiparty negotiations started almost two years later, agreed on a clear vision for the future and the desired political economy of South Africa. More important, it had decided to play a constructive role in the transition process and to commit significant resources to this end.

The Early Nineties: Active Participants in Establishing Peace and Democracy

With the start of the peace and constitutional negotiation processes, the broader business community started to participate actively in the transition to democracy.

Engaging the ANC Leadership on the Economy and Development

Realizing the necessity of a forum for senior business and ANC leaders to interact, CBM organized a meeting between some of the top leadership of the ANC and about 350 business leaders at the Carlton Hotel in Johannesburg in May 1990 (before the release of Mandela). The agenda included the nationalization versus privatization debate, and changed it from being largely rhetorical to a "deeper one about the nature of the mixed economy and ways to transform the political economy constructively and in partnership with each other" (CBM 1997, 17–18).

It also produced a degree of congruence and acceptance that the upcoming political transformation enjoyed the support of business, and that it would not be successful unless it was accompanied by an equivalent transformation of the economy (CBM 1997). This was followed a year later, in June 1991, by a national workshop on development that involved 250 senior representatives from a range of organizations. These and other encounters led to discussions with the ANC on its envisaged Reconstruction and Development Programme (RDP) and were part of an informed dialogue on economic growth and development.

The Peace Process

The high levels of political violence at the beginning of the nineties made the need for a national peace conference undeniable. The political dynamics and power struggle between the government and the ANC (and some of the other parties) presented a complicated problem regarding who had the power to convene such a conference. The impasse was broken when, through a combined effort, CBM and the South African Council of Churches (and other churches), as well as trade unions, facilitated a process that led to an inclusive peace process.

The first meeting of the formal peace process was convened at the offices of Barlow Rand Ltd . . . (and) co-chaired by John Hall (a Barlow executive and Chairman of the Chamber of Commerce) and Archbishop Desmond Tutu. This was the start of a long process in which business leaders played an active (but by no means exclusive) part in working with political parties, women's groups, religious groupings, NGO's, and labour unions to foster a climate of peace. (Fourie and Eloff 2005, 41)

After the signing of the Peace Accord by political parties in September 1991, business leaders played an active role in supporting the implementation of the National Peace Accord and ultimately local businessmen and women became involved in hundreds of local peace committees across the country.[1]

Managing Change: The Role of Business in Transition

In 1993 CBM published a book called *Managing Change: A Guide to the Role of Business in Transition.* This was done while the Multi-Party Negotiations were still in progress. In the publication, the more than one hundred CBM member companies were called to play an active role in the transition in four areas: the constitutional negotiations, the ownership and management base, effective and legitimate business practices, and the interface between business and community. The motivation for this was that the future of business was at stake and that the foundations for future prosperity should be laid. The material to compile the book resulted from a series of workshops that the national "Role of Business in Transition" Team conducted with 217 business executives across the country.

The Constitutional Negotiations

When it was agreed in November 1991 by the government and the ANC (as well as the other parties) to pursue multilateral constitutional negotiations, CBM was requested to render "process and secretariat services." This was a consequence of the organization's credibility and legitimacy built over a number of years (CBM 1997). "CBM's formal involvement with the constitutional negotiation process began with the . . . organisation for CODESA 1[2] in December 1991, and afterward continued with the CODESA process in 1992. . . . This formal . . . role was initially an administrative and secretarial one, but as trust in the CBM's political sensitivity and objectivity grew, it became more than that—facilitating the process in a quiet 'backroom' way" (CBM 1997, 25).

After the CODESA 2 deadlock in June 1992, the CBM leadership continued to keep contact with the different political parties, facilitating debate when almost no contact existed after the dark days of Boipatong and Bisho.

Acting as a "shuttle diplomat," CBM facilitated several meetings aimed at establishing what could be done to break the deadlock and identify obstacles to the resumption of negotiations. Most of the parties welcomed the CBM initiatives, and the ANC political leadership encouraged the business leaders to continue with this process (CBM 1997).

After the ANC and NP had resolved the impasse and signed the Record of Understanding in 1992, the new process started in March 1993 with the Planning Conference for Multi-Party Talks. At this meeting, CBM was formally asked by the parties to act as the administration of the Multi-Party Negotiating Process (as opposed to its mainly secretarial role in CODESA) (CBM 1997).

While the Multi-Party Negotiations Process was in progress, CBM continued in its shuttle diplomacy role, ensuring that potential stumbling blocks were identified and dealt with by the parties in timely fashion. For instance, CBM gathered a group of international and local constitutional experts for a workshop process of three weeks, resulting in a report, *Regions in South Africa: Constitutional Options and Their Implications for Good Government and a Sound Economy.* The wording in this report about the powers of the provinces was adopted into the South African constitution almost verbatim.[3]

When international mediation to get the Inkatha Freedom Party (IFP) into the election failed just before the elections in 1994, an informal shuttle diplomacy process was started by one of the lower-profile international mediators, with intense support from CBM. A corporate jet was used to shuttle national leaders from different parties to secure buy-in one week before the election (Fourie and Eloff 2005). It was fitting that business leaders also played a significant role in removing this one last stumbling block on the road to the new South Africa (Friedman and Atkinson 1994).

The National Economic Forum (Leading to NEDLAC)

In August 1990, CBM launched the Economic Project. During early 1991 (while violence racked the country), a series of regional economic workshops were held, with themes such as poverty and inequality; development, growth, and redistribution; South Africa and the world economy; and the roles of state, markets, business, and labor. This process helped the debate to mature significantly in a relatively short period of time. While real differences remained, parties had begun to debate far more complex issues.

CBM was asked in January 1992 to facilitate a meeting between stakeholders, and eventually the National Economic Forum (NEF) was formally launched in October 1992. The NEF came to play an important role in developing common positions among the key economic stakeholders. CBM provided secretariat services to the NEF until it was absorbed into the National Education, Development and Labour Council (NEDLAC) in 1995. CBM was also requested by the mandated business organizations to act as secretariat for the Business Forum, the business input into the NEF (CBM 1997).

The Business Election Fund

In the run-up to the democratic elections in 1994, business leaders realized there was a need for an initiative whereby companies could give money not to political parties but to ensure that the election would be as free and fair as possible, serving the aims of democracy. CBM initiated the Business Election Fund (BEF), with the slogan "Business stands for building a great Nation." With CBM as its secretariat, the BEF eventually raised a total of R14 million in cash and R32 million in in-kind commitments, cementing business's commitment to the process of transition (BEF 1994; Fourie and Eloff 2005).

Business in the Early Nineties

Realizing that a different approach was necessary, even the mandated business organizations came into the transition process in the early nineties. The catchphrase became "The business of business is to stay in business." The underlying philosophy was not merely a liberal do-gooder one but "enlightened self-interest," and therefore sustainable in terms of both effort and resources. The South African business community had, out of dire necessity, started to practice (some of) the principles of the triple bottom line, before it was formally propagated.

It is interesting that none of the "grand accounts" of the negotiations and transition (e.g., Friedman and Atkinson 1994; Sparks 1994; Waldmeier 1997) gives much (if any) recognition to the role that business played (albeit behind the scenes), probably because the events described were largely seen through politicians' eyes. Slabbert gives slightly more recognition to the role of business and "predicts" that mediating and facilitating organizations such as the Institute for a Democratic Alternative for South Africa (IDASA), CBM, and the Urban Foundation "could play an increasingly important role" (1992, 54). As stated earlier, CBM not only facilitated "externally" but also played an important role in informing, influencing, and exhorting the broader business community to become involved and play a constructive role.

The historical record (especially through the unpublished documentation on the work of CBM) is clear on the role that the business community played in the political transition. In 1997, the ANC stated: "We acknowledge . . . that the business community in South Africa played an important role in the 1980s in setting our country on a path towards a negotiated transition" (1). No mention, however, is made of the specific interventions described above (with the exception of the Anglo American visit to Lusaka in 1985).

BUSINESS IN THE NEW SOUTH AFRICA: THE FIRST FIFTEEN YEARS OF DEMOCRACY (1994–2009)

Expectations in the New South Africa

With the first democratic election in April 1994, the expectations of all South Africans were very high. These did not coincide fully, but to a large extent everyone wanted peace, freedom, stability, and the protection of human rights. In hindsight, it can be observed that the majority of South Africans (essentially the disadvantaged) hoped that everything would change immediately, while the minority (essentially the advantaged) hoped that nothing would change significantly. Both sets of expectations were far from realistic, as it is clear that many things changed fairly rapidly, while quite a number of things took longer to change (or even remained the same).

The newly elected ANC government (with the full support of the other two partners in the Government of National Unity, the NP and the IFP) tried to embody the hopes and expectations of the majority in the RDP. The RDP was an ambitious program of socioeconomic delivery, but lacking an economic policy to act as foundation or driving force.

Business Engaging the new South Africa Actively

On a more general front, the period after the democratic elections (1994–99) saw business engaging the new South Africa in three ways:

- It made full use of the new economic and commercial opportunities brought about by the democratic South Africa, arguably also to the advantage of the country as a whole.
- It worked actively, through the mandated business organizations, in bringing about a new and more democratic labor and socioeconomic dispensation, especially through NEDLAC and its consensus-building efforts, before proposed legislation went to Parliament (Adam, Slabbert, and Moodley 1997).

- Through business-based organizations such as the National Business Initiative (NBI), it contributed to the socioeconomic development, stability, and success of the new South Africa (Eloff 1999b). Notable examples are the formation of Business Against Crime (BAC) in 1996 and the establishment of the R1 billion Business Trust in 1999—both in partnership with government.[4]

Business Support for the Reconstruction and Development Programme

In meetings with various political leaders shortly after the 1994 election, it became clear to CBM's leadership that support for the RDP was critical. Although business urged a greater emphasis on the interdependence of economic growth and socioeconomic reconstruction, business acknowledged the RDP's visionary and integrated approach.

Building on CBM's Role of Business in Transition project, it was agreed in May 1994 to convene a series of RDP summits around the country with input from business, government, and labor. Agenda issues included global competitiveness, restructuring of industry, private sector funding and involvement in reconstruction, technological advancement, and human resource development.

"The outcome of these valuable discussions was used to compile a *Building a Winning Nation: Companies and the RDP* (CBM 1994). This book was published in the commercial market and several thousand copies were sold . . . This initiative of the CBM concluded its major projects" (CBM 1997).

Establishment of the National Business Initiative

After the democratic election in 1994, CBM initially considered closing down, as its mission of facilitating a peaceful transition had been accomplished. But both business and government leaders felt strongly that the expertise assembled in CBM was too valuable to lose. The same was true of the Urban Foundation.[5] Consequently, the two organizations were merged into the National Business Initiative for Growth, Development, and Democracy. The new business organization, often called business's socioeconomic delivery arm, was launched and endorsed by President Nelson Mandela in March 1995 (NBI 2005).

In a foreword to a publication commemorating the first ten years of the NBI's existence, former president Mandela summed up its work as follows:

"The NBI is not very well known . . . to the wider public. . . . But the NBI and its work are well understood and appreciated at the highest levels of government, and in senior business circles. . . ." Just like its predecessors, the NBI had the support of most of the large and medium-sized companies in South Africa.[6]

Business Against Crime

Fourie and Eloff describe the formation of BAC, which was co-founded by the NBI and Business South Africa (the mandated national umbrella body of business organizations), as follows:

In 1996 nearly 500 business leaders met . . . in Johannesburg to deliberate on how the private sector could contribute to the fight against crime. . . . Following intense dialogue with (then President) Nelson Mandela, a new organisation called Business Against Crime was established to partner with the government in dealing with this major threat to safety and security in the new democracy. . . . The NBI facilitated this process and served as the managing agency of BAC until the organisation was eventually set up as a separate legal entity. (2005, 43)

BAC is still an active partner of government and has had several successful projects.[7]

The Business Trust

The Business Trust was co-founded by the NBI, the South African Foundation, and the Black Business Council. Fourie and Eloff write:

In 1998 a grouping of business leaders and organizations . . . (had) intense discussions with the government on the challenges of economic growth and job creation. A firm foundation of the initiative was the broader concern among leading business people about unemployment. An important outcome of the dialogue was the formation of the R1-billion (approximately $140 million[8]) Business Trust, a five-year project designed to focus on the creation of jobs and building human capacity. An early key focus was to develop a stronger business approach to the international tourism marketing of the country, as a basis for sustainable job creation. . . . By 2002, SA was the world's fastest growing tourist destination, international tourist arrivals having increased by 20.2%. (2005, 43)

Both the Business Trust and BAC are active partnerships between business and government. They are examples of how business can be involved in more than corporate social responsibility, for the good of the country—but also in its own (enlightened) interest.[9]

Moving from the RDP to GEAR

On the macroeconomic and political fronts, from 1997 on, the socioeconomic drive of the RDP (especially in terms of the provision of housing, water, and electricity) made way for a new Growth, Employment, and Redistribution policy (GEAR). In hindsight, this was probably inevitable, as the wave of globalization also swept over South Africa. The process through which GEAR was established was not without its problems (Gumede 2005). Some commentators, although acknowledging that the new South Africa could not ignore the strong globalization trends, described GEAR as a "Thatcherite discourse of fiscal discipline and market forces," while conceding its "refreshing non-dogmatism" (Adam, Slabbert, and Moodley 1997, 161). This move was, however, generally welcomed by business, as it was seen as being necessary to build the economy, so that jobs could be created and socioeconomic development initiatives could be funded.

The voices of the mandated business organizations, such as the South Chamber of Business (SACOB), the Afrikaanse Handelsinstituut (AHI), and the National African Federation of Commerce and Industry (NAFCOC), became more audible, with predictable calls for either privatization (SACOB and AHI) or black economic empowerment (NAFCOC). Business unity was, however, still an elusive concept.

Moving from GEAR to Transformation and Black Economic Empowerment

During 2000–2004 another macroeconomic change occurred. Even though GEAR was, through a number of policies and in practice, still very much in place, after 1999 it was slowly but surely supplemented by a new political call for transformation and black economic empowerment (BEE). With the wave of sectoral charters on empowerment, business had to reconcile its core business objectives (including global competitiveness) with

the needs of the country in terms of empowerment and equity transformation. No single industry was able to shy away from this new political call.
The drive for transformation and BEE was complemented by legislation,
primarily in the form of the Black Economic Empowerment Act (Act 53
of 2003). The results of these efforts were mixed. In some industries, good
examples of success can be given. In most others, there was a sense either
of not (yet) enough empowerment or of empowerment (enrichment) of
only a few.

Business Organizations

During this time, business had also succeeded in uniting its mandated
organizations in Business Unity South Africa (BUSA). It is essentially a federal organization, with the constituent parts (such as SACOB, the AHI, and
NAFCOC) retaining a large degree of independence. BUSA's establishment
indicates progress, although much remains to be done, especially at local
level.

The business-based organizations, such as the NBI, the Business Trust,
and BAC, continued to play a facilitating and mobilizing role, in partnership with government structures, during the first fifteen years of democracy.
An important development in terms of business organizations was that the
old-style South African Foundation, an organization of the chief executives of the fifty top South African companies, was transformed into Business Leadership South Africa (see "Business's Task to Create a Stable Environment" below).

It was also agreed between government and senior business leaders that
the Business Trust (originally planned as a five-year project) should continue.
In its second term (2004–9), the trust would support the drive to halve
the unemployment rate by 2014 and would have a direct impact on more
than one million South Africans through supporting the government's expanded public works program, investing in communities, and supporting
enterprise development, in terms of business process outsourcing and programs to catalyze investment in depressed communities.[10]

The Presidential Big Business Working Group

During this period (and emerging out of the formation of the Business
Trust) the Big Business Working Group (BBWG) was established. Through its

formation, senior business leaders (about twenty in number) met regularly with President Mbeki and key ministers to discuss policy and other strategic issues. This was a significant development, clearly signaling that government and business had become partners at the highest level. For instance, a joint press statement issued after a two-day workshop of the BBWG in April 2003 stated, "The purpose of the meeting was to explore how to accelerate the rate of growth and development in South Africa, and to ensure open and constructive communication between government and large corporations. . . . Government and business agreed that the relationship between them had improved significantly, . . . Both parties agreed that there was scope for deeper consultations on long-term strategies that could contribute effectively to raising the rate of growth, development and employment creation" (BBWG 2003).

Expectations of the New South Africa Fifteen Years after Apartheid

The expectations of the disadvantaged majority for socioeconomic delivery were met in some areas. Examples of good delivery were water provision in rural areas, electricity provision, and housing (in some provinces). Relative success had also been achieved in establishing a peaceful democracy and a legitimate judicial system, with the maintenance of human rights (South African Government 2003).

However, fifteen years after the end of apartheid, many problems remain or have become worse. Here one can cite the levels of unemployment, levels of crime (especially violent crime), the lack of proper basic education, the slow pace of land reform, the lack of adequate job creation, and the lack of basic health services (including measures to combat HIV-AIDS). In general, delivery at the local government level had become a problem, often because of a lack of capacity and maintenance (and not a lack of funding).

Business's hopes for the new South Africa had been fulfilled to a larger extent, in that the peaceful transition helped to create a stable and conducive environment for doing business, and economic growth had started to pick up—at least until the beginning of 2008. Safety and security, however, remain a concern, as do the growing skills shortage and ever-increasing legislative requirements for doing business in South Africa.

Therefore, on a broad front, by the 2009 elections the majority's expectations had not been met. These challenges are awaiting the next ANC government.

BUSINESS AFTER THE 2009 ELECTION

Business by and large reacted slowly to the political change in the late eighties, but since then it has been an active (and sometimes even enthusiastic) social partner in the building of the new South Africa. This statement applies to both individual companies and mandated business organizations. Their role was amply supported by business-based and business-funded organizations such as the CBM, NBI, BAC, and the Business Trust. Having come through both the political transformation and the start of the socioeconomic transformation, there are indications that South Africa had entered a period of sustained economic growth.

In 2005, former president Mandela, both praising business for the role it had played in the first years and exhorting it to play an even bigger one in the next phase, stated, "The contribution of the business sector to South Africa, through the work of the NBI, other business organisations, and individual companies, has been significant. But a new decade brings with it new challenges, as well as new opportunities. I am sure, given its past record, that business, and business leadership will not be slow to come forward, with ideas, expertise and resources, to play their part in making South Africa a great place to live, learn, to work and do business" (NBI 2005, 1).

The Political Context

Since 2003, the political context in South Africa was dominated by intense political power plays within the ruling ANC that started with the prosecution of Jacob Zuma, then deputy president of the country and deputy president of the ANC. Zuma was axed as deputy president of the country by President Mbeki but survived as ANC deputy president and eventually succeeded in becoming the ANC president at the Polokwane Conference in December 2007. This left Mbeki as a lame duck president, eventually "recalled" (fired) by the ANC leadership under Zuma in September 2008. Such political infighting had enormous impact on the business climate in South Africa, and only when the ongoing court proceedings against Zuma were dropped two weeks before the national elections in April 2009 did the climate start to change. By then, however, the country was in the grip of its first recession in seventeen years.

The uncertainty in the economic climate and drop in business confidence were aggravated by the fact that Zuma's support in the ANC came primarily from the left. Zuma was carried by the South African Communist

Party (SACP) and the Congress of South African Trade Unions (COSATU) to victory over Mbeki at Polokwane, and a certain political debt was created that Zuma would have to pay once he became president of the country. The formation of the Congress of the People (COPE) as a breakaway party from among the leadership of the ANC, especially Mbeki followers, also created uncertainty with regard to the election.

Despite the economy and the negative impact of the split between Mbeki and Zuma, the ANC maintained its enormous political following at the polls on 22 April 2009. Although it lost its two-thirds majority in Parliament, it still succeeded in winning 65 percent of the vote, with the next largest party, the Democratic Alliance, receiving 17 percent of the vote, and COPE receiving 8 percent.

In its country overview after the April 2009 elections, the *Economist* noted that "Foreign investors remain nervous about the influence that COSATU-affiliated ministers may wield in Mr Zuma's new government." It also pointed out that the ANC, with its declared market-friendly macroeconomic policies, was "hitting back against its supposed ally" (*Economist* 2009). These tensions will have to be managed carefully.

The Concept of the Developmental State

Even though South Africa should "formally and constitutionally" be described as a liberal democracy (Adam, Slabbert, and Moodley 1997, 83), the concept of a developmental state emerged during the Mbeki years (Esterhuyse 2005). This concept is based on the view that market forces alone cannot reduce entrenched poverty and inequality, and that "without a powerful countervailing force, the shadow of history will dictate opportunities, entitlements and outcomes" (*Economist* 2007). This prediction was echoed in the ANC's 2009 election manifesto: "The developmental state will play a central role in the economy. We will ensure a more effective government, improve the coordination and planning efforts of the developmental state by means of a planning entity to ensure faster change" (ANC 2008). In his first State of the Nation address, President Jacob Zuma (2009) also referred to the important role of the developmental state. This is a fundamental premise of the new government.

But in describing the mammoth task that the South African government has set for itself in terms of social grants, running water, sanitation, roads, electricity provision, and a social security scheme by 2010, the *Economist* pointed out that already by 2007 the capacity of the developmental state to spend faster had become problematic: "Even if the government were to throw all caution to the wind, it would struggle to spend faster. The state raises revenues more efficiently than it spends them. Provinces and munici- palities . . . routinely underspend their capital budgets. Local governments struggle to hire managers and engineers, leaving many essential posts un- filled. The central government is trying to strengthen municipalities, but the pace of change is slow. The developmental state it dreams about is still in the developmental stage" (*Economist* 2007).

Freund makes a compelling case that, so far, the developmental state model is a superficial one in South Africa, He points out that the govern- ment has failed to increase skill levels, to create jobs, or to tackle poverty in a substantial way. He concludes that in these aspects, "we are very far from the world of the developmental state. . . . The problem in South Africa today is not so much that the vision of a developmental state is such a poor one. But it remains far too narrowly based and its implications have barely begun to be thought out by our governors. Its limitations make its progress fragile and uncertain" (Freund 2007, 197).

It will be one of the Zuma administration's biggest challenges to create the capacity and will in government structures to make the dream of the development state a reality. And the fact that many of these undertakings have been restated in the president's first State of the Nation address will un- doubtedly create further expectations.

Globalization and International Competitiveness

The influential World Economic Forum's Global Competitiveness Index (GCI) for 2008–9 again puts South Africa in forty-fifth place. The report gives the country an overall score of 4.4 out of 7, and ranks it in twelve pillars of competitiveness as shown in table 4.1

The report continues, "South Africa, ranked 45th overall, remains the highest ranked country in sub-Saharan Africa, with a very stable perfor- mance. Among the country's strengths is the large size of the economy . . . (ranked 23rd in the market size pillar). The country continues to receive good marks in more complex areas measured by the GCI, such as intellectual prop- erty protection (23rd), the quality of private institutions (25th), and goods (31st), as well as financial market efficiency (24th), business sophistication (33rd), and innovation (37th). . . . These combined strengths explain South Africa's position at the top of the regional ranking."

In pointing out the obstacles to competitiveness, the report mentions poor labor market flexibility (129th), poor labor-employer relations (119th),

Table 4.1 Global Competitive Index (South Africa)

	Rank out of 134	Score (1–7)
Basic requirements	69	4.4
1. Institutions	46	4.6
2. Infrastructure	48	4.2
3. Macroeconomic stability	63	5.1
4. Health and primary education	122	3.8
Efficiency enhancers	35	4.5
5. Higher education and training	57	4.1
6. Goods market efficiency	31	4.8
7. Labor market efficiency	88	4.2
8. Financial market sophistication	24	5.2
9. Technological readiness	49	3.7
10. Market size	23	4.8
Innovation and sophistication factors	36	4.1
11. Business sophistication	33	4.6
12. Innovation	37	3.6

Source: World Economic Forum, 2008, *The Global Competitiveness Report 2008–2009.*

a low university enrollment rate (93rd), deteriorating infrastructure (46th place), organized crime (126th place), and the business costs of crime and violence (134th). According to the report, the greatest obstacle remains the health of the workforce (ranked 129th out of 134 countries). "These are areas that must be tackled in order to improve South Africa's competitiveness outlook" (World Economic Forum 2008).

The IMD 2009 *World Competitiveness Yearbook* puts South Africa at number 48 out of 57 countries for 2009, up from the 53rd place in 2007 and the only African country to feature on the list (IMD 2008). The IMD has designed what it calls a "stress test": an analysis of which countries are better equipped to come through the crisis and increase their competitiveness in future. This is done on the basis of the relevant forecast and opinion survey criteria in the 2009 *World Competitiveness Yearbook* database, divided into four categories: key forecasts for the economy in 2009, and opinions assessing the attitude, readiness, and the resilience of government, business, and society in confronting the future.

South Africa is put at number 45 (three better than its competitiveness rankings), but it is significant that its economic forecast/perspectives score, at 56, is the second worst in the group, while for government it scores a respectable 36, for business a better 23, and for society an equally respectable 32.

Two deductions can be made from this: if its economic performance can be better than expected, South Africa could improve substantially its competitiveness in future. Second, as the IMD notes, "Smaller economies are often more fit to adapt and rebound in difficult times" and "smaller nations, which are export-oriented, resilient and with stable socio-political environments are better equipped to benefit immediately from the recovery" (IMD 2009). This could also be true of South Africa, given its present profile.

Economic and Social Context

Economic Growth Prospects and Job Creation

Up to the middle of 2008, the government's economic policy had started to show success, resulting in strong and consistent economic growth and net job creation. The unemployment rate had decreased to 21 percent in 2007, and GDP was 5.3 percent and 5.1 percent, respectively, in 2006 and 2007 (South African Reserve Bank 2009). However, the quarterly report from Statistics South Africa (2009) indicates that the good growth levels until mid-2008 took a sharp downward trend in the third quarter of 2008, declining even further in the first quarter of 2009. There were hopes that the downturn had reached its lowest point and that 2010 would see a slow recovery. From the *Economist*'s 2009 country overview a fairly stable picture emerges, given the global recession (*Economist* Intelligence Unit 2009). But despite the (now modest) progress of the last few years, there is consensus that the levels of unemployment, at just over 20 percent, are still too high (Gouws 2006). Business will be called on to play its part in creating jobs and alleviate unemployment and poverty.

The Accelerated and Shared Growth Initiative for South Africa

Following on the government's goal to halve poverty and unemployment by 2014, the Accelerated and Shared Growth Initiative for South Africa, or ASGISA (with its subproject the Joint Initiative on Priority Skills Acquisition, or JIPSA), was launched as a joint initiative of government, business, labor, and relevant players from civil society (such as higher education), with the NBI as its secretariat. It aimed to achieve the 6 percent growth rate by better coordination of the work of the various government departments, the private sector, and organized labor. It was led, significantly, by the deputy-president (South African Government 2007b).

ASGISA marked a new challenge for business, but one it was more accustomed to. Delivery, growth, efficiency, and effectiveness seemed to be the new slogans at the beginning of 2007. According to the first report on ASGISA by the deputy-president, it had shown limited progress in the short time it was operational (South African Government 2006).

Gouws (2006) points out that to achieve the ASGISA goals, "government calculates that growth of around 5% on average is required between 2005 and 2014." Contogiannis (2007) is of the opinion that ASGISA had a good chance of achieving its goals, and Parsons (2009, 5–8) observes that the ASGISA framework is still a helpful and necessary one.

Unfortunately—and this is generally applicable to a host of other partnership initiatives between government and business—with the uncertainty before the ANC Polokwane conference and the governing paralysis that followed it, ASGISA did not progress much further. It is also doubtful that the Zuma administration will take it forward enthusiastically. JIPSA has already been transformed into a Department of Education–coordinated Human Resource Development Council—although still made up of stakeholders from labor, the private sector, and higher education. On the other hand, as Robbins (2009) notes, Jacob Zuma, during his tenure as MEC (provincial minister) of KwaZulu-Natal, had firsthand experience with the constructive role a stakeholders' forum can play when he supported the creation of a Regional Economic Forum. Perhaps this memory will weigh stronger than the taint of the Mbeki-initiated ASGISA.

HIV/AIDS

If poverty and crime are the two main problems facing the country, HIV/AIDS must be the third. The *Economist* Intelligence Unit states that "Combating HIV/AIDS is . . . South Africa's chief social and economic challenge, as the disease is already having an impact on the health, welfare and education systems, as well as on the economy" (2007). There are indications that the government has made a turnaround on this issue and is now actively working toward preventing and treating the disease, if not yet at the levels needed (Mlambo-Ngcuka 2007). President Zuma, in contrast to his predecessor, specifically acknowledged HIV/AIDS as a challenge in his first State of the Nation address (Zuma 2009). Business feels the impact of HIV/AIDS, especially in the ever-increasing skills shortage, the costs of absenteeism, and the costs of prevention and treatment.

Other factors completing the economic and social context include broad-based black economic empowerment (BBBEE), pressure on infrastructure, skills shortages, and corruption. These are dealt with in other essays in this volume.

Strengthening South Africa's Institutions

There is growing consensus that to sustain growth and effect socio-economic delivery, South Africa needs to strengthen what the World Economic Forum (2008) calls its institutions. These include government structures at all three levels, state-owned enterprises (such as Eskom), and links to what has been called the developmental state (see "The Concept of the Developmental State" above). As Contogiannis states, "There is no doubt that a country's legal, political, social and economic institutions affect the rate of economic growth. . . . getting the institutions right, is the major and the key factor for a sustainable economic growth and stability" (2007, 43).

Parsons sums it up well: "We need to accept that the real challenge facing government is not the availability of financial resources, but the effectiveness of delivery. We are now basically in a position where too much money is chasing too little capacity—whether in generating electricity, in social services, urban housing, fighting crime, alleviating poverty or creating jobs. . . . Our public institutions need to be strengthened and made to perform. This means better functioning state departments—including local authorities" (2008, 13).

In this context, business will face specific challenges to function well. For instance, if government delivery at local level has come to a standstill, or if state tender procedures are seriously deficient, the business environment cannot be said to be optimal. The negative effect of the ongoing Eskom power cuts and load shedding is another case in point.

The Cost of Doing Business in South Africa

The cost of doing business in South Africa covers not only material costs but also opportunity costs and the trouble of complying with a wide range of legislative and other requirements, including charter responsibilities, employment equity, BBBEE requirements, tender requirements, and World Trade Organization imperatives. Add to these the "environmental costs" and the "societal costs," such as corporate social investment (CSI), HIV/AIDS and crime prevention, and the complexity definitely increases.

Another cost of doing business is corruption, as it negatively affects business's working environment. The Heritage Foundation (2009) puts South Africa's "Freedom from Corruption" at only 51 percent and South Africa is placed 46th out of 158 countries in Transparency International's Corruption Perceptions Index for 2005. Gouws points to the fact that corruption "[a]t local government level . . . is one of the reasons for poor service and lack of delivery" (2006, 20). Corruption therefore remains a huge challenge for business. And while it is true that there can be no "one-sided" corruption, and that many companies succumb to the lure of providing corrupt officials with the demanded bribes in order to "just get the job done," it must also be stated that governments at all levels have the first and primary responsibility to ensure that officials do not invite and practice corruption.

BAC has increased its efforts to help the government to improve its capacity to combat crime and corruption. In 2006, the presidency and the BBWG (with the secretarial support of BAC) agreed to increase efforts to combat crime. But the effective "shutting down" of government between 2007 and 2009 because of internal strife in the ANC and the removal of former president Mbeki also influenced the work of BAC negatively.[11]

WHAT ROLE WILL BUSINESS (HAVE TO) PLAY IN THE NEXT TEN YEARS?

Numerous hopes and aspirations have not been realized in the fifteen years since apartheid ended. If business wants to contribute to the success of South Africa, it will have to address the hopes and aspirations of the majority of South Africans, directly or indirectly.

Business should, in the first instance, focus on its "primary" role, creating wealth for its shareholders (and through that, for its stakeholders, which means creating jobs). To be able to sustain that, business must, second, assist in creating and maintaining a stable and conducive environment, among other means by entering into partnerships with government and other stakeholders to address the various societal issues that are barriers to the fulfillment of the hopes and aspirations of South Africans. Third, business must address inequality and empowerment actively, especially in its own environment. Finally, business must assist in community development (and poverty alleviation) through its own specific corporate social investment programs.

Business's Task to Create Wealth (and Jobs)

The level of economic growth had been consistently around 5 percent until mid-2008. This growth had initially been driven by consumer spending, but the lead factor became investment in infrastructure, especially by government (Bruggemans 2007). This strong growth had even resulted in net job creation, in which business's own job creation was supplemented well by government through various labor-intensive initiatives. But this momentum was dramatically interrupted by the worldwide recession and downturn at the end of 2008 (South African Government 2007a). The medium-term outlook, however, still looks positive.

As stated in the previous section, the environment in which business will have to create wealth and jobs will consist of positive and negative factors. The fact that former minister of finance Trevor Manuel has been retained in the cabinet (as minister with oversight for planning in the presidency) gives business some reassurance of continuity in macroeconomic policy. In addition, new minister of finance Pravin Gordhan has built up a good reputation as commissioner of revenue.

However, sustainable economic growth and (net) job creation will depend on factors such as bringing crime and corruption under control, delivering socioeconomic services at local level, providing more and better skills to the economy though the secondary and tertiary education systems, and improving the health situation (including combating HIV-AIDS). In addition, fiscal, monetary, and industrial policy, including inflation targeting, will remain crucial, as is pointed out in the useful selection of essays on economics under the Zuma government edited by Raymond Parsons (2009). In this regard, Abedian and Ajam state, "we caution against a populist and welfarist fiscal framework that is detrimental to the sustainable upliftment of the poor within the society and inimical to the performance of the economy" (2009, 101).

Business's Task to Create a Stable Environment

It is incontestable that it is in business's interest to help create a stable environment. Fourie and Eloff make the point that "a better business environment in the form of good social, economic and physical infrastructure represents potential direct business benefits. . . . A better educated workforce, less crime and violence, improved housing conditions and stronger social cohesion can also reduce the cost and risk of doing business and thus improve the competitiveness of corporations" (2005, 47).

To be able to achieve this, business leadership is needed. Coetzee highlights the importance of leadership that "understands the interconnectedness of the world, the integrated nature of development and societal issues and the importance of the private sector's role in development" (2006, 2). This sentiment is also echoed by McKay (2006), who makes a strong case that business should play a role in poverty alleviation (through its core business) and that business should act collectively.

Parsons strongly emphasizes the need for strong business leadership in the term of the new government: "there has never been a more propitious time than now to reshape and renew the business agenda to meet the new challenges in South Africa that, like the waves on the beach, will keep coming. Organised business should be seen as a 'foul weather friend' to its members" 2008, 14).

Although the business sector will never be the unified and cohesive force that other sectors of society often suspect it to be, it must surely be in the interest of major corporations to develop the ability to think and act more consciously as a business *community.* Bernstein, Berger, and Godsell argued as far back as 1998 that the business community needs to become a more self-conscious actor in engaging the state and broader society. For business to be able to play this broader role, it must also organize itself properly and act collectively.

As stated above, business unity has been achieved to some extent with the formation of Business Unity South Africa (BUSA). But even though the organization is the primary business organization for policy coordination, it is struggling with capacity and lack of leadership. For instance, when accessed on 31 March 2007, its website was last updated in July 2006, and when accessed on 18 June 2009, the last message was for 2008, the calendar had 2008 dates, and there was only one new policy document posted for 2009.[12] With a new president in the person of veteran Andre Lamprecht, BUSA may still play the role it was intended to.

The separate formation of an overarching body for local chambers (CHAMSA) and the continued separate existence of historically separate chambers did not work. A recent positive development is that the chambers have now decided to affiliate directly to BUSA, who will be responsible for mandated policy positions of business.[13]

With regard to business acting collectively through business-based organizations, the picture is slightly better with a range of strong organizations in existence (e.g., NBI and BAC). These organizations are generally in a position to enter into macro-partnerships with government (and labor, where applicable).

In addition, Business Leadership South Africa (the former South African Foundation) has started playing a stronger role. As an independent association of the chief executive officers and chairmen representing the diversity of South African big business leadership (some eighty in number), as well as the major multinational investors in South Africa, it describes itself as "a body of engaged and committed South African leaders, together with key foreign investors . . . (that) endeavours to actively support the effective pursuit of key national goals." It facilitates an effective business dialogue with government and is concerned with issues of collective interest to business, the economy and the society as a whole.[14] Business Leadership South Africa

Enough has been said above about the Business Trust and the BBWG, as well as about BAC and the NBI. While it is true that the effective "closing down" of government after the Polokwane conference had an impact on the effective functioning of these partnerships, it can still safely be said that South Africa has an impressive array of business-led and business-based organizations with the ability to assist government in creating a stable environment. The capacity and willingness of the Zuma government to engage productively with these is, for the time being, not clear. It has not yet been made clear exactly what the new government is expecting of business and its organizations.

Business's Task to Address Inequality and Empowerment

The South African business community is, by legislation, compelled to address inequality (among other ways through the Employment Equity Act) and ensure BBBEE (among others through the BEE Act). The *Economist* Intelligence Unit (2009) sums up the thrust of government policy well: "Black economic empowerment (BEE), correcting social imbalances and job creation—within the context of fiscal and monetary discipline—are the main aims of the government's economic policy."

In addition, the various sectoral charters are vehicles to achieve these and other redress aims. Barker 2005) describes the aims of the sector "charters" as being "to encourage the transformation of sectors, and more specifically to empower historically disadvantaged persons. . . . Generally, these Charters deal with issues such as skills development, employment equity, procurement and ownership. [They are] an innovative new (African) mechanism to achieve certain social objectives."[15]

While generally welcomed, the charters have also had unintended (and unwelcome) consequences (Hay 2004). Some of the charters have realistic equity targets, but others (such as the agricultural charter) are so politically driven that it will probably frustrate rather than encourage the establishment of successful black farmers. While the overall motivation for the charters is probably positive and in some cases innovative (see the charter of the

Business Map Foundation [2005]), it constitutes another complexity factor to doing business in South Africa. And the acute high-level skills shortage among especially black South Africans will not make reaching the charter targets easy.

Business's Task to Assist in Community Development and Poverty Alleviation through Corporate Citizenship

The general case for business being involved in developmental issues has been made above. A compelling case for business's engaging with broader societal issues can also be made, precisely because business and society are interdependent.

This can only be done if business transforms its former corporate social responsibility programs into something more concrete and part of its core business. Indeed, Coetzee (2006) points out that a review of the literature shows that the initial concept of corporate social responsibility has been broadened to embrace corporate citizenship, including the notion of sustainable development and the triple bottom line.

Parsons emphasizes the role of organized business in this regard, especially at a local level: "There needs to be much better engagement in future—'partnership' if you like—between organised business and local authorities simply because so many of the solutions lie at the local level. . . . Business therefore needs to use the tools and institutions closest to it to empower the organised business movement to influence the course of events and produce better outcomes, whether locally or nationally. By supporting and building capacity in our public and private institutions we strengthen confidence in the results. That is the way to create a better life for all by mobilising the talents of the whole community" (2008, 14).

The South African website *SA Good News* reiterates that "a growing number of South African businesses are moving beyond cosmetic corporate philanthropy towards a strategic approach to social investment. Increasingly, Corporate Social Investment (CSI) is being regarded as a business imperative. . . . mov(ing) away from 'cheque book' CSI towards a more integrated approach. Instead of making an annual cash contribution to a wide variety of initiatives, businesses are being more proactive and involved in a few flagship projects that are aligned with the company's core business" (South African Government Communication Service 2005).

According to McKay, there "is now a greater appreciation among all parties that what is good for business is good for development. Underpinned by a more rigorous and in-depth understanding of what the private sector really brings to the poverty alleviation equation, this growing consensus is providing an international framework for more effective public-private sector partnerships" (2006, 1). Coetzee (2006) proposes that business enter into "Corporate Sustainable Development Programmes" in close cooperation with governments and experienced development agencies. These should be aimed at supporting self-reliance and self-sufficiency.

The website *SA Good News* makes the point that the greatest CSI challenge lies in encouraging employee volunteering during working hours. The aim of this suggestion is to bring about better understanding and "trust between racial groups, trust between business and government and trust between the many strata of our society . . . one of the most important lessons we can learn from an examination of economic life is that a nation's sustainable well being, as well as its ability to compete, is conditioned by a single, evasive cultural characteristic: the level of trust inherent in the society"(South African Government Communication Service 2005).

In summary, business has a responsibility and an interest in community development and alleviating poverty. It can do this through corporate citizenship and corporate social investment initiatives aligned with its core business and the triple bottom line—economic, social, and environmental. This should further be done through public-private sector partnerships or compacts. If successful, such efforts will also build the crucially needed levels of trust among sectors of society.

CONCLUSION: WHAT ARE THE PROSPECTS FOR BUSINESS'S CONTRIBUTING TO MEETING THE EXPECTATIONS OF THE MAJORITY OF SOUTH AFRICANS?

Given the record of business's engagement in the ending of the old South Africa and the beginning of the new, as well as its track record in the first fifteen years of democracy, the prospects of business continuing to play a constructive role must be rated high. This will be done with the motivation of "enlightened self-interest," which is arguably a stronger motivation than pure philanthropy.

There are, of course, a number of "ifs" in this equation that have been dealt with in this essay. Despite these well-known obstacles to economic growth and prosperity, the economic outlook is reasonably positive in the medium term. And this means that business and its mandated and collective bodies will continue to help give momentum to economic growth and job creation.

Business expenditure on corporate social investment in South Africa is already substantial (Coetzee 2006). The website *SA Good News* notes that the "sincerity with which South African managers take their social responsibility is reflected in the World Competitiveness Yearbook 2005, where South African business's social commitment ranks eighth out of sixty nations" (South African Government Communication Service 2005).

With regard to a stable environment, business has numerous mandated and collective business organizations in place: BUSA for policy matters, BLSA for high-level interaction with government and society, BAC for partnering with government on crime prevention, the NBI on matters of a socioeconomic and sustainability nature, and the Business Trust on large-scale partnership projects. South Africa is probably a world-class example of business-government partnerships.

With regard to the impact of the political situation on business's contribution, the initial uncertainty around the Zuma government's policy stance is slowly receding. It appears that any macroeconomic changes will be minimal and are not likely to have permanent detrimental effects on the other positive factors.

In summary, the next several years could see more of the expectations of both the majority of South Africans and of business met. And business will play a significant and positive role in this regard.

NOTES

1. For a full exposition of the role of business in the peace process, see Gastrow (1995).

2. Convention for a Democratic South Africa, the country's first round of constitutional negotiations in December 1991, followed by the second (CODESA 2) in June 1992.

3. Constitution of the Republic of South Africa, 1996, section 146.

4. National Business Initiative, *Annual Report,* 1995–96, 1997, 1999–2000, and 2002–3, http://www.nbi.org.za (accessed 28 July 2006).

5. The Urban Foundation was founded in 1977, shortly after the Soweto uprisings. While positioning itself as a development organization, the Urban Foundation was largely business funded and well supported by business leadership. In the late seventies and eighties it played a crucial role, not only in raising intellectual critique against apartheid but also engaging in concrete programs (such as hous-

ing and education) to improve the lives of ordinary (mostly black) South Africans (NBI 2005).

6. National Business Initiative, *Annual Report,* 1998–2004, http://www.nbi.org.za (accessed 28 July 2006).

7. For a full account of the work and ongoing achievements of BAC, see NBI (2005), as well as the BAC website at www.bac.org.za.

8. Exchange rate from Oanda, http://www.oanda.com/convert/classic (accessed 16 November 2009).

9. For a full account of the work and ongoing achievements of the Business Trust, see NBI (2005), the NBI's annual reports from 1998–99 to 2003–4, as well as the Business Trust's website at www.btrust.org.za.

10. Information is at the website http://www.btrust.org.za.

11. Michael Spicer, interview, 8 June 2009, Johannesburg.

12. The website for Business Unity South Africa is http://www.busa.org.sa.

13. Spicer, interview.

14. Information is at the Business Leadership South Africa website, www .businessleadership.org.za (accessed 30 March 2007).

15. Led by the Financial Services Charter, there are now several other charters. For a good overview of the initial charters, see "Key Empowerment Charters," 29 October 2004, www.southafrica.info. For a full exposition of the Sectoral Transformation Charters and Scorecards, see the Cliffe Dekker BEE regulatory team's website at www.cliffedekker.co.za.

BIBLIOGRAPHY

Abedian, Iraj, and Tania Ajam. 2009. "Fiscal Policy beyond 2008: Prospects, Risks and Opportunities." In Parson, *Zumanomics,* 79–102.

Adam, H., F. Van Zyl Slabbert, and K. Moodley. 1997. *Comrades in Business.* Cape Town: Tafelberg.

African National Congress (ANC). 1997. *Submission to Special Truth and Reconciliation Commission Hearing on the Role of Business.* Johannesburg: ANC.

———. 2008. *ANC 2009 Election Manifesto.* Johannesburg: ANC.

Barker, F. 2005. "Expanding Social Protection through Sector Charters: The South African Experience." Paper presented at the Fourth African Regional Conference of the International Industrial Relations Association, Chamber of Mines of South Africa, South Africa, 28–30 November.

Bernstein, A., P. L. Berger, and B. Godsell. 1998. "Introduction: Business and Democracy: Cohabitation or Contradiction?" In *Business and Democracy,* ed. A. Bernstein and P. L. Berger. London: Pinter.

Big Business Working Group. 2003. Joint press statement after the Big Business Working Group Indaba held at Fancourt, George, South Africa, 28–29 March.

Bruggemans, C. 2007. "Growth Surprises on Upside." 28 March. www.fnb.co.za/ economics (accessed 11 April 2007).

Business Election Fund. 1994. "Final Report: Business Stands for Building a Great Nation." Unpublished report, Business Election Fund, Johannesburg.

Business Map Foundation. 2005. "Financial Services Charter spurs innovative answer to finance conundrum." Update 5 May.

Coetzee, Stef. 2006. "Corporate Social Responsibility: Towards a New Paradigm." Leader's Angle address, University of Stellenbosch Business School, 24 February.

Consultative Business Movement. 1988. "The Broederstroom Encounter." Unpublished manuscript, Consultative Business Movement, Johannesburg.

———. 1993a. "Regions in South Africa: Constitutional Options and Their Implications for Good Government and a Sound Economy." Unpublished confidential report for discussion with political parties, Consultative Business Movement, Johannesburg.

———. 1993b. *Managing Change: A Guide to the Role of Business in Transition.* Johannesburg: Ravan.

———. 1994. *Building a Winning Nation: Companies and the RDP.* Johannesburg: CBM.

———. 1997. "The Consultative Business Movement: 1988–1994." Unpublished submission to the Truth and Reconciliation Commission, Consultative Business Movement, Johannesburg.

Contogiannis, T. 2007. "Economic Growth, Constraints and Prospects for the South African Economy." *Discourse* 35, no. 2 (December).

Economist. 2007. "South Africa"s Economy." 22 February. http://www.economist.com (accessed 4 April 2007).

Economist Intelligence Unit. 2007. "Country Data, 26 February 2007." http://www.economist.com (accessed 4 April 2007).

———. 2009. "Country Data, 6 May 2009." http://www.economist.com (accessed 18 June 2009).

Eloff, T. 1999a. "The Role of Civil Society, specifically Business, in Conflict Resolution, Constitution-Making and Transition in Divided Societies." Paper presented at the Bellagio Conference, Italy, 15–19 February.

———. 1999b. "From Honest Broker to Constructive Partner." In *People Building Peace,* 331–35. Utrecht: European Centre for Conflict Prevention.

———. 2001. "Partnerships between Business, Government and NGO's: Lessons from the NBI Experience." Paper presented at the World Bank Conference on Evaluation and Development, Washington, DC, 23–24 July.

Esterhuyse, W. P. 2005. "Whereto with the Developmental State (DS)? Or: The Struggle for the 'Soul' of the ANC." *Politics* (Institute for Futures Research) 15, no. 6 (July).

———. 2006. "The New Left: Force or Farce?" *Politics* (Institute for Futures Research) 16, no. 4 (April).

Fourie, A., and T. Eloff. 2005. "The Case for Collective Business Action to Achieve Systems Change." *Journal of Corporate Citizenship* 18 (Summer).

Freund, B. 2007. South Africa as a Developmental State? Part Two. Policy and Political Choices. *Africanus* 37, no. 2.

Friedman, S., ed. 1994. *The Long Journey: South Africa"s Quest for a Negotiated Settlement.* Johannesburg: Ravan.

Friedman, S., and D. Atkinson. 1994. *The Small Miracle. South Africa's Negotiated Settlement.* Johannesburg: Ravan.

Gastrow, P.1995. *Bargaining for Peace: South Africa and the National Peace Accord.* Washington, DC: United States Institute of Peace Press.

Gouws, R. 2006. "South Africa and the challenge of globalization." Presented at the conference "Globalisation and Economic Success: Policy Options for Africa," Cairo, 13–14 November.

Gumede, W. M.2005. *Thabo Mbeki and the Battle for the Soul of the ANC.* Cape Town: Zebra Press.

Hay, S. 2004. "Charters Could Do Well to Follow the Process of Precedence." *Empowerment,* 7 October.

Heritage Foundation. 2009. "Index of Economic Freedom 2009." http://www.heritage.org (accessed 15 June 2009).

IMD. 2009. "Announcing 2009 Results. *World Competitiveness Yearbook.*" http://www.imd.ch/research/publications (accessed 12 May 2009).

McKay, G. 2006. "Africa and the G8: A Business Perspective on Progress One Year Later," 24 July. www.ethicalcorp.com.

Mlambo-Ngcuka, P. 2007. Keynote Address to the National Conference to Finalise the National Strategic Plan (NSP) on HIV and AIDS, 2007–2011, 14 March.

National Business Initiative. 2005. "Building a South African Future: The First Ten Years of the National Business Initiative." Unpublished manuscript, National Business Initiative, Johannesburg.

Parsons, R. 2008. "The South African Economy: Will It Survive the 'Perfect Storm'?" *Management Today* 24, no. 4 (May).

———, ed. 2009. *Zumanomics: Which Way to Shared Prosperity in South Africa? Challenges for a New Government.* Auckland Park, SA: Jacana.

Robbins, Glen. 2009. "Industrial Policy and National Competitiveness." In Parsons, *Zumanomics,* 117–28.

Sparks, A. 1994. *Tomorrow Is Another Country.* Johannesburg: Struik.

Slabbert, F van Z. 1992. *The Quest for Democracy: South Africa in Transition.* London: Penguin.

South African Reserve Bank. 2006. *Quarterly Bulletin.* Pretoria: South African Government, September.

———. 2007. *Quarterly Bulletin.* Pretoria: South African Government, March.

———. 2009. *Quarterly Bulletin.* Pretoria: South African Government, March.

South African Government. 2003. *Towards a Ten Year Review.* Pretoria: The Presidency.

———. 2006. *Accelerated and Shared Growth Initiative for South Africa.* Annual Report. Pretoria: South African Government.

———. 2007a. "SA Creates More Jobs, Better Jobs," 30 March. www.southafrica.info (accessed 6 April 2007).

————. 2007b. "Accelerated and Shared Growth Initiative." www.info.gov.za/asgisa (accessed 2 April 2007).

South African Government Communication Service. 2005. "Profound Potential of Corporate Citizenship in South Africa." http://www.sagoodnews.co.za/news letter, July (accessed 30 March 2007).

Sparks, A. 1994. *Tomorrow Is Another Country. The Inside Story of South Africa"s Negotiated Revolution.* Johannesburg: Struik.

Spicer, M. 2004. "The Role of Business in Sustainable Development." Paper presented at the Johannesburg +2 Sustainability Conference, Johannesburg, 1–3 September.

Statistics South Africa. 2009. Labour Force Survey September 2000 to May 2009 historical series of revised estimates, Statistical release P0210, 26 May.

United Nations Human Development Reports. http://hdr.undp.org (accessed 16 June 2009).

Waldmeier, P. 1997. *Anatomy of a Miracle.* New York: Viking.

World Bank. 2006. World Development Indicators database, July.

World Economic Forum. 2008. *World Competitiveness Report 2008–2009.* Geneva: World Economic Forum.

Zuma, J. G. 2009. State of the Nation address. Joint sitting of Parliament, Cape Town, June.

Macroeconomic Policy and Its Governance after Apartheid

Janine Aron

THE OBJECTIVES OF MACROECONOMIC POLICY

The last decade and a half have been notable for South Africa's greater integration with the international economy, domestic political stability, and the gains made in the governance and stability of macroeconomic policy-making. This essay reviews the institutional changes that have aligned the conduct of monetary and fiscal policy closely with recent international practices designed for more transparent, credible, and accountable policy and operating over a longer horizon. It also evaluates the significant improvements in fiscal and monetary performance—remarkable given the initial conditions faced by the postapartheid government and a volatile external economic environment. These gains are likely to be sustainable within the new frameworks for policy, if evolving institutional design helps entrench the practices. The notable success in the management of financial stability by the National Treasury and the South African Reserve Bank (SARB), as well as the "fiscal space" created by a prudent fiscal policy, has left South Africa relatively well placed to weather the 2008–9 global financial crisis. This situation contrasts with that of many emerging market countries, and indeed of some industrialized countries, such the UK, where regulation and financial supervision has been far too lax and fiscal policy far too loose for the past five years.

Following the elections of April 1994, the initial objectives of macroeconomic policy were detailed in two highly publicized macropolicy plans. The broad goals of the Reconstruction and Development Programme (RDP), launched by the African National Congress (ANC) in January 1994, were re-inforced by the ANC government's Growth, Employment and Redistribu-tion strategy (GEAR), announced in June 1996.[1] Fiscal prudence, tax reform, increased transparency of administration, a reorientation of spending to so-cial sector spending, and longer-term expenditure planning were hallmarks of both the RDP and the GEAR plans. There has been a remarkable consis-tency in fiscal policy since 1994. The well-articulated fiscal objectives of these plans were entrenched in the 1996 constitution,[2] and subsequent legislation addressed the many constitutional imperatives, including the restructuring of key organizations, such as the (renamed) Revenue Authority. Extensive tax reform followed the recommendations of a specially appointed commis-sion, the Katz Commission, and successive annual budgets sought to meet the fiscal objectives.

The inherited fiscal position after apartheid was believed to be unsus-tainable, with a large and growing domestic debt and budget deficit (the lat-ter reaching nearly 8 percent of GDP by 1992–93).[3] Historical intergovern-mental relations were dysfunctional, with overly complex provincial and municipal structures. Both plans sought to cut the budget deficit through fiscal consolidation, improved debt management, and more efficient tax collection (while also reducing the tax burden), with the objective of re-ducing inflationary pressures and ultimately real interest rates. In creating greater macrostability, the aim was to reduce uncertainty for investment as well as to cut the cost of capital. A more realistic fiscal position was also seen as facilitating the sustainability of the RDP over time. Both plans aimed to decrease government dissaving, which was contributing to the nation's very low domestic savings rate, thus entailing greater dependence on "for-eign savings" in the form of volatile capital inflows to fund investment. Both plans also aimed (though initially observing fiscal constraints) to substitute investment for consumption expenditure (e.g., spending on infrastructure), and to alter the composition of expenditure from military expenditure and debt service toward social expenditure, such as health, pensions and grants, housing, and education. The spending goals and some of the redistribution goals aimed to address the pervasive supply-side constraints on medium-term economic growth.

The fiscal aims of the two plans were reinforced by global pressures, as the postapartheid economy progressively opened to trade and capital flows and international credit markets. Sovereign ratings and capital flows are strongly influenced by international perceptions of the soundness of fiscal and monetary fundamentals. Financial globalization has created pressures to reform fiscal policy institutions and budgetary systems, to reduce deficits, to engage in tax reform to broaden the tax base (while lowering marginal rates), and to restructure public sector enterprises (Abedian 1998; Calitz 2000).

In contrast to the detailed fiscal policy objectives, there was a rather cursory treatment of monetary policy in the RDP and GEAR plans. After 1994, monetary policy continued to be governed by the South African Reserve Bank Act (no. 90 of 1989), detailing the powers and functions of the central bank. Unfortunately, and again in contrast to fiscal policy under the two plans, little emphasis was given to improving the transparency of monetary policy, which had been opaque under the preceding government. An important step forward was the constitutional granting of instrument independence to the central bank for the first time, in setting monetary policy under the act.[4] Yet the plans and the interim and final constitutions expressed the monetary policy objectives differently, and until mid-1996 there was no clear prioritization among these objectives (see "The Governance of Monetary and Fiscal Policy" below).[5] A prioritization of objectives became important with the opening of the capital account with unification of the dual exchange rate system from 1995, and the consequent large capital inflows.[6] Under such circumstances, a policy trade-off can arise in which a sustained intervention to support the nominal exchange rate may occur at the cost of higher inflation, higher interest rates, and eventually reduced output (e.g., Obstfeld 1996). The third section of this essay ("The Performance of Monetary and Fiscal Policy") argues that after the capital account was opened in 1995, Governor Stals had dual and conflicting objectives for monetary policy, with an explicit monetary and an *implicit* exchange rate target, promoting a classic exchange rate crisis in 1996.

The firefighting GEAR plan of June 1996 was formulated to raise international credibility by clarifying the objectives of macropolicy, after the monetary policy errors in 1994–96 culminated in a damaging exchange rate crisis in early 1996. Yet the GEAR's section on monetary policy focused mainly on reiterating that there would be a prudent liberalization of domestic exchange controls to alleviate pressure on the exchange rate. It interpreted the long-term monetary policy objective as keeping the real effective exchange rate at a competitive level. But while it endorsed the objective of keeping inflation low (and it was committed to positive real interest rates), it did not explicitly rule out sustained exchange rate interventions to influence the nominal exchange rate. Thus, the potential for dual and conflicting objectives remained. An amendment to the Reserve Bank Act in March 1996 and an alteration in the final constitution (December 1996) finally clarified that the primary objective of monetary policy was to "protect the value of the currency of the Republic in the interest of balanced and sustainable economic growth in the Republic."

The weakness in monetary policy thereafter (until the adoption of inflation targeting in 2000) lay in poor transparency about the means of achieving this constitutional objective, which encouraged discretionary and secretive policy. Monetary policy lacked a transparent and credible target and hence a benchmark by which to hold the SARB fully accountable for its interest rate decisions. The monetary targets on which the SARB was purportedly firmly basing its anti-inflation strategy even by 1996 (Stals 1996) relied on outdated and discredited monetarism that functioned poorly, if at all, in the context of liberalized domestic financial markets.[7] These targets were largely bypassed and replaced by an eclectic set of indicators, including the exchange rate, asset prices, output gap, balance of payments, wage settlements, credit growth, and the fiscal stance (Stals 1997). But the weights on the many new indicators were never made public, and monetary policy was thus opaque.[8] There were no formal structures for communicating and explaining *all* interest rate decisions immediately after every meeting (i.e., including those meetings where interest rates were not changed, for these were never announced).

The governor and his deputies had carte blanche to intervene to influence the exchange rate, which they did in 1994–96 and again in 1997 and 1998, though to no avail. Prior to 1996, there was also no transparency about the extent of forward foreign exchange market intervention to influence the exchange rate, which officially was deemed to be freely floating. The heavy intervention eventually proved extremely costly to the fiscus, as in the absence of meaningful foreign reserves, intervention was undertaken via forward foreign exchange contracts, which disadvantaged the government when the exchange rate collapsed (see Kahn and Leape 1996). Moreover, setting very high policy interest rates badly damaged economic growth and curtailed investment (see "The Performance of Monetary and Fiscal Policy" below). With growth falling to half a percent in real terms during 1998, this monetary policy was hardly compatible with the objective of "balanced and sustainable economic growth."

Inflation targeting, a monetary policy framework already successfully implemented in a dozen countries (Loayza and Soto 2002), was introduced at the behest of the minister of finance, Trevor Manuel, in February 2000, and under a new SARB governor, Tito Mboweni. This finally provided the *means* for achieving the constitutional primary objective for monetary policy to be realized, through an announced, credible target range for inflation. Maintaining the value of the currency under inflation targeting involves achieving price stability as well as stable conditions in the financial sector as a whole (the successful approach to the latter is touched on in the concluding section of this essay). The framework relies on instituting mechanisms for a high level of policy transparency (see "Governance of Monetary and Fiscal Policy" below). There are no conflicting policy goals under inflation targeting, and the exchange rate floats freely. The SARB may accumulate foreign currency reserves, but cannot under this mandate undertake sustained interventions to influence the currency in a particular direction without inflationary implications for meeting its target. The inflation targeting system has seen several improvements with evolving institutional design since 2000 (Mboweni 1999; Van der Merwe 2004; Aron and Muellbauer 2009).

Monetary and fiscal policy targets and goals typically operate over one to three years, that is, over a relatively short-term horizon. Macropolicy, however, also feeds into growth objectives, where the time scale is typically far longer. Both the RDP and the GEAR plans aimed at a supportive fiscal-monetary policy mix to create an environment of macroeconomic stability conducive to long-term growth. Acquiring and keeping credibility and a good reputation in macropolicy reduces economic uncertainty and is a key for attracting foreign investment and encouraging long-term domestic investment favorable for growth (Aron and Muellbauer 2005). Since 1994, fiscal policy, and only more recently under Mboweni, monetary policy, have been successful in achieving their stabilization objectives. Many of the important drivers of growth, such as a healthy and educated workforce and an efficient infrastructure (both currently constraining growth in South Africa), can only be improved over the longer term—and appropriate fiscal allocation is only part of the story (see "Growth Performance" below).

This essay specifically evaluates monetary and fiscal policy relative to the government's original objectives and more general benchmarks. It begins by exploring the constitutional and legal background to the better governance of fiscal and monetary policy, providing transparency indicators for monetary policy, and contrasting parliamentary scrutiny of monetary policy in South Africa with international standards. The following section illustrates the improvements in monetary policy performance, and fiscal policy reform and outcomes. South Africa's recent growth trends and the relative contributions to growth of labor and capital accumulation and efficiency are discussed next. Emphasis is given to South African empirical evidence for the contribution of stable monetary and fiscal policy to the positive growth outcomes, though monetary policy errors prior to inflation targeting significantly impeded growth. Growth has been hamstrung, too, by the poor microdelivery of some fiscal services (e.g., health, education, and housing) and unfortunately by delayed infrastructure expenditures (e.g., electricity generation, ports, and railways). The essay concludes with an assessment of future challenges to macropolicy under the new Zuma-led government, and the impact of the global crisis.

THE GOVERNANCE OF MONETARY AND FISCAL POLICY

There has been an increased focus internationally in the last decade on good governance in economic policy, particularly by the multilateral international institutions, and a range of private organizations monitoring transparency, the ease of doing business, the rule of law, and levels of corruption (e.g., Freedom House and Transparency International). The International Monetary Fund (IMF) has prescribed codes on a mix of transparency and accountability measures for fiscal, monetary, and financial policy (available on its website). The World Bank has tried to establish linkages between economic performance and institutional indicators of good governance in recent World Development Reports (beginning in 1997, and reports on investment and institutions in 2002 and 2005). A large empirical literature has sought to demonstrate statistically, using a range of subjective and objective measures of political and economic governance, that improved growth is dependent on well-functioning institutions (e.g., surveyed in Aron 2000).

Demonstrating good governance carries rewards through access to cheaper international finance for sovereign and private national entities, and greater and more stable net capital inflows. Currency ratings and sovereign and corporate debt ratings by international ratings agencies explicitly or implicitly incorporate governance measures in determining risk ratings. These ratings significantly influence private flows to emerging markets and developing countries, and the terms at which debt can be acquired. For countries with very low domestic saving rates, such as South Africa, sustained external finance to fund investment is vital. South Africa, with its large current account deficit (see "Conclusions" below), is vulnerable to a halt in inflows, let alone their reversal.

In line with these trends, many countries have constrained discretionary policy through formalizing the objectives of national economic policy and the priorities among these objectives, and in some cases, have limited potential political interference through statutory independence of decision-making bodies. For improved accountability of the independent decision-makers, a greater emphasis has been placed on the transparency of the procedures of decision making, on explaining and publicizing policy decisions, and on making data available that allow an evaluation of policy and whether the objectives have been met. Greater transparency facilitates a broader accountability not only through providing more detailed information for national audits and parliamentary subcommittees, and perhaps limiting "capture" of monitoring bodies, but also through monitoring by the wider economic community, such as the financial sector, media and academics, and international observers of the type discussed above.

Transparency can help reduce economic uncertainty through making policy more predictable and credible: providing more systematic and timely information on policy, the risks facing policy, and what procedures are followed when objectives are not met. For instance, recent economic thinking suggests that greater transparency of policy influences the effectiveness of monetary policy. Anchoring agents' inflationary expectations around a credible target facilitates a more moderate approach to shocks by the central bank, as agents will discount short-term volatility. By increasing the predictability of interest rate policy, market interest rate volatility is reduced, lowering uncertainty in the economy and promoting economic investment. Enhanced transparency to the public may also serve to protect central bank independence (Blinder et al. 2001).

The ANC government has embraced these global trends, significantly enhancing the transparency, accountability, and predictability of both fiscal and monetary policies.

Monetary Policy Governance

We begin with an assessment of monetary policy transparency and accountability. The governance of the SARB is prescribed by the constitution (Act no. 8 of 1996), which specifies a primary objective, its instrument independence, and that its powers are defined by an act of Parliament. The relevant act is the South African Reserve Bank Act (no. 90 of 1989) and its subsequent amendments. Operational independence was achieved initially through an exchange of letters between the government and the bank. But before the interim constitution, there were no explicit arrangements or contracts between the government and the SARB on instrument independence. By the Reserve Bank Act, only the governor and deputy governors can vote on monetary policy matters; however, in practice, under inflation targeting, decisions are made by "consensus" in a monetary policy committee (MPC).

Central bank transparency is defined as the disclosure of information about monetary policy. Theoretical and empirical evidence on central bank transparency has been surveyed by Geraats (2002), and a comprehensive empirical framework has been applied in the context of OECD countries by Eijffinger and Geraats (2006). Aron and Muellbauer (2008) apply and extend the framework to contrast transparency under the SARB's Governor Mboweni in 2007,[9] and under his predecessor, Governor Stals, in early 1994.[10] The different channels of central bank transparency are organized by political, economic, procedural, policy, and operational aspects of central banking.[11] Information disclosure by central banks is used to score the five channels, creating a total transparency index. By capturing *observed* behavior, these measures are not subject to the criticism of empirical measures of central bank independence, which are typically based on de jure statutes and not on de facto independence. Central bank transparency has substantially improved since 1994 in South Africa, largely as a result of the adoption of inflation targeting in 2000. Eiffinger and Geraats weight all categories equally, and with this weighting the SARB's transparency has improved from a score of 5 in 1994 to 10 in 2007 (out of a possible 15). This result is robust to the application of different weighting systems to the various categories (see Aron and Muellbauer 2008, table 1 and appendix). Transparency is superior to Australia's and, on Plenderleith's chosen weighting,[12] not far off the experienced targeters, New Zealand and the UK (figure 5.1).

Parliamentary scrutiny of the SARB is provided for in the Reserve Bank Act. Monthly statements of assets and liabilities, annual financial statements, and an audit report have to be submitted to the Department of Finance, and later are tabled in Parliament by the minister of finance (section 32 of the act). The governor is also required by the act to submit an annual report to the minister on the implementation of monetary policy. Periodically, the governor and senior staff appear before the Parliamentary Portfolio Standing Committee on Finance to account for monetary policy, an appearance that is now televised. The important change is that with the advent of inflation targeting, there are now benchmarks and far more information with which to hold the SARB accountable. The targeting framework itself makes provision for regular reporting and explanations of policy decisions in public and media forums, encouraging a broader debate and questioning of its policies. The well-developed financial sector and financial press are regular commentators on the SARB's performance.

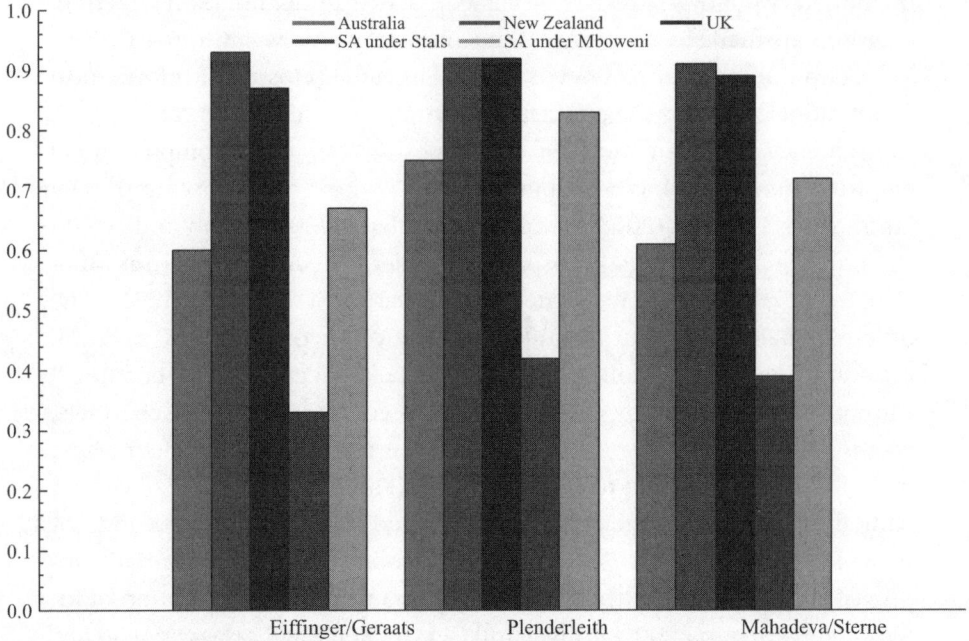

Figure 5.1   Central bank transparency ratings under different weighting schemes
Source: South African data and reweighted data for the other countries are from Aron and Muellbauer (2008). Original data for Australia, the UK, and New Zealand are from Eiffinger and Geraats (2006). There are equal weights under the Eiffinger-Geraats scheme. Plenderleith's weights assign a zero weight to the publication of minutes, voting records, and the disclosure of an explicit policy inclination after every policy meeting. The final set of weights are derived by the authors from Mahadeva and Sterne (2000, chap. 4).

For a qualitative comparative assessment of the current degree of parliamentary scrutiny of the SARB, we have applied the survey of Sterne and Lepper (2002). The question and results for 2006 are given in the appendix to this essay. When the results for South Africa are compared with the findings of Sterne and Lepper, it appears that the number of parliamentary appearances, three per annum, falls within the norm for purely monetary policy–related appearances, with the governor attending all of these in South Africa, as is the case in Canada, New Zealand, the Czech Republic, and Australia. More important than the number of meetings is the effectiveness or quality of parliamentary oversight, which is more difficult to measure. Sterne and Lepper try to gauge the competence of the committee by the number of technically trained participants, and the extent of external advice sought by the committee. South Africa's committee is unusual in receiving no technical or analytical support, at least by comparison with the nine countries surveyed in Sterne and Lepper, and unusual too in apparently having no part-time external advisers. One-off briefings are sometimes given to the committee on chosen topics by external economists, though *after* the governor's address to the committee. The survey thus suggests that the quality of parliamentary scrutiny in South Africa could be improved.

Sterne and Lepper document cases in which special circumstances may trigger the prearranged requirement of an explanation by central banks, such as cases in which targets are missed. In South Africa, under the Reserve Bank Act, the Ministry of Finance has recourse to the Supreme Court should it judge the SARB as having deviated from its mandate, where it has not appropriately responded to written instructions to rectify matters from the Ministry (section 37 of the act). Further, to help correct inflationary expectations for the special case of supply shocks under inflation targeting, an "explanation clause" was developed in November 2003 (see Aron and Muellbauer 2007a). The SARB may inform the public of the monetary policy response should an exogenous shock cause deviations from the target.

Sterne and Lepper find that government is involved in the appointment of monetary policy decision makers in all countries surveyed (except Canada, where the central bank board chooses the governor, and the appointment is approved by the minister of finance). In South Africa, too, the president, after consultation with the minister of finance and the board, appoints the governor and deputy governors.[13] In common with most other countries in the Sterne and Lepper survey (the exceptions being Japan and the United States), parliament does not have the power to veto the appointment of the chairman or governor of the SARB. As Nel and Lekalake (2004) point out, the act stipulates conditions for tenure of bank directors (including the bank's governor), but it does not explicitly give criteria for the removal of directors from office. Since late 1999, the governor appoints the members of the MPC, and there is no provision in the Reserve Bank Act for the composition of this committee.[14] There are no external members to the MPC as for the Bank of England, where they are appointed for three-year periods by the Treasury and scrutinized by the Parliamentary Treasury Committee, and are personally accountable for their minuted votes on monetary policy decisions. Some have argued that appointing external members would improve credibility and accountability in the monetary policymaking process in South Africa (Du Plessis 2005).

Finally, there is one other avenue of accountability. The Reserve Bank is unusual in being one of only three central banks that is still privately owned (see, e.g., Rossouw 2004). The SARB is internally governed by a board of fourteen directors, seven appointed by the president (of whom one is the governor and three are deputy governors) and seven by public shareholders. The SARB is thus also required to be accountable to its shareholders: the annual report and accounts are approved by them in annual meetings. It has been argued that ambiguity of accountability is introduced by the chair of the board also being the governor of the SARB (Nel and Lekalake 2004; see the rejoinder by Rossouw 2004). However, the minister of finance has powers of regulation in relation to good governance by the board (section 35).

Fiscal Policy Governance

The improvements in monetary policy transparency have mainly come via the adoption of an inflation-targeting framework in the context of instrument independence under the constitution (though inflation targeting has not itself been the subject of legislation). However, in South Africa, unusually, the ideals of good fiscal governance are constitutionally entrenched. The 1996 constitution mandated that budget processes promote transparency, accountability, and effective financial management at national, provincial, and municipal levels (chapter 13, secs. 215–17). Legislation was required to characterize the form of these budgets and when they were tabled. The National Assembly of the Parliament was charged with providing mechanisms to enforce oversight for greater accountability (chapter 4) and oversight over budget formulation and implementation. The establishment of a National Treasury was mandated under the constitution to apply recognized accounting practices, classifications, and norms for transparency and expenditure control at all three levels of government, and when financing the deficit through increased public debt (sec. 216). Procurement at each level was expected to be "fair, equitable, transparent, competitive and cost-effective"—though preferential allocation in some cases was allowed for.[15]

Ajam and Aron (2007, 2009) describe in detail the improved governance via legislation, new institutions, and organizations, and the consequent benefits for the fiscal process. A few key points are summarized here. The Public Finance Management Act of 1999 provided the legislation to address the above constitutional requirements. As pointed out by Calitz and Siebrits (2004), the act did not prescribe numerical fiscal rules but emphasized "regular financial reporting, sound internal expenditure controls, independent audit and supervision of control systems, improved accounting standards and training of financial managers, and greater emphasis on outputs and performance monitoring." This act also provided for multiyear budgeting toward improved planning, and the Medium-Term Expenditure Framework was introduced in 1998–99 with three-year rolling budgets for national and provincial governments. In 2003, the Municipal Finance Management Act extended similar budget reforms to local government.

Revenue-raising powers under the constitution are highly centralized, with the most productive taxes, VAT or general sales taxes, income taxes, and excise taxes, being vested in the national government. The Financial and Fiscal Commission is an independent body,[16] established in terms of the constitution (chapter 13, secs. 220–22), that is required to make recommendations to Parliament on equitable allocations to national, provincial, and local government from nationally collected revenues. For greater provincial expenditure control, provision was made for halting for up to four months the transfer of national funds to those provinces in breach of legislation, pending parliamentary approval and a report from the auditor general. But with centralized revenue, and expenditure responsibilities decentralized to provincial governments, the mismatch between financing and local implementation has in practice resulted in coordination problems (Ajam and Aron 2007).

Most other constitutions confer only civil and political rights on their citizens. The South African constitution also confers justiciable socioeconomic rights. The Bill of Rights (secs. 7–39) details the obligations of the state to ensure progressive realization of the right to housing (sec. 26), the right to health care, food, water, and social security (sec. 27), and the right to education (sec. 29). Ajam and Aron argue that future budget allocations and central government grants need to be efficiently delivered, rather than simply allocating sufficient funds for health, education, and other social expenditure.

THE PERFORMANCE OF MONETARY AND FISCAL POLICY

South Africa has improved fiscal policy transparency, accountability, and predictability at all tiers under the ANC government by consolidating budgetary institutions, improving expenditure management at the provincial level, and engaging in multiyear planning at all tiers (Ajam and Aron 2009). This was supported by comprehensive tax reform and improved revenue collection via the new South African Revenue Services (SARS), unifying the previous administrations for tax and customs, introducing computerized systems, and enhancing capacity for debt recovery and investigation and prosecution of tax evaders. Horton (2005) summaries international evidence on the most sustainable types and sequencing of fiscal reform in terms of favorable macroeconomic effects, and classifies South Africa as having adopted durable and credible reforms. Similarly, monetary policy has become more transparent, and hence more accountable, since 2000. In this section we examine the performance of monetary and fiscal policies consequent on the reforms.

Monetary Policy

The process of interest rate setting by the MPC can broadly be described by Svensson's recommended moderate policy of flexible and forward-looking inflation targeting (Svensson et al. 2002), and so copes reasonably well with supply shocks.[17] Inflation is not controlled at the shortest possible horizon by aggressive and volatile policy but rather at a longer horizon of two to three years. The flexible approach aims also to stabilize the business cycle and hence the output gap. In the short term, inflation may therefore deviate, and sometimes significantly, from the target.[18]

One of the goals of an inflation-targeting system is to improve communication and transparency so as to improve the *effectiveness* of monetary policy. Transparency has scored high. There is also encouraging evidence for the improved credibility of monetary policy since 2000. Aron and Muellbauer (2008) examine the evolution of inflation expectations after the adoption of inflation targeting, using the new survey of inflation expectations from the Bureau of Economic Research (Kershoff 2000).[19] The authors find that different agents' expectations have converged on the target, though the arguably better-informed analysts' views converged earlier than those of the business sector and trade unions. The convergence holds even when correcting for backward-looking expectations of inflation.

As well as being more credible, the evidence suggests that monetary policy is both reasonably predictable in the inflation-targeting regime and more predictable than in the preceding regime. Aron and Muellbauer (2007a, 2008) use regression analysis with monthly interest rate expectations data and daily forward market interest data for the targeting period to assess how well these proxies for market forecasts capture changes in the policy rate of the SARB. They find the new monetary policy framework was well entrenched in agents' expectations by late 2001, and policy interest rates were predictable, with errors usually well below 1.25 percent. Interest rate policy rules were also estimated from 1990 covering both types of monetary policy regime. The authors find *stable* monthly models for the policy interest rate during 1999–2006, but *unstable* and far worse-fitting models for 1990–98 or 1994–98, before targeting began. Models for the latter periods show a weak response to inflation but a strong response to exchange rate changes, and there is a big jump in the exchange rate coefficient in 1996 and 1998, suggesting that a constant policy rule was not being followed. Clearly, 1999 marks a new regime, made explicit by the formal adoption of inflation targeting in 2000, during which interest rates have become far easier to predict.

Macroeconomic aggregates and their volatility are compared in table 5.1 for the tenure of three consecutive governors of the SARB—de Kock, Stals, and Mboweni, with Stals spanning two different governments. The data in the table exclude the period from mid-2008, with the onset of the global financial crisis. Nevertheless, the volatility and performance indicators in table 5.1 are hard to interpret without taking into account the varying size and nature of the shocks in the different periods. Mboweni's regime from August 1999 coincided with the period of inflation targeting, which saw sizable external shocks: exchange rate shocks in 1998 Q3 (and the extreme policy reaction to it) and 2001 Q4, shocks to U.S. producer prices, as well as shocks to U.S. output, equity prices, and interest rates. Hence it is a creditable achievement that inflation and output volatility declined, with a strong improvement in the growth rate.

Under Governor Mboweni there was a decline in nominal currency depreciation, in nominal interest rates, and in inflation, though interest rates rose from mid-2006 and double-digit inflation returned in March 2008 under global pressures. Both growth and per capita GDP growth improved significantly, particularly when compared with the substantial declines in output per capita under de Kock and in the first Stals period. The volatility of output growth and of real interest rates declined under Mboweni. Real interest rates on average were lower than in the second Stals period, but substantially higher than under de Kock and in the first Stals period. The volatility of changes in nominal interest rates and in CPI inflation[20] was, however, higher than in the second Stals period, given larger exchange rate and food and energy price shocks. The record under Governors Stals and Mboweni for inflation, real interest rates (not tax-adjusted), and real growth, is also illustrated in figure 5.2. The new regime paid dividends in bringing down inflation from double-digit figures to within the target range of 3–6 percent from 2003, despite considerable external volatility and an exchange rate shock in 2001–2. More recently, with large external shocks from rising food prices and particularly oil prices, inflation[21] exceeded this range, marginally in 2007 and substantially in 2008, before falling after September 2008 with collapsing global demand in the credit crisis. The SARB reduced nominal interest rates by 4.5 percentage points from mid-2008, in light of the fall

Table 5.1   Overview of macro-aggregates by regime of central bank governor

	National Party government		ANC government	
Macrovariable	De Kock (1981 Q1– 1989 Q2)	Stals (1989 Q3– 1994 Q1)	Stals (1994 Q2– 1999 Q2)	Mboweni (1999 Q3– 2007 Q4)
Nom. exchange rate change (%)*	–11.0	–5.7	–9.0	–2.5
NEER (level) *volatility*[†]	0.16	0.06	0.11	0.12
Real exchange rate change (%)	–1.4	2.5	–3.6	1.1
REER (level) *volatility*	0.12	0.03	0.07	0.09
Inflation rate (CPI, %)[‡]	14.7	13.3	8.0	5.2
Inflation rate (CPI) *volatility*	2.5	2.2	2.4	3.6
Inflation rate (CPD, %)	14.9	14.6	8.1	6.0
Inflation rate (CPD) *volatility*	2.7	2.4	2.5	1.8
Inflation rate (CPIX, %)	—	—	—	6.3
Inflation rate (CPIX) *volatility*	—	—	—	1.7
Nominal interest rate (%)	17.1	19.0	19.2	13.3
Nominal interest rate *volatility*	4.4	1.7	1.7	2.4
Real interest rate (%)	2.2	4.4	11.2	7.4
Real interest rate *volatility*	5.7	1.6	2.9	2.2
Growth rate (%)	1.8	–0.2	2.6	4.2
Growth rate *volatility*	3.7	2.4	1.7	1.4
Growth rate per capita (%)	–0.6	–2.6	0.5	3.1

Sources: SARB's *Quarterly Bulletin* and (IFS) International Monetary Fund. By permission of Oxford University Press. Table reproduced with permission from from J. Aron, B. Kahn, and G. Kingdon, eds., *South African Economic Policy Under Democracy* (Oxford: Oxford University Press, 2009), table 3.1.

Governor De Kock began his tenure on 1 January 1981, Governor Stals on 8 August 1989, and Governor Mboweni on 7 August 1999. Figures shown are average annual percentage changes during the period of governance identified for each governor.

* Nominal (NEER) and real (REER) effective exchange rates are the latest measure excluding Zimbabwe, spliced in 1990 to the preceding measure, which includes Zimbabwe.

† The volatility measures are defined as follows: e.g., for inflation, *the absolute value* of the annual percentage change in inflation less annual percentage change in inflation one year earlier. This measure places less emphasis on outliers than the conventional standard deviation does.

‡ Unlike the CPI, the consumer price deflator (CPD) does not contain an interest rate component, nor does the CPIX (for "metropolitan and urban areas"), but the latter is available from 1994 only. The real prime is defined using CPD to approximate the CPIX, and is not tax-adjusted. For comparison, see figure 5.1 for the real prime rate defined using a constructed measurement of CPIX (Aron and Muellbauer 2004).

in growth, which reached negative territory early in 2009 for the first time since 1993. Both official SARB and surveyed private sector expectations predicted a return of inflation to the target range by 2010.

Although real interest rates fell relative to the period prior to inflation targeting, some critics have argued that inflation targeting has resulted in real interest rates being kept too high, with a consequent cost in lower growth

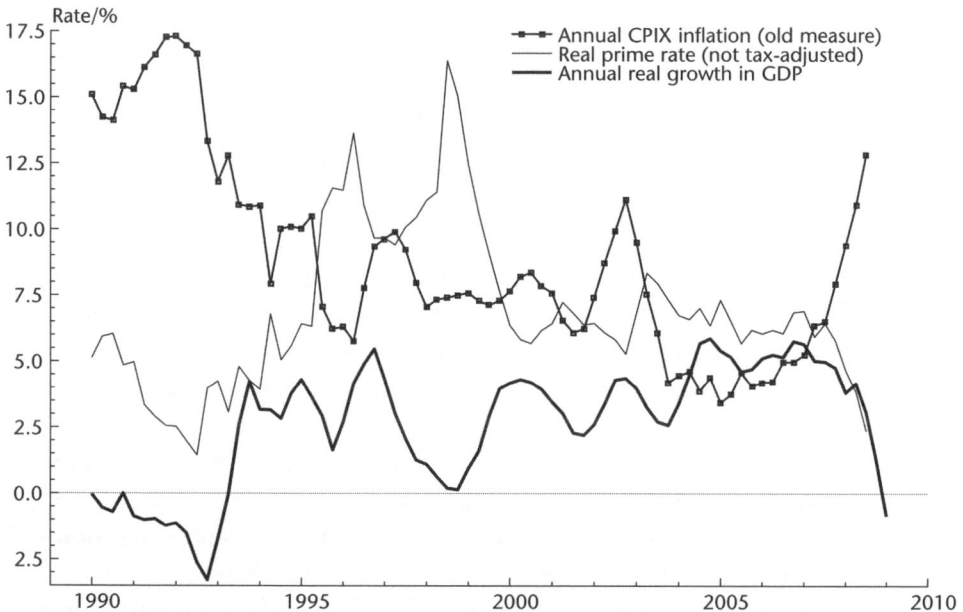

Figure 5.2 Real growth, CPIX inflation, and real prime interest rate in South Africa, 1990–2010

Sources: The prime rate is from IFS (International Monetary Fund). Real GDP, seasonally adjusted, is from the SARB's *Quarterly Bulletin*. The CPIX measure is our constructed (seasonally unadjusted) measure for metropolitan and urban areas (Aron and Muellbauer 2004), spliced in February 2000 (when targeting began) to the seasonally unadjusted CPIX measure, obtained from *Statistics South Africa*. Changes are annual percentage changes based on quarterly data. *Note:* The final available CPIX data point, before a new measure of CPI was introduced in January, 2009, was October 2008. Annual inflation on the new CPI measure in 2009Q1 averaged 8.4 percent. In May 2009 it was 8 percent.

and high unemployment. However, the relevant interest rate for companies is the *real* and *after-tax* rate, as interest payments by companies are tax-deductible (Jansen 2004). In Aron and Muellbauer (2009), South Africa's tax-adjusted real interest rates are compared with those of the United States, UK, Australia, Chile, and Brazil to the end of 2007.[22] South Africa's *real* domestic tax-adjusted cost of borrowing to companies does not seem strongly out of line with competitors' rates. For instance, South Africa's tax-adjusted real rates largely lie below Chile's, and are below Australia's in every year except for 2001; they are substantially below Brazil's rates (except in 2003, though bank margins are so high in Brazil that bank lending rates always exceed South Africa's); they lie below those of the UK, except in 2003 and 2004; but they usually exceed those of the United States, where real policy rates were negative in the aftermath of the 2001 recession and the events of 9/11.

The management of exchange rate shocks since 1994 can be evaluated by contrasting the policies of the two consecutive governors of the SARB, under their different monetary policy and governance regimes. Governor Stals faced considerable exchange rate pressure from the strong resumption of capital inflows after the 1994 elections from a negligible base after the sanctions era, which later reversed in a classic exchange rate crisis in 1996. Later crises ensued from contagion during the Asian crisis of 1997–98. In each case interest rates were sharply raised and there was substantial, costly foreign exchange intervention to support the depreciating currency. The necessary adjustment to a more appreciated real exchange rate commensurate with the new positive level of capital inflows after 1994 was resisted by Stals through intervention (only some of which was sterilized), though it was officially claimed that the exchange rate floated freely. Aron and El-badawi (1999) argue that the SARB had dual policy objectives prior to the first currency crisis in February 1996: to contain inflation through an interest rate policy based on explicit monetary targets, and to stabilize the nominal exchange rate by preventing appreciation of the currency. However, the steady bilateral exchange rate in the face of huge net capital inflows was viewed by investors as an implicit, "one-sided" nominal target (e.g., Union Bank of Switzerland 1996 [February]). The exchange rate intervention was judged to be unsustainable; investors expected an announcement in the February 1995 budget speech for the removal of remaining exchange controls to alleviate the upward pressure on the currency. This expectation precipitated a sudden capital outflow, and from mid-February to late April, the bilateral rand depreciated by 20 percent. The SARB intervened heavily to avoid the depreciation of the currency. Of a net cumulative intervention of US$5.3 billion (mid-February to the end of April), about US$3.5 billion occurred via the forward market (Kahn and Leape 1996). Interest rates rose sharply further with the onset of the crisis (see fig. 5.1).

There were later currency crises in October 1996, November 1997, and April 1998, linked to "contagion" from other emerging market crises. The prime rate rose to 20.25 percent and remained at that level until the end of 1997, falling to 18.25 percent just prior to the April 1998 crisis, when it rose as high as 25.5 percent (see fig. 5.1). Further forward market intervention failed to halt the fall of the rand. Considerable losses were incurred from uncovered forward intervention, as forward contracts drawn up when the rand was stronger then had to be settled at a much-depreciated value of the currency. These losses accrued to the fiscal authorities. To give an idea of the size of the losses, forward intervention drove the net open forward position (NOFP)[23] from $12 billion to $23 billion between April and August, 1998—a change equivalent to about 8 percent of GDP. By contrast, Australia passed relatively unscathed through the 1998 global currency crisis, without heavy intervention or high interest rates, believing that with slow pass-through from the exchange rate to consumer prices and with the deflationary terms of trade and demand shocks, no rise in interest rates was necessary (Caballero, Cowan, and Kearns 2005).

The contrast with the MPC's moderate response to the large exchange rate shocks under inflation targeting is striking, and a good illustration is provided by the 2001 exchange rate shock. Fairly early in Mboweni's governorship, after an eighteen-month period of stasis in nominal interest rates and relative stability in real interest rates, the rand depreciated by 42 percent against the U.S. dollar (from the beginning of September to the end of December 2001). The Myburgh Commission (2002) has examined the causes of this episode, with emphasis on two factors. First, the SARB had signaled its intention to retire the expensive NOFP accumulated by Stals and his predecessors. This entailed the SARB persistently buying U.S. dollars and created the impression of a "one-way bet" for investors in the foreign exchange market. Second, a tightening of foreign exchange regulations in October 2001 resulted in a sharp reduction in liquidity in the foreign exchange market. In thin markets, volatility is likely to increase. Together with the perception of the one-way bet, the result was a sharp fall in the value of the rand.

Given the information available to Mboweni's MPC, their interest rate responses were hard to fault. The MPC raised the policy rate (repurchase or "repo" rate) from 9.5 to 10.5 percent at a special meeting in January 2002, a very moderate response to the turmoil on the foreign exchange market, to 11.5 percent in March, 12.5 percent in June, and 13.5 percent in September, a level sustained until June 2003. Aron and Muellbauer (2007a) assess the monetary policy stance by calculating the real repo rate using the SARB's own one-year ahead inflation forecasts, and find policy was tightest from about mid-2002 to mid-2003. The authors criticize the SARB only for not lowering interest rates sooner, for instance in March 2003, once they were aware of a data error by *Statistics South Africa* overstating the inflation data (Stopford 2003).[24]

In summary, interest rate policy has become more transparent, credible, and predictable under Mboweni's inflation targeting regime with its clear procedures, priorities, and governance. Shocks have been handled with greater moderation and far less lasting damage to the economy. Macrostability and key economic aggregates have improved, lowering uncertainty and the real after-tax cost of capital for investment.

Fiscal Policy

Ajam and Aron comment on the remarkable degree of fiscal discipline in South Africa in light of theories of public expenditure. These theories suggest that, in countries with highly unequal income distributions, the extension of voting rights to lower-income groups is likely to strongly increase the growth of redistributive public expenditure. Rather than commit itself to fixed fiscal rules, South Africa followed "target-guided discretion" during 1994–98 and "transparency-based discretion" thereafter, with an underlying strong commitment to fiscal prudence (Calitz and Siebrits 2004). These authors argue that the flexible nature of these regimes has proved beneficial in a volatile external environment of currency crises, political democratization, and strong popular pressure for more expansionary policies. Moreover, the discretionary nature of fiscal policy has not cost the Treasury credibility, as its fiscal discipline has been consistent.

During the fiscal adjustment under the RDP and then the GEAR plans, the fiscal authorities established credibility by announcing and meeting deficit targets through a mix of expenditure cuts, revenue gains, and improved administration. Detailed discussions of the annual policies followed are given in Horton (2005) and Ajam and Aron (2007, 2009). The budget deficit fell from 7.3 percent of GDP in 1992–93 to 1.1 percent in 2002–3, and by 2005–6 the deficit was as little as 0.4 percent of GDP. In the fiscal years 2006–7 and 2007–8, the fiscal authorities posted surpluses of just under 1 percent of GDP. Some of the discipline in spending was due to an inability of departments to spend the money and was therefore unintentional. Unfortunately, this extended mainly to spending on infrastructure and on maintenance, two areas that have come home to bite in recent years. Moreover, revenue collection under SARS has time and again exceeded that which was forecast.

The reduced primary balance (i.e., the fiscal balance before interest payments) also reflects improved debt management (which focused on extending the maturities of government foreign and domestic debt, consolidating debt instruments, and introducing inflation-indexed bonds). Domestic debt fell from 50 percent to below 25 percent of GDP between 1998–99 and 2007–8, and debt service has correspondingly fallen from 6 percent to below 3 percent of GDP. National government foreign debt remains a small proportion of its overall debt, though it rose from 1 percent to over 4 percent of GDP between 1993–94 and 2007–8, reflecting increased borrowing (at longer maturities) and the effects of the rand depreciation. With better management of interest rates under inflation targeting and reduced volatility, perceived currency and sovereign credit risks have fallen, also aided by the elimination of the NOFP, lowering international borrowing costs for South Africa.

Ajam and Aron (2009) update an earlier exercise by Horton (2005) to assess the government's fiscal stance purely as a result of discretionary fiscal policy. This requires a correction to remove the cyclical economic factors that may have affected revenue and expenditure.[25] The annual change in the fiscal stance is termed the fiscal impulse, and it reveals whether policy tightened or loosened at the various stages of the business cycle. The analysis suggests that discretionary fiscal policy was tightened from 1992–93, with a combination of expenditure cuts and revenue gains by 1998–99. Sharp expenditure cuts are especially evident in 1993–94 and 1997–98, and moderate cuts ensued in the following three years. In 1998–99, the impact of the establishment of SARS and associated reforms is apparent with significant revenue raised, and also in 2001–2, 2004–5, and 2005–6. The rise in budgeted social and investment spending after 2001–2 loosened the fiscal stance, despite the revenue gains. Comparing the gap between trend and actual output, with the fiscal impulse, suggests that before about 2002–3, policy had been largely pro-cyclical (i.e., with fiscal tightening occurring even in a period of falling output), but fiscal policy has fortunately been able to become more countercyclical in the most recent years.

The reorientation of spending away from defense, administration, and subsidies and a much-reduced debt burden have freed spending for social services and increased capital investment, under the constraint of the overall fiscal targets. Despite intentions to increase spending, actual expenditure was often well below that budgeted, mainly due to lack of spending *capacity* at the provincial level (e.g., Ajam and Aron [2007] document the disappointing delivery of social services in education and housing, despite substantially raised fiscal allocations). Although South Africa is a high spender on education among middle-income countries, the quality of the educational outcomes is significantly inferior to that in comparable developing countries. Despite massive resource shifts to black schools in the postapartheid period, overall learning achievement levels (as measured by matriculation pass rates) have not improved, and the mainly black schools—which constitute the majority of schools—continue to have extremely low pass rates with high variability. Moreover, the percentage of teenagers taking higher-level mathematics in high school has been falling, measured since 1994. The analysis of Van der Berg (2009) implicates school management rather than fiscal allocations, suggesting improved utilization of existing resources, increased attention to non-personnel expenditure (the overwhelming proportion of postapartheid resource increases in education went to teachers in the form of higher salaries), and generating learning achievement data regularly to inform both policymakers and parents, to reduce information asymmetries, and to foster school accountability.

"Social services" jointly consume the bulk of non-interest consolidated national and provincial expenditure, averaging just below 60 percent of total expenditure. Of this, education expenditure and social security and welfare expenditure are the two largest items, followed by health expenditure. Social welfare expenditure, which includes means-tested child support grants, disability grants, and universal old age grants, is expected to rise by the Medium Term Expenditure Framework's projected figures. South Africa has a substantial system of state-provided social assistance, exceptional compared with many other middle-income countries (Case and Deaton 1998; Agüero, Carter, and Woolard 2007). Means-tested noncontributory old age pensions and disability pensions are provided, the former to women over sixty and men over sixty-five, and research confirms that grants significantly alleviate poverty among the elderly and their dependants (National Treasury 2007). Moreover, following the Lund Committee's recommendations (established in late 1995), the child support grant in 1998 replaced an earlier State Maintenance Grant, which only 0.2 percent of African children received (Agüero, Carter, and Woolard 2007). This child-focused grant is paid to the primary caregiver (98 percent of whom are women), and coverage has been progressively extended. As of April 2005, it has been given to children under the age of fourteen, and the uptake is about half of age-eligible children, with increases outstripping inflation. The 2009 budget further extended the child support grant to age fifteen years, with the feasibility of further extension to eighteen years under investigation (and there was also a further rollout of old age grants). Agüero, Carter, and Woolard (2007) have found robust evidence that these targeted unconditional payments have bolstered early childhood nutrition as measured by child height for age, and they also present evidence for the likely beneficial long-term greater earnings based on these short-term transfers. Ambitious new social security and retirement reforms have been proposed following National Treasury investigations to extend access and improve incentives for retirement saving by the poor (National Treasury 2007).

GROWTH PERFORMANCE

While there has been much focus on raising the growth rate in South Africa, under the government's 2006 plan, the Accelerated and Shared Growth Initiative for South Africa (ASGISA),[26] it is important to recognize that the past decade—until the onset of the global financial crisis in mid-2008—has been a relative success story: growth performance and the stability of growth improved, and investment performance began to rise. Table 5.1 shows that in a comparison of the apartheid government's regime with the period under the ANC until 2007 Q4, the annualized real growth rate rose strongly in the second period. The growth pickup has been even greater under Mboweni when measured from mid-1999 (following the 1998 currency crisis with punitive interest rate rises under Stals). Growth volatility dropped substantially under the ANC government, and real per capita growth rose from negative territory in the apartheid era to an average of 3.1 percent during mid-1999 to 2007. Annual expenditure on fixed investment has improved under the ANC government, at 16.5 percent of GDP on average between 1994 and 2007, and exceeded 21 percent of GDP in 2007, though it remains low by international standards.

Several recent studies on South Africa have employed "growth accounting" to investigate the underlying relative contributions to long-run economic growth of factor accumulation in labor and capital (including human capital) and of efficiency gains (Fedderke 2002; Arora 2005; Du Plessis and Smit 2009). The method typically uses a Cobb-Douglas production function, with data on gross fixed capital accumulation and employment. It is assumed that there are constant shares to labor and capital over time (proxied by shares in national income), and various assumptions may be made concerning the contribution of human capital over time. Real GDP growth is attributed to labor and capital growth via this function. The residual is assumed to represent improved technology and efficiency of production, and is known as total factor productivity (TFP) growth.

The results of the exercise are shown in table 5.2 for the two more recent studies covering slightly different time periods. The relative contributions of labor and capital to growth differ across studies, depending on assumptions about human capital accumulation. Using the results of Du Plessis and Smit (for assumptions on human capital, see table 5.2), labor's contribution declines and capital's is virtually static, contrasting the tenures of the ANC and the preceding government. The common and notable result is that the

Table 5.2   Growth contributions using growth accounting

Estimated growth contributions, by study	Average in percentage points, by period	
Du Plessis and Smit (2009)	1985–1994	1995–2004
Real GDP growth	0.8	3.1
TFP[a]	−0.28	1.86
TFP[b]	−0.76	1.60
TFP[c]	−1.14	1.53
Labor[c]	1.49	0.95
Capital[c]	0.45	0.62
Arora (2005)	1980–1994	1995–2003
Real GDP growth	1.2	2.9
TFP	−0.4	1.3
Labor	0.7	0.9
Capital	0.8	0.7

Sources: Annualized real GDP growth, Quarterly Bulletin, SARB. Survey of Employment and Earnings from Statistics South Africa.

Note: TFP measures a, b, and c are respectively treating employment as not adjusted for changes in human capital, adjusted via years of schooling measure, and adjusted via skills differentiation; see Du Plessis and Smit (2009).

TFP contribution to growth has increased strongly in each study across the two periods. At over 50 percent it is the largest contributor to actual growth in the later period. Du Plessis and Smit also find the aggregate level results for TFP broadly hold at the level of *sectors*, specifically the (manufacturing) subsectors in the South African economy.

An important caveat is that the method unfortunately is sensitive to the poor quality of the South African employment data (see, e.g., Klasen and Woolard 1999).[27] Nevertheless, some interesting conclusions can be drawn from these findings related to the dominant role of improved technology and efficiency of production, or TFP growth. First, Arora (2005) contends that stronger TFP growth contribution than the other factors is significant because it is more sustainable in the longer run, not being subject to demographic constraints and diminishing returns to scale. Second, institutional and regulatory changes under the ANC government, as well as regime changes in monetary and fiscal policy and in trade liberalization, can indeed help to explain the stronger TFP performance. Du Plessis and Smit (2009) survey empirical studies for South Africa and some international studies to try to adduce which determinants are responsible for the notable growth of TFP and the lower relative contribution of capital and labor. They find that the increased openness of the economy, driven by trade liberalization[28] from

1990 onward, has been a leading cause of TFP growth. Arora (2005) concurs on openness, citing empirical work by Arora and Bhundia (2003). Further, the 40 percent larger post-1994 share of equipment and machinery in private investment, compared with the previous decade, suggests that spillover effects from imported technology may be helping to drive TFP both directly and indirectly via the imports in which they are embedded.[29] Arora (2005) also suggests that greater private participation in the economy through deregulation and privatization, as evidenced by the 20 percent greater share of private sector investment in overall investment, has raised the scope for TFP influences on growth.

Du Plessis and Smit also partly attribute the revival of investment expenditure as a contributing factor to growth after 1994, to greater trade openness and openness to international capital flows. Their survey finds compelling evidence for South Africa that a lower user cost of capital and lower systemic and sectoral uncertainty through more stable macropolicy are consistent with the recovery in investment. Reduced policy volatility (or reduced uncertainty) should indeed be associated with faster growth (e.g., Fatjas and Mihov 2003). The somewhat static contribution of investment growth as a contribution to overall growth (table 3, up to 2004), may partly be explained by the timing of the macrostability outcomes for South Africa. The fiscal transparency and accountability improvements bore fruit early on (see the preceding two sections of this essay). But the lower real interest rates and reduced sovereign risk spreads, improved reserves position, and increased credibility and predictability of monetary policy that have collectively helped to reduce economic uncertainty, only materialized some years after the adoption of inflation targeting in 2000 (see again the preceding two sections). The full impact of reduced uncertainty on promoting investment was probably still to be felt, just prior to the onset of the global financial crisis in the second half of 2008. On the other hand, South Africa's policy on Zimbabwe and its underinvestment in infrastructure resulting in power cuts, as well as high levels of crime, were among important impediments to private investment.

Increased openness also features strongly in the South African labor market literature, helping explain the lackluster employment growth since 1994. Formal labor markets have contracted, partly as a result of retrenchment from cost cutting, given the greater competitiveness faced by manufacturing firms after trade liberalization.[30] In the drive for increased productivity, there has been a relative increase in demand for skilled workers over unskilled labor (Nattrass 2000; Barker 2003).[31] Skills deficiencies or mismatches have also hindered expansion in a range of firms. Originating in poor standards of education and educational infrastructure in the apartheid era, they are difficult to reverse rapidly despite increased fiscal allocations, as discussed above. Reduced public sector hiring, and declining public infrastructure spending with fiscal consolidation after 1994, also contracted employment. Du Plessis and Smit's survey finds the empirical evidence is ambiguous as to whether the high level of real wages may have induced unemployment. Insofar as the increased credibility of monetary policy has helped stabilize and reduce inflationary expectations (see "The Performance of Monetary and Fiscal Policy" above), this may have curtailed the size of wage settlements. Arora and Ricci (2005) cite evidence that employment generation has been impeded by regulation-induced labor market rigidities, including hiring and dismissal costs and policies that particularly disadvantage small businesses (see also Edwards 2001).[32]

In sum, these authors suggest openness to trade and capital flows, lower macropolicy uncertainty, and lower interest rates mainly explain South Africa's growth recovery since 1994. The important role of the fiscal and monetary policy mix is apparent in reducing uncertainty and sovereign risk ratings through the greater credibility, transparency, and predictability of policy and lower and less volatile real interest rates in the short to medium term. This achievement has to be balanced against poor results concerning some of the longer-term factors influencing growth, on which fiscal policy has a bearing. Delayed government expenditure on infrastructure has impeded growth, as has poor delivery of microservices such as education, though fiscal allocation is only a small part of the story for the latter (see "The Performance of Monetary and Fiscal Policy" above).

CONCLUSIONS, AND THE BALANCE OF PAYMENTS CONSTRAINT ON RADICAL MACROPOLICY CHANGES

The ANC government has undoubtedly made large gains in the governance and performance of fiscal and monetary policy. Moreover, these gains were achieved despite the considerable transitional challenges of normalizing international relations in credit and foreign currency markets and in trade, after years of isolation under apartheid. Sovereign reputation and credibility have been restored, as reflected in international credit ratings and domestic investment. Monetary policy since 2000 has operated in a more transparent institutional framework with clear policy priorities for the first time, and a flexible and forward-looking monetary rule that has made monetary policy more credible and predictable. By contrast, the nontransparent conduct of monetary policy prior to the inflation-targeting regime damaged credibility, confidence, and economic growth. Inflation targeting has stabilized consumer price inflation at lower levels than under the preceding regime, with the exception of 2008, when high global food and oil prices had a persistent upward influence on South African inflation. The closure in 2003 of the large NOFP position created by the previous monetary policy regime is an important achievement, freeing the SARB to accumulate foreign exchange reserves to limit short-term exchange rate instability, and further stabilize inflation and interest rate volatility. Despite a dismal inherited position, fiscal policy, with its underlying institutional governance reforms, has strongly supported monetary policy with an impressive fiscal prudence and reorientation of expenditure, debt reduction and better debt management, and more transparent longer-term planning. This has allowed a redirection of spending to social services, including extending old age pension and disability grants and creating a child support grant with wide coverage and take-up. It has also opened the way for the large public sector infrastructural investments envisaged by ASGISA. Empirical evidence suggests that the reduction in macroeconomic policy uncertainty and the technological spillovers from greater economic openness have helped restore investment and growth and improve the "initial conditions" for promoting future investment and growth. Thus, fiscal and monetary policy design aimed to fulfill the original objectives of the RDP and GEAR plans, and has followed these plans closely, particularly in fiscal policy.

Outside monetary policy and the stabilizing achievements of fiscal policy, the policy record, particularly on the supply side of the economy, has been less impressive. Implicitly this has been recognized in the ASGISA 2006 Summary. The document recognizes South Africa's poor record on bringing down unemployment (Kingdon and Knight 2009).[33] One of the major growth constraints listed is "the cost, efficiency and capacity of the national logistics system" resulting in part from backlogs in infrastructure and investment. To a degree, these are the results of past curbs on government expenditure, as well as disarray in industrial policies including poor regulation of former public utilities (for a critique, see Black and Roberts 2009). There has been a long-term decline in infrastructure investment and capital stock, with real investment per capita falling by 72 percent from 1976 to 2002 (Bogetić and Fedderke 2006). Yet in line with international evidence, infrastructure in South Africa has been found to influence growth, with electricity having the greatest and most robust impact (e.g., Fedderke, Perkins, and Luiz 2006).

Arvantis (2005) finds foreign direct investment (FDI) flows to South Africa to be affected by the quality of infrastructure, inter alia. The public capital constraint is only belatedly receiving extensive policy attention, with significant expansions first planned in the 2005 budget. Backlogs in electricity maintenance and investment in generation capacity caused power outages in early 2008, with mines being forced to shut down for two weeks. This had an impact on the exchange rate as foreign investors noted the emergence of electricity supply constraints in mining and manufacturing production affecting the growth outlook. Planned infrastructure spending escalated massively in the 2009 budget, with investment tabled at R787 billion over the Medium Term Expenditure Framework, to be funded about half by nonfinancial public enterprises, such as Transnet, responsible for rail, ports, and pipelines, and Eskom, for electricity.[34]

Ajam and Aron (2007) also suggest that the hard-won fiscal stability gains may be threatened in the future unless the mediocre quality and scope of service delivery are addressed through strengthening the management capacity for delivery. In an environment of low employment and persisting poverty, inequality, and deprivation, the government may otherwise face pressure to extend cash-based entitlements, which would prove fiscally extremely costly. Disappointing service delivery has been recognized in the ASGISA (2006) document, which acknowledges "weaknesses in the way government is organized, in the capacity of key institutions, including some of those providing economic services"; local government and service delivery are among those highlighted. A case in point is the delivery of education and skills training. While this is rightly attributed to the legacy of apartheid, the relative failure of the majority of schools used by the mass of the population to deliver hoped-for improvements in levels of literacy, numeracy, and other skills is becoming a pressing issue.

The "shortage of suitably skilled labour" is another major supply-side constraint on growth highlighted by ASGISA (2006), discussed above. The ASGISA document fails to acknowledge that the rapid implementation of affirmative action employment policies has contributed to the exodus from South Africa of skilled professionals, managers, and artisans, whose shortages now constrain growth and public service delivery, especially at provincial and municipal levels.

It has recently been argued (IMF 2007) that a neutral rather than an expansionary fiscal policy stance is sensible, in view of South Africa's current account balance to GDP, which has escalated from a small surplus in 2002 to a deficit of 7.4 percent of GDP in 2008. Indeed, fiscal consolidation has been a key structural reform in Australia, aimed at addressing its own persistently large current account deficit. The main driver of the South African deficit prior to the 2008–9 global financial crisis, with an appreciated exchange rate influenced by high commodity prices, was strong domestic demand for imports from booming investment spending and credit-driven consumer spending.[35]

The deficit is funded mainly by portfolio inflows, raising worries about a stoppage or sudden reversal of flows. South Africa's vulnerability has increased with the turbulent state of the global economy in 2008–9, and greater risk aversion by foreign investors. Studies of early warning indicators of capital flow reversals and currency crises (surveyed in Chui 2002) include current account deficits as high on the list of reliable indicators. Institutional differences amongst emerging markets should be noted, however, before applying a 'one-size-fits-all' approach to assessing vulnerability (Belkar, Cockerell, and Kent 2007). Australia, with a large current account deficit, averaging 5.3 percent of GDP during 2003–8, and a relatively large net external debt, has not experienced currency crises. Belkar, Cockerell, and Kent (2007) argue that Australia possesses particular features making it fairly resilient to large external shocks and which "underpin the stability which encourages sizeable capital inflows in the first place." South Africa shares many of these features, including a stable government with credible and sustainable monetary and fiscal policies (at least until the time of writing), a commitment to low and stable inflation, no (recent) debt defaults,[36] and a robust financial system with deep, liquid financial markets underpinned by efficient regulation and supervision.[37] However, Australia has more transparent and open markets for factors of production and outputs.[38]

Another feature is that a significant proportion of Australia's current account appears to be funded by more long-term FDI flows, supposedly reducing its vulnerability. However, Leape and Thomas (2009) argue that South Africa's low levels of FDI reflect the relatively highly developed nature of South Africa's domestic financial markets which facilitates portfolio investment as an *alternative* to direct investment. While the pattern of investment in the bond market reflects high-frequency trading, portfolio equity inflows especially have been relatively stable and long term in nature. However, the resiliency feature most highlighted is that of Australia's net external debt, around 40 percent of which is denominated in Australian dollars ,while most of the remaining net exposure is hedged, thereby insulating domestic residents against exchange rate fluctuations. South Africa, again, shares some of these features, which have helped cushion it from the worst excesses of the 2008–9 global crisis. Levels of South Africa's total foreign debt are low (29 percent of GDP in 2008), reducing the "fear of floating" (Calvo and Reinhart 2002), as the balance sheet effects of a sharp depreciation are limited. Leape and Thomas (2009) demonstrate that significant shifts in the external balance sheet toward predominantly *rand*-based liabilities (42 percent of total South African foreign debt in 2008) make South Africa better placed than previously to manage external shocks. Further, their evidence of "home bias" and, importantly, the shift to prudential regulation of foreign exposures by residents suggests that risks associated with destabilizing resident outflows have also been greatly reduced. Hedging is not yet fully efficient in South Africa, and efficient financial markets to allow domestic residents to hedge foreign exposures at a reasonable cost can only be expected to evolve fully under a flexible exchange rate regime (Caballero, Cowan, and Kearns 2004).

Evidence also shows that the flexible exchange rate regime has provided a timely and automatic mechanism to cushion against external shocks in Australia, with a modest impact on inflation. While Frankel, Smit, and Sturzenegger (2006) acknowledge South Africa's relative strengths, for instance with mainly rand-based portfolio inflows, they suggest that the real exchange rate should become an objective of the SARB (p. 10) and that monetary policy, instead of focusing on its primary target under inflation targeting, should additionally actively and persistently dampen real exchange rate appreciations. The feasibility of this partly depends on one's view on the permanence of the factors appreciating the rand. If there are *temporary* shocks appreciating the rand, then there may be a case for a temporary ironing out of such fluctuations, following the example of the inflation-targeting Reserve Bank of Australia, which has made profits (Becker and Sinclair 2004) by intervening only at extremes of the exchange rate to stabilize the rate, but not to influence it persistently in any direction.[39] If the shocks are more permanent, however, intervention will fail in the medium run (see above points on Stals's 1994–6 intervention). During the protracted period of booming commodity prices prior to August 2008, Chile had far less exchange rate appreciation than the rand, aiming to prevent commodity-related appreciation from devastating non-mining areas of export growth (the so-called "Dutch disease"). Chile prevented appreciation mainly by keeping export earnings offshore and encouraging foreign investors to externalize dividends. With South Africa targeting manufacturing growth as an important, low-skill contributor to employment growth, a weaker exchange rate is desirable. The

Chilean policy offers an alternative to attempting unsuccessfully to manipulate the currency by monetary means in the medium term.

It is vital to improve the domestic saving rate in South Africa, and thereby reduce the heavy reliance on foreign investors for "foreign savings" or potentially volatile capital inflows (long argued by Aron and Muellbauer 2000, 2006a, 2006b). The saving-growth connection goes both ways, and there is controversy over how strong the saving-to-growth channel is (Deaton 1999). Even while the government moved from dissaving to saving under the ANC, households have moved to a dissaving position, and corporate saving has fallen. Raising the saving rate should bring down the cost of capital and help growth. More incentives should be provided for savers. The new pensions reforms outlined above and the new cooperative banks bill under consideration, which aims to help bank the half of South African adults that are unbanked, should aid a rise in saving. Consumption has been driven by easy credit and perceived increases in wealth with higher asset and house prices. Prudent regulation of credit extension, especially to new borrowers, is important, and the National Credit Act of June 2007 is an important step in this direction.[40]

The above discussion makes clear that the balance of payments remains a key continuing constraint on domestic macropolicy under the new Zuma-led government in 2009. Hence, reliance on foreign investment to finance the large current account deficit will likely, as in the first fifteen years of the ANC government, forestall radical macropolicy changes that might damage internationally perceived macrostability. The continued presence in the new 2009 cabinet of internationally respected former finance minister Trevor Manuel in a planning role would have been designed with this in mind; similarly the appointment of Pravin Gordhan as the new finance minister, respected by the financial markets for his efficiency in raising tax revenue as head of SARS.

Prior to the May 2009 elections and after the ousting of Mbeki as president in September 2008, there were fears that the stable macroeconomic policy framework might be under threat. The *apparent* direction of future ANC macroeconomic policy, gauged from several documents[41] of the ANC-COSATU-SACP Alliance (the Congress of South African Trade Unions and the South African Communist Party), looked radically different. The apparent departures from the macroeconomic policy of the previous era lie mainly in the objectives of monetary policy and a far more expansionary fiscal policy, aimed at a developmental and welfarist state. As regards monetary policy, there is unfortunately a continued lack of understanding among some alliance players about the long-term nature of the principal drivers of growth, and the highly limited role of monetary policy in influencing medium-term growth (except insofar as it creates favorable initial conditions for growth with sustained macro-stability). There is widespread international consensus among economists on this fact, as pointed out by Du Plessis (2009, 75), who remarks of the South Africa debate, "This debate might have been more salutary if it didn't seem so ill informed." There is little understanding too of the significant *gains* from the ANC's monetary policy under inflation targeting. Despite the threat of political interference or of changing the mandate of monetary policy, no robust alternatives to inflation targeting have been offered. Vague statements about exchange rates and interest rates needing "to be calibrated to take account of industrial policy imperatives" (*Declaration of the Alliance Economic Summit* 2008) fail to recognize that the exchange rate floats in South Africa as a necessary part of a transparent monetary policy,[42] while cognizance is already fully taken of the output gap in setting interest rates. Fortunately, in the early months after the appointment of the new cabinet,[43] most public statements were of the a pragmatic or practical variety, carefully stressing intended continuity of the macropolicy stability gains to international investors.

However, under inflation targeting, interest rate policy will be challenged by the large fiscal stimulus, with proposed expenditure on a greater social safety net, sustained public sector incomes and jobs, new jobs, infrastructure, a developmental state, improved microdelivery, and reduced crime, among others. Fiscal experts Abedian and Ajam (2009) warn that while judicious past fiscal policy has bought "fiscal space" in the short term, fortuitous given the sudden global financial and economic crisis in 2008, this will be rapidly dissipated. They advise extreme caution in creating further social entitlements well known to create fiscal rigidities, and hence fiscal risk, in a volatile and deteriorating economic climate. They note that the present number of beneficiaries is over twelve million, and increasing at a far more rapid rate than the number of tax-payers, while SARS is reaching diminishing returns in ensuring compliance from the existing tax bases. The huge projected rise in debt to pay for expenditure will create expensive debt servicing, crowding out social expenditures, as in the position inherited after apartheid. Any departure from perceived stable macroeconomic policy may alter international risk aversion toward South Africa and credit ratings, significantly raising the costs of acquiring and servicing such debt.

Thus, the challenge for fiscal policy is to support South Africa's transparent monetary policy through a sustainable delivery of resources for social upliftment, infrastructure spending, and a better quality of microservice delivery, such as in education, without jeopardizing a prudent fiscal position and past gains from macrostability. Meeting commitments on public services and reducing unemployment through improving the supply-side determinants of growth could thus take very many years, undermining political credibility if unrealistic political promises are made. As a final point, the contention of Abedian and Ajam (2009) is highlighted: the *binding* constraint on service delivery, and hence a key constraint on growth, is South Africa's poor institutional capacity for efficient implementation. The apparent inclination to continue the past trend of expansion in resources ("throwing money at the problem") will achieve little impact and value for money. They remark, "The temptation should be resisted to seek the solution for government failure in the realm of policy development or in organisational re-configuration, simply because these are more politically visible and effected more quickly and expediently, rather than grapple with the fundamental but more intractable dilemmas of improving managerial and technical skills, and other institutional capabilities" (101).

APPENDIX: PARLIAMENTARY SCRUTINY OF THE SOUTH AFRICAN RESERVE BANK

1a. How many separate times did central bank officials appear before Parliament or its representatives in the last year? (Please count joint appearances by two or more officials at the same hearing as a single appearance.)

 None, 1–5, 6–10, 11–20, 21–30, 31–40, 41–50, 51–100, 100+

 1–5 (There were 3 parliamentary hearings.)

1b. What percentage of these appearances were by the chairman/governor of the central bank (either alone or accompanied by other central bank officials)?

 1–20, 21–40, 41–60, 61–80, 81–100

 81–100 (All meetings were attended by the governor, with 1 or 2 officials.)

1c. What percentage of the total number of hearings was, in the main, related to monetary policy concerns?

 1–20, 21–40, 41–60, 61–80, 81–100

 81–100 (The hearings may address any aspect published in the central bank's *Quarterly Bulletin*.)

1d. Is this number of hearings, division of subjects, and percentage of appearances, representative of a typical year? (If not, please explain; e.g. does it vary owing to the state of the economy?)

>Yes.

2a. How many members of staff work full-time for the parliamentary committee(s) responsible for holding the central bank to account?

>1–5, 6–10, 10–25, 25–50, 50+

>>1–5 (2 full-time staff members.)

2b. What percentage of this staff provides research/analytical support?

>1–20, 21–40, 41–60, 61–80, 81–100

>>No staff members are currently providing analytical or technical support.

2c. Does anybody advise the committee(s) on a part-time basis; if so, who? (e.g., in the UK Parliament a panel of expert economists briefs the Treasury Committee in advance of hearings on monetary policy).

>No.

3 How is the number of appearances before Parliament, made by central bank officials, decided?

>By statute (i.e. set out in law); by the parliamentary committee; both; other.

>Both (but not in the Reserve Bank Act of 1989).

4a. Who is responsible for appointing the chairman/governor of the central bank?

>The central bank board; Parliament; Council of Ministers; prime minister/finance minister; other.

>>The president, after consultation with the minister of finance and the board.

4b. Does Parliament have the power to veto the appointment of the chairman/governor of the central bank?

>No.

5a. Who in the central bank is responsible for determining monetary policy?

>Chairman/governor; committee of officials including the chairman

>>Committee of officials and the governor, known as the Monetary Policy Committee (MPC). By the Reserve Bank Act, only the governor and deputy governor(s) can vote on monetary policy matters, but in practice decisions are made by "consensus."

5b. Who is responsible for appointing the members of the committee?

>Central bank board; Parliament Council of Ministers; prime minister or finance minister; other.

>>The governor appoints members to the MPC (there is no provision in the Reserve Bank Act for the composition of the committee).

5c. Does Parliament have the power to veto appointments to the committee?

>   No.

6. What is the principal objective of the parliamentary committee when it holds hearings with central bank officials?

>   To account for monetary policy decisions.

7. How many members of Parliament make up this committee, how many attend meetings with central bank officials, and how many have any formal economic expertise?

>   There are 13 members of the Portfolio Committee on Finance; on average 10 members attend and 8 members have academic training (at different levels).

8. How often does the parliamentary committee request that the central bank provide written evidence on the conduct of monetary policy?

>   The committee thus far has not requested any written evidence on the conduct of monetary policy.

Survey adapted from Sterne and Lepper, "Parliamentary Scrutiny of Central Banks in the United Kingdom and Overseas" (2002). Results for South Africa pertaining to 2006 were kindly provided by Andre Herman (South African Parliament) and Brian Kahn (South African Reserve Bank).

NOTES

I am very grateful to Brian Kahn (South African Reserve Bank), John Muellbauer (Nuffield College), Gavin Keeton (Rhodes University), Dennis Dykes (Nedbank), and Andre Hermans (South African Parliament) for comments and advice. I acknowledge funding from the Department for International Development (UK), grant no. R8311, but the views and opinions expressed are mine alone. My website is http://www.economics.ox.ac.uk/index/php/staff/aron.

1. These plans are available on the web; see also Hirsch (2005) and Nowak and Ricci (2005).

2. An interim constitution was adopted in 1994 and the final constitution in December 1996.

3. Admittedly, the 1992–93 and 1994–94 fiscal deficits had also been boosted by one-time payments related to refunding the government pension fund.

4. Section 224 (2) of the constitution states: "The SARB, in pursuit of its primary object must perform its functions independently and without fear, favour or prejudice, but there must be regular consultation between the Bank and the Cabinet member responsible for national financial matters."

5. Under Governor Stals, a mission statement published in 1990 entrusted the protection of the domestic *and* external value of the rand to the bank. Carried through to the interim constitution (1994), this could be interpreted as monetary

policy having *both* a price and an exchange rate target, but without explicit prioritization.

6. A separate exchange rate for nonresidents' transactions was operative from the early 1960s until 1995, except for two years in the 1980s, and was called the "financial rand" from 1979.

7. Prior to inflation targeting, pre-announced monetary target ranges were used from 1986 on, for a broad definition of money. Monetary targets had, however, long been abandoned as unworkable by the UK and United States.

8. Aron and Muellbauer (2002) apply an extension of the Taylor Rule model (Taylor 1993) to try to estimate the weights applied to different indicators in the interest rate rule during 1986–97.

9. Institutional change is slow, and this position had not altered materially by 2009.

10. Nel and Lekalale (2004) evaluate whether the SARB adheres to the IMF's codes on transparency and accountability. They address similar issues, though without constructing indexes of transparency.

11. There are three questions for each of the five aspects of transparency. The three questions each have equal weight and a maximum score of one.

12. Alternative weights suggested by Plenderleith, deputy governor of the Reserve Bank, 2003–6 (and inaugural member of the Bank of England's MPC), assign a zero weight to the publication of minutes and of voting records, and to the disclosure of an explicit policy inclination after every policy meeting. Other weights are derived by the authors from chapter 4 in Mahadeva and Sterne (2000); see the appendix to Aron and Muellbauer (2007a).

13. As late as July 2009 no successor to Mboweni, whose term was due to end in August 2009, had been announced, creating uncertainty. The choice of successor was an important signal to the nature of future monetary policy objectives supported by the Zuma government (see the conclusion). Gill Marcus succeeded Mboweni in November 2009.

14. The structure of the MPC has changed since its formation in October 1999, as has the frequency of its meetings. In 2007, it comprised seven SARB officials, chaired by the governor. The MPC met six times per year as of 2004, and monthly as of March 2009 in the face of the global financial crisis.

15. These include policies that restrict tendering for contracts to achieve targets for black empowerment or affirmative action employment.

16. In the 1996 constitution, the mandate of the Financial and Fiscal Commission is given in section 2.2, while the later Financial and Fiscal Commission Act of 1998 explains the organization's structure and functions.

17. This section draws on research on South African monetary policy conducted with John Muellbauer; see Aron and Muellbauer (2005, 2007a, 2007b, 2009).

18. As of January 2009, with the introduction of a new measure of the consumer price index (CPI), the inflation target is for a rate of increase in the CPI of between 3 and 6 percent per year, on a continuous basis.

19. There are no inflation expectations surveys available before targeting began. The monthly Reuters survey, which presents analysts' inflation expectations at various ranges ahead, also begins only in 2000.

20. The volatility of inflation, when measured using the consumer expenditure deflator, which excludes interest rates and which we use to approximate the targeted CPIX given the absence of data before 1994, was lower under Mboweni.

21. The CPIX measure was replaced in January 2009 by a new CPI measure. There are no historical data before 2008, and the two series cannot be directly compared. See footnote to figure 5.2.

22. We employ short-term market interest rates and, for comparability, backward-looking annual inflation rates, adjusting nominal rates for tax using the KPMG annual survey on corporate tax rates.

23. The net open foreign currency position (NOFP) refers to the accumulation by the South African Reserve Bank of foreign currency obligations through forward market intervention that were far in excess of its net international foreign currency reserves.

24. The official downward revision to the CPI from *Statistics South Africa,* however, came out only on 30 May 2003.

25. A measure of the output gap (potential or trend output minus actual output) was used to adjust revenue and expenditure values relative to GDP to the amounts needed to maintain revenue and expenditure at the level of a neutral or base year, that is, a year when potential and actual output approximately coincided. The chosen base year was the fiscal year 2000–2001, when the output gap was close to zero. Subtracting these neutral levels of revenue and expenditure from actual levels of revenue and expenditure gives the revenue stance and expenditure stance. The fiscal stance is calculated as the difference between the revenue stance and the (non-interest) expenditure stance, or the *primary* balance relative to its neutral value. The assumptions for the calculation of neutral values are that neutral revenue grows at the rate of GDP, while neutral non-interest expenditure grows at the rate of trend GDP (as in Horton 2005).

26. The 2006 Summary of ASGISA can be found at http://www.info.gov.za/asgisa/asgisa.htm.

27. Prior to March 2003, the Survey of Employment and Earnings had serious limitations, excluding information particularly from the services sector. By excluding significant sectors from the underlying survey, the employment data used to proxy labor input are unreliable. The result is that labor's contribution to growth is understated and that of the residual, or TFP, is overstated, even where informal sector employment is included. The Quarterly Employment Statistics, published from June 2005, now covers all companies registered for income tax.

28. The nature of trade liberalization in South Africa since 1990 is detailed by Hviding (2005), Edwards (2005), and Aron and Muellbauer (2007b), and there remains scope for further liberalization.

29. Pertinent also to the importance of TFP growth, the role of research and

development and of human capital in driving innovation patterns in South Africa has been explored by Fedderke, de Kadt, and Luiz (2000).

30. Despite greater trade openness, various industries are highly concentrated, and the associated pricing power introduces inefficiencies. Fedderke, Kularatne, and Mariotti (2007) find pervasive pricing power in a wide range of industries, linked to concentration. Fedderke and Szalontai (2009) and Fedderke and Naumann (forthcoming) find that the consequences of high concentration extend to poor employment and investment performance in South African industry.

31. The issue is contentious: Fedderke, Shin, and Vaze (2009) find that trade liberalization has had a positive impact on labor demand—but that it has been associated with labor-saving technological changes.

32. An example of the latter is that minimum wages are set by the extension system in collective bargaining for the largest employers, and may not reflect productivity differences in smaller firms.

33. The 2006 ASGISA Summary cites irrational patterns of population settlement stemming from apartheid, resulting in the poor often living far from places of work, as a contributing factor. But it also includes the administration of labor law under the heading of the "regulatory environment and the burden on small and medium businesses," which it recognizes has contributed to "the mediocre performance of the small, medium and micro business sectors in terms of contribution to GDP and employment."

34. Infrastructure expansion will come under strain following the global crisis of 2008–9, and new difficulties for Eskom and Transnet to borrow in the foreign markets. Should South Africa's credit rating deteriorate, this will also make foreign funding of infrastructure more expensive. The infrastructure plans may thus be in jeopardy or delayed.

35. The deficit contracted somewhat from late in 2008 as a result of the global crisis, when weakened exports were more than counteracted by lower imports through falling demand and a lower oil price.

36. A major external debt crisis occurred in 1985 under the apartheid government.

37. For instance, see Mboweni (2004) on the resiliency of the South African banking sector under the ANC government.

38. By contrast, "barriers to entry, limits to competition and limited new investment opportunities" are listed as a serious constraint by ASGISA in its 2006 Summary, with the high degree of firm concentration in South Africa noted.

39. Their intervention strategy is small daily interventions with frequent changes in direction (often described as "testing and smoothing") to less frequent but larger-scale intervention once the exchange rate had moved a long way (see Reserve Bank of Australia website for operational detail).

40. The IMF recommends a careful following of differentiated credit indicators, especially mortgage refinancing and household debt by income category, as

well as prudential steps to lower loan to value and loan to income ratios to borrowers (IMF 2007).

41. These documents are the proceedings of the ANC's 52nd National Conference in Polokwane, December 2007; the *Declaration of the ANC-COSATU-SACP Alliance Economic Summit,* promulgated in October 2008; and the ANC's 2009 election manifesto (closely linked to the first two). The SACP also raised concerns about the conduct of fiscal policy and the key role of the National Treasury (2008 document). From the incumbent cabinet, there were budget statements in October 2008 and March 2009, and the document *Framework for South Africa's Response to the International Economic Crisis,* of February 2009.

42. Even the Treasury's "International Panel (Harvard)" had to substantially water down vague proposals on "including the exchange rate" in monetary policy.

43. The new cabinet, appointed in May 2009, has five key portfolios for macroeconomic policy: finance and trade and industry portfolios, plus three new portfolios: overall planning, monitoring and evaluation, and economic development. How these will interplay remains a matter of development and debate.

BIBLIOGRAPHY

Abedian, I. 1998. "Fiscal Policy and Economic Growth." In *Economic Growth in South Africa: Selected Policy Issues,* ed. I. Abedian and B. Standish, 25–54. Cape Town: Oxford University Press.

Abedian, I., and T. Ajam. 2009. "Fiscal Policy Beyond 2008: Prospects, Risks and Opportunities." In *Zumanomics: Which Way to Shared Prosperity in South Africa?,* ed. R. Parsons, 79–102. Auckland Park, SA: Jacana.

Agüero, Jorge M., Michael R. Carter, and Ingrid Woolard. 2007. "The Impact of Unconditional Cash Transfers on Nutrition: The South African Child Support Grant." Working Paper no. 39, International Poverty Centre, Brazilia, September.

Ajam, T., and J. Aron. 2007. "Fiscal Renaissance in a Democratic South Africa." *Journal of African Economies* 16, no. 5: 745–81.

———. 2009. "Transforming Fiscal Governance." In *South African Economic Policy Under Democracy,* ed. J. Aron, B. Kahn, and G. Kingdon, 92–117. Oxford: Oxford University Press.

Aron, J. 2000. "Growth and Institutions: A Review of the Evidence." *World Bank Research Observer* 15, no. 1: 99–135.

Aron, J., and I. Elbadawi. 1999. "Reflections on the South African Rand Crisis of 1996 and Its Consequences." WPS/1999–13, Centre for the Study of African Economies, Oxford University.

Aron, J., and J. Muellbauer. 2000. "Personal and Corporate Saving in South Africa." *World Bank Economic Review* 14, no. 3: 509–44.

———. 2002. "Estimating Monetary Policy Rules for South Africa." In *Monetary Policy: Rules and Transmission Mechanisms, ed.* Norman Loayza and Klaus Schmidt-

Hebbel, 427–75. Vol. 4 in Series on Central Banking, Analysis and Economic Policies, Central Bank of Chile, Santiago.

———. 2004. "Construction of CPIX Data for Forecasting and Modelling in South Africa." *South African Journal of Economics* 72, no. 5: 1–30.

———. 2005. "Monetary Policy, Macro-stability and Growth: South Africa's Recent Experience and Lessons." *World Economics* 6, no. 4: 123–47.

———. 2007a. "Review of Monetary Policy in South Africa since 1994." *Journal of Africal Economics* 16, no. 5: 705–44.

———. 2007b. "Inflation Dynamics and Trade Openness." Working Paper Series no. 6346, Centre for Economic Policy Research, London.

———. 2008. "Transparency, Credibility and Predictability of Monetary Policy under Inflation Targeting in South Africa." Paper presented at the 23rd Meeting of the European Economic Association, Milan, Italy, 27–31 August.

———. 2009. "The Development of Transparent and Effective Monetary and Exchange Rate Policy." In *South African Economic Policy Under Democracy,* ed. Aron, J., B. Kahn, and G. Kingdon, 58–91. Oxford: Oxford University Press.

Arora, V. 2005. "Economic Growth in Post-apartheid South Africa: A Growth Accounting Analysis." In *Post-Apartheid South Africa,* ed. N. Nowak and L. Ricci, 13–22. Washington, DC: International Monetary Fund.

Arora, V., and A. Bhundia. 2003. "Potential Output and Total Factor Productivity Growth in Post-Apartheid South Africa." IMF Working Paper no. WP/03/178, International Monetary Fund, Washington, DC.

Arora, V., and L. Ricci. 2005. "Unemployment and the Labour Market." In *Post-Apartheid South Africa,* ed. N. Nowak and L. Ricci, 23–47. Washington, DC: International Monetary Fund.

Arvantis, A. 2005. "Foreign Direct Investment in South Africa: Why Has It Been So Low?" In *Post-Apartheid South Africa,* ed. N. Nowak and L. Ricci, 64–65. Washington, DC: International Monetary Fund.

Barker, F. S. 2003. *The South African Labour Market,* 4th ed. Pretoria: Van Schaik Publishers.

Becker, Chris, and Michael Sinclair. 2004. "Profitability of Reserve Bank Foreign Exchange Operations: Twenty Years after the Float." Research Discussion Paper 2004–06, Economic Research Department, Reserve Bank of Australia, September.

Belkar, Rochelle, Lynne Cockerell, and Christopher Kent. 2007. "Current Account Deficits: The Australian Debate." Research Discussion Paper 2007–02, Economic Research Department, Reserve Bank of Australia, March.

Black, A., and S. Roberts. 2009. "The Evolution and Impact of Industrial and Competition Policies." In *South African Economic Policy under Democracy,* ed. J. Aron, B. Kahn and G. Kingdon, 211–43. Oxford: Oxford University Press.

Blinder, A., C. Goodhart, P. Hildebrand, D. Lipton, and C. Wyplosz. 2001. *How Do Central Banks Talk?* Geneva Reports on the World Economy 3. London: Centre for Economic Policy Research.

Bogetić, Z., and J. W. Fedderke 2006. "International Benchmarking of South Africa's Infrastructure Performance." *Journal of Development Perspectives* 2: 7–31.

Caballero, R., K. Cowan, and J. Kearns. 2005. "Fear of Sudden Stops: Lessons from Australia and Chile." *Journal of Policy Reform* 8, no. 4: 313–54.

Calitz, E. 2000. "Fiscal Complications of the Economic Globalisation of South Africa." *South African Journal of Economics* 68, no. 4: 564–606.

Calitz, E., and F. K. Siebrits. 2004. "Should South Africa Adopt Numerical Fiscal Rules?" *South African Journal of Economics* 72, no. 4: 759–83.

Calvo, G., and C. Reinhart. 2002. "Fear of Floating." *Quarterly Journal of Economics* 117, no. 2: 379–408.

Case, A., and A. Deaton. 1998. "Large Cash Transfers to the Elderly in South Africa." *Economic Journal* 108: 1330–61.

Chui, Michael. 2002. "Leading Indicators of Balance of Payments Crises." Working Paper 171, Bank of England, London.

Deaton, Angus. 1999. "Saving and Growth." In *The Economics of Saving and Growth,* ed. Klaus Schmidt-Hebbel and Luis Serven. Cambridge: Cambridge University Press.

Declaration of the Alliance Economic Summit. 2008. http://www.anc.org.za/show .php?doc=ancdocs/pr/2008/pr101g.html.

Du Plessis, S. A. 2005. "Proposals for Strengthening the SARB's Inflation Targeting Regime." *South African Journal of Economics* 73, no. 2: 337–54.

———. 2009. "Inflation Targeting: A Pillar of Post-Polokwane Prosperity." In *Zumanomics: Which Way to Shared Prosperity in South Africa?,* ed. R. Parsons, 57–78. Auckland Park, SA: Jacana.

Du Plessis, S. A., and B. Smit. 2009. "Accounting for South Africa's Growth Revival after 1994." In *South African Economic Policy under Democracy,* ed. J. Aron, B. Kahn, and G. Kingdon, 28–57. Oxford: Oxford University Press.

Edwards, L. 2001. "Globalization and the Skills Bias of Occupational Employment in South Africa." *South African Journal of Economics* 69, no. 1: 40–71.

———. 2005. "Has South Africa Liberalised Its Trade? *South African Journal of Economics* 73, no. 4: 754–75.

Eijffinger, S., and P. Geraats. 2006. "How transparent are central banks?" *European Journal of Political Economy* 22, no. 1: 1–21.

Fatjas, A., and I. Mihov. 2003. "The case for restricting fiscal policy discretion." *Quarterly Journal of Economics* 118, no. 4: 1419–47.

Fedderke, J. W. 2002. "The Structure of Growth in the South African Economy: Factor Accumulation and Total Factor Productivity Growth 1970–1997." *South African Journal of Economics* 70, no. 4: 612–46.

Fedderke, J. W., R.H.J. de Kadt, and J. M. Luiz. 2000. "Uneducating South Africa: The Failure to Address the Need for Human Capital." *International Review of Education* 46, nos. 3–4: 257–81.

Fedderke, J. W., C. Kularatne, and M. Mariotti. 2007. "Mark-up Pricing in South African Industry." *Journal of African Economies* 16, no. 1: 28–69.

Fedderke, J. W., and D. Naumann. Forthcoming. "An Analysis of Industry Concentration in South African Manufacturing, 1972–2001." *Applied Economics.*

Fedderke, J. W., P. Perkins, and J. Luiz. 2006. "Infrastructural Investment in Long-Run Economic Growth: South Africa 1875–2001." *World Development* 34: 1037–59.

Fedderke, J. W., Y. Shin, and P. Vaze. 2009. "Trade and Labour Usage: An Examination of the South African Manufacturing Industry." Mimeo.

Fedderke, J. W., and G. Szalontai 2009. "Industry Concentration in South African Manufacturing Industry: Trends and Consequences, 1970–1996." *Economic Modelling* 26, no. 1: 241–50.

Frankel, J., B. Smit, and F. Sturzenegger. 2006. "South Africa: Macroeconomic Challenges after a Decade of Success." CID Working Paper no. 133, Harvard University.

Geraats, P. 2002. "Central Bank Transparency." *Economic Journal* 112:F532–65.

Hirsch, A. 2005. *Season of Hope: Economic Reform under Mandela and Mbeki.* Pietermaritzburg: University of KwaZulu Press/IDRC.

Horton, M. 2005. "Role of Fiscal Policy in Stabilization and Poverty Alleviation." In *Post-Apartheid South Africa,* ed. N. Nowak and L. Ricci, 79–112. Washington, DC: International Monetary Fund.

Hviding, Ketil. 2005. "Liberalising Trade and Capital Transactions." In *Post-Apartheid South Africa,* ed. N. Nowak and L. Ricci, 133–41. Washington, DC: International Monetary Fund.

Loayza, N., and R. Soto. 2002. *Inflation Targeting: Design, Performance and Challenges.* Vol. 5 in Series on Central Banking, Analysis and Economic Policies, Central Bank of Chile, Santiago.

IMF. 2007. "South Africa: Article IV Consultation." IMF Country Report no. 07/274, August.

Jansen, Z. 2004. "Note on the Funding Structure of Non-Financial Companies, 1990–2003." *Quarterly Bulletin* (South African Reserve Bank), June: 61–66.

Kahn, B., and J. Leape. 1996. "Managing the Rand's Depreciation: The Role of Intervention." *Quarterly Review* (Centre for Research into Economics and Finance in Southern Africa, London School of Economics), April.

Kershoff, G. 2000. "Conducting Inflation Expectation Surveys in South Africa." Mimeo, Bureau for Economic Research, Department of Economics, University of Stellenbosch, October.

Kingdon, G., and J. Knight. 2009. "Unemployment: South Africa's Achilles' Heel." In *South African Economic Policy Under Democracy,* ed. J. Aron, B. Kahn, and G. Kingdon, 300–26. Oxford: Oxford University Press.

Klasen, S., and I. Woolard. 1999. "Levels, Trends and Consistency of Employment and Unemployment Figures in South Africa." *Development Southern Africa* 16, no. 1: 3–16.

Leape, J., and L. Thomas. 2009. "Capital Flows and the External Balance Sheet." In *South African Economic Policy under Democracy,* ed. J. Aron, B. Kahn, and G. Kingdon, 118–50. Oxford: Oxford University Press.

Mahadeva, L., and G. Sterne, eds. 2000. *Monetary Frameworks in a Global Context.* New York: Routledge.

Mboweni, T. T. 1999. "Inflation Targeting in South Africa." *South African Journal of Economics* 67, no. 4: 221–25.

———. 2004. "The South African Banking Sector: An Overview of the Past 10 Years." http://www.bis.org/review/r041231f.pdf.

Myburgh Commission. 2002. *Commission of Inquiry into the Rapid Depreciation of the Exchange Rate of the Rand and Related Matters. Final Report.* Pretoria: Government of the Republic of South Africa, 30 June.

National Treasury. 2007. "Social Security and Retirement Reforms. Second Discussion Paper." Pretoria: Republic of South Africa, National Treasury, February.

Nattrass, N. 2000. "The Debate about Unemployment in the 1990s." *Journal for Studies in Economics and Econometrics* 24, 3: 73–89.

Nel, H., and K. Lekalake. 2004. "Monetary Policy Transparency in South Africa." *South African Journal of Economics* 72, no. 2: 349–64.

Nowak, N., and L. Ricci, eds. 2005. *Post-Apartheid South Africa.* Washington, DC: International Monetary Fund.

Obstfeld, M. 1996. "Models of currency Crises with Self-fulfilling Features." *European Economic Review* 40: 1037–47.

Rossouw, J. 2004. "A Brief Note on Nel and Lekalake, Monetary Policy Transparency in South Africa." *South African Journal of Economics* 72, no. 5: 1097–1104.

South African Reserve Bank. 2000. *A New Monetary Policy Framework: Appendix, Statement of the Monetary Policy Committee.* Pretoria: South African Reserve Bank, 6 April.

Stals, C. 1996. "The Challenges for Monetary Policy." Address to the 19th Annual Investment Conference, Frankel Pollak (Pty) Limited, Johannesburg, 20 February.

———. 1997. "Effect of the Changing Financial environment on Monetary Policy in South Africa." Address to the Annual Dinner of the Economic Society of South Africa, Pretoria Branch, 15 May.

Sterne, Gabriel, and Jonathan Lepper. 2002. "Parliamentary Scrutiny of Central Banks in the United Kingdom and Overseas." *Bank of England Quarterly Bulletin,* Autumn.

Stopford, J. 2003. "Inaccurate Statistics a Threat to the Economy." *Business Day* (Johannesburg), 23 April.

Svensson, L., K. Houg, A. Berg, H. Solheim, and E. Steigum. 2002. "An Independent Review of Monetary Policy and Institutions in Norway." Norges Bank Watch, Centre for Monetary Economics, BI Norwegian School of Management, September.

Taylor, J. 1993. "Discretion versus Policy Rules in Practice." *Carnegie-Rochester Conference on Public Policy* 39: 195–214.

Union Bank of Switzerland. 1996. "Economic Research Note," 13 February.

Van der Berg, S. 2009. "Apartheid's Enduring Legacy: Inequalities in Education." In *South African Economic Policy Under Democracy,* ed. J. Aron, B. Kahn, and G. Kongdon, 327–54. Oxford: Oxford University Press.

Van der Merwe, E. 2004. "Inflation Targeting in South Africa." Occasional Paper no. 19, South African Reserve Bank, Pretoria, July.

PART II

Health and Social Welfare

AIDS Policy in Postapartheid South Africa

Nicoli Nattrass

AIDS policy is one of the most notorious features of postapartheid South Africa. In 1990, when the ban against the African National Congress (ANC) was lifted and South Africa began the transition to democracy, HIV prevalence was less than half a percent, but rising rapidly. ANC military commander Chris Hani warned at the time that if left unattended, AIDS would "result in untold damage and suffering by the end of the century" (quoted in Thom and Cullinan 2004). Unfortunately, his dire prediction came true: by 2009 almost one in five adults was infected with HIV. Although it would have been impossible to prevent the already rampant African AIDS epidemic from crossing into South Africa over that country's long and porous borders (Iliffe 2006), better policies could have saved hundreds of thousands of lives.

Both the late apartheid government and the Mandela presidency (1994–99) were slow to react to the AIDS epidemic, but these failures were dwarfed by those of the Mbeki years (1999–2008). The apartheid government assumed for too long that AIDS was an isolated gay epidemic, and neither it nor the Government of National Unity that followed confronted the heterosexual epidemic squarely or effectively. Mandela himself shied away from the topic when he was president, apparently having been told that to mention it was risky politically (Nattrass 2007, 40). To some extent, these early government failures are understandable, insofar as South Africa was in the throws of a democratic transition (complete with violent episodes) at just the time the AIDS epidemic was becoming visible. Furthermore, the power of antiretroviral drugs to help prevent new infections—especially the transmission of HIV infection from mother to child—had yet to be demonstrated. Thus, the only weapon in the fight against AIDS at the time was AIDS awareness and safe sex campaigns—neither of which were compelling topics for politicians, given the stigmatizing nature of HIV disease and the difficulties inherent in addressing an epidemic that affected Africans more than other racial groups (Lieberman 2009).

Mbeki, however, had more options. By the time he became president in June 1999, it was clear that a short course of zidovudine (AZT) or nevirapine for pregnant HIV-positive women could substantially reduce the risk of HIV transmission from mother to child (see review of early published studies in Brocklehurst 2002 and Volmink et al. 2007). Pilot mother-to-child transmission prevention (MTCTP) programs were already up and running in South Africa, and one of the first things the new health minister, Manto Tshabalala Msimang, did was visit Uganda, from where she returned enthused about that country's cost-effective MTCTP programs (Coovadia 2009). This momentum, however, ground to a halt after Mbeki's first address to the National Council of Provinces, in which he raised doubts about the safety of AZT, asked the health minister to find out "where the truth lies," and advised the assembled ministers to access material about AZT through the Internet (Mbeki 1999; Nattrass 2007, 54–55). Mbeki and his health minister subsequently rejected reports from South Africa's regulatory authority, the Medicines Control Council (MCC), about the safety of AZT. They also resisted the use of all other antiretrovirals, whether for MTCTP, for postexposure prophylaxis for rape victims, or for highly active antiretroviral therapy (HAART), citing discredited claims by AIDS denialists that antiretrovirals were "toxic." It took sustained civil society mobilization, protest, and court action before their bizarre resistance to the use of antiretrovirals was broken (Nattrass 2007; Geffen 2010).

Although MTCTP and HAART were rolled out nationally in the public sector only from 2002 and 2004, respectively, the Western Cape Province defied the national government by offering MTCTP services from 1999 in key hospitals, and by initiating in 2001 (in partnership with Médecins Sans Frontières) a pilot HAART project in Khayelitsha, Cape Town's largest African township (Naimak 2006). Using the ASSA2003 demographic model, it is possible to estimate that if the national government had rolled out antiretrovirals for prevention and treatment at the same rate as the Western Cape Province, around 171,000 new HIV infections and 343,000 deaths could have been prevented between 1999 and 2007 (Nattrass 2007, 136–39, 2008a). This ballpark figure was supported by a subsequent study, performed using a different methodology, which found that between 2000 and 2005 there were 330,000 unnecessary deaths and 35,000 babies unnecessarily born with HIV (Chigwedere et al. 2008). In short, we can be confident in concluding that hundreds of thousands of lives were lost as a result of Mbeki's AIDS policies. It was, as Peter Mandelson (2002) once put it graphically, a form of "genocide by sloth." Moreover, these estimates are conservative, as they do not include the lives lost through sowing confusion about the efficacy of antiretrovirals and the promotion of untested alternatives (Nattrass 2008a; Cullinan 2009; McGregor 2009; Ndaki 2009; Thom 2009; Geffen 2010).

Why did South Africa take such a dramatically wrong turn on AIDS policy? One set of explanations suggests that there must have been an economic rationale: either the state lacked the funding to provide antiretroviral drugs or the ANC had a direct economic interest in rival therapies. Another set of arguments highlights issues of leadership, notably Mbeki's AIDS denialism, his obsession with race, his Africanism, and his revolutionary socialization.

Which of these explanations is correct has implications beyond setting the historical record straight. It has direct bearing on the question of what is likely to happen in South Africa under the new Zuma government. If the problem was Mbeki's beliefs about HIV in general and antiretroviral drugs in particular, then the key questions would be, what are Zuma's attitudes toward these drugs, and what room for maneuver does he have to influence AIDS policy going forward? If the problem was economic, then the question would be whether there is room for any president to pursue an aggressive agenda in combating HIV infection. This essay discusses these rival explanations, arguing that Mbeki's beliefs were the central constraint but that the legacy of his resistance to antiretroviral drugs, and the undermining of the scientific governance of medicine that resulted, is a key challenge for the Zuma government. Because of Zuma's support for Mbeki's policies in the past and his promotion of traditional values and practices, unregulated cures and confusion over medicinal efficacy are likely to continue for some time.

AN ECONOMIC RATIONALE?

The first possible explanation for Mbeki's resistance to antiretrovirals, and one I seriously considered myself, was that it had to do with resource constraints. During the late 1990s, as successive health ministers claimed that South Africa could not afford MTCTP, it seemed reasonable to suppose that the policy problem was an economic one. However, after exploring the economics of MTCTP, I concluded that the government would actually *save* money if it were implemented (Nattrass 2004, 66–98). This is because the costs of testing pregnant women and providing antiretroviral prophylaxis were substantially lower than the costs of dealing with large numbers of AIDS-sick children. Yet government resisted this logic, even rejecting internal reports making the same case (e.g., Hensher 2000) and the recommendations of the parliamentary health committee (Govender 2009, 45), and opted instead to fight a legal challenge from the Treatment Action Campaign (TAC) and its allies all the way to the Constitutional Court. To suggest that the government may have been resisting the use of antiretrovirals for cost-related reasons makes little sense: by not rolling out an MTCTP program, the government was increasing the burden on the health sector and letting children die unnecessarily. Yet Mbeki and his health minister fought against an MTCTP rollout tenaciously. Only after all the legal options had been exhausted did the government finally set in motion a national MTCTP program.

Was the problem, then, perhaps, that the ANC feared that MTCTP would open the floodgates to demands for expensive, long-term HAART for AIDS-sick people? Given the excessive prices of patented antiretrovirals at the time, such a scenario could legitimately be viewed as unaffordable. However, by the time TAC won its battle over MTCTP in 2002 and started to push for a HAART rollout, generic formulations had reduced drug prices to much more manageable proportions. Nathan Geffen, TAC's research head, and I calculated in early 2003 that a HAART rollout was economically feasible, although some increase in tax revenue was probably needed (Geffen, Nattrass, and Raubenheimer 2003; Nattrass 2004, 99–131). Yet Mbeki's health minister, Tshabalala-Msimang, continued to resist, and it was only after a bruising TAC civil disobedience campaign and a cabinet revolt in October 2003 that the government committed to a HAART rollout.

But despite further sharp declines in antiretroviral prices and growing evidence of the cost-effectiveness of providing HAART (Nattrass and Geffen 2005; Badri et al. 2006), the rollout proceeded at a disappointingly slow pace. Each year Tshabalala-Msimang failed to spend the resources allocated to her for this purpose by the finance minister (Nattrass 2007, 134–35). She ignored evidence from Khayelitsha that HAART could restore AIDS-sick people to health, even in resource-poor environments (e.g., Abdullah 2005; Naimak 2006), and instead described antiretrovirals as "poison," promoted untested alternative remedies and nutritional interventions, refused to condemn or halt illegal "trials" by the Rath Health Foundation (in which people were encouraged to stop taking antiretrovirals and start taking Rath's vitamins instead), and undermined efforts by provincial governments to access international funding for HAART (Nattrass 2007; Geffen 2010).

The story, in short, suggests that the government actively resisted the rollout of HAART, even though it was affordable and donor funding was available to support the rollout. But even so, the scale of the necessary response, together with institutional constraints, may well have been a factor predisposing the government to "delay and obfuscation" (Butler 2005, 612; see also Fourie 2006). After all, with South Africa topping the international charts for the number of people needing HAART (more than half a million by 2004), it is possible that the government felt it simply could not cope. However, because other hyperepidemic countries at lower levels of development had achieved higher levels of HAART coverage, the resource constraint argument should not be accepted at face value. The issue is more appropriately addressed through cross-country regression analysis on HAART coverage to see which countries performed better or worse than international norms, after key individual characteristics such as the size and distribution of the HIV-positive population, state capacity, the reach of the health sector, donor funding, per capita income, and so forth are taken into account. Such analyses consistently show that South Africa performs significantly below expected levels and is one of the worst performers globally (Nattrass 2006, 2008b). In other words, judging by international standards, and taking into account South Africa's resources and demographic challenges, a far higher level of HAART coverage could have been achieved.

Another possible "economic" rationale for South Africa's AIDS policies is more venal and conspiratorial. Could Mbeki and Tshabalala-Msimang simply have been blowing smoke, biding their time until an alternative treatment, one in which the ANC had a direct stake, came into production? James Myburgh (2009) insinuates as much in his account of the Virodene saga. This scandal first came to public attention in 1997 when University of Pretoria scientists Ziggie and Olga Visser informed the health minister (then Dlamini-Zuma) that dimethylformamide, an industrial solvent they called "Virodene," appeared to help AIDS patients but that the "AIDS establishment" was blocking their research. The health minister responded by inviting the Vissers and some of their patients to a cabinet meeting. Writing in the ANC magazine *Mayibuye,* Mbeki described what a "privilege" it was "to hear the moving testimonies of AIDS sufferers who had been treated with Virodene, with seemingly very encouraging results" (Mbeki 1998). After giving the Vissers a standing ovation, the cabinet resolved to help them win approval for a scientific drug trial.

In this respect, there are distinct similarities to the Kenyan experience, where on the basis of initial (and faulty) trials of alpha-interferon (dubbed "Kemron"), President Moi threw his weight behind this supposed miracle cure (Hyden and Lanegran 1993). However, unlike the Kenyan case, and to Mbeki's evident dismay (Mbeki 1998), the Medicines Control Council (MCC) found fault with the Vissers' underlying scientific rational for the study and with their proposed clinical trial design. Despite political pressure and a subsequent restructuring of the MCC by the health minister, the body continued to turn down subsequent applications for a Virodene trial because they lacked scientific merit and posed clear risks for patients (Myburgh 2009). Mbeki, however, continued to support the Vissers—including, it would appear, facilitating additional funding for them, channeled through the ANC and ANC-aligned businessmen, to continue funding Virodene trials in London and Tanzania (ibid.).

Court records indicate that the ANC had a 6 percent "stake" in Virodene, though Mbeki denied this (Mbeki 1998). Myburgh, however, points out that it was only after Virodene had been shown to be ineffective against HIV in 2002 that the ANC altered its stance toward antiretrovirals for the first time. The strong insinuation of his story is thus that the motivation for Mbeki's AIDS denialism and reluctance to roll out other antiretrovirals may well have been rooted in his support for, and material interest in, Virodene. His AIDS denialism in this context would have been useful as a marketing strategy (by denigrating existing antiretrovirals) and as a cover or excuse for undermining the MCC, which had blocked the South African Virodene trials.

MBEKI'S AIDS DENIALISM

According to Myburgh, it was the Vissers who introduced Mbeki to AIDS denialist claims about antiretrovirals when they alerted Mbeki to an exchange of newspaper articles between Anthony Brink (a magistrate with no training in medical science) and the president of the Southern African HIV/AIDS Clinicians Society, Dr. Des Martin. In his article "AZT: A Medicine from Hell," Brink (1999) defended the health minister's decision not to make AZT available for MTCTP, saying that AZT was so toxic that prescribing it "was akin to napalm-bombing a school to kill some roof-rats." Martin responded by pointing out that ART had resulted in a 40 percent decline in U.S. AIDS mortality between 1995 and 1997, and that AZT has been shown to cut maternal-child transmission by 67 percent. He agreed that the toxicity of AZT was a "very real issue" requiring constant vigilance on the part of clinicians. However, its benefits for MTCTP rendered the drug, in his view, "a medicine from heaven" (Martin 1999).

In some respects, this "debate" rehearsed the often emotional clash of perspectives over AZT in the United States during the early 1990s (Epstein 1996). But by 1999, the proven success of AZT had shifted the scientific consensus firmly in its favor. The claims by AIDS denialists such as Peter Duesberg that AZT caused AIDS rather than helped prevent or treat it had by this time been thoroughly discredited (see Cohen 1994; Galea and Chermann 1998). This shift, however, had no discernible impact on the die-hard AIDS denialists, who continued to assert that AZT was dangerous and that none of the evidence to the contrary should be believed (see Nattrass 2007). This is why they are known in the scientific community as AIDS denialists rather than by the term they would prefer for themselves, "AIDS dissidents." AIDS denialists reject the scientific cannon and claim (without any evidence) that HIV is harmless, if it exists at all, and that AIDS is caused by antiretrovirals themselves or by "lifestyle" factors, such as drug abuse in the West, and by poverty or exposure to bacterial infections in Africa (Gevisser 2007, 727–67; Nattrass 2007, 15–37).

One of the first things Mbeki did as president was to magnify the debate by setting up the Presidential AIDS Advisory Panel, half of whose members were conventional scientists and the other half AIDS denialists. As the eminent immunologist John Moore observed dryly about the extraordinary weight given to this small group of discredited denialists, the panel comprised "pretty well everyone . . . who believes that HIV is not the cause of AIDS, and about 0.0001 per cent of those who oppose this view" (quoted in Cherry 2000, 405).

In his opening address to the panel, Mbeki described how he had "ploughed through lots and lots of documentation" in an effort to understand the "controversy around these matters" (Mbeki 2000). Such self-education in science is reminiscent of the way that early AIDS activists in the United States came to understand their disease and engage research scientists about treatment (Epstein 1996, 229–30). But unlike those early AIDS activists, Mbeki was head of state and living in a context in which the science of AIDS was well established. And, instead of drawing on the advice of South African scientists—including Malegapuru Makgoba, an immunologist and head of the Medical Research Council—he chose to challenge them with the views of AIDS denialists from the United States and Australia. He subsequently engaged in an unproductive debate with Makgoba and Michael Cherry (a zoologist and part-time correspondent for *Nature*) over AIDS science and included AIDS denialists in the correspondence (Cherry 2009).

When there is a stand-off of this kind, the issue of whom to believe boils down to credibility and scientific authority. Most nonspecialists opt to trust mainstream science, on the reasonable assumption that evidence-based scientific enquiry, coupled with peer review, generates the best available information. While it is true that scientific advances may be shaped by commercial interests, that people with an intellectual or material stake in an existing paradigm may resist the implications of new evidence as long as possible (Kuhn 1962), and that the construction of scientific fact is a contested social process (Epstein 1996; Fassin 2007), major scientific advances (such as the discovery that AIDS is caused by HIV and that antiretrovirals help fight it) are ultimately achieved through evidence-based science. AIDS denialists, however, refuse to accept such findings. Thus, despite being presented with evidence from South African scientists showing that HIV-infected babies succumbed rapidly to AIDS and that antiretrovirals reduced the rates of maternal transmission of HIV substantially (Presidential AIDS Advisory Panel 2001, 22, 33), the denialists on Mbeki's panel simply asserted that "AIDS would disappear instantaneously if all HIV testing was outlawed and the use of antiretroviral drugs was terminated" (ibid., 15, 79, 83).

The AIDS panel served as a means for Mbeki and his health minister to portray AIDS science and policy formation as deeply contested, and contestable. This in turn provided them with the space to resist the introduction of AZT and other antiretrovirals on the grounds that "more research was needed" into their toxicity and effectiveness. However, despite turning down two reports from the MCC concluding that the benefits of AZT outweighed the risks, Mbeki and his health minister were eventually forced to concede ground. They were ridiculed in the mainstream media, ran into increasing opposition within their own ranks, and were challenged in court and on the street by the TAC (Nattrass 2007). In mid-October 2000, Mbeki announced his "withdrawal" from the public debate over AIDS science. However, he continued to dispute death statistics attributed to AIDS and, when asked on television in April 2001 if he would take an AIDS test, he refused on the grounds that it would be "setting an example within the context of a particular paradigm" (in Gevisser 2007, 727). Mbeki also co-authored an AIDS denialist tract (Mbeki and Mokaba 2002), an updated version of which he sent to Mark Gevisser, who was writing Mbeki's biography. (The denialist tract was produced anonymously, but the document's electronic signature links it to Mbeki—hence he is believed to be its primary author. Mokaba is also acknowledged as an author as it was he who circulated it in the ANC; see below.) For Gevisser, the message Mbeki was delivering was clear: "He was now, as he had been since 1999, an AIDS dissident" (Gevisser 2007, 737). Gevisser draws attention to the fact that Mbeki's beliefs that poverty was a cause of AIDS for poor people and that richer people with AIDS had probably become ill through repeated exposure to bacterial infections from sexually transmitted diseases (ibid. 762–63) closely mirrored denialist claims about "lifestyle" factors driving AIDS.

Why did Mbeki champion the cause of such a fringe group and at such cost to society and to himself politically? Perhaps the answer is relatively simple: AIDS denialism resonated with him intellectually, and then, for reasons relating to his arrogant personality, he refused to concede ground (Van der Vliet 2004; Gumede 2005, 167; Gevisser 2007, 727–65). According to Gumede, in the first biography of Mbeki, he, like the other AIDS denialists, "stoically believes that he is a modern-day Copernicus who will ultimately be vindicated, even if posthumously" (Gumede 2005, 159). Gevisser (2007, 735) makes a similar point in his biography:

> Thabo Mbeki is a prophet-in-the-wilderness. This is what gets him up in the morning. This is what gets him through the day. He was the one who said, when nobody else believed it, that the ANC had to embrace the market and the West if it was to survive. He was deeply unpopular for it, but he was proven right. He was the one who said, at the height of the conflict, "Lay down your guns and talk to the enemy." He was called a traitor, an *impimpi,* a black Englishman in tweeds. But he was right, again. Now, in the era of the dream deferred, in the difficult transition, he found himself once more in a tiny minority of free-thinking dissidents. Once more, he might by overwhelmed by conventional thinking. But once more, in the long run—he believes, with absolute conviction—he will be proven correct.

Others argue that Mbeki's denialism is best understood not as some inherent psychological flaw but as part of a political struggle with civil society. According to this perspective, once Mbeki encountered resistance from scientists, AIDS activists, and health professionals—all of whom could mobilize different forms of social and political capital—he found himself locked into a battle over the nature of state power itself (Schneider 2002). But while this description of the situation is plausible, it does not address the prior question of why he put himself in the position of having to struggle against mainstream opinion on AIDS in the first place.

Another interpretation also focusing on political determinants emphasizes Mbeki's revolutionary political socialization, which may have predisposed him to see science as corrupted by industrial interests (Lodge 2002; Sheckels 2004; Gevisser 2007). Even so, none of this explains why he fought the battle so hard, even when it was costing him political support, or why his supposedly revolutionary AIDS policy was so out of step with his own support for the government's orthodox economic policies. Gevisser suggests that Mbeki's appropriation of a radical critique of the pharmaceutical industry may have been an attempt to find a home for his left-wing heritage that had been lost through his orthodox stance on economics (2007, 742), but this is speculative and ultimately unsatisfying as an explanation.

THE POLITICS OF AIDS

A different set of explanations for Mbeki's position on AIDS highlights his anticolonial, Africanist ideology and his desire not to see Africa "blamed" for a sexually driven epidemic (Mbali 2004; Cameron 2005; Fassin 2007; Gevisser 2007). Several authors have pointed to the use of medical science by colonial powers to justify oppressive interventions in understanding Mbeki's suspicion of science (Fassim and Schneider 2003; Scheckels 2004; Mbali 2004; Fassin 2007). But as Phillips (2004) points out, what distinguishes AIDS from earlier epidemics is the degree to which biomedicine had already permeated South African society. The trade unions especially were strongly supportive of scientific approaches to medicine. As the health and safety coordinator of the National Council of Unions put it, "We in the unions pledge our support to the roll-out of scientifically proven medication where and when necessary and we oppose those who peddle untested nostrums on a pseudo scientific basis" (quoted in Bell 2006). If Mbeki was appealing to some underlying antiscientific stance within his support base, this was probably a mistake.

Similarly, those who attempt to construct Mbeki's thinking on AIDS as reflecting a broader important cultural and historical vein in society (e.g., Fassin 2007) or as reflecting "the reality of politics in his country" (Lieberman 2009, 163) cannot account for his isolation on this issue within his own party, or the widespread support for TAC, the use by many Africans (including members of Parliament) of antiretrovirals through the private health sector, and the huge demand for HAART once it became available through the public health sector. To be sure, Mbeki evoked a racialized discourse rail- ing against antiretrovirals—but this in itself does not mean that he was re- flecting a wider cultural or ideological perspective. All it tells us is that he was playing the race card for all it was worth.

And in the end, the race card did not work. Despite attempts by Mbeki and his supporters to frame (or represent) the TAC as being run by "white" men and as a stooge for the pharmaceutical industry, this did not resonate among TAC supporters. Indeed, the fault lines within TAC were more along gender and sexual orientation than along race (Stephen 2009). Furthermore, internal accounts of Mbeki's influence over AIDS policy in the early 2000s do not emphasize constructions of HIV, race and sex as politically important but rather point to misplaced confidence by ANC members in Mbeki's intel- lect, blind loyalty to the leader, and fear of speaking out against the presi- dent (see Feinstein 2007; Govender 2009). Pregs Govender, a former ANC MP, recalls how ANC members would talk to her about AIDS in their families while doing nothing to contradict Mbeki:

> What did it mean to be a loyal party member when mothers, fa- thers, daughters, sons, brothers and sisters, husbands and wives were dying of AIDS? Over and over again the same thing was repeated: "The president is a very intelligent man. He is extremely well read. He does his homework"—until I wanted to scream out "Yes, but he's not infal- lible. He needs to look at what's actually happening. He doesn't need de- fenders, we're not out to destroy him—we want him to beat HIV/AIDS and end economic apartheid everywhere." In the ANC caucus and in Parliament I looked at Thabo Mbeki, son of Govan and Epainette, and wanted him to open his eyes to what was happening to women who have HIV/AIDS and use his power for their lives. (2009, 42)

When Mbeki's AIDS policies were resisted at the provincial level, this was because of the recognized power of antiretrovirals to save lives. In Feb- ruary 2002, while the government was still appealing the original court verdict on MTCTP, KwaZulu-Natal premier Lionel Mtshali finally lost pa- tience with the national AIDS policy and with his ANC MEC for health. In a speech to the provincial legislature, he announced that he would be accept- ing Boehringer Ingelheim's offer of free nevirapine and would be rolling out MTCTP. He said the population was being decimated by AIDS and thou- sands of children had died unnecessarily because of the delayed MTCTP program:

We had to act, and may God forgive us for waiting so long. We shall not wait one day longer, nor allow any space for further excuse, delaying tactic or preposterous theory which may get in the way of saving our children. . . . For me this is a matter of principle and common decency. I have turned upside-down the scientific facts to find a reason which can justify the failure to act and ameliorate the suffering and reduce the death of so many of our children, [and] I have found none. The undisputed facts before me are that there are sound scientific bases on which Nevirapine is recommended, which include that it is effective in reducing the number of HIV/AIDS infected babies born to HIV-positive mothers. It is cost-effective in that it is more expensive not to treat and it is safe. There to me is where the issue stops. (Mtshali 2002)

Even some ANC-controlled provinces rebelled against the government's legal campaign to delay MTCTP programs (Gauteng, Eastern Cape, Limpopo). On 18 February 2002, the premier of Gauteng announced that the province had expanded its MTCTP program and would be rolling it out to all hospitals in the coming year (Shilowa 2002). Despite an ANC NEC resolution in March 2002 that the decision to extend the use of nevirapine for MTCTP beyond the pilot sites had to be "taken collectively" by national ministers and provincial MECs, the national government had by this time effectively lost control over the provinces. MTCTP programs were rolling out in South Africa in early 2002, well before the final Constitutional Court judgment.

Mbeki and his health minister also faced ongoing resistance elsewhere from within the ANC. For example, when NEC member Peter Mokaba circulated an AIDS denialist document linked to Mbeki at an ANC NEC meeting (Mbeki and Mokaba 2002), the ANC's national health secretary, Saadiq Kariem, responded furiously, saying, "Anyone who believes the claims made in it might as well believe the moon is made of green cheese" (quoted in Le May 2002). In 2001, Parliament's Joint Monitoring Committee on the Improvement of the Quality of Life and Status of Women held public hearings, to which TAC and others made submissions about what could be done to reduce the impact of AIDS on women. The report, penned by its chair, ANC MP Pregs Govender, adopted the scientific approach on AIDS and found that women had a right to MTCTP (Govender 2004, 2009). Despite discussion of this report within the ANC being delayed by the leadership, it was eventually welcomed by the ANC caucus in March 2002.

Govender (2004) attributed the long time it took for the ANC to formulate a position contrary to that of Mbeki's to "groupthink," which entails "the naive and unquestioning acceptance of the leader as infallible." But as the folly of Mbeki's position became increasingly evident, and as Mandela himself announced support for antiretrovirals (at a March 2002 press conference designed to show ANC unity on AIDS policy; Heywood 2004, 110), the ANC caucus and cabinet started to shift the antiretroviral policy terrain. The mass civil disobedience campaign of 2003 and concerns that Mbeki's views were seriously eroding the ANC's electoral support (Nattrass 2007, 118–19) gave the process greater momentum, and in October 2003 the government announced it would be rolling out HAART.

Even so, Mbeki's health minister continued to undermine the program, among other means by supporting unproven alternative therapies and by describing antiretrovirals as "poison" (Nattrass 2007; Geffen 2010). It was only in late 2006, after embarrassing criticisms of Tshabalala-Msimang's policies at the Toronto International AIDS conference, that responsibility for AIDS policy was transferred (by a cabinet decision) to the deputy president, Phumzile Mlambo-Ngcuka. The deputy health minister, Nozizwe Madlala-Routledge, subsequently spoke out in favor of HAART and condemned past government policies as being hamstrung by "denialism at the highest levels." While Tshabalala-Msimang was on sick leave, Madlala-Routledge and the interim health minister, Jeff Radebe, started working more constructively with civil society organizations and health professionals—a process resulting in a new National Strategic Plan to cut HIV infections in half and to increase HAART coverage dramatically to 80 percent by 2011. This remained official policy even after Tshabalala-Msimang returned to work, a post she held until she was replaced by Barbara Hogan in 2008, and then by Aaron Motsoaledi in 2009 as part of Zuma's cabinet reshuffle.

But while the benefits of antiretrovirals for prevention and treatment have been clearly affirmed, the damage caused during the Mbeki presidency to the scientific governance of medicine has yet to be rectified. One of the most pernicious legacies of AIDS denialism (which sees AIDS science as irredeemably corrupted by corporate interests) has been the undermining of scientific approaches to understanding the AIDS epidemic and to regulating purported alternative and traditional therapies for it (Nattrass, 2007; Ndaki 2009). The MCC has been steadily stripped of its power and resources, and there is widespread confusion over which products count as medicines and which need to be regulated (Geffen 2010). In 2006, Mbeki established the Presidential Task Team on African Traditional Medicine, headed by Herbert Vilakazi (a man with direct interests in the untested herbal AIDS "cure" Ubhejane) and which included Mbeki's AIDS denialist associate Christine

Qunta. This task team remains in place. In 2008 the new health minister, Barbara Hogan, challenged the team to come up with concrete proposals as to how to deal with the "daily emergence of charlatans" (quoted in Ndaki 2009, 155). This challenge has yet to be addressed, and the regulation of medicine in South Africa remains inadequate.

How is President Jacob Zuma likely to address AIDS? It is still early, but there is cause for concern. First, Zuma has framed himself as a traditionalist, happy to appear in the media in traditional garb and to promote "traditional values," including respect for tribal authority and traditional medicine. It is thus likely that he will continue to provide space for untested traditional or alternative remedies to be marketed in South Africa. And, with regard to antiretrovirals, Pregs Govender tells a worrying story in this regard. Back in 2002, she recalls, MPs were asked to join then deputy president Jacob Zuma in an HIV/AIDS candlelighting ceremony. Candles were passed around, and then Zuma pointed to two young people on either side of him, telling the audience that they were HIV-positive and healthy, and were looking after themselves "naturally" with "no ARVs." Govender describes the exercise as a "crude propaganda exercise" against antiretrovirals (2009, 52). Zuma has also demonstrated an alarming lack of understanding about HIV, most infamously when he claimed, while on trial for raping an HIV-positive woman, that he had taken a shower afterward to protect himself against HIV infection. This, coupled with his traditionalism and his role in denigrating antiretroviral drugs, is certainly cause for concern. However, as he is a shrewd politician, Zuma will probably bend with the wind. By the end of 2010, more than a million South Africans were on HAART, and the country was on track to reach 80 percent coverage by 2012. As long as these people continue to fight for access to HAART, the political incentives to provide it will remain strong.

BIBLIOGRAPHY

Abdullah, Faried. 2005. "The Complexities of Implementing Antiretroviral Treatment in the Western Cape Province of South Africa." Development Update. http://www.sarpn.org.za/documents/d0001195/13-ARV_rollout_W-Cape -Fareed_Abdullah.pdf.
Badri, Motasim, Gary Maartens, Sundhiya Madalia, Linda-Gail Bekker, John Penrod, Robert Platt, Robin Wood, and Eduard Beck. 2006. "Cost-Effectiveness of Highly Active Antiretroviral Therapy in South Africa." *PLoS Medicine* 3, no. 1 (January): 48–56.
Bell, Terry. 2006. "Rath and Company Is an Assault on the Working Class." *Busi-*

ness Report, 17 March. http://www.busrep.co.za/index.php?fSectionId=559&f ArticleId=3163411.

Brink, Anthony. 1999. "AZT: A Medicine from Hell." *Citizen,* 17 March.

Brocklehurst, Peter. 2002. "Interventions for Reducing the Risk of Mother to Child Transmission of HIV infection." *Cochrane Database of Systematic Reviews,* issue 1, art. no. CD000102.DOI:10.1002/14651858.CD000102.

Butler, Anthony. 2005. "South Africa's AIDS Policy: 1994–2004. How Can It Be Explained?" *African Affairs* 104, no. 417: 591–614.

Cameron, Edwin. 2005. *A Witness to AIDS.* Cape Town: David Philip.

Cherry, Michael. 2000. "South Africa Turns to Research in the Hope of Settling AIDS Policy." *Nature* 405 (May 11): 105–6. http://www.nature.com/nature/journal/ v405/n6783/full/405105a0.html.

———. 2009. "The President's Panel." In Cullinan and Thom, *The Virus, Vitamins and Vegetables,* 16–35.

Chigwedere, Pride, George Seage, Sofia Grusin, Tun-Hou Leee, and Max Essex. 2008. "Estimating the Lost Benefits of Antiretroviral Drug Use in South Africa." *Journal of Acquired Immune Deficiency Syndrome* 49, no. 4: 410–15.

Cohen, Jon. 1994. "The Duesberg Phenomenon." *Science* 266 (9 December): 1642–49.

Coovadia, Ashraf. 2009. "The Fight to Prevent Mother-to-Child HIV Transmission." In Cullinan and Thom, *The Virus, Vitamins and Vegetables,* 58–6.

Cullinan, Kerry. 2009. "Government's Strange Bedfellows." In Cullinan and Thom, *The Virus, Vitamins and Vegetables,* 91–111.

Cullinan, Kerry, and Anso Thom, eds. 2009. *The Virus, Vitamins and Vegetables.* Auckland Park, SA: Jacana.

Epstein, Stephen. 1996. *Impure Science: AIDS, Activism and the Politics of Knowledge.* Berkeley and Los Angeles: University of California Press.

Fassin, Didier. 2007. *When Bodies Remember: Experiences and Politics of AIDS in South Africa.* Berkeley and Los Angeles: University of California Press.

Fassin, D., and H. Schneider. 2003. "The Politics of AIDS in South Africa: Beyond the Controversies." *British Medical Journal* 326 (1 March): 495–97.

Feinstein, Andrew. 2007. *After the Party: A Personal and Political Journey inside the ANC.* Cape Town: Jonathan Ball.

Fourie, Peter. 2006. *The Political Management of HIV and AIDS in South Africa: One Burden Too Many?* New York: Palgrave Macmillan.

Galea, P., and J. Chermann. 1998. "HIV as the Cause of Aids and Associated Diseases." *Genetica* 104: 133–42.

Garrett, Laurie. 2002. "Anti-HIV Drug Poison, Summit Told." *The Age,* 9 July. http:// www.theage.com.au/articles/2002/07/08/1025667115671.html.

Geffen, Nathan. 2010. *Debunking Delusions: The Inside Story of the Treatment Action Campaign.* Johannesburg: Jacana.

Geffen, Nathan, Nicoli Nattrass, and Chris Raubenheimer. 2003. "The Cost of HIV Prevention and Treatment Interventions in South Africa." Working Paper no. 28, Centre for Social Science Research, Oxford University.

Gevisser, Mark. 2007. *Thabo Mbkei: The Dream Deferred.* Cape Town: Jonathan Bau.

Govender, Pregs. 2004. "Experiments in a Politics of Love and Courage. Ruth First Memorial Lecture." *Network News,* July, 9–12. http://www.getnet.org.za/Network_news_july2004.pdf.

———. 2009. "Love, Courage, Insubordination and HIV/AIDS Denialism." In Cullinan and Thom, *The Virus, Vitamins and Vegetables,* 36–57.

Gumede, William. 2005. *Thabo Mbeki and the Battle for the Soul of the ANC.* Cape Town: Zebra Press.

Hensher, Martin. 2000. "Confidential Briefing: The Costs and Cost Effectiveness of Using Nevirapine or AZT for the Prevention of Mother to Child Transmission of HIV: Current Best Estimates for South Africa." 19 April.

Heywood, Mark. 2004. "The Price of Denial." *Development Update* 5, no. 3: 93–122. http://www.sarpn.org.za/documents/d0001195/4-The_Price_of_Denial-Mark_Heywood.pdf.

Hyden, G., and K. Lanegran. 1993. "AIDS, Policy and Politics: East Africa in Comparative Perspective." *Policy Studies Review* 12, nos. 1–2 (Spring–Summer): 47–65.

Iliffe, John. 2006. *The African AIDS Epidemic: A History.* Cape Town: James Currey and Double Storey.

Kuhn, Thomas. 1962. *The Structure of Scientific Revolutions.* Chicago: University of Chicago Press.

Le May. 2002. "ANC Divided over Dissident AIDS Report." *Independent Online,* 22 March. http://www.iol.co.za/index.php?set_id=1&click_id=13&art_id=ct20020323190611345C620685.

Liberman, Evan. 2009. *Boundaries of Contagion: How Ethnic Politics Have Shaped Government Responses to AIDS.* Princeton, NJ: Princeton University Press.

Lodge, Tom. 2002. *Politics in South Africa: From Mandela to Mbeki.* Bloomington: Indiana University Press.

Mandelson, Peter. 2002. "Genocide by Sloth." *New Statesman,* 18 February.

Martin, Des. 1999. "AZT: A Medicine from Heaven." *Citizen,* 31 March.

Mbali, M. 2004. "AIDS Discourse and the South African State: Government Denialism and Post-Apartheid AIDS Policy Making." *Transformation* 54: 104–22.

Mbeki, Thabo. 1998. "ANC has no financial stake in Virodene." *Mayibuye,* March. http://www.anc.org.za/ancdocs/pubs/mayibuye/mayi9801.html#Contents.

———. 1999. Address to the National Council of Provinces, Cape Town, 28 October. http://www.anc.org.za/ancdocs/history/mbeki/1999/tm1028.html.

———. 2000. Remarks at the First Meeting of the Presidential Advisory Panel on AIDS, Pretoria, 6 May. http://www.anc.org.za/ancdocs/history/mbeki/2000/tm0506.html.

Mbeki, Thabo, and Peter Mokaba. 2002. "Castro Hlongwane, Caravans, Cats, Geese, Foot and Mouth Statistics: HIV/AIDS and the Struggle for the Humanisation of the African." Report circulated to ANC branches, 1–132. http://www.virusmyth.net/aids/data/ancdoc.htm.

McGregor, Liz. 2009. "Garlic, Olive Oil, Lemons and Beetroot." In Cullinan and Thom, *The Virus, Vitamins and Vegetables,* 130–42.

Mtshali, Lionel. 2002. "The War on HIV/AIDS in KwaZulu Natal." State of the Province speech to the KwaZulu Natal Provincial Legislature, 25 February. http://www.afrol.com/Countries/South_Africa/documents/mtshali_aids _2002.htm.

Myburgh, James. 2009. "In the Beginning There Was Virodene." In Cullinan and Thom, *The Virus, Vitamins and Vegetables,* 1–15.

Naimak, Trude. 2006. "Antiretroviral Treatment in the Western Cape: A Success Story Facilitated by the Global Fund." Centre for Social Science Research Working Paper no. 161, University of Cape Town. http://www.cssr.uct.ac.za/pubs _cssr.html.

Nattrass, Nicoli. 2004. *The Moral Economy of AIDS in South Africa.* Cambridge: Cambridge University Press.

———. 2006. "What Determines Cross-Country Access to Antiretroviral Treatment?" *Development Policy Review* 24, no. 3 (May): 321–37.

———. 2007. *Mortal Combat: AIDS Denialism and the Fight for Antiretrovirals in South Africa.* Pietermaritzburg: University of KwaZulu-Natal Press.

———. 2008a. "AIDS and the Scientific Governance of Medicine in Post-Apartheid South Africa." *African Affairs* 107, no. 427: 157–76.

———. 2008b. "Are Country Reputations for Good and Bad AIDS Leadership Deserved? An Exploratory Quantitative Analysis." *Journal of Public Health* 30, no. 4: 398–406.

Nattrass, Nicoli, and Nathan Geffen. 2005. "The Impact of Reduced Drug Prices on the Cost-Effectiveness of HAART in South Africa." *African Journal of AIDS Research* 4, no. 1: 65–67.

Ndaki, Kanya. 2009. "Traditional Alternatives?" In Cullinan and Thom, *The Virus, Vitamins and Vegetables,* 143–56.

Phillips, Howard. 2004. "HIV AIDS in the Context of South Africa's Epidemic History." In *AIDS and South Africa: The Social Expression of a Pandemic,* ed. K. Kauffman and D. Lindauer, 31–47. New York: Palgrave Macmillan.

Presidential AIDS Advisory Panel. 2001. *Presidential AIDS Advisory Panel Report: A Synthesis Report of the Deliberations by the Panel of Experts Invited by the President of the Republic of South Africa, the Honourable Thabo Mbeki.* Johannesburg. http://www.info.gov.za/otherdocs/2001/aidspanelpdf.pdf.

Sheckels, Tom. 2004. "The Rhetoric of Thabo Mbeki on HIV/Aids: Strategic Scapegoating?" *Harvard Journal of Communication* 15: 69–82.

Schneider, Helen. 2002. "On the Fault line: The Politics of AIDS Policy in Contemporary South Africa." *African Studies* 612, no. 1: 145–67.

Shilowa, Mbhazima. 2002. Address by Premier Mbhazima Shilowa at the opening of the Gauteng Provincial Legislature, 18 February. http://www.info.gov.za/ speeches/2002/0202181246p1001.htm.

Stephen, Janine. 2009. "Saints and Sinners: The Treatment Action Campaign." In Cullinan and Thom, *The Virus, Vitamins and Vegetables,* 157–74.

Thom, Anso. 2009. "The curious Tale of the Vitamin Seller." In Cullinan and Thom, *The Virus, Vitamins and Vegetables,* 112–29.

Thom, Anso, and Kerry Cullinan. 2004. "Responses to HIV/AIDS." *Health-e News,* 28 November. http://www.health-e.org.za/news/article.php?uid=20031154.

Van der Vliet, Virginia. 2004. "South Africa Divided against AIDS: A Crisis of Leadership." In Kauffman and Lindauer, *AIDS and South Africa: The Social Expression of a Pandemic,* 48–96.

Volmink, Jimmy, Nandi Siegfried, Lize van der Merwe, and Peter Brocklehurst. 2007. "Antiretrovirals for Reducing the Risk of Mother to Child Transmission of HIV Infection." *Cochrane Database of Stematic Reviews,* issue 1, art. no. CD003510. DOI: 10.1002/145651858/CD003510.pub2.

The Role of Social and Economic Rights in Supporting Opposition in Postapartheid South Africa

Lauren Paremoer and Courtney Jung

In 1995, Courtney Jung and Ian Shapiro published an article about South Africa's democratic transition.[1] In it they argued that South Africa's negotiated settlement had yielded a constitution that was more focused on guaranteeing representation for minority whites than on entrenching opposition. The interim constitution included power-sharing clauses that reserved seats in the executive branch for all of the major parties and had very weak mechanisms for ensuring a strong institutionalized opposition, either from minority parties or from dissenting back-benchers within the major parties. Jung and Shapiro argued that a strong institutionalized opposition was the key to a healthy democracy, and they were not alone in warning that the gravest danger to South African democracy would be the lack of opposition to the African National Congress (ANC).

Although the final constitution did not include many of the articles they had been most critical of, most important dropping the guarantee of power sharing, it retained all of the constitutional provisions that strengthened the ruling party and weakened the opposition. The National Party (NP) dropped out of the executive in 1996 to take up the role of opposition, but in the 1999 election the ANC won an even larger majority of the vote. The NP subsequently disintegrated, and the Democratic Party took up the mantle of official opposition, positioning itself as a watchdog party. Since renamed the Democratic Alliance, the party retained the role of the dominant opposition party in the 2009 election by winning 16.7 percent of the national vote, an outright majority in the Western Cape Province and the second-highest share of votes in four provinces. The third largest party, the Congress of the

People (COPE), was a breakaway faction of the ANC that formed in 2008 and captured 7.5 percent of the national vote and the official opposition in four provinces in 2009.

Despite the consolidation of two stronger opposition parties between 1994 and 2009, the ANC still controls just under two-thirds of all parliamentary seats. Given the strong institutional incentives created by the South African electoral system to prioritize party loyalty, legislative oversight of an ANC executive is likely to remain limited even in the presence of a more consolidated opposition.

This does not mean, however, that the ANC faces no opposition. In 1995, Jung and Shapiro speculated that opposition to the ANC might in the future come from within the party itself, and that the party might split among its competing constituencies. The ANC, they noted, was a broad church. The party's liberation struggle heritage carried sufficient moral weight that it could encompass social groups with opposing interests, but they anticipated that disaffection with the ruling party could soon break out into open opposition from civil society groups affiliated with the ANC.

In the period since 1994, opposition has been most consistently voiced by community groups and nongovernmental organizations whose members come from the ANC or from breakaway factions of the ANC. This trend is likely to continue. South African civil society has been vocal in its opposition to many government policies, taking the ANC to task for failing to provide adequate housing, abrogating its commitment to health care, failing to provide sufficient jobs, failing to guarantee a living wage, and failing to deliver the social and welfare services it has promised. Although this is not the kind of institutionalized opposition that Jung and Shapiro had in mind in 1995, it is certainly opposition, and it is playing an important role in maintaining democratic participation and deliberation. Despite ANC hegemony in Parliament, civil society has sometimes succeeded in holding the ANC accountable (Mattison 2004; Ballard, Habib, and Valodia 2006).

One reason why popular participation has been effective in playing this role is that, while the final constitution dropped the guarantee of power sharing, it added a commitment to a raft of justiciable social and economic rights. Section 24 of the constitution guarantees everyone's right to a safe and healthy environment and requires the state to protect the environment. Section 25(5) requires the state to enable citizens to gain equitable access to land. Section 26 provides a right to access to adequate housing and prohibits arbitrary evictions. Section 27 guarantees access to health care services, sufficient food and water, and social security, and prohibits the refusal of emergency medical treatment. Section 28(1)(c) entrenches children's rights to shelter and basic nutrition, social services, and health care services. Section 29 provides a right to education, and section 35(2)(e) guarantees the right of detained persons to be provided with adequate nutrition, accommodation, medical care, and reading material.

The ANC government has nevertheless failed to secure many of the social and economic rights that are promised by the constitution. The constitution itself does not promise an absolute guarantee of such rights, and the Constitutional Court has ruled that such rights are only protected to the extent the government can afford them. The rights of some must be balanced against the rights of others, limiting the degree to which constitutionally enshrined social and economic rights can produce a robust social welfare net in developing countries.

As a result, there may be reasons to be skeptical of the wisdom of relying on a constitutional guarantee of rights to contribute to consolidation in nascent democracies. Legal scholars have been wary of the role of rights in closing down politics. The existence of constitutionally enshrined rights is said to remove issues that ought properly to be decided through the democratic process to the realm of the courts (Waldron 1984). Even more critically, some scholars argue that the emancipatory veneer of rights masks an underlying tendency to preserve and legitimate the status quo (Gabel and Kennedy 1984).

Some have been even more skeptical of social and economic rights than they are of civil and political rights. They point out that, unlike civil and political rights, which ostensibly impose a negative obligation, social and economic rights impose a positive obligation on the state—an obligation that most states lack the capacity to honor. If a constitution promises rights the government does not uphold, then such rights are in fact not guaranteed, and should not be called rights. If governments are under limited obligation to ensure compliance with socioeconomic rights, and lack the capacity to do so in a way that is justiciable, such rights may be meaningless. Even worse, social and economic rights may actually be pernicious to the extent they undermine the conceptual legitimacy of rights altogether (Sunstein 1993).

We argue instead that social and economic rights have played an important role in opening up the political space of oppositional politics in South Africa. We propose that social rights may be different from political and civil rights in the sense that they are measured ordinally rather than categorically. Whereas people either possess or lack civil and political rights, their access to social and economic resources is always a matter of degree. As a result, these "second-generation" rights may be less susceptible to the limiting logic that has made many theorists critical of the political use of rights.

In particular, such rights have enhanced the quality of democratic deliberation and entrenched the concept of government accountability. They do so in four ways. First, Constitutional Court cases involve the production of evidence and arguments that become part of the public record and can, as a result, enhance deliberation. Second, the Court's refusal to endorse the concept of a minimum core obligation has kicked the scope of government obligation back into the sphere of democratic debate. Third, the Court has nevertheless demonstrated a willingness to review government policy, assessing it for "reasonableness" and for coherence between intention and outcomes. Fourth, the Court has recognized the necessity for balancing competing rights, and resolved such calibrations in favor of majoritarian principles.

We advance an argument regarding the role of social and economic rights in generating deliberation and accountability in three steps. First, we review debates regarding the political and transformative potential of rights and argue that, notwithstanding the pitfalls many scholars have noted, constitutionalizing social and economic rights can contribute to democratic consolidation in nascent democracies. Second, we show that court cases alone often enhance both deliberation and accountability by providing documents, evidence, and arguments that become part of the public record and put the government on notice that it cannot implement policy unilaterally. As such, courts and legal battles are an important location of political opposition rather than an alternative to politics. We support this contention with evidence from two well-known Constitutional Court cases, *Soobramoney* and *Grootboom*. Third, we nevertheless note that the scope of law alone is limited. We propose therefore that social and economic rights best play an opposition-enhancing role when a legal strategy is supplemented by a political strategy. To support this claim, we show how the Treatment Action Campaign (TAC) has used political and legal strategies to support and enhance one another.[2]

In South Africa, the constitution, and the social and economic rights it enshrines, have played an important role in motivating and sustaining political participation and opposition. A "transformative constitution," committed to the "progressive realization" of social and economic well-being, may challenge the commonly held conception of constitutions as fundamentally conservative pre-commitment strategies, designed to limit the excesses of democratic majoritarianism (Klare 1998). Rather than acting as a curb on democracy, such constitutions may be used to deepen and extend a commitment to a society based on democratic values, social justice, and fundamental human rights. In particular, in the context of the global spread of neoliberal economic policies whose discourse ostensibly relieves the state of many social and economic welfare responsibilities, the existence of constitutionally enshrined socioeconomic rights legitimates demands for government-provided welfare and services.

THE PROMISE AND THE LIMITS OF RIGHTS

As a weapon against the indiscriminate use of power, rights have come under intense scrutiny in recent years. Starting in the 1970s, some scholars associated with the field of critical legal studies (CLS) issued an important critique of the transformative potential of legal rights. They took the position that engaging in rights discourse was fundamentally incompatible with a broader strategy of social change. Although the extension of rights may energize struggle and produce apparent victories in the short run, ultimately it legitimates the dominant structure of class, race, and gender inequality. Rights, they argued, reinforce existing social arrangements. Because they are indeterminate, they are subject to interpretation and contextual grounding, which most often protects the status quo. According to Mark Tushnet (1984), people lose sight of their real objectives when they abstract concrete experiences of discrimination and injustice into legal rights discourse. Peter Gabel and Duncan Kennedy (1984) have argued that rights are an illusion that bind people to an imaginary political community of citizens and legitimate state power by appearing to offer grounds for redress.

Embedded as they are in the evolution of liberal theory, rights also play an important role in framing the public sphere as a space of interaction among free and equal individuals. Patrick Macklem has noted that human rights law privileges individual civil and political rights over collective social and cultural rights. As he notes, "Rights bearers overwhelmingly are individuals, and their entitlements protects a zone of individual liberty from the exercise of public power" (2006, 489). Ross Poole argues that rights isolate claims from public debate (1999, 126). Wendy Brown has shown that rights have historically acted "as a mode of securing and naturalizing dominant social powers—class, gender, and so forth" (1995, 99).

Critical race theorists, on the other hand, have been more sympathetic to the political use of rights, defending the strategic use of rights discourse, and of the law, in the civil rights movement. Kimberlé Crenshaw argues that many CLS scholars disregarded the transformative significance of rights in "mobilizing black Americans and in generating new demands" and ignored "the transformative potential that liberalism offers. Although liberal legal ideology may indeed function to mystify," she continues, "it remains receptive to some aspirations that are central to black demands" (Crenshaw 1995, 110). The existence of rights, she argues, forces a crisis in hegemonic legitimacy when "powerless people force open and politicize a contradiction between the dominant ideology and their reality" (111). "Rather than using the contradiction to suggest that American citizenship was itself illegitimate or false, civil rights protestors proceeded as if American citizenship were real and demanded to exercise the 'rights' that citizenship entailed" (111).

Crenshaw insists in particular that it is the very fact that rights are enshrined in the prevailing ideology that makes them useful as an oppositional tool. "Merely critiquing the ideology from without or making demands in language outside the rights discourse," she argues, "would have accomplished little" (117). Her critique seems especially poignant in the context of neoliberal political agendas that threaten to erase the role of government altogether, undermining the sovereign power—and obligation—of states to carry out reform or development. As she argues, "Some critics of legal reform movements seem to overlook the fact that state power has made a significant difference—sometimes between life and death—in the efforts of black people to transform their world. Attempts to harness the power of the state through the appropriate rhetorical and legal incantations should be appreciated as intensely powerful and calculated political acts" (117).

Crenshaw and others simultaneously recognize, however, that the same rights used to push reform in the civil rights era were pushing back against the advances of the civil rights movement in the 1980s. "Yet today," she says, "the same legal reforms play a role in providing an ideological framework that makes present conditions facing underclass blacks appear fair and reasonable" (117). The ostensible race neutrality of the legal system creates the illusion that racial disparities are the result of individual and group merit (117). Despite its emancipatory potential, the use of rights may ultimately limit oppositional politics, offering a degree of formal equality that masks underlying, and persistent, structural injustice. There are dangers, she warns, "both in engaging the dominant discourse and in failing to do so. What subordinated people need is an analysis that can inform them about how the risks can be minimized and how the rocks and the very hard places can be negotiated" (112).

Between them, critical legal scholars and critical race theorists map the possibilities and pitfalls of using rights as a strategy of social transformation. Even as rights have played an important role in protecting vulnerable individuals and minority groups from the indiscriminate use of majority power, so have they entrenched the status quo by substituting formal for real equality. Crenshaw's diagnosis, that we need to find ways of harnessing the emancipatory potential of rights without falling prey to their limiting logic, precisely describes the challenge facing political activists in the present age.

Many observers of South Africa's postapartheid constitutional jurisprudence have pointed out that the Constitutional Court has actually been fairly conservative in its interpretation of social and economic rights (Klare 1998; Brand 2005). Justices have not, for the most part, delivered decisions, or engaged in reasoning, that would force the government to commit funding or make policy changes that support a transformative interpretation of social and economic rights. As Theunis Roux has pointed out, the Constitutional Court has consistently declined to endorse the view that socioeconomic rights mandate judges to second-guess the budgetary allocations to the areas of social provision protected by particular rights (Roux 2003, 92, quoted in Wilson 2004, 438 n52).The Constitutional Court has also refused to interpret the existence of social and economic rights as imposing a minimum core obligation on the state, even though the concept of a minimum core is central to international law on social and economic rights. Cass Sunstein has described the Court's decisions as "restrained," "respectful," and even "deferential" to the state (Sunstein 2001, 123), and Danie Brand argues that the courts have been acutely aware of the constraints under which they operate (Brand 2005, 20–25).

Brand and others (e.g., Michelman 2003) put this down to what is called a "separation of powers" constraint. Courts are reluctant to enforce positive rights, it is argued, for three reasons that have to do with maintaining the independence of the judiciary and the separation of powers. The court justifies its conservatism with reference to its lack of technical capacity (to decide issues of funding allocation), its lack of democratic accountability, and a concern with maintaining the institutional integrity of the court (Brand 2005, 22–23). These arguments, which are marshaled against including positive rights in constitutions more generally, have also been used to critique the South African constitution in particular.

Michelman (2003) focuses attention on the second of these constraints, calling it the democratic objection. It seems there are a number of objections to constitutionalizing social and economic rights that might fall under the rubric of "democratic" objections. First, the courts are not democratically elected. Therefore, allowing the courts to make decisions that are otherwise made by elected legislators is anti-democratic. Second, if the judiciary issues positive enforcement orders, it does so against the prevailing political will (Michelman 2003, 16) by compelling the democratically elected government to enact policy against its will. By naming social citizenship a constitutional right, Michelman says, we impose "a far-flung constraint on policy choice by majority rule" (2003, 29). Third, viewing the problem from below, Dennis Davis has argued that justiciable socioeconomic rights might "erode the possibility for meaningful political participation in the shaping of the societal good" (Davis 1992).[3]

Michelman argues, however, that the majoritarian objection against constitutionalizing socioeconomic rights holds only if we employ a narrow definition of democracy that is not the only, or best, one available to us (2003, 13). "The point of naming social citizenship a constitutional right is to give a certain inflection to political public reason", he says (34). "'Democracy' then would name the practice by which citizens communicatively form, test, exchange, revise, and pool their constitutional-interpretive judgments" (34). By moving the location of democracy from the legislature to civil society, Michelman proposes that democracy—that is, deliberation in the public sphere—will in fact be strengthened through the constitutionalization of socioeconomic rights.

THE CONSTITUTION, THE COURT, AND DEMOCRATIC OPPOSITION

The Constitutional Court has played an important role in producing accountability and improving the quality of democratic deliberation in at least four ways. First, as Michelman observes, Court cases involve the production of evidence and arguments that become part of the public record and can, as a result, enhance deliberation. Social rights litigation has produced a formal and contemporary record of government failures in conceptualizing and implementing social policy. This record consists of sophisticated technical evaluations as well as affidavits containing extremely personal narratives of the objectionable conditions in which many South Africans live and work every day.

Second, while the Court has been criticized for its consistent refusal to endorse the concept of a minimum core obligation, this refusal has also kicked the scope of government obligation back into the sphere of democratic politics. There is an additional danger that a minimum core could morph from a floor to a ceiling, doing more to limit than provide a baseline for government obligations.

Third, the Court has nevertheless consistently maintained the position that it has the right to review government policy and assess it for "reasonableness" and for coherence between intention and outcomes. Litigation has therefore forced the government to provide citizens with publicly articulated, recorded, and justified responses as to the adequacy of its policies. This legal process has arguably yielded more productive analyses of social policy and deliberation on the nature of South African democracy than comparable parliamentary debates during 1994–2004. The willingness and capacity of the Court to review government policy has generated not only accountability itself but also the idea, now widespread in South African civil society, that the government can be held accountable for its actions.

Fourth, the Court has recognized the necessity of balancing competing rights and has resolved such calibrations in favor of majoritarian principles. It has also embraced an obligation to safeguard the rights of the most vulnerable segments of society. Significantly, the extent and quality of government engagement with social rights litigation contrast sharply with its uneven and sometimes punitive responses to street protests, parliamentary hearings, or reports from parliamentary standing committees, the other main forums for opposition politics during this period. Court cases based on social rights claims have provided citizens with a mechanism, other than elections, for demanding government accountability.

Soobramoney: Social Rights Should Address "the Larger Needs of Society"

Any evaluation of social rights claims involves a two-stage process (Govender 2006, 101). First, the court has to assess whether a violation of rights has in fact occurred. The onus of proof falls on the party making the claim (typically directed against the state), who may argue that a particular law is unconstitutional (e.g., *Khosa and Others v. Minister of Social Development*), that state conduct is inconsistent with a constitutional right (e.g., *Minister of Health and Others v. Treatment Action Campaign and Others*), or that the opposing litigant's argument relies on a legal rule that is inconsistent with the general tenor of the Bill of Rights (as argued, e.g., in *Afrox Health Care (Pty) Ltd. v. Strydom*) (Brand 2005, 19–20). Legal arguments demonstrating these claims effectively try to elaborate a record of policy failure.

Second, the court must assess whether the limits placed on social rights, where these exist, are reasonable and justifiable in a "democratic and open society in which government is based on the will of the people and every citizen is equally protected by law" (Constitution of the Republic of South Africa 1996, Preamble). The burden of providing such justifications typically falls on the state and requires that it justify its policies in terms of the democratic commitments set out in the constitution. "In effect, the Court assesses the importance of the right against the purpose of the limitation and assesses whether the means chosen to achieve the objective is proportionate and reasonable" (Govender 2006, 101; see also Constitution of the Republic of South Africa 1996, sec. 36).

Soobramoney was the first social rights case argued before the Constitutional Court in which the government and an affiliated service provider would have to account for their policies in these terms. It concerned the section 11 and section 27 rights of Mr. Thiagraj Soobramoney, a chronically ill man who had been denied access to lifesaving dialysis treatment by Addington Hospital in KwaZulu Natal.

To make optimal use of its twenty dialysis machines, which served the whole of KwaZulu Natal and patients from parts of the Eastern Cape Province, this public hospital had developed a protocol that gave priority to patients who would most benefit from dialysis. Mr. Soobramoney did not qualify for dialysis treatment on any of the grounds set out in the protocol and was thus denied treatment. He responded by making an urgent application to the Durban and Coast Local Division of the High Court for an order obliging Addington Hospital to provide him with dialysis treatment. The matter was heard by Judge Combrinck, who ruled against Mr. Soobramoney and dismissed the application. The plaintiff then took the case to the Constitutional Court, which ruled that the right to life had not been violated.

In its decision, the Court deferred to the judgment of the medical doctors at Addington Hospital, describing itself as "slow to interfere with rational decisions taken in good faith by the political organs and medical authorities whose responsibility it is to deal with such matters" (*Soobramoney* 1997, para. 29). It justified its noninterference on the grounds that Soobramoney's exclusion from the dialysis treatment service was not arbitrary but based on both rational and reasonable considerations articulated by the Provincial

Health Department in its budgeting process and by the medical staff at Addington Hospital in their treatment guidelines.[4]

The *Soobramoney* decision is sometimes interpreted as conservative and unduly deferential to existing state policy. The decision effectively interpreted certain rights, such as the right to life, as circumscribed by resource constraints rather than as absolute.[5]

We argue that *Soobramoney* nevertheless laid down important markers for how the Court would decide social rights cases in the future and shows more continuity with future cases, such as *Grootboom* and *TAC*, that were decided against the government, than is commonly acknowledged. First, the Court signaled its willingness to review government policy. The fact that it found such policy nonarbitrary, rational, and reasonable suggested that, in the future, if the Court did not so find, it would be willing to use such standards to decide against government policy.

Second, the Court also noted that a commitment to social rights involved a balancing act. In noting that the state's obligation to facilitate the right to life (section 11) should be understood in the context of the resource limitations noted in sections 26 and 27 of the Constitution (*Soobramoney* 1997, para. 11), the Court signaled a context-sensitive approach to legislating social rights, where broader social and political concerns were considered as important as technical legal questions in reaching decisions. Most significant, the Constitutional Court argued that ruling in favor of the plaintiff would have a negative impact on the state's capacity to fulfill its obligations to "the larger needs of society" (*Soobramoney* 1997, para. 31). The *Soobramoney* decision thus made explicit that specific individuals would not be able to use social rights provisions to secure access to costly social services. In balancing the competing health needs of South African citizens in an atmosphere of limited resources, the Court embraced majoritarian principles.

Grootboom

What the *Soobramoney* judgment failed to explain was the normative commitments that would allow the Court to distinguish, on grounds other than cost, between vulnerable groups that could legitimately be denied social services in some contexts and groups that should otherwise be prioritized because of their marginalized status.[6] The *Grootboom* case took this matter up as its central issue. In this decision the Court began to elaborate the conditions under which the state had "the obligation to devise, fund, implement and supervise measures to provide relief to those in desperate need" (*Grootboom* 2000, para. 96).

The *Grootboom* case was precipitated by a land takeover in which three hundred people living in appalling conditions moved onto land previously earmarked for low-cost housing. Their settlement was then bulldozed by the provincial government without warning, leaving them with no alternative housing. Lawyers for the community brought a case to the Cape High Court, arguing that the eviction violated sections 26 and 28 of the constitution, guaranteeing the circumscribed right to equal housing and the rights of children to shelter and parental or family care.

In its decision, the High Court found against the government, stating that it had violated the rights of children under section 28. The High Court nevertheless also found that plaintiffs had not made a convincing case that their section 26 rights had been violated in the context of a government policy the Court deemed fair and rational. The High Court referenced *Soobramoney* in cautioning against an excessively generous approach to social rights in cases where the existence of relevant policies demonstrates that the government is not actively disregarding its duty to progressively realize social rights.

In appeal, the government brought the case to the Constitutional Court in May 2000, arguing, among other things, that the Court had neither the skills nor the authority to make decisions regarding social policies. The Court nevertheless ruled that the state's existing housing policy did not adequately fulfill the obligations laid out in section 26(2) because it did not "provide relief for those in desperate need." As the ruling went on, "They are not to be ignored in the interests of an overall programme focused on medium and long-term objectives" (*Grootboom* 2000, para. 66)

Unlike *Soobramoney,* the *Grootboom* judgment evaluated the reasonableness of government policy not only in terms of its fiscal implications but also with regard to the quality and effects of implementation. The Community Law Centre (CLC), arguing for the amici curiae, contended that government's one-size-fits-all housing policy unintentionally exacerbated existing socioeconomic inequalities because it imposed unreasonable limitations on the rights of adults in crisis situations to access either housing or shelter.

The CLC's argument significantly emphasized the criteria the Court could use to judge the degree of deference it owed the executive and legislature. These guidelines emphasized that the groups adversely affected by extant housing policy, "children and the very poor," were "two of the most vulnerable in society." Quoting John Hart Ely, the CLC argued that "those whose rights need particular protection through the courts are 'those groups in society to whose needs and wishes elected officials have no apparent interest in attending'" (Community Law Centre 2001, para. 108–9). Children are in this position because they may not vote, and impoverished citizens because they often cannot vote or participate in politics when their civil and political rights are enforced but not their social rights. The CLC also argued that the degree of deference the Court owed the legislature and executive depended on the extent to which policies, or decisions about their enforcement, resulted from "thorough and consultative" processes consistent with politics in a democratic society.

This argument highlighted government's obligation to justify its actions and decisions, to be transparent in its decision-making processes, and to give due consideration to the interests of minor citizens and the poor. Framing the case in this manner exposed the ways in which government had fallen short of these standards of conduct at both the national and provincial levels. It also set out a justification for prioritizing marginalized groups on the basis of their inability to otherwise participate effectively in the democratic process, and not solely on the basis of a history of discrimination, a factor legitimately highlighted in the preamble of the constitution and several policy documents as grounds for promoting social rights. The CLC's argument was thus important from the perspective of accountability and opposition because it hinges the Court's duty to assess the reasonableness of policy, and thus the degree of deference owed to government, on government's compliance with broadly democratic procedures and concerns.

In its judgment, the Court endorsed the CLC's framing of rights claims, most significantly by ruling that citizens' section 26 rights had been violated.[7] It explicitly endorsed their conception of social and political rights as interdependent (*Grootboom* 2000, para. 23), as well as the state's obligation, at all levels of government, to implement policy in a legal, transparent, and humane manner, consistent with the vision of democracy expressed in the Bill of Rights (*Grootboom* 2000, paras. 39–44, 83–90). The ruling also pointed out that the legislation drawn up to "respect, protect, promote and fulfill" the right of access to housing was not "contextually fair" (Brand 2005, 5), as it in fact left the most destitute citizens worse off than their impoverished, but sheltered, counterparts.

Grootboom thus refigured the basis on which social rights claims would be judged "reasonable" by stipulating that government programs were not constitutionally reasonable "if the measures, though statistically successful, fail to respond to the needs of those most desperate" or to situations of crisis. The fact that the government had a housing policy in place was not sufficient. In the future, housing policy would have to meet standards of flexibility, coherence, and effective implementation.

Although the Court showed its willingness to find against the government in this case, the decision nevertheless rejected the concept of a minimum core obligation. Instead, it emphasized that social rights should be protected in a manner that was "socially fair." The Court made four arguments against importing the concept of a minimum core into the South African context.

First, the Court stated that rights are related and must be read together. In both *Soobramoney* and *Grootboom* (and later again in *TAC*), it rejected the notion that sections 26 and 27 of the constitution imposed two distinct positive obligations on the state: "one an obligation to give effect to the 26(1) and 27(1) rights; the other a limited obligation to do so progressively through "reasonable legislative and other measures, within its available resources." Instead, the Court argued that these sections should be read together, and that 26(2) and 27(2) limited the rights that can be claimed under 26(1) and 27(1), given the lack of available resources the government has at its disposal (paras. 29–32).

Second, the Court argued that rights should be read in context. The Court insisted that it is not the provisions of the International Covenant on Economic, Social, and Cultural rights that matters most in the South African context but the reasonableness of the state's attempts to fulfill these rights. Thus, minimum core in the South African context should function, they argued, as a reference point in assessing the reasonableness of policy, and not as a guarantee of a basic or minimum package of services to which everyone is entitled in the short term.

Third, the Court referred to its lack of institutional expertise in deciding the content of a minimum core. As it stated, the Court is not "institutionally equipped to make the wide-ranging factual and political enquiries necessary for determining what the minimum-core standards called for by the first and second amici should be, nor for deciding how public revenues should most effectively be spent." This argument nevertheless included a temporal dimension. The Court made reference to the fact that it was relatively new, suggesting that it might introduce a minimum core doctrine in future, when its jurisprudence is more refined.

Finally, and in a related vein, the Court invoked its concern over separation of powers limitations. It argued that deciding in favor of a minimum core obligation might infringe on the role of other branches of parliament in fulfilling social rights (*TAC* 2002, paras. 33–35).

In *Grootboom,* the Court additionally demonstrated that it was less concerned with the so-called technical proficiency of social policy designed to protect social rights than it was with the outcome of such policies.[8] The decision made repeated references to the dignity the state should afford citizens in a democratic order. The *Grootboom* case thus gave content to the conception of reasonableness the Court would use in subsequent jurisprudence.

In the wake of *Grootboom,* judges at all levels of the judicial system began to criticize the government's lack of engagement with marginalized citizens prior to litigation, as well as the poorly reasoned responses to their claims presented in court. This suggests that some members of the judiciary started to see the courts as a forum for holding government accountable not only for policy failures but also for its tendency to embrace a narrowly procedural approach to democratic participation. In the wake of *Grootboom,* many courts thus began to function not only as mechanisms of accountability but also as sites where embattled communities could take the government to task for the poor quality of public deliberation regarding public policies.

In *Permanent Secretary, Department of Welfare, Eastern Cape Provincial Government v. Ngxuza* (2001), for example, Justice Cameron referred to state–civil society engagement preceding the trial as "a pitiable saga of correspondence, meetings, calls, appeals, entreaties, demands and pleas by public interest organizations" (Cameron in Heywood 2003, 279). In *City of Cape Town v. Neville Rudolph and Others* (2003), Judge Selikowitz of the Cape High Court described the city's denial that a community was living in crisis conditions as "astonishing" and its presentation of the facts of the case as "indicative of a state of denial . . . and a failure [by the city] to recognize and acknowledge that there is, in fact, any category of persons to which it has any obligation beyond the obligation to put them on the waiting list for housing in the medium to long term" (Selikowitz in Wickeri 2004, 29–30). These critiques are distinct from judicial assessments of government policy, condemning instead government bureaucracies and their representatives for failing to be responsive to citizen demands in accordance with the commitments to participatory and deliberative democracy included in the constitution.

Although the *Soobramoney* and *Grootboom* cases played an important role in enhancing deliberation and accountability, the precedents they established have nevertheless had a narrow impact. Although the transformative potential of *Soobramoney* was probably negligible, *Grootboom* might conceivably have been used as a springboard for redefining the resources government should provide to landless citizens or citizens living in informal settlements, and even for thinking critically about the spatial integration of apartheid cities and towns. Instead, the *Grootboom* ruling has been used in a minimalist manner to fight illegal evictions by local governments in an incremental and piecemeal fashion. It has been taken up as a baseline, used by citizens to defend their "right" to live on sites with little or no services, infrastructure, or stable housing structures. Local governments have also tried to use *Grootboom* to justify evictions, for example by arguing that a particular group of squatters is not destitute or in crisis (Oldfield and Stokke 2004, 26–27).[9]

The Treatment Action Campaign Case

Both *Soobramoney* and *Grootboom* used social rights in the classical sense—as legal grounds for demanding redress through the courts. In contrast, the *TAC* case suggests that social rights claims may be particularly effective when deployed as a political strategy—as a source for organizing and mobilizing a political constituency, and for gaining access to senior government representatives. The organization has used social rights as a basis for litigation only as a last resort. Its success in this regard suggests that the strategic potential of social rights for forging new political debates, conceptions of reasonableness, and mechanisms of accountability is latent, and is best exploited when social rights claims are coupled with strategic political action.

In August 2001, then deputy chairperson of TAC, Siphokazi Mthathi, filed an affidavit against the minister of health and provincial MECs for health in the Transvaal Provincial Division of the High Court.[10] TAC's affidavit contested whether (1) the government was entitled to refuse to make nevirapine available to HIV-positive women who give birth in the public health sector and (2) whether it was obliged, as a matter of law, to set out clear time frames for a national program to prevent mother-to-child transmission (MTCT) of HIV (*TAC* 2002, paras. 20–21).[11] It argued that the state's continued reluctance to implement a coherent, cost-effective, and comprehensive MTCT prevention (MTCTP) program violated (1) the government's 1994 commitment to provide children under the age of six and their pregnant mothers with "free medical care in every state hospital and clinic where such need exists," (2) the provisions set out in the "National AIDS Plan for South Africa, 1994–1995" for preventing perinatal transmission of HIV—an agreement to which two postapartheid health ministers were party, (3) the National Patients' Rights Charter of 1996, (4) the HIV/AIDS Strategic Plan for 2000–2005, and (5) a commitment by Dr. Nkosazana Dlamini Zuma, after a joint meeting with the TAC on 30 April 1999, to take steps to lower the price of MTCTP measures. It also constituted a breach of several constitutional provisions and international conventions the government had ratified.[12]

The Constitutional Court's decision in *TAC* followed both *Soobramoney* and *Grootboom*, refraining once again from defining a minimum core set of social rights. Lawyers for TAC argued that sections 26 and 27 of the constitution state rights and obligations separately. Subsection (1) of each clause establishes an individual right, vested in everyone. The lawyers claimed that this right identifies a minimum core to which every person in need is entitled (paras. 26–28). The Court held that, in keeping with its own prior decisions regarding the minimum core, the Court was more concerned with generating government accountability and responsiveness than it was with determining the substance of government obligations:

> The state is obliged to take reasonable measures progressively to eliminate or reduce the large areas of severe deprivation that afflict our society. The courts will guarantee that the democratic processes are protected so as to ensure accountability, responsiveness and openness, as the Constitution requires in section 1. As the Bill of Rights indicates, their function in respect of socio-economic rights is directed towards ensuring that legislative and other measures taken by the state are reasonable. As this Court said in Grootboom, "It is necessary to recognise that a wide range of possible measures could be adopted by the State to meet its obligations." (para. 36)

Echoing *Soobramoney*, the Court nevertheless asserted its power to review health policy, rejecting the government's argument that the separation of powers doctrine limited it from doing so or, as the government argued, from making any other than declaratory orders. It also rejected the government's contention regarding constrained resources, and dismissed all government arguments regarding safety and efficacy. Although the Constitutional Court declined to exercise supervisory jurisdiction in *TAC*, it ordered the government to devise and implement a comprehensive MTCTP program and mandated immediate removal of restrictions on nevirapine. The Court ordered the government to make the drug available in the public sector, to provide training for counselors, and to take reasonable measures to extend testing and counseling facilities and services throughout the public health sector.

The ruling was thus much broader and more detailed than the one handed down in *Grootboom*. The *TAC* judgment also reiterated the Court's obligation "to guarantee that the democratic processes are protected so as to ensure accountability, responsiveness, and openness, as the Constitution requires," by ensuring that the state act reasonably to provide access to socioeconomic rights on a progressive basis (*TAC* 2002, paras. 35–36). It thus reaffirmed the sentiments of the *Grootboom* decision that social rights could be used not only to document and remedy policy failures but also as mechanisms for strengthening democratic accountability.

Two dimensions of the *TAC* case are particularly interesting for thinking about the use of social rights as a political strategy. These are TAC's use of litigation as one component of a broader political campaign and its influence on public discourse surrounding HIV/AIDS.

Mobilization and Litigation Strategies

The *TAC* case was preceded and accompanied by a high level of popular mobilization around improved access to drugs preventing MTCT of HIV/AIDS.[13] In both the High Court and Constitutional Court cases, TAC packed the Court with supporters in its trademark "HIV-positive" t-shirts and organized demonstrations outside the Court. Constitutional Court clerk Steven Budlender claimed that "within the Court, it was impossible not to consider the actual impact of the decision, as is sometimes the case in the insulation of the country's highest court. The TAC would literally be outside with placards, organizing support for a favorable decision and mobilizing the media to cover the case's outcomes" (Budlender 2002).

Because it works through the courts, and has tried to engage cooperatively with the Ministry of Health and other government ministries and bureaucracies, TAC has been accused of being too reformist, and of being insufficiently critical of the ANC (Jones 2004). TAC has nevertheless been willing to deploy its record of cooperation with government as legitimate grounds for encouraging civil disobedience and legal sanction of government policies.

Among civil society organizations with grassroots membership structures active in South Africa today, TAC has been most committed to using litigation as a component of political activism. It explicitly defines litigation as a strategy of political action rather than an alternative to such action. Although taking the government to court is a risky strategy, likely to anger high-level officials and hardly guaranteed to win, TAC sees litigation not only as an opportunity to change government policy and demand accountability but also as a vehicle for educating civil society and shaping public deliberation. It has also been involved in South African case law as a friend of the court, providing evidence and support in a number of cases that it has not brought directly. TAC treasurer Mark Heywood has described TAC's commitment to litigation in combination with activism as follows:

> For the TAC, litigation both emerges from and feeds back into a social context. Resort to litigation is not exclusive of other strategies. Litigation can also help to catalyse mobilisation and assist public education on the contested issues, as well as bring about direct relief to individuals or classes of applicants. . . . However, support within TAC for a strategy of litigation could not be taken for granted. Internally numerous workshops were conducted with TAC volunteers to explain the case [before taking government to court for its MTCTP program]. (Heywood 2003, 300)

The organization has proved particularly adept in furthering its rights claims by creating opportune moments to alternately transgress and embrace national and international laws governing property regimes, import/export regulations, distribution and manufacture of biomedical treatments for HIV/AIDS and related illnesses, and provision of social rights. It is against this broader approach to political activism that TAC's 2002 Constitutional Court victory against the South African government should be interpreted (Greenstein 2003; Achmat 2004).

Two seemingly contradictory uses of law illustrate TAC's political approach to legal strategies. In 1998 TAC entered a case filed by the Pharmaceutical Manufacturers' Association (PMA) against the South African government as amicus curiae (Treatment Action Campaign 1998)—on the side of the state. The PMA challenged the constitutionality of an amendment to the Medicines and Related Substances Control Act that was intended to make essential medicines more affordable. The legal papers filed by TAC quickly became the focal point of the case. The impact of the case was extended beyond the court by TAC activists, who used it to mobilize political support in South Africa and the United States (Heywood 2001).

In direct contrast to its use of litigation in 1998, in 2001 TAC publicly and illegally imported fluconazole, a generic alternative to a brand-name drug used to treat systemic thrush in persons living with AIDS. This action was part of the Christopher Moraka Defiance Campaign, named for a recently deceased HIV-positive activist, targeted at convincing Pfizer to lower the price of the drug or to give the South African government a voluntary license to distribute it locally (Treatment Action Campaign 2000).

Both campaigns also contributed to the success of TAC's 2001–2 MTCTP case by eliciting a drop in the price of antiretroviral drugs. Most dramatically, Boehringer Ingelheim offered to provide free nevirapine to the government for a period of five years. The government's refusal to accept free nevirapine would subsequently make it impossible for it to claim that an expanded MTCTP program would prove prohibitively costly. The "resource constraints" argument that had proved crucial in the *Soobramoney* case was thus reduced to a non-issue through activism preceding the MTCTP case, even though both cases were brought on virtually identical rights claims.

During this same period TAC also supported the Western Cape Province government and Médecins Sans Frontières in successfully undertaking a highly active antiretroviral treatment (HAART) program in Khayelitsha. In so doing the organization helped to demonstrate that much more complicated ARV treatment regimes than the single dose of nevirapine required to prevent MTCT could be feasible and effective in resource-poor settings (Heywood 2003; Médecins Sans Frontières et al. 2003; Fourie 2006, 105–72). TAC later benefited from this amicable relationship with the Western Cape provincial government in building its Constitutional Court case against the national government. The Western Cape MEC for Health provided TAC, and the minister of health, with detailed information about the practical considerations that affected the success of large-scale MTCTP programs (Heywood 2003, 292). TAC used this information to modify the claims for a national treatment program it eventually submitted to the Constitutional Court (Heywood 2003, 295–96).

Through campaigns and relationships such as these, which preceded and sustained the High Court and Constitutional Court cases, TAC refined its use of litigation as a political strategy. Taken together, these measures prepared the ground for success in TAC's Constitutional Court case, generating empirical evidence, a normative consensus, and evidence of technical capacity. TAC has both transgressed and used the law to great effect as a space for reforming notions of reasonableness and for holding government accountable to the constitution, as well as to its own promises and policies.

The Changing Discourse on HIV/AIDS

TAC's combination of litigation and mobilization also refigured public perceptions of HIV/AIDS, effectively reframing the epidemic as a national health concern rather than a symptom of individual immorality and a matter of personal responsibility (Friedman and Mottiar 2005, 531). More specifically, it allowed TAC to cast the MTCTP policy as the primary incarnation of this "national concern," using sustained mass action to forge a normative consensus and demonstrate public support for government action (Heywood 2003, 286; Achmat 2004; Johnson 2006).

By the time of its application to the High Court in 2001, TAC could thus convincingly argue that government had no "rational or lawful basis" (*TAC* 2002, para. 22.11) for substituting "a *blanket* official decision for decisions made by medical professionals who are well qualified to make those decisions in the light of the circumstances of their individual patients" (*TAC* 2002, para. 162, emphasis in text). Doing so produced "catastrophic results for the people affected, and for the country" (*TAC* 2002, para. 162).

The wording of TAC's claims is significant because it portrayed HIV/AIDS as a health issue affecting the national interest rather than focusing attention on the small number of pregnant women who were the potential beneficiaries in the case. It appealed therefore to the majoritarian principles already established by the Court in *Soobramoney*.

The TAC application also insisted that government inaction forced hospital administrators "to act in a manner which is perceived to be contrary to the official policy" (*TAC* 2002, para. 126.3). By framing doctors' violations of policy as "perceived" transgressions of "official policy," TAC's affidavit effectively invoked the well-known apartheid dilemma of choosing between adherence to formal law versus a "higher" moral law on the MTCTP policy.[14]

TAC's impact on the public discourse surrounding HIV/AIDS was particularly important in establishing the legitimacy of these demands for public sector antiretroviral programs, and for a more expansive MTCTP policy in particular. As Friedman and Mottiar (2005, 531) point out,

> The fact that people living with HIV and AIDS came to be seen as persons deserving of sympathy demanding a basic human right was the result of the strategy of the TAC and its allies [which include HIV-positive Supreme Court of Appeals Judge Edwin Cameron], not an asset they inherited. . . . HIV/AIDS was not a popular issue among South African policymakers—it was seen as at best a diversion from the pressing tasks of

creating a democracy on the ashes of minority rule . . . South Africa is
a socially conservative society with pressing development needs occasioned by both the demand of organized black interest groups for racial redress and by the acknowledged need to address severe social inequalities. AIDS could well have been seen as a symptom of its victims'
inability to control their sexual impulses and thus a consequence of social deviance which ought not to be rewarded by the public purse—or,
at best, as a luxury which a society with pressing challenges could not
afford. . . . The fact that AIDS activist Gugu Dlamini was beaten to death
by a mob enraged by her open acknowledgement of her HIV status is el-
oquent testimony to the depths of potential resistance.

A 2006 Afrobarometer briefing paper confirmed the steadily increasing
importance of HIV/AIDS as a mainstream concern during the period 1994–
2004 (Afrobarometer 2006). What is more, 63 percent of respondents who
prioritized either unemployment or HIV/AIDS thought that the government, rather than any other agency or institution, had the capacity to address these problems "within the next few years."

The fact that several provinces expanded their public sector MTCTP programs during the period between the High Court and the Constitutional
Court decisions, despite then Justice Minister Penuell Maduna asserting the
provinces' "right" to ignore the Pretoria High Court's execution order ("Justice Minister" 2002), exposed the lack of popular and political support for
the government's MTCTP policy. By the time it resorted to litigation, TAC's
demands enjoyed widespread legitimacy—among ordinary citizens, physi-
cians working in the public sector, and even senior members of provincial
administrations.

TAC's popular support and moral authority were enhanced by its ability
to position itself as more committed to the democratic process than government officials, given its record of cooperation with government officials who
reneged on various commitments to expand treatment programs. In court
proceedings, members of civil society organizations could thus speak with
more authority about the integrity of their attempts to change the MTCTP
policy through conventional political channels than the government itself.
Ostensibly in response to political campaigns surrounding the Constitutional Court case, the government tried to partly preempt the Court's decision by announcing a plan to roll out universal provision of antiretroviral
drugs, committing to the treatment of all uninsured HIV-positive citizens,
not only the subset of pregnant women covered by the case.

The government's announcement of a universal HAART plan might additionally have been spurred by dramatic testimony regarding the impact of the disease and the limitations of public health services described in supporting affidavits by HIV-positive women and medical doctors included in TAC's High Court application. These accounts effectively illustrated the stakes involved in refusing to expand the MTCTP program and in failing to develop a general HAART program.

In the affidavits, two nurses detailed the large number of persons they counseled in relation to HIV/AIDS—about sixty per month, according to one—and expressed frustration at their inability to offer them any treatment (Mahlonoko 2001; Matebula 2001). The nurses' affidavits also demystified MTCTP treatment, stating that nevirapine required no more skill or knowledge to administer than any other drug distributed at primary health facilities (Mahlonoko 2001).[15]

Most dramatically, the affidavits detailed the arbitrariness of the obstacles pregnant women faced in accessing treatment. Some had access to nevirapine and gave birth to HIV-negative children merely because they lived in neighborhoods located in a pilot site. In one affidavit a nurse described how a woman in labor had to take three taxis and walk over a footbridge in order to access nevirapine at Baragwanath Hospital, after she had initially shown up at Kopanong Hospital. Kopanong Hospital, which did not distribute nevirapine at the time, is in Vereeniging, on the border of Gauteng and the Free State. The Chris Hani Baragwanath Hospital is in Soweto, forty-three kilometers away.

In another case a woman named Sarah Hlale was given a nevirapine tablet some months before her child's birth, but she went into premature labor and forgot the tablet at home. The hospital where she delivered her baby was prohibited from distributing the drug and did not have an ambulance available to transport the infant to a site where it was available. They offered instead to transport the premature infant to Baragwanath Hospital by bus, an offer the mother refused because she felt it unsafe. During the course of the Constitutional Court case, Sarah Hlale died of AIDS-related illnesses. Three days after her widely reported death, the government unexpectedly released a statement on HIV/AIDS that promised a universal rollout plan for antiretrovirals, to be implemented as soon as possible (Heywood 2003, 309–10).

These women's accounts graphically illustrate the implications of the dry legalistic claim that government policy was unreasonable because it arbitrarily excluded some citizens from accessing health care services. Though highly specific and extremely dramatic, it is unlikely that these experiences were uncommon, given the extremely limited scope of the existing MTCTP program and South Africa's high HIV infection rate. The announcement of the antiretroviral rollout plan after Sarah Hlale's death suggests that the experiences of these women—which had been exposed and made part of the official record through the court case—exerted some pressure to publicly endorse conventional AIDS science, and to promise a universal treatment program (Heywood 2003, 310). Such accounts also helped TAC to frame the existing treatment policy as arbitrary, and therefore potentially threatening to the legitimacy of the democratically elected government.

In the context of South Africa's postapartheid institutional landscape, which will continue to undermine the formation of a strong institutionalized opposition for the foreseeable future, representative democracy alone will produce neither robust deliberation nor credible government accountability. The existence of justiciable social and economic rights has nevertheless allowed the Constitutional Court to play a partial role in filling that gap, enhancing deliberation and generating a presumption of accountability that fulfills many of the functions of a democratic opposition. Even more persuasively, some civil society organizations have expanded the sphere of social and economic rights beyond the Court, combining political and legal strategies to demand government transparency and accountability.

The case study material presented here demonstrates how social rights can be deployed to reframe policy as well as the normative consensus that surrounds them. The processes of drafting affidavits, sourcing personal and technical evidence of policy failures, exercising the right to access government documents, and mobilizing political support for a social rights claim have proved invaluable in improving the quality and scope of deliberation about the kind of government residents of the Republic of South Africa desire. Social rights litigation frames concrete experiences of discrimination and injustice as important considerations in constitutional law. It also demands that government provide a reasoned response as to the adequacy of policies that aim to limit government responsiveness to citizen demands. In cases where courts recognize a breach of social rights obligations, detailed decisions, particularly ones that include structural or supervisory interdicts, can compel the government to change its policy in a timely manner and give the court the authority to "hold the state to its own undertakings" (Berger 2008, 71).

We propose that social rights are different from civil and political rights in the sense that they are measured ordinally rather than categorically. They operate on a scale to measure progress in attaining some idealized goal. Social rights can be realized to a greater or lesser extent, a fact that is implicitly recognized in the constitutional commitment to the "progressive realization" of such rights. Because the content of social rights is less easily determined than that of civil and political rights, especially in contexts where courts are unwilling to elaborate a minimum core obligation, their realization depends on constant political engagement.

Social and economic rights are therefore less likely to limit oppositional politics in the way that civil and political rights have been shown to do. Civil and political rights have a categorical character. Once marginalized citizens are formally awarded civil and political rights—once they are formally incorporated into the political community—it is extremely difficult to demonstrate the ways in which their formal status might nevertheless be circumscribed in practice. Social rights cannot be awarded through such simple categorical moves, and consequently function as more open-ended grounds for ongoing political struggles.

The argument presented here suggests that the transformative potential of constitutions may not be limited to the law. Constitutions may also be politically transformative to the extent that they offer grounds for an immanent critique of democratic governance. By enshrining rights, constitutions offer a standard by which societies can measure their progress toward goals they themselves have set. Constitutional rights also offer grounds on which oppositions can constitute themselves, and by which they can offer a critique of government policy with internal legitimacy. By providing the soil for domestic oppositions to take root, constitutionalism may open up, rather than close down, the space of politics.

NOTES

We thank conference participants for valuable comments on earlier versions of this paper, and Patrick Macklem for helpful discussions regarding legal controversies over social and economic rights.

1. At the time, Jung was a graduate student, and the experience of co-authoring a paper with Shapiro was invaluable. When Shapiro invited Jung to participate as an author in this edited volume, ten years later, she asked Lauren Paremoer, a graduate student, to co-author the paper, in tribute to Shapiro, as a way of paying back, by passing along, his generous mentorship. In part, this essay builds on Jung and Shapiro's original article.

2. This essay focuses on three of the most prominent social and economic rights cases since the enactment of the 1996 constitution. We argue that *Soobra-*

money, Grootboom, and *TAC* are important because they legitimated socioeconomic rights jurisprudence as a strategy citizens could use to demand government accountability between elections. These cases informed civil society strategies for engaging the state and defined the court's approach to socioeconomic jurisprudence in postapartheid South Africa. For a more comprehensive review of judicial decisions where either claimants or the court refer explicitly to socioeconomic rights, see Berger (2008).

3. Note, however, that, as a judge, Davis decided the High Court judgment in *Grootboom.*

4. Paragraph 25 of the *Soobramoney* decision reads as follows: "By using the available dialysis machines in accordance with the guidelines more patients are benefited than would be the case if they were used to keep alive persons with chronic renal failure, and the outcome of the treatment is also likely to be more beneficial because it is directed to curing patients, and not simply to maintaining them in a chronically ill condition. It has not been suggested that these guidelines are unreasonable or that they were not applied fairly and rationally when the decision was taken by the Addington Hospital that the appellant did not qualify for dialysis."

5. For critiques of the reasoning used in *Soobramoney,* particularly the purely negative interpretation of section 27(3) of the constitution, see Pieterse (2004, 899–902), Liebenberg (2002), and Scott and Alston (2000).

6. In an assessment of South Africa's progress on health care rights, Karrisha Pillay (2003, 20–21) notes that the white paper on health (Department of Health 1997) gives special attention to meeting the needs of the poor, underserved, aged, women, and children—all groups considered to be among the most vulnerable. The 2004 National Health Act includes all these groups, except the poor or underserved, and adds people with disabilities to its list of examples of "vulnerable groups." Pillay points out that the white paper, in effect at the time of the *Soobramoney* case, "gives no insight as to how this determination was made and it is unclear why it does not, for instance, specifically include people living with HIV/AIDS, people with disabilities, etc. Instead it uses vague terminology like the 'under-served' with little guidance as to exactly who would be included in such a category. A severe shortcoming is accordingly the failure of the national health framework to determine the criteria in terms of which 'vulnerable groups' are identified." Furthermore, government policy does not explicitly target all persons included in these groups but specific subsets, such as pregnant women or children under age six. In this sense the groups listed, and policies devised to serve them, are essentially arbitrary, though their inclusion makes intuitive sense to most South Africans. As noted above, this lack of clarity regarding criteria for assessing patients' vulnerability and its impact on their access to medical resources is echoed in the *Soobramoney* decision. It is particularly important to develop more explicit principles for prioritizing access to health care services as the kinds of groups judged "most vulnerable" or "underserved" are likely to change over time with the emergence of new public health concerns and new socioeconomic configurations and status hierarchies in South

African society—particularly if government succeeds at progressively realizing socioeconomic equality.

7. This is in contrast to the Cape High Court ruling, which had recognized only that a narrower right, children's right to shelter, had been violated.

8. The Court's emphasis on equality of outcomes is significant insofar as the government typically is silent on the inequalities generated by its neoliberal economic policy, which favors economic growth and stability above job creation and redistribution, and its market-based approach to the provision of social services and land redistribution.

9. See Oldfield and Stokke (2004) for an account of the obstacles citizens face in using this legal baseline to defend their right to stay in underserviced informal settlements in the Western Cape Province. They note that "experience with legal struggles is mixed. Successes have required, not only external assistance . . . but extensive energy and human and financial resources. Even where cases have been won, the possibilities for appeals and continued delays are large. At the same time, legal cases are a form of struggle which state officials take seriously and where there is a potential for progressive policy change in conjunction with a range of other forms of direct action" (Oldfield and Stokke 2004, 27).

10. The arguments considered in the High Court and Constitutional Court cases were largely similar, with the latter case involving an additional set of disputes pertaining to a judicial order issued in favor of TAC by Justice Botha that instructed government to allow nevirapine to be prescribed in cases where it was "medically indicated" and where the relevant medical superintendent ruled there was capacity to do so. It further ordered government to formulate an effective and comprehensive MTCTP program and to present it to the Court before 31 March 2002 (Heywood 2003, 301).

11. The government responded to TAC's case by arguing that it would be unaffordable to extend its comprehensive MTCTP program, which included the provision of formula to those unable to afford it, that the efficacy and safety of nevirapine had not been sufficiently verified, that the public health system did not have the capacity to expand this service, and that widespread provision of the drug might lead to resistant strains of the virus and thus a public health catastrophe.

12. These were listed in the affidavit as sections 9 (the right to equality and freedom from discrimination on the basis of socioeconomic status and race), 10 (the right to human dignity), 11 (the right to life), 12, (the right to make choices and decisions concerning reproduction) 27 (the right of access to health care services), 28 (the right of children to basic health care services) and 195 of the constitution. It argued government policy was in violation of the Universal Declaration of Human Rights, the International Covenant on Civil and Political Rights, the International Covenant on Economic, Social and Cultural Rights, the African Charter on Human and People's Rights, the Convention on the Elimination of Discrimination Against Women, the Convention on the Rights of the Child, and the Convention on the Elimination of All Forms of Racial Discrimination.

13. Achmat, quoted in Friedman and Mottiar (2005, 524), describes the demographic profile of TAC'S members as "80 percent unemployed, 70 percent women—the group most affected by HIV, domestic violence and violence in schools—70 percent in the 14–24 age group and 90 percent African." Women make up half the staff and about a third of TAC officeholders, but the public face of the organization remains predominantly male. TAC's formal structure provides for internal representative democracy. In practice, however, major strategic decisions are initiated and financial control strictly exercised by national leadership. Interviews with TAC members suggest that ordinary members' influence on and participation in key decisions are somewhat uneven (ibid., 517–21, 526).

14. This way of framing the issue forced the Court to elaborate on the limits of political authority vis-à-vis other domains of expertise, that is, on the scope of democratically elected officials' right to settle scientific and other epistemological debates through legislation or other democratic procedures. In discussing this question on the limits of the political, the Constitutional Court stipulated that the minister of health's concerns regarding the efficacy of nevirapine were not "supported by the data" or the "wealth of scientific material produced by both [TAC and government]," and that her concerns regarding the safety of the medication amounted to no more than a "hypothetical issue" (*TAC* 2002, paras. 58, 60). Political consensus among members of government about the undesirability of nevirapine, in other words, did not trump medical consensus regarding the safety and efficacy of the drug in the Court's estimation, whereas in *Soobramoney* the government and the medical community were on the same side. In both cases the Constitutional Court deferred to the medical community.

15. In her affidavit, senior nurse Tshidi Mahlonoko (2001) asserted the capacity of appropriately trained nurses to administer nevirapine in the following terms:

I have heard that some of the reasons provided as to why Nevirapine cannot be made available more widely at clinics and hospitals are difficulties of controlling the administering of the drug. In my opinion we should not restrict the control system by stocking Nevirapine at one hospital with one person in charge of the drug. I think that it is possible and advisable to make NVP available at all levels of the health system. . . . Like with all other diseases and treatments, nurses can be trained on possible side effects of the drug and how to deal with this. . . . As a nurse who is responsible for setting up systems of control for drugs of this nature, I would suggest the following workable system. The patient starts with the counselor, and the doctor can confirm the patient's status with the consent of the patient. The patient is monitored and given all the relevant information. The nurse will administer Nevirapine at the appropriate time, and ensure that the relevant information is recorded on the drug register available. This register is used for potentially harmful toxic drugs like Valium and morphine. As I understand it, every drug has side effects. Even aspirin has side effects, and can cause an adverse reaction in some people depending on their immune system, threshold of tolerance for a drug, etc.

BIBLIOGRAPHY

Achmat, Zackie. 2004. "HIV/AIDS and Human Rights: A New South African Struggle." John Foster Lecture. The Miriam Rothschild and John Foster Human Rights Trust, London, 10 November.

Afrobarometer. 2006. "The Public Agenda: Change and Stability in South Africans' Ratings of National Priorities." Afrobarometer Briefing Paper no. 45, June. http://www.afrobarometer.org/papers/AfrobriefNo45.pdf.

Ballard, Richard, Adam Habib, and Imraan Valodia, eds. 2006. *Voices of Protest: Social Movements in Post-Apartheid South Africa.* Scottsville, South Africa: University of KwaZulu-Natal Press.

Belani, Aarthi. 2004. *The South African Constitutional Court's Decision in TAC: A "Reasonable" Choice?* Center for Human Rights and Global Justice Working Paper: Economic, Social and Cultural Rights Series, no. 7, New York University School of Law. http://www.chrgj.org/publications/docs/wp/Belani%20The%20South %20African%20Constitutional%20Court's%20Decisions%20in%20TAC.pdf.

Berger, Jonathan. 2002. "Litigation Strategies to Gain Access to Treatment: The Case of South Africa's Treatment Action Campaign." *Wisconsin International Law Journal* 20: 595–614.

———. 2008. "Litigating for Social Justice in Post-Apartheid South Africa: A Focus on Health and Education." In *Courting Social Justice: Judicial Enforcement of Social and Economic Rights in the Developing World,* ed. Varun Gauri and Daniel M. Brinks, 38–99. Cambridge: Cambridge University Press.

Brand, Danie. 2005. "Introduction to Socio-Economic Rights in the South African Constitution." In *Socio-Economic Rights in South Africa,* ed. Danie Brand and Christof Heyns, 1–56. Pretoria: Pretoria University Law Press.

Brown, Wendy. 1995. *States of Injury.* Princeton, NJ: Princeton University Press.

Budlender, Geoff. 2002. "A Paper Dog with Real Teeth." *Mail and Guardian,* 12 July.

Community Law Centre. 2001. "Government: Heads of Argument on Behalf of the Amici Curiae." http://www.communitylawcentre.org.za/Court-Interventions %20/grootboom-right-to-adequate-housing-the-rights-of-the-child.

Constitution of the Republic of South Africa. 1996. Act no. 108. http://www .concourt.gov.za/site/theconstitution/english.pdf.

Crenshaw, Kimberlé Williams. 1995. "Race, Reform, and Retrenchment: Transformation and Legitimation in Antidiscrimination Law." In *Critical Race Theory: The Key Writings that Formed the Movement,* ed. Kimberlé Crenshaw, Neil Gotanda, and Gary Peller. New York: New Press.

Davis, Dennis. 1992. "The Case against the Inclusion of Socioeconomic Demands in a Bill of Rights Except as Directive Principles." *South African Journal on Human Rights* 475: 488–90.

Department of Health, Government of the Republic of South Africa. 1997. "White Paper for the Transformation of the Health System in South Africa." http://www.info.gov.za/whitepapers/1997/health.htm.

Fourie, Pieter. 2006. *The Political Management of HIV and AIDS in South Africa: One Burden Too Many?* New York: Palgrave MacMillan.

Friedman, Stephen, and Shauna Mottiar. 2005. "A Rewarding Engagement? The Treatment Action Campaign and the Politics of HIV/AIDS." *Politics and Society* 33: 511–65.

Gabel, Peter, and Duncan Kennedy. 1984. "Roll Over Beethoven." *Stanford Law Review* 36: 1–55.

Govender, Karthy. 2006. "Assessing the Constitutional Protection of Human Rights in South Africa during the First Decade of Democracy." In *State of the Nation: South Africa 2005–2006,* ed. Sakhela Buhlungu, John Daniel, Roger Southall, and Jessica Lutchman. Pretoria: HSRC Press.

Greenstein, Ran. 2003. "State, Civil Society, and the Reconfiguration of Power in Post-Apartheid South Africa." Paper presented at the WISER Seminar, 28 August. http://wiserweb.wits.ac.za/PDF%20Files/state%20-%20greenstein.PDF.

Heywood, Mark. 2001. "Debunking 'Conglomo-Talk': A Case Study of the Amicus Curiae as an Instrument for Advocacy, Investigation and Mobilisation." *Law, Democracy and Development* 5: 133–62.

———. 2003. "Preventing Mother-to-Child HIV Transmission in South Africa: Background, Strategies and Outcomes of the Treatment Action Campaign Case against the Minister of Health." *South African Journal of Human Rights* 19: 278–315.

Johnson, Krista. 2006. "Framing Aids Mobilization and Human Rights in Post-Apartheid South Africa." *Perspectives on Politics* 4: 663–70.

Jones, Peris. 2004. "A Test of Governance: Rights-Based Struggles and the Politics of HIV/AIDS Policy in South Africa." Research Notes 01/2004, Norwegian Centre for Human Rights at the University of Oslo. http://www.humanrights.uio.no/forskning/publ/rn/2004/0104.pdf.

Jung, Courtney, and Ian Shapiro. 1995. "South Africa's Negotiated Transition: Democracy, Opposition and the New Constitutional Order." *Politics and Society* 23: 269–308.

"Justice Minister Rubbishes Court's Aids Ruling." 2002. *Mail and Guardian,* March 26. http://www.aegis.com/news/DMG/2002/MG020326.html.

Klare, Karl. 1998. "Legal Culture and Transformative Constitutionalism." *South African Journal on Human Rights* 14: 146–88.

Liebenberg, Sandra. 2002. "South Africa's Evolving Jurisprudence on Socio-Economic Rights: An Effective Tool in Challenging Poverty?" *Law, Democracy and Development* 6: 159–92.

Macklem, Patrick. 2006. "Militant Democracy, Legal Pluralism, and the Paradox of Self-Determination." *International Journal of Constitutional Law* 4: 488–516.

Mahlonoko, Tshidi. 2001. Personal affidavit of Tshidi Mahlonoko submitted alongside TAC founding affidavit on MTCT. Filed on 21 August 2001 at the Pretoria High Court. http://www.tac.org.za/Documents/MTCTCourtCase/cctmahlo.txt.

Matebula, Vivienne Nokuzola. 2001. Personal affidavit of Vivienne Nokuzola Matebula submitted alongside TAC founding affidavit on MTCT. Filed on 21 August 2001 at the Pretoria High Court. http://www.tac.org.za/Documents/MTCT CourtCase/ccmvmate.txt.

Matisonn, Heidi Leigh. 2004. "Beyond Party Politics: Unexpected Democracy-Deepening Consequences of One-Party Dominance in South Africa." *Theoria* 51, no. 3.

Médecins Sans Frontières South Africa, Department of Public Health at the University of Cape Town and the Provincial Administration of the Western Cape. 2003. *Antiretroviral Therapy in Primary Health Care: Experience of the Khayelitsha Programme in South Africa. Perspectives and Practice in Antiretroviral Treatment. Case Study.* Geneva: World Health Organization. http://www.who.int/hiv/pub/prev_care/en/South_Africa_E.pdf

Michelman, Frank. 2003. "The Constitution, Social Rights, and Liberal Political Justification." *International Journal of Constitutional Law* 1: 13–34.

Oldfield, Sophie, and Kristian Stokke. 2004. "Building Unity in Diversity: Social Movement Activism in the Western Cape Anti-Eviction Campaign." Paper presented as a case study for the UKZN project, "Globalisation, Marginalisation and New Social Movements in Post-Apartheid South Africa," a joint project of the Centre for Civil Society and the School of Development Studies, University of KwaZulu-Natal. http://folk.uio.no/stokke/Publications/CCS.pdf.

Pieterse, Marius. 2004. "Possibilities and Pitfalls in the Domestic Enforcement of Social Rights: Contemplating the South African Experience." *Human Rights Quarterly* 26: 882–905.

Pillay, Karrisha. 2003. "Tracking South Africa's Progress on Healthcare Rights: Are We Any Closer to Achieving the Goal?" *Law, Democracy and Development* 7. http://www.communitylawcentre.org.za/clc-projects/socio-economic-rights/ research/socio-economic-rights-transformation-in-sa/2003-vol-7-law -democracy-and-development/Tracking%20South%20Africas%20progress%20 on%20health%20care%20rights%20Karrisha%20Pillay%2019%20March.pdf.

Poole, Ross. 1999. *Nation and Identity.* London: Routledge.

Roux, Theunis. 2003. "Legitimating Transformation: Political Resource Allocations in the South African Constitutional Court." *Democratization* 10: 92–111.

Scott, Craig, and Philip Alston. 2000. "Adjudicating Constitutional Priorities in a Transnational Context: A Comment on *Soobramoney*'s Legacy and *Grootboom*'s Promise." *South African Journal of Human Rights* 16: 206–68.

Sunstein, Cass. 1993. "Against Positive Rights." *East European Constitutional Review,* Winter: 35–38.

———. 2001. "Social and Economic Rights? Lessons from South Africa." *Constitutional Forum* 11: 4.

Treatment Action Campaign. 1998. "The Pharmaceutical Manufacturers' Association of South Africa and Others v. The President of the Republic of South Africa, The Honorable Mr. N.R. Mandela N.O. and Others, and Treatment Action Campaign (Amicus Curiae): Heads of Argument on Behalf of the Treatment Action Campaign." http://www.tac.org.za/Documents/MedicineActCourtCase/pharmace.txt.

———. 2000. "Introduction to the Christopher Moraka Defiance Campaign Against Patent Abuse and AIDS Profiteering by Drug Companies: Defy Trade Laws That Place Profits Before Health." http://www.tac.org.za/Documents/Defiance Campaign/defiancecampaign.htm.

Tushnet, Mark. 1984. "An Essay on Rights." *Texas Law Review* 62: 1363–1403.

Waldron, Jeremy, ed. *Theories of Rights.* Oxford: Oxford University Press.

Wickeri, Elizabeth. 2004. *Grootboom's Legacy: Securing the Right to Access to Adequate Housing in South Africa?* Center for Human Rights and Global Justice Working Paper: Economic, Social and Cultural Rights Series, no. 5, New York University School of Law. http://www.chrgj.org/publications/docs/wp/Wickeri%20 Grootboom%27s%20Legacy.pdf.

Wilson, S. 2004. "Taming the Constitution: Rights and Reform in South African Education System." *South African Journal on Human Rights* 20: 418–47.

LEGAL REFERENCES

Afrox Health Care (Pty) Ltd. v. Strydom, 2002 (6) SA 21 (SCA).

City of Cape Town v. Neville Rudolph and Others, 2003 (11) BCLR 1236 (C).

City of Cape Town v. Various Occupiers of the Road Reserve of Applicant Parallel to Sheffield Road, Phillipi, 2003. Unreported judgment delivered 30 September, 2003, Case no. A 5/2003.

Government of the Republic of South Africa and Others v. Irene Grootboom and Others, CCT11/00, 2000(1) SA 46. http://www.constitutional.org.7a/Archimages/2798 .pdf.

Khosa and Others v. Minister of Social Development, CCT 12/03.

Minister of Health and Others v. Treatment Action Campaign and Others (No. 2) CCT 9/02 (18 April 2002).

Minister of Public Works v. Kyalami Ridge Ratepayer's Association, 2001 (3) SA 1151 (CC).

Modderklip Boerdery (Pty) Ltd. v. Modder East Squatters and Another, 2003 (4) SA 385 (W).

Ngxuza and Others v. Permanent Secretary, Department of Welfare, Eastern Cape, and Another, 2001 (2) SA 609 (E).

Speaker of the National Assembly v. De Lille and Another, SCA 297/98.

Thiagraj Soobramoney v. Minister of Health (KwaZulu Natal). Case CCT 32/97, 27 November 1997. http://www.law-lib.utoronto.ca/diana/TAC_case_study/Soobra money.pdf.

PART III

The Rule of Law

The Pasts and Future of the Rule of Law in South Africa

David Dyzenhaus

In 1996, the constitution of the Republic of South Africa marked the beginning of a new era in South African law (sec. 1(c)). It lists among the founding values of the new republic the "supremacy of the constitution and the rule of law" and, while it entrenches standard liberal rights and freedoms, it also goes well beyond. For example, it gives a right to fair labor practices, to an environment that is not harmful to health, to adequate housing, and to just administrative action (secs. 23(1), 24(a), 26(1), 33(1)).

The sections that entrench socioeconomic rights—for example, the right to adequate housing—do make it clear that the state's duty to fulfill the right is subject to the availability of adequate resources. But it seems clear that the state is obliged to take action, and with some rights—for example, the right to just administrative action—the state was put under an explicit duty to enact national legislation giving effect to that right. The constitution does permit the state to justify limitations of entrenched rights by showing that the limitations are "reasonable and justifiable in an open and democratic society" (sec. 36). But at the same time it sets out a proportionality test for deciding whether a limitation is justified, thus making it clear that judges have the final word on the constitutionality of legislation.

Writing in 2000, Heinz Klug drew attention to how surprising this constitutional turn was in the African postcolonial era—the embrace of judicial review in place of the customary postcolonial grant in Africa to government of "nearly untrammeled legislative authority." He also commented that what he perceived to be the success of South Africa's constitutional project had been "reinforced" by the "judicious politics" of the Constitutional Court—

the apex of the judiciary on constitutional matters. That Court, Klug concluded, had "repeatedly asserted its right to decide central questions of governance, while simultaneously limiting its role to a clearly specified judicial function which pays open respect and deference to the new democratic institutions and politics" (Klug 2000, 178). In this essay, I discuss Klug's conclusion through an inquiry into the constitutional principle of legality. My discussion in general supports his conclusion. But it also indicates some troubling trends on the part of government.

Klug correctly emphasizes that the success of constitutionalism in a postcolonial setting must depend on the judicious politics of the courts in establishing their democratic legitimacy; in other words, it depends on a sense of the project of constitutionalism as primarily about cooperation and collaboration rather than confrontation. But, as they say, it takes two to tango. While the Constitutional Court has continued to play that role, it is not so clear that the government is willing to continue the dance. I indicate in my conclusion that the tensions exposed in this account of the politics of the rule of law in South Africa are not confined to the particular context of a government and a judiciary seeking to manage a transition from an authoritarian past to a democratic future. They illuminate quite general questions about the nature and worth of the rule of law.

THE PRINCIPLE OF LEGALITY

The commitment in new-order South Africa to the supremacy of the constitution and the rule of law does not, in itself, mark a departure from the past. The apartheid legal order implemented a racist ideology through law but formally was no less committed than the new order to both the supremacy of the constitution and the rule of law. If one ignored the ideology and focused on the formal features of the apartheid legal order, it replicated the constitutional structure of the British legal order (Corder 1984; Forsyth 1985).

Apartheid South Africa had a Parliament elected by the enfranchised part of the population—adult whites. The politicians from the political party with the majority of seats formed the government and governed only as long—more than forty years!—as they enjoyed the confidence of the majority of parliamentarians. All government or executive action required a warrant in law.[1] An independent judiciary had the task of interpreting the law and so could determine when government officials were acting within the scope of the authority delegated by the legislature, but did not have the authority to invalidate statutes.[2] In sum, if the rule of law exists when the principle of legality is observed, not only did the apartheid legal order acknowledge the supremacy of the constitution, but by virtue of the kind of constitution it acknowledged—one based on the principle of legality—it also established the rule of law.

The fact that law was used as an instrument of apartheid ideology could then simply show that the principle of legality or the rule of law is by itself morally insignificant. What matters is the content of the law—the nature of the ideology of which the law is the instrument. It would follow that the explicit commitment in the constitution to the supremacy of the constitution and the rule of law is not what marks the difference from the apartheid era, since such a commitment is merely formal, requiring that any exercise of public power be authorized by law. Rather, what marks the difference is the fact that the constitution also guarantees a list of rights and liberties and utterly rejects the discriminatory ideology of the previous order.

However, an inquiry into the rule of law in South Africa since 1996 is productive because of reasons that relate to the apartheid past of the rule of law, to its present state, and to its future.

In regard to the past, it mattered a great deal during apartheid that there were lawyers and judges who did not accept that the principle of legality imposes requirements of form alone. Lawyers who mounted challenges to government oppression through law often argued before the courts that the judiciary should read statutes in the light of common-law presumptions protective of the individual interest in liberty and the equality of those subject to the law. On this view, only to the extent that a statute explicitly requires that these interests are not to be protected by the statute should judges countenance that the legislature intended to subvert rather than serve the interest of all those subject to the law in liberty and equality. The idea is that the commitment of the legal order to the supremacy of the constitution and to the principle of legality includes constitutional commitments to protecting these interests, expressed in a common-law legal order in principles developed by judges. Should officials implement statutes in ways that violate these commitments—if they violate, that is, the common-law principle of legality—judges should find that the officials acted outside the scope of their legal authority. Thus in issue during apartheid was whether the legal order was committed to a substantive or merely formal conception of legality or the rule of law.

The substantive conception was accepted by only a small minority of a bench that was all white until just before the formal end of apartheid, and from the end of the 1950s the National Party government ensured that the Appellate Division, South Africa's highest court, was for the most part stocked with judges who subscribed to a formal conception of legality. In their view, the only limits on any legislative delegation of authority to an official were the limits explicitly stated in the statute, plus some formally understood and very limited grounds of review of decisions: bad faith, bias, and utter irrationality.[3] So on almost all of the few occasions when lower court judges decided a matter on the basis of the substantive conception, one could predict that the Appellate Division would overrule them.[4] Moreover, it was just as predictable that the government would almost always use its power in Parliament to override any politically inconvenient judgment and would also ensure that its statutes in the future made it explicit that Parliament's intention was that such implicit limits did not apply. Nevertheless, the efforts of this minority of lawyers and judges are generally thought to have supported a sense within the leadership of the African National Congress (ANC) and other groups committed to ending apartheid that the substantive rule of law is an ideal to which legal orders should generally aspire.

In addition, one should not underestimate the importance of the guarantees provided by the formal conception of legality. That most South African lawyers and judges subscribed during apartheid to the formal conception, and that the government officially subscribed to that same conception, meant that the courts would come to the aid of those able to mount a challenge to official exercises of power when these clearly fell outside the scope of the authority delegated by the relevant statute. Indeed, one study of the Appellate Division concludes that the court decided in favor of challenges to the government in more or less the same ratio as apex courts in other jurisdictions (Haynie 2003).[5] In sum, no illegal act of a public official could be rendered legal by executive fiat. Thus, the apartheid state was not the "Prerogative State," as Ernst Fraenkel termed the Nazi state in which officials had the authority to displace legal controls whenever they thought this appropriate (Fraenkel 1941).

However, a legal order that maintains only the formal conception can undermine its commitment to legality. Consider that decisions in the early 1960s by the Appellate Division signaled to the officials of the apartheid state that as long as they had a bare formal warrant in law for their decisions in important areas of government policy, including security, the courts would not generally act to control them. As I have argued elsewhere, those decisions allowed the government to have its cake and eat it too. Because the courts were ready to equate the rule *of* law with rule *by* law, the government could have statutes enacted that gave its officials authority to act in a legally uncontrolled fashion at the same time as the courts endorsed the officials' actions as in accordance with the rule of law (Dyzenhaus 1991).[6] In other words, pockets of the prerogative state can emerge within the law if courts subscribe to the formal conception alone and the legislature does not impose explicit rule of law controls on public officials, or even indicates, more or less explicitly, that it does not intend such controls to apply. The officials have formal authority to act as they do, so do not, as in the prerogative state, have the power simply to sidestep the law when its controls seems inconvenient. But the authority they wield seems so barely limited that within their mandate they seem virtually uncontrolled.

Nevertheless, as long as the formal conception is maintained, officials can be called to account when it can be shown that they have acted illegally, even on the rather bare understanding of legality espoused by the formal conception. If judges do not uphold the law, on any conception of the rule of law, and if public officials do not regard it as their duty to implement the law, the very existence of legal order is in doubt. In addition, the existence of the formal conception always contains the promise of the substantive conception. It gives lawyers and judges minded to do so a toehold for working up the substantive conception, until the point where the judges are overruled by higher courts or overridden by statute.

It might still seem that the rule of law has no independent role to play in legal discourse after a constitution such as South Africa's is entrenched, since the rights and liberties guaranteed by the constitution include not only all the substantive content of the rule of law but much more besides. However, the rule of law has remained an important and controversial topic within South Africa's constitutional jurisprudence, and debate about its details is likely, if anything, to become even more contentious, as I indicate in a brief epilogue.

As I will now show, a commitment to the substantive conception of the rule of law cannot settle contention about the rule of law, since the content of that commitment remains controversial. But the problems that attend the rule of law in South Africa go well beyond this kind of controversy. Indeed, they pertain to the maintenance of the rule of law, on any conception.

LITIGATING THE RULE OF LAW: *MINISTER OF HEALTH V. NEW CLICKS SOUTH AFRICA (PTY) LTD.*

The Constitutional Court of South Africa was established because the parties to the constitutional negotiations concluded that it was necessary to have a specialized court dedicated to transforming the law of the land in accordance with the values entrenched in the new constitutions, initially the interim constitution and then the final constitution (Spitz and Chaskalson 2000). The parties had agreed that the old-order judges would keep their jobs in the new order. However, judges who for the most part had been complicit not only in implementing apartheid law but also in facilitating its implementation by their allegiance to a merely formal conception of the rule of law were not considered fit to undertake the transformative task. In addition, if the court charged with transformation had been staffed by judges drawn from the almost exclusively male, white bench of the old order, no matter the rule-of-law credentials of each judge, the court would have enjoyed little legitimacy. Finally, the issue was not merely that the Constitutional Court had to aspire to representing South Africa as a whole. It was also considered important to have people on the bench whose personal experience gave them an understanding of what transformation involved which would not readily be available to judges entrenched in the thought-ways of the past.[7]

The question then arose about how to allocate jurisdiction. The interim constitution answered that question by depriving the Supreme Court of Appeal, the successor to the Appellate Division, of jurisdiction to hear constitutional challenges. Nonetheless, the Supreme Court of Appeal retained its status as the final court of appeal on all the matters on which it had previously decided. And that raised the question whether it was the final court of appeal on challenges to the validity of government decisions on the basis that they did not accord with the common-law principle of legality. So the possibility existed of the South African legal order's having two systems of constitutional law: on the one hand, the unwritten constitution, presided over by the Supreme Court of Appeal, which covered challenges to government officials for noncompliance with common-law principles of judicial review and, on the other, the written constitution, presided over by the Constitutional Court. That possibility was politically fraught, as litigants could attempt to forum shop and the Supreme Court of Appeal could abet this attempt by casting challenges to government officials in a common-law mould. In fact, in a series of cases, the Supreme Court of Appeal attempted to preserve its jurisdiction as the final court of appeal on matters to do with the common-law principle of legality, until the Constitutional Court put an end to what was shaping up as an ugly turf war in *Pharmaceutical Manufacturers* (2000). There, in direct response to the jurisprudence of the Supreme Court of Appeal, it stated that:

There are not two systems of law, each dealing with the same subject matter, each having similar requirements, each operating in its own field with its own highest court. There is only one system of law. It is shaped by the Constitution which is the supreme law, and all law, including the common law, derives its force from the Constitution and is subject to constitutional control. (*Pharmaceutical Manufacturers*, 2000, para. 44)

This decision ensured that the Constitutional Court, not the Supreme Court of Appeal, was the final court of appeal on any matter to do with the legal control of public power. But it also seemed to assert that the common-law principle of legality has no independent role to play in the South African legal order. The content of legality has the written constitution as its source, which means the constitution as it is definitively interpreted by the judges of the Constitutional Court, judges who have been appointed because they are keenly aware of their transformative role and supposedly best suited to ensure that that role is carried out.[8]

Under the final constitution, the Supreme Court of Appeal has a wide jurisdiction to hear constitutional matters.[9] In addition, it is now the case that the majority of its members are new-order judges, by which I mean that their first appointment to the bench was during the new order. But tensions about jurisdiction and conceptions of the rule of law continue, not only because the question of the content of the rule of law is controversial, but also because in South Africa that controversy is inevitably affected by the politics of transformation. My discussion of this point relies on just one case, but, as we will see, it acted as a kind of lightning rod for tensions that show little sign of abating in the new South Africa.[10]

The litigation in the matter I will refer to as *New Clicks* arose out of amendments to the Medicines Act of 1965, a statute that had been enacted to achieve quality control of the supply of medicines to the South African public. In 1997, the ANC government introduced new measures into the act, directed toward making medicines more affordable. After a troubled history of governmental bungling, the measures came into force in May 2003, through a proclamation following the Medicines and Related Substances Amendment Act, no. 59 of 2002. The measures, and their place within the statute, were not, as the Constitutional Court was to point out, carefully designed (*Minister of Health v. New Clicks South Africa (Pty) Ltd.*, 2006, para. 2; hereafter *New Clicks* CC).

In 2004, retail pharmacies—the stakeholders in the pharmaceutical industry affected by the legislation—mounted a challenge to the regulations made to give effect to the pricing system established by the act. These regulations were made by the minister of health on the recommendation of the Pricing Committee, itself established by the act. The stakeholders challenged the functioning of the Pricing Committee, its procedures, and the substance of the regulations promulgated by the minister on the Pricing Committee's recommendation. The core of their argument was the claim that fees prescribed for dispensing medicines would require pharmacies to run at a loss, thus threatening the viability of the dispensing profession. Indeed, claims were made that pharmacies were being forced to close because of the dispensing fee set by the government.[11] The matter was thus treated as a matter of urgency by all the parties and by the Cape High Court.

In early June, the stakeholders were granted interim relief, which suspended the operation of the regulations pending a final determination. Later in June, the matter was heard by a panel of three judges, which included the judge president, Judge Hlophe, who joined in the judgment of Judge Yekiso dismissing the challenge, and reinstating the regulations. Judge Traverso dissented (*New Clicks South Africa [Pty] Ltd. v. Tshabalala-Msimang*, 2005; hereafter *New Clicks* Cape).

The stakeholders immediately sought leave to appeal against the order of the Cape High Court, and on 20 September 2004 argument was heard. The Cape High Court reserved judgment instead of making, in accordance with practice, an immediate order. In October the stakeholders wrote to the registrar of the court asking when Judge Hlophe, who had indicated at the hearing that he would hand down the judgment, might give his ruling. They received no reply. By November they had become frustrated by the apparent unwillingness of the Cape High Court to give its judgment on their application for leave, and they decided to apply directly to the Supreme Court of Appeal for leave to appeal. They tried first to meet with Hlophe to explain their reasons, but he was, for what the Court called "unknown reasons," unable to meet them (*Pharmaceutical Society of South Africa v. Tshabalala-Msimang*, 2005, para. 5; hereafter *New Clicks* SCA). They then applied to the Supreme Court of Appeal and the next day were informed by Hlophe that he was finalizing his reasons, but he gave no indication of when he would deliver the judgment, or any explanation of the delay. The Court agreed to hear the matter and set it down for argument on 30 November and 1 December. On 29 November, Hlophe announced that he would deliver judgment on 3 December, which he did. He refused leave to appeal, a judgment in which he was joined by Judge Yekiso, with Judge Traverso again dissenting (*Phar-

maceutical Society of South Africa v. Tshabalala-Msimang, 2005; hereafter *New Clicks* leave to appeal).

It was clear that the government's lawyers thought that if any appeal against the Cape High Court's decision was to be heard it should be heard directly by the Constitutional Court, as the matter was urgent and the case turned on constitutional issues that would be determined ultimately by the Constitutional Court, whatever the Supreme Court of Appeal's decision. Indeed, they had urged the stakeholders to avoid asking for leave to appeal to the Supreme Court of Appeal and instead to go directly to the Constitutional Court with the government's support, a route that did not require applying to the Cape High Court for leave to appeal.[12] It was also clear that they thought that their case would be best heard in the Constitutional Court, not the Supreme Court of Appeal, and Judge Hlophe expressed a similar view in his judgment refusing leave to appeal (*New Clicks* leave to appeal, 236).[13] Finally, Hlophe was obviously offended that the applicants had approached the Supreme Court of Appeal with a view to finding out the availability of hearing dates.[14]

The government's lawyers contended that the Supreme Court of Appeal had no jurisdiction to hear the appeal as the Cape High Court had not yet given its decision. But the Supreme Court of Appeal directed that the question of jurisdiction and the merits be dealt with at one hearing. At the hearing itself, following their minister's instructions, the government's lawyers declined the Supreme Court of Appeal's requests to address the merits; indeed, they declined an invitation to postpone the hearing so that they could have time to prepare argument on this issue, essentially the same argument they had made in June to the Cape High Court.

Judge of Appeals Harms, who gave judgment for a five-judge panel, held that the Cape High Court had constructively refused leave to appeal, that it was in the interests of justice to hear argument as to the merits as well as the other issues at one hearing, and that the regulations were invalid (*New Clicks* SCA). He chastised the government lawyers in strong terms for their lack of respect for the Supreme Court of Appeal, and he accused Hlophe of undermining the rule of law through his dilatory stance (*New Clicks* SCA, paras. 12–14, 39). He also seemed offended by the belief, which he perceived to be shared by the government lawyers and Hlophe, that the Supreme Court of Appeal was not the appropriate forum to decide constitutional claims (*New Clicks* SCA, para. 10).

The Constitutional Court heard the appeal on 15–16 March 2005. It took until 30 September 2005—an unusually long period of time—to deliver judgment, and its judgment of 241 pages is unusually long by its own standards, as well as compared to the length of the Supreme Court of Appeal's judgment of thirty pages. While the eleven-judge panel of the Constitutional Court differed both in the details of how it reached its particular conclusions and in regard to the particular conclusions, it upheld the Supreme Court of Appeal's jurisdiction to hear the matter and its decision to hear argument on the merits of the appeal, even though the Supreme Court of Appeal had not heard argument from the government's lawyers on this issue. In various combinations, the Constitutional Court upheld several of the stakeholders' challenges, dismissed others, or found that it could cure defects in the regulations by reading phrases in or out. In addition, Chief Justice Chaskalson expressed his displeasure with the attitude of the government lawyers and the minister to the Supreme Court of Appeal (*New Clicks* CC, para. 82), though no judge of the Constitutional Court ventured to comment directly on the dispute between the Supreme Court of Appeal and the Cape High Court.

RACE, JURISDICTION, AND TRANSFORMATION

Well before the matter reached the Constitutional Court, it had become politically charged. For example, Zachie Achmat of the Treatment Action Campaign, a leading AIDS activist, commented that the case was a "test. . . . If the constitutional court backs off and supports Judge Hlophe on process, they are killing off the SCA; if they support him on substance, the government can do what it likes." Another "senior legal source" said, "this is a watershed divide between executive-minded judges and the rest" (Dawes 2004a). In addition, a rumor that Hlophe and not Yekiso had written the majority judgment of the Cape High Court surfaced at one point. Hlophe concluded the hearing on leave to appeal with a warning to those who were spreading the rumor. He went on to complain in interviews about "a calculated attempt to undermine the intellect and talent of African [black] judges," and there was speculation that he thought that Judge Traverso, the only white judge of the three, was the source of the rumor.[15] Hlophe reacted publicly, claiming that such rumors were proof of white resistance to transformation of the judiciary.[16]

Thus, Chief Justice Chaskalson felt compelled to comment in his judgment (the last he gave) that, because the case pitted industry against government policy, it had come to be seen as a "test of [the court's] independence, implying that if it finds against the government it will be independent, but not if it finds for it".[17] Chaskalson immediately rejected this impression, saying that the case was not "about the wisdom of public policy" (*New Clicks* CC, para. 32). All the courts had to do was assess on the basis of detailed legal submissions "whether the regulations [had] been made in accordance with the requirements of the Constitution and the law." There was, he said, "nothing unusual about this. Our courts have frequently been called on to deal with similar questions in the past and will no doubt be called upon to do so in the future. This is the role of courts in a democracy" (*New Clicks* CC, para. 33).

Chaskalson claim that the Court is doing law, not politics, is a standard judicial trope when judges are forced into the political arena. But it does not follow that his or the other judges' reasoning simply masks a political stance. While the politics of the rule of law in the postapartheid era are affected by the politics of race and of the transition, the issues remain distinctly legal. At stake is the issue of what the "similar" and thus normalizing or legitimating "past," to which Chaskalson refers, is. Is it the immediate past of the postapartheid constitutional jurisprudence of the Constitutional Court or the past—more accurately the different pasts—of legality during the apartheid era?

Two distinctions play an important role in the political context of this and other cases in which government policy is challenged. The first is between old- and new-order judges, between the judges who had been appointed during the apartheid era and who remained in office after 1994 and the judges who were appointed after that date by Presidents Mandela and Mbeki, on the advice of the Judicial Service Commission.[18] The second distinction, a delicate one to discuss, not least because it relies on the racist categories of the past, is between white judges and all others, either black South Africans or South Africans of Indian or mixed descent. The old-order judges were, as I have indicated, almost all white and male. In the new era, the government has been determined to transform the judiciary by appointing judges who are black or from other racial groups than white, and also by appointing female judges.

The two distinctions do not map neatly onto each other since new-order judges include both female and male whites. But race affects perception of allegiance. For example, the fact that the sole dissenting judge in the Cape High Court was the only white judge on the panel meant that she, despite being both new order and female, could be perceived as "untransformed" by those who regard any decision against the government as evidence of the grip on power of an old-order judiciary determined to frustrate progressive change.[19]

Of the five-judge panel in the Supreme Court of Appeal, two of the judges were new order. One of these is black, the other of mixed race: respectively, Judge Mthiyane, appointed to the bench in 1997 and to the Supreme Court of Appeal in 2001, and Judge Navsa, appointed to the bench in 1995 and to the Supreme Court of Appeal in 2000. Of the white judges, Judge Harms, who gave the judgment of the court, is an old-order judge, having been appointed to the bench in 1986 and to the Supreme Court of Appeal in 1993. While Judge Cloete (1991) and Judge Brand (1992) were appointed to the bench in the last years of the old order, they were appointed to the Court during the new order: Brand in 2001 and Cloete in 2003. However, the fact that the panel was dominated by whites and led by an old-order judge could give rise to a perception that the decision was one of a court still rooted in the old order. In contrast, of the eleven judges of the Constitutional Court who decided the matter, only four are white and all are new-order judges.

Not only are such perceptions common in South Africa,[20] but in this matter they could latch on to what seem to be clear differences between the jurisprudential approach of the Supreme Court of Appeal and the Constitutional Court, as well as within the Constitutional Court itself. To some extent, these differences are reflected in the mere fact of the difference in length of the judgments. While the length of the Constitutional Court's judgment is partly the product of the fact that all eleven judges had something to say, while the Supreme Court of Appeal's judgment was given by Harms alone, it is noteworthy that Chaskalson judgment is ninety-three pages to Harms's thirty, and that of the thirty pages Harms devoted only seventeen to the merits, the rest being taken up with the dispute between the Supreme Court of Appeal, the government lawyers, and the Cape High Court.

Of course, it is the case that Harms was responding to the urgency of the matter, so wrote and delivered his judgment in around three weeks. It is also the case that the extreme length of the Constitutional Court's judgments makes them difficult to follow, indeed probably impossible for any lay person, and the delay in issuing its judgment meant that almost seventeen months had elapsed in all from the time of the first hearing before the Constitutional Court to the time of final judgment. Nevertheless, as the legal columnist of the *Mail and Guardian,* "Serjeant at the Bar" (2005), commented, "the final product of the court does serve as a partial mitigation for this delay."

For when it came to the merits, Harms had little to say about the relationship between constitutionalism and the rule of law and chose to bypass altogether a question that had occupied the Cape High Court and was to occupy the Constitutional Court: whether the Promotion of Administrative Justice Act 2 of 2000 (PAJA) governed the regulations made by the Pricing Committee. PAJA had been enacted in order to comply with section 33 of the constitution, which entrenched the right to administrative action that is "lawful, reasonable and procedurally fair," but also required that within three years legislation be enacted to give concrete expression to that right (Currie 2006). Harms said that he did not have to deal with the question of whether PAJA applied because all agreed that the regulations had to "withstand the test of legality" and it was "unlikely that this Act, written in light of the Constitution and supposedly written to codify administrative justice principles, reduced the level of administrative justice" (*New Clicks* SCA, para. 94).

It was by no means obvious that PAJA did apply to the making of regulations by an executive body, and the judges in the Constitutional Court divided on this issue: five judges, including Chaskalson, held that PAJA did apply,[21] five held that they did not have to determine this issue, while Sachs held that PAJA did not for the most part apply, but that the constitutional principle of legality governed.

Even though the outcome did not turn on whether PAJA was applicable, Harms's cursory treatment of the issue is symptomatic of a general lack of attention to the nuances of the legal situation that confronted the courts. He did not deal at all with the question of the standard of review, that is, the content of legality, nor did he make much attempt to understand the Pricing Committee's work in the context of a complex administrative state into which it has been inserted in order to carry out a rather important mandate. Finally, he did not confront the question of whether the constitution makes a difference to judicial review, other than to make the following remark about the challenge to the dispensing fees, which the statute required to be "appropriate":

What is appropriate was not left to the discretion of the minister and also not to that of the committee. In this regard there is a clear break from the approach adopted in matters such as security legislation during the pre-Constitutional era. There, the jurisdictional fact was quite often the opinion of one or other functionary and, provided the functionary held the opinion, courts were rather hamstrung. Here the jurisdictional fact is not someone's opinion but an objective fact, namely a dispensing fee that must be "appropriate". Whether it is appropriate can be tested judicially. (*New Clicks* SCA, para. 75)

Harms's remark glosses over the fact that the courts of the apartheid era were partly responsible for hamstringing themselves.[22] While the apartheid government went out of its way to write statutes that would eviscerate review for legality, most of the judges were, as I have indicated, entirely on side with this process. Moreover, it is not clear why he should use as his contrast class security legislation, which is often regarded as exceptional, when in issue before him was an altogether "ordinary" legislative delegation of power.[23]

The irony is that in the new, constitutional era, Harms moves from the old-order formal view of legality to a view that is so substantive it looks as though he is applying a correctness standard. In his view, a "brief analysis of the evidence on record" showed "that there is no bona fide dispute of fact" (*New Clicks* SCA, para. 89). But the lengthy analyses of several of the judges of the Constitutional Court of the record show that there was at the very least a bona fide dispute and, in addition, that it was by no means as easy as Harms seemed to find it was to conclude that the entire regulatory scheme was not authorized by the statute.[24] So the claim that there was no bona fide dispute gives the unfortunate appearance, compounded by the language of "objective facts," that the judge was taking sides on correctness.

Thus, despite some perfunctory remarks disclaiming this role (*New Clicks* SCA, para. 41), Harms laid himself open to the charge of second-guessing the legislature and the executive as to the wisdom of policy.[25] His judgment is the exact converse in this respect of Yekiso's in the Cape High Court, since Yekiso spent most of his judgment on the issue of whether PAJA applied and then provided scanty reasons to support the government's arguments.[26]

In contrast, in the Constitutional Court, Chief Justice Chaskalson took great care to show that the constitutional standard for review was one of reasonableness, a more exacting standard than the one that prevailed during the apartheid era, even in ordinary administrative law, of utter irrationality. He reasoned that this new standard was supported by the general value commitments of the constitution and by PAJA, an enactment of the national legislature in fulfillment of those commitments. But at the same time he wanted to emphasize that the standard was reasonableness in the context of the statute, and so he was anxious, with the other Constitutional Court judges, to assist as far as possible the working of the regulatory scheme and the executive's understanding of the best way to implement it, and, in addition, to remit to the executive, insofar as this was possible, issues for it to work out in the light of problems detected by the Court. Both his and the other Constitutional Court judges' willingness to undertake this task and their effort to understand the positive role of the administrative state in a constitutional order are what account for the striking difference in length of the judgments (*New Clicks* CC, paras. 98–420).

In addition, the majority of the Constitutional Court was careful to avoid the appearance of correctness review. Both Chief Justice Chaskalson and Judge Ngcobo found that the Pricing Committee had not provided a sufficient answer to the pharmacies' claim that the dispensing fee would destroy the viability of the pharmacies and impair access to health care. Since the pharmacies had a sufficient body of evidence to show that this was a real possibility, the applicants were under an obligation to provide this information. As Chaskalson put it, "'Accountability, responsiveness and openness' on the part of government are foundational values of our Constitution" (*New Clicks* CC, para. 404). And Ngcobo, while he recognized that the Supreme Court of Appeal had a basis for determining that the fee was inappropriate, preferred to put his judgment on the basis that the record showed that the Pricing Committee had not properly applied its mind to the factors it was bound to consider.[27] Similarly, Judge Sachs commented that because the state

> was embarking upon an important new regulatory enterprise . . . the principle of accountability imposes on it a special responsibility in the particular circumstances to show that it has taken all reasonable steps to assess, take account of and justify the potential knock-on effects on the pharmacy profession of its new intervention. The more the risk, the greater the precaution. . . . In the long run the Ministry, the profession and the public will be better served by calculations that are manifestly reasonable, than by assertions that might or might not be true but lack convincing substantiation. (*New Clicks* CC, paras. 663–64)

In contrast, Judge Moseneke found that the dispensing fee was appropriate. He painstakingly went through the expert evidence on both sides in order to show that the pharmacies had failed to establish a conclusive case that the pricing regulations would lead to the closure of "most or many or some of the pharmacies" (*New Clicks* CC, para. 783). Given this, he found that the regulations were appropriate—they were

> lawful in as much as they are rationally connected to the admittedly legitimate purpose of rendering medicines and Scheduled substances affordable and accessible to the public. Finally, keeping in mind the reasonableness test articulated in *Bato Star,* I am unable to find that the decision of the Pricing Committee and of the Minister is one *that no reasonable person could have arrived at.* (*New Clicks* CC, para. 786, my emphasis)

However, if by the reasonableness test in *Bato Star* Moseneke meant the test he quoted from that decision earlier in his judgment (*New Clicks* CC, para. 725, quoting from para. 45 of *Bato Star Fishing (Pty) Ltd. v. Minister of Environmental Affairs,* 2004), this was not the test he applied in *New Clicks.* The Constitutional Court in *Bato Star* established a test whose application depends on the circumstances of the case. Judges would have to take into account a range of factors, including "the nature of the decision, the identity and expertise of the decision-maker, the range of factors relevant to the decision, the reasons given for the decision, the nature of the competing interests involved and the impact of the decision on the lives and well-being of those affected" (*New Clicks* CC, para. 43).

The point is not one about mere wording[28] but about how that wording is implemented, even though one should not underestimate the signal sent by the apparent citation of the irrationality test. What Moseneke neglects is the fact, emphasized by Chaskalson, as well as by Ngcobo and Sachs, that the Pricing Committee had not undertaken the task of demonstrating that its regulations were reasonable. Indeed, it would be fair to say that far from observing the requirement that judges should not second-guess the government when it comes to the wisdom of policy choices, he took on the job of doing the work the Pricing Committee had failed to do.

Tamar Kahn, the science and health editor of *Business Day,* called the judgment "truly Solomon-like, one that preserves the good in the disputed laws, while giving precise instructions to remedy the flaws" (2005),[29] while Pat Sidley, head of communications at the Council of Medical Schemes, said in the *Mail and Guardian* that the Constitutional Court "finally saw to it that a well-intentioned piece of law designed to help consumers would see the light of day" ("At Last, the Law Inscribed" 2005). In general, the judgment is viewed as having provided the impetus to get government and the pharmacies to negotiate in good faith a dispensing fee that would implement the objective of making medicine more affordable while sustaining the infrastructure necessary to deliver the medicine to the public.[30] However, had the majority of the Court found the dispensing fee appropriate, there would have been no such impetus. As "Serjeant at the Bar" commented, the "most important lesson to be drawn from this saga" lay in the "different levels of deference that certain of the judges revealed to the state" (2005).

I have pointed out the irony in Judge Harms's move from the formal conception of legality to a conception so substantive that his judgment might be thought to support fears that only the Constitutional Court would take seriously the transformative aim of the Pricing Committee within the new, transformed legal order. In a context still charged with the politics of race and transformation, it was inevitable that his judgment would be perceived as a double "klap" (the Afrikaans, more onomatopoeic, word for a slap) to both a black judge below and a black government, and could thus be perceived as a vindication of the government lawyers' determination to cut the Supreme Court of Appeal out of the constitutional loop.

But at the same time, the Cape High Court's stance, especially its efforts to prevent any appeal to the Supreme Court of Appeal, presented not an appearance but the reality of a future in which the promise of the constitution to guarantee the supremacy of law and the rule of law would begin to look rather empty (J. Lewis 2005, 127). Indeed, had the Constitutional Court upheld the Cape High Court's judgment on the merits and had it refrained from endorsing the Supreme Court of Appeal's stance on procedure, there would have been, as Achmat warned, some reason to believe that South Africa was on the path to becoming, despite the constitution, a prerogative state, though one disguised by a veneer of legality.[31]

Yet there is also an irony in Chaskalson's judgment. Unlike Harms, he does not assert a radical discontinuity between the present and the past of a "pre-Constitutional era." Indeed, to find that PAJA required a reasonableness standard, he had to deal with the fact that PAJA seemed to stipulate exactly the standard of review—irrationality—that Chaskalson thought characterized the old era (*New Clicks* CC, paras. 186 and 187, relying on *Bato Star Fishing (Pty) Ltd. v. Minister of Environmental Affairs,* at paras. 44–45).[32] He thus had to read what looked like a legislative interpretation of the standard of review contemplated by section 33 of the constitution not literally but in the light of section 33 and of the general structure of the constitution. In addition, not only could the legislature be interpreted as having attempted to reduce the content of legality suggested by section 33 but, on a literal interpretation, its definition of reviewable administrative action left out much of what the administrative state does. Indeed, so much was left out that if it followed that what was left out was not susceptible to control by the principle of legality, PAJA itself would be vulnerable to challenge on constitutional grounds. Such a challenge would be embarrassing for the Constitutional Court, as it would be forced to face concluding that the government had sought by statute to reduce the control of the rule of law over its actions to the point where it had violated its constitutional commitments.[33]

Chaskalson's strategy avoids the path that leads to this conclusion by bringing rule- or regulation-making within the scope of PAJA and by reinterpreting the standard of review stipulated by PAJA. In doing so, he harked back to a different past—the past of the small minority of South African judges who, during the apartheid era, tried their utmost to interpret statutes as if they were intended to comply with constitutional commitments to a substantive conception of the rule of law. But at the same time, in seeking to support rather than thwart the regulatory scheme, he invoked the more recent past of his court's interpretation of both the interim and final constitutions—a past that differs from that of the apartheid era, since judges in the new order have an authentic basis for assuming that the national legislature and government are involved in an effort to realize their constitutional commitments to the rule of law.

However, it is important to know that Moseneke is thought to be the chief justice in waiting and that Madala, Mokgoro, Skeweyiya, and Yacoob concurred in his judgment. That is, the majority of six judges who concurred that the dispensing fee was inappropriate included *all* the white judges of the court as well as two black judges, Ngcobo and Langa. In addition, as discussed in the next two sections, serious concerns have arisen about the government's commitment to the rule of law, on any conception of that rule. And, as I will indicate, such concerns will be addressed appropriately only if the judiciary remains both fiercely independent and anxiously vigilant. These sections will show that there are threats to the authenticity of the assumption that all the institutions of government are involved in a cooperative project of maintaining the rule of law. Judges might at some point have to engage more in the politics of the klap instead of the politics of deference when it looks like government or even parts of the judiciary no longer subscribe to that assumption.

GLEICHSCHALTUNG OR TRANSFORMATION?

Gleichschaltung was the word used in Germany after 1933 to describe the process of bringing into gear or synchrony all organs of state so as to ensure an efficient machine for the unchecked implementation of the regime's policy. While any such analogy is deeply provocative, it seems clear that transformation risks becoming like *Gleichschaltung* in the face of both deep resentments about persisting white privilege and the government's tendency "to play the race card" by equating any opposition to its power and policies as yet another attempt to reassert such privilege. Indeed, the government seems prepared to use its control over legislation—indeed, sometimes over the constitution, since it, until the most recent election, commanded the numbers to amend the constitution—to ride roughshod over institutional checks.

A troubling example in the context of this essay arose out of the 2005 annual conference of the ANC, shortly after the Supreme Court of Appeal gave its judgment in *New Clicks*. On 8 January 2005, the National Executive Committee of the ANC spoke to the issue of transformation of the judiciary, saying that while much had been done, it was still "confronted by the . . . important challenge to transform the collective mindset of the judiciary to bring it into consonance with the vision and aspirations of the millions who engaged in struggle to liberate our country from white minority domination." The statement went on:

> The reality can no longer be avoided that many within our judiciary do not see themselves as being part of the masses, accountable to them, and inspired by their hopes, dreams and value systems. If this persists for too long, it will inevitably result in popular antagonism towards the judiciary and our courts, with serious and negative consequences for our democratic system as a whole.[34]

While the target of these remarks is wider than the Supreme Court of Appeal's judgment, there is no doubt that the judgment played a role in prompting them.[35] The ANC responded to adverse comment on its statement by claiming that the remarks were neither a "threat" to judges nor an "'attack' on white judges"; rather, the statement amounted to an "honest assessment of the state of transformation within the judiciary."

The minister of justice subsequently put forward legislation that would give the government control over the administration of justice, a control some thought could include deciding which judges should sit on particular panels. In addition, she proposed amending the constitution to remove potential obstacles to a constitutional challenge to such a system of control of the judiciary, and to deprive judges of the authority to suspend legislation found to be in violation of the constitution. Finally, she proposed legislation to take away from the Judicial Service Commission the authority to appoint judges president and their deputies and to give that authority to the president; to make the Constitutional Court the final court of appeal on all matters; to improve judicial education; and to make judges accountable through an improved disciplinary system.

Among this rather mixed bag of measures, several are no doubt badly needed. For example, Judge Hlophe has been in the news again because it transpired that he was accepting payments from an asset management group at the same time that he was involved in deciding an application by that group to sue one of his fellow judges for defamation ("DA Calls for Hlophe Probe" 2007).[36] In addition, the Supreme Court of Appeal has made it clear in a number of judgments that some of the decisions of the lower courts that it is reversing are not only wrong but incompetent, a fact that led fifteen black judges to complain to the Judicial Service Commission about the fact that it had discussed these judgments—their fear being that such discussion could hamper further promotion (Rickard 2007).[37]

Moreover, there is a sense among senior South African judges that it is now time to move toward establishing one apex court for South Africa on all matters (C. Lewis 2005), a move that might do much to remove the jurisdictional politics that still attends the relationship between the Supreme Court of Appeal and the Constitutional Court, but which would also require that the Judicial Service Commission and the president transform their understanding of transformation. An apex court that is the final court of appeal on all matters is a generalist court that has to be staffed by judges who have a deeper experience of the practice of law than many of the appointees to the Constitutional Court.

However, the bills were put forward without any process of prior consultation with lawyers or the judiciary. While initially the government seemed determined to rush these proposals through Parliament, a storm of protest from the judiciary (which included threats of judicial resignations), from lawyers, from opposition parties, as well as from the International Bar Association led to a government decision to allow time for more debate, even though President Thabo Mbeki expressed his puzzlement that there could be such opposition (Moya 2006; Temkin 2006).

The minister of justice indicated in April 2005 that she was willing to engage in discussions with the judiciary, and in October 2005 it was reported that the government had decided to shelve the package of bills, apart from the bill dealing with the administration of the courts ("Judicial Bills on Hold" 2005). However, on 14 December 2005, the bill amending the constitution and the bill dealing with court administration were gazetted with much of the content that had previously come under fire, with a deadline of 15 January 2006 for public comment. When it was suggested that the timing during the Christmas holiday break was intentional, the Department of Justice responded that it was "really just a coincidence" ("Publication of Judges' Bill" 2006).

A second public outcry about the short period given for consultation led to a three-month extension, during which time the general council of the bar of South Africa held a conference, attended by several senior judges, including Chaskalson (the now retired chief justice) and Langa (the present chief justice), at which both the substance of the proposed legislation and the government's attempts to shield it from expert comment were severely criticized. Chaskalson, for example, said that the "[e]volving process of judicial independence essential to a constitutional state, has been stopped and reversed, and a great deal of control has now been placed in the hands of the Minister" (Chaskalson 2006, 33). He went on:

> It is the early incursions into checks and balances which have historically been shown to open the way for later incursions to be made. Nobody knows what the future holds for us, but once you accept you can eat into protections which are there, and that you can erode fundamental principles of the Constitution, sometime, somebody else can take it further. So any attempt to do so, no matter how small, is open to objection. (ibid., 33–34)

Both he and Langa emphasized that the bills had nothing to do with transformation (ibid., 33; Langa 2006, 65).

Subsequently, the government has put forward bills on judicial education and training that appear to be far more acceptable to the judiciary and the profession, and seems to have shelved the bills discussed at the conference (Hartley 2007). But the fact that the government did appear to be so determined to chip away at the independence of the judiciary and to weaken the constitutional safeguards of all South Africans, and moreover to do so in a fashion calculated to avoid public deliberation, does not bode well for the future of the rule of law in South Africa. I now turn to a discussion of an even more dismal situation.

FAILURE TO IMPLEMENT THE LAW

In *Ngxusa v. Permanent Secretary* (2001), Judge Froneman wrote:

> Prior to 1994 the South Africa Act of 1909 in effect created a bifurcated State whereby the white minority was governed by a system of parliamentary democracy whilst the majority of black South Africans were subject to administrative rule. . . . The fact that our Constitution now explicitly provides the foundation and means for the Courts to act as instruments of democracy is no reason for complacency. Some social theorists argue that the bifurcated State bequeathed to post-independent Africa by colonialism and apartheid is alive and well in post-colonial form, thereby presenting a real threat to the future democracy in Africa. . . . This case is an illustration of the dangers associated with unaccountable administrative rule. (621)

The case that led to this comment arose out of some examples of the comprehensive failure of the Eastern Cape provincial administration to deal with its mandate to provide social assistance to indigent people within its jurisdiction. In *Vumazonke v. MEC For Social Development* (2005), a matter decided four years later, Judge Plasket had to decide similar instances in which individuals had not received responses to their applications for social assistance. He noted that in one week in 2004 he had had to deal with 102 matters in which applicants made more or less the same claim in social assistance cases against the Eastern Cape provincial government; that is, they had asked the court to order the government to make decisions about their claims. In many of these cases the government not only failed to make decisions within its own prescribed period of three months but had refused to respond to the applicants' own inquiries and, when they resorted to legal assistance, to their lawyers.

Plasket pointed out that this was not an unusual week for his court. This practice had persisted for several years, and judges had been commenting adversely on the performance of the government, without any response. Indeed, the government seemed far more ready to expend vast resources fighting the judicial orders against it to the level of the Supreme Court of Appeal than to devote any energy to internal reform (*Vumazonke v. MEC For Social Development,* 2005, paras. 1–2). Plasket summed up as follows:

Notwithstanding that literally thousands of orders have been made against the respondent's department over the past number of years, it appears to be willing to pay the costs of those applications rather than remedy the problem of maladministration and inefficiency that has been identified as the root cause of the problem. . . . [T]he courts are left with a problem that they cannot resolve: while they grant relief to the individuals who approach them for relief, they are forced to watch impotently while a dysfunctional and apparently unrepentant administration continues to abuse its power at the expense of large numbers of poor people. . . . What escalates what I have termed a problem into a crisis is that the cases that are brought to court represent only the tip of the iceberg. (*Vumazonke v. MEC For Social Development,* 2005, para. 10)

He went on: "The administration does not have a free hand to behave as it wishes. It is constrained by the Constitution and the law, and a network of constitutional institutions are created to ensure that it operates within the limits of the Constitution and the law" (*Vumazonke v. MEC For Social Development,* 2005, para. 11). Thus he not only granted the relief he thought appropriate, he also ordered that copies of his judgment be served on the premier of the Eastern Cape Province, the chairperson of the Social Development Standing Committee of the Eastern Cape provincial legislature, the minister of social development in the national government, the chairperson of the Human Rights Commission, and the chairperson of the Public Service Commission.

I said at the beginning of this essay that if public officials do not regard it as their duty to implement the law, the very existence of legal order is in doubt. The practice of the public officials of the Eastern Cape Province subverts not only the constitution but the rule of law, on any conception. It displays a contempt not only for the constitution and the courts but, more important, for the people most in need of the benefits of a transformed social and political order.[38]

CONCLUSION

Etienne Mureinik has written that

If the new Constitution is a bridge away from a culture of authority, it is clear what it must be a bridge to. It must lead to a culture of justifica-

tion—a culture in which every exercise of power is expected to be justified; in which leadership given by government rests on the cogency of
the case offered in defence of its decisions, not the fear inspired by the
force at its command. The new order must be a community built on per-
suasion, not coercion. (1994, 32)

These hopeful words of South Africa's leading public lawyer of the time were
meant to elaborate the commitment expressed in the interim constitution
to a new legal order, and their eloquence meant that they were cited frequently in South Africa in the early years of constitutional adjudication. In
addition, Mureinik's idea that the ideal of legality is the expression of a "culture of justification" has become something of a term of art among judges of
apex courts in the Commonwealth. It even informs the argument of a recent
work on China and the West in the twenty-first century.[39] When Plasket ordered that copies of his judgment be served on various institutions of the
legal order, as well as public officials, he was placing his faith in that same
commitment.

How long such faith can last is an interesting question. I have argued
that Klug's optimism in 2000 remains justified: the Constitutional Court
continues to assert its right "to decide central questions of governance,
while simultaneously limiting its role to a clearly specified judicial function
which pays open respect and deference to the new democratic institutions
and politics" (Klug 2000, 178). In addition, the courts, now dominated by
new-order black judges, together with the bar, sympathetic journalists, and
others in civil society, have proved resilient in seeing off the government's
attempt to bring the judiciary into line. Finally, the elaborate constitutional
furniture put in place by the constitution would be a standing rebuke for
anything less. One might say not only that the fundamentals are more than
sound but also that the will to maintain them remains, except at times on
the part of the government.

That is, however, a rather large exception, and a pessimist might predict
that gradually the government will succeed in chipping away at the institutional checks. The temptation to turn transformation into *Gleichschaltung*
on the part of the ANC central government, as well as of the provincial governments,[40] suggests a yearning for the more traditional postcolonial form
of African rule of nearly untrammeled executive discretion in a state dominated by one party. Moreover, that tendency is perversely twinned with the
kind of comprehensive failure to obey the law, even contempt for the law

and the courts, on the part of the ANC-led Eastern Cape provincial government. Finally, if one adds to this the possibility of a future Constitutional Court, or whatever apex court replaces it, unwilling to call senior public officials to account, one might predict a dire future for the rule of law.

Thus, Judge Froneman's comment about the resurgence of the unaccountable administrative state—the prerogative state disguised as a rule-of-law state—has to be taken seriously. All it might take is a more deferential apex court, which is the final court of appeal on all matters, and which is not only unwilling to uphold the constitution when in issue is the constitutionality of a statute or government action but is also unwilling to resist the government's desire to move the constitutional furniture around or to get rid of a piece here or there.[41] All one can safely predict is that legitimate issues around the transformation of the judiciary are and will remain vexed into the future.[42]

However, it should not be thought that the tensions discussed in this essay are limited to the South African context or to the context of transitional societies. Precisely this point is well made in the work just referred to on China and the West in the twenty-first century.

There Will Hutton argues that the Chinese experiment with capitalism will fail if it is not buttressed by the institutions of what he calls the "soft infrastructure of capitalism," including the rule of law. But Hutton is as anxious to argue that these same institutions are under threat in the West (Hutton 2007). One might rephrase this point by saying that it is worth keeping in mind that transitions can go in different directions—that is to say, the transition in Western societies can steer them away from institutions like the rule of law and democratic accountability. Especially since 9/11, there has been a marked decline in the West of executive accountability to the legislature, and judges of apex courts who are reacting to what we can think of as 9/11 statutes and executive action find it difficult to steer a path between giving too much and too little deference to the executive and the legislature. They often err on the side of too much, as governments make the claim that they enjoy something like a prerogative power when it comes to questions of national security. While these problems are not complicated by the politics of the apartheid racial divide, they are by the politics of pluralism, when the terrorist "other" becomes identified with Arabs or with Islam, or both. It is also deeply troubling that as secure and stable a democracy as the United States of America does not seem able to afford the risk of prosecutions of senior members of George W. Bush's regime for complicity in torture and other crimes committed during the "war on terror." If that country cannot uphold the rule of law when senior figures might have committed serious crimes, why should South Africa be held to a different standard?

In these contexts, there should therefore be as much concern about a decline in the culture of justification as is sparked by the rather halting progress toward creating such a culture in societies that are seeking to escape an authoritarian past. It might be ironic, but not all that surprising, that the lens afforded by the ideal of justification that came out of the South African transition helps to direct light not just on developments in that country, but also on the countries which are—supposedly—the guardians of the Western ideal of the rule of law.

EPILOGUE

I indicated earlier that the topic of the rule of law is likely to become even more contentious in the near future. Consider, for example, a list of just a few of the factors that are currently stoking a fevered public debate in South Africa:

1. The decision of the National Prosecuting Authority just prior to the 2009 election to drop the prosecution of Jacob Zuma, even though the prior conviction of his associate indicated that Zuma's conviction on serious charges of corruption was in the cards. This decision is a serious blow to the rule of law, on any conception, especially in a country in which corruption is endemic.

2. John Hlophe faced charges by thirteen permanent and acting judges of the Constitutional Court of attempting to influence two of them in the case against Zuma. However, he successfully used tactics to avoid confronting these charges that were worryingly reminiscent of the tactics relied on successfully by Zuma. Moreover, the ANC has been accused of packing the Judicial Service Commission, in order both to achieve this result and to ensure that the short list of judges to be appointed to the Constitutional Court consisted largely of judges friendly to Zuma.

3. Hlophe was one of the judges nominated for consideration for appointment to the Constitutional Court and was backed by a vigorous lobby group, who accused critics of his checkered career of racism. His appointment was considered a real possibility, and the Judicial Service Commission in its public interviews of the nominees seemed to give Hlophe and other "Africanist" judges a rather easy ride compared to the others.

4. The idea that candidates for public office can be divided between Africanists and others means that there is a new fracture line in political debate. It is no longer the case that one's ethnicity and past role in the struggle against apartheid make one immune to the charge of being a racist. Rather, one's allegiance to some ill-defined agenda of transformation is what counts, a factor that might well have played a role in the episode recounted next.

5. Dikgang Moseneke, who, as I mentioned, was widely regarded as the new chief justice of the Constitutional Court in waiting, was not appointed to this position. It is widely thought that this was punishment for having said at his birthday party in 2007 that judges are not beholden to any political party, including the ANC.

However, before one foretells doom, one has to take into account that the culture of justification is well entrenched in South Africa, and that one of the new appointments to the Constitutional Court is Johan Froneman, one of whose judgments is discussed above.

NOTES

I thank Jonathan Berger, Edwin Cameron, Arthur Chaskalson, Alfred Cockrell, Hugh Corder, Jacques De Ville, Richard Goldstone, Cora Hoexter, Jonathan Klaaren, Carole Lewis, Jonathan Lewis, Denise Meyerson, Frank Michelman, Christina Murray, Kate O'Regan, Mike Taggart, Albie Sachs, and Bashier Vally for comments on a draft of this essay. Because it seemed fitting to publish this essay in a South African venue as well, I secured the permission of Ian Shapiro, editor of this volume, and of the *South African Law Journal* to submit it to both the volume and the journal. (See *South African Law Journal* 124 [2007]: 734–61.) In view of the highly contentious nature of the issues I discuss, I would like readers to take seriously the disclaimer that all the views in this chapter are my own and were often deeply—indeed vehemently—contested by my commentators. I also thank Linda van de Vijver for research assistance, Helena Gluzman for converting the essay from one house style to another, and the participants in the Yale "After Apartheid" conference for two sets of very stimulating discussions, especially Susan Hyde for a very perceptive commentary.

1. Save for the existence of a prerogative (or legally uncontrolled) power in certain matters that was itself derived from the British tradition.

2. Though the highest court during the apartheid era did invalidate two statutes that sought to bypass the entrenched protection of people of mixed race on the general voters roll: *Harris v. Minister of the Interior* (1952) and *Minister of the Interior v. Harris* (1952). See Ian Loveland (1999).

3. See Hoexter (2004, 165) for a compelling account of how South African judges went about abdicating their role to uphold the rule of law even in "ordinary" administrative law matters. See further Klaaren and Penfold (2002).

4. For explorations of the theme of judicial resistance to apartheid, see Abel (1995) and Dyzenhaus (1991). For the tale of judicial complicity in the attempt to crush resistance, see Ellman (1992).

5. This is an interesting but highly problematic observation because the bare statistic tells us nothing unless we know something qualitative about each case. A judge whose formal conception of the rule of law leads to a finding that public officials are acting illegally makes the law more effective, not less. Indeed, this point informs the argument of legal positivists that strict observance of the formal requirements of legality will make morally obnoxious laws worse. Haynie does not have a firm grip on such issues, as is evidenced in her discussion of the positions taken in the jurisprudential debate about adjudication during apartheid at 15–23. For example, in her discussion of Raymond Wacks, she equates legal positivism and Ronald Dworkin's approach, and in her discussion of my work she attributes to me a view of adjudication that I explicitly reject. However, the most troubling aspect of her study is the half-explicit thought that the judges of the Appellate Division were correct to uphold the government's argument in the high-profile cases where judges declined to uphold the substantive conception of the rule of law. Her idea seems to be that because the judges could anticipate that the government would use statute as a brute instrument to override their judgments, they decided correctly. If anticipation of government reaction is made the criterion of correct judgment, the rule of law—on any conception—is in peril.

6. Consider how the U.S. Supreme Court has asserted federal jurisdiction over aspects of the Bush administration's "war on terror," but has done so in a way that permits the administration to get away with a bare minimum of legal controls, so that in substance the fate of, for example, "enemy combatants" seems at the whim of the administration.

7. For an illuminating discussion of transformation in the South African context, see Klare (1998, 146).

8. For an outstanding analysis of South Africa's postapartheid constitutional jurisprudence on the rule of law, see Michelman (2002).

9. Section 167(5) stipulates that the Constitutional Court is the apex court on constitutional matters, which leaves the Supreme Court of Appeal the apex court on all other matters (sec. 161(3)).

10. It is, of course, true that one's assessment of *any* of the judges discussed below might change if one looked not just at his or her decision in *New Clicks* in the context of that case but at the judge's record over a range of cases. My inquiry is not into the overall performance of any judge, however, but into tensions that affect perceptions of the judiciary and the rule of law. I also do try to show that these tensions latch on to reality, in that the way judges reasoned in this case provides a basis

for the tensions. That is, the issue is not just perceptions but conduct that fuels the perceptions. Put differently, and using the term suggested to me by my commentator, the case was not a "perfect storm." Rather, the case was a storm waiting for the right conjunction of factors.

11. See, e.g., Bolin (2004), quoting a New Clicks executive to the effect that small retail pharmacies will soon be extinct in South Africa unless new regulations governing medicine pricing and dispensing margins are changed. It was also claimed that the regulations could lead to a rise in the cost of medicines.

12. However, this route risked the Constitutional Court refusing to hear the appeal on the ground that it preferred to have the benefit of the Supreme Court of Appeal's views before it decided the matter, as the Supreme Court of Appeal pointed out in its judgment—*New Clicks* SCA, paragraph 10.

13. As Chaskalson was to point out, in *New Clicks* CC paragraph 74, this view was rather inconsistent with Judge Hlophe claim that there were no grounds for appeal.

14. *New Clicks* leave to appeal, 233–34, where he said that the stakeholders' stance "borders on contempt for this Court."

15. An article in the *Mail and Guardian* stated that it "spoke to several lawyers with different attitudes to the transformation debate, but none of them was prepared to be quoted on the record on the merits of the appeal or the reasons for the delay. Citing the sensitivity of the current situation [. . .]" (Dawes 2004b).

16. Eventually Pius Langa, who had succeeded Chaskalson as chief justice of the Constitutional Court, stepped in, in a bid to quiet the brewing race storm by discussing Hlophe's allegations with him at a meeting of the heads of the country's courts. See Maclennan (2005).

17. The first bench of the Constitutional Court contained six old-order judges, including Ismail Mahomed, who was first appointed to the bench in 1995.

18. The commission, established under section 178 of the constitution, is given an independent role in advising the national government on any matter relating to the judiciary or the administration of justice. It is presided over by the chief justice and composed of judges, lawyers, and elected politicians, including the minister of justice.

19. Deputy Judge President Traverso (1994) was the second woman appointed to the bench in South Africa.

20. Dawes (2004a) quotes one "leading advocate" as having said that, because Judge Harms had been compromised by his role in 1990 as head of the Harms commission, which failed to uncover the truth about apartheid death squads, the final message would need to come from the Constitutional Court: "If one hopes for a society where the judiciary is independent it may depend on where people like [Constitutional Court Judges] Ngcobo and Moseneke, who have some credibility with the government, come down. If they agree with the SCA, this whole race thing will go away," he said.

21. Judge Ngcobo, unlike the other four, did not hold that PAJA applied to all rule- or regulation-making, but that it did apply to this particular exercise undertaken by the Pricing Committee and the minister (*New Clicks* CC, para. 470).

22. See Hoexter (2004) for the argument that the traits of formalism and parsimony that characterized apartheid-era jurisprudence still affect the reasoning of South Africa courts, even in some of the landmark decisions on legality by the Constitutional Cout. She also shows the strong impact of these traits on PAJA.

23. I do not however accept this distinction between the exceptional and the ordinary—for detailed argument, see Dyzenhaus (2006).

24. Indeed, Harms's wholesale dismissal of the regulatory scheme might give the impression that the Court was in some sympathy with the general antipathy of the main expert witness for the stakeholders toward regulatory interventions into the free market.

25. For a sophisticated discussion of deference in the South African context, see De Ville (2003). At 13–21, De Ville concludes very tentatively that the Constitutional Court is more ready to defer in an appropriate fashion than the Supreme Court of Appeal. He also comments at 21 on a reluctance on the part of the Supreme Court of Appeal to engage with PAJA, which he regards as a refusal "to enter into a debate with Parliament."

26. In *New Clicks* Cape, Judge Yekiso dealt with the merits in around twenty-five pages of a forty-two-page judgment. But there is very little analysis in these pages. As in the rest of the judgment, he mostly describes the history of particular legal measures and gives their details.

27. See *New Clicks* CC, especially paragraphs 543 and 576. Ngcobo's reasoning exposes the Supreme Court of Appeal's missed opportunity. That is, Harms at times spoke of the problem in the calculation of the dispensing fee in terms of a failure of justification or explanation, but preferred in the end to decide on the basis that the Pricing Committee had been wrong.

28. See, for example, Judge Ngcobo's statement of the reasonableness test, *New Clicks* CC, paragraph 522: "Such a fee would have to be challenged on the ground that it is one that a reasonable decision maker could not fix".

29. See also her follow-up piece (Khan 2006).

30. However, the issue is far from resolved, as a search for "pharmacies" in the archive of *Business Day Online* reveals. See, e.g., Musgrave (2006).

31. In *New Clicks* leave to appeal, Judge Hlophe suggested at 237 that no other court was likely to differ from the majority decision in *New Clicks* Cape because of the importance of the objective of making medicine affordable to all. He invoked the value of *ubuntu* or community as an interpretative principle in aid of this proposition. His judgment thus evoked the worst examples of the apartheid-era judgments, in which national spirit seemed to animate interpretation.

32. See Hoexter (2006) for an analysis of the deficiencies of PAJA, in particular the fact that it seems to set a threshold for what counts as administrative action for the purposes of review that excludes vast swathes of the activity of the admin-

istrative state. While Hoexter praises Judge Chaskalson's judgment in *New Clicks,* she also expresses concern that the Constitutional Court did not resolve the issue of threshold (2006, 322–24). With her, I take Chaskalson's, Ngcobo's, and Sachs's judgments to entail that there is one unified system of administrative law with the issue of the content of legality to be determined according to particular contexts. In another essay, Hoexter notes that during the "early days of the constitutional negotiations, it was dispiriting to find that the ANC, then a liberation movement, supported just the sort of test that might have found favor with the National Party government: a standard of 'such gross unreasonableness . . . as to amount to manifest injustice.'" See Hoexter (2006b, 62). Two essays in this same volume discuss *New Clicks* CC: Corder (2006) and Klaaren (2006). For further discussion, see Davis (2006, 23).

33. For a discussion of PAJA's constitutionality, see Klaaren and Penfold (2002, 63-5, 63-8).

34. See further the minister of health, Manto Tshabalala-Msimang, commenting that the case raised issues about the "transformation of the judiciary" (2005).

35. See Dawes and Moya (2005). They identify three positions in the ANC. The first, associated with the minister of health, Tshabalala-Msimang, "felt the judiciary was too independent and an obstacle to the will of the executive. Another, ANC officials said, was 'concerned primarily with what it saw as that slow pace of change in the racial composition of the judiciary, particularly in the lower courts.'" A third body of opinion "maintained the more traditional ANC line that a lack of transformation manifested itself as a lack of access to justice for the poor, and the failure of too many judges to demonstrate empathy for people who lived in circumstances alien to them. This group essentially believed that only through more thorough transformation could constitutional values be more fully realised."

36. In an earlier episode, the Judicial Service Commission accepted Judge Hlophe's claim that he had oral permission from the late minister of justice, Dullah Omar, to accept a post with this group. Joubert (2006b) reported that the commission, in reaching this result, split on racial lines.

37. Rickard describes the Supreme Court of Appeal's rebuke to these lower court judges as a "klap." She points out that among the judges klapped were white judges. The same point is made by "Serjeant at the Bar" (2007): "The 15 black judges complain that the appeal court criticism is targeted against black judges, yet the Supreme Court of Appeal has been equally rude to a number of white judges. This is not to deflect the point made by the 15 judges, nor does it excuse rudeness, but it is to show that the pathology of which they complain may be owing more to a form of judicial arrogance than racism."

38. Curiously, the Supreme Court of Appeal sought to undermine the efforts of the South Eastern Cape courts to get the administration to do its job in *Jayiya v Member of the Executive Council for Welfare* (2004), where Judge Conradie for the Court in a very technical and narrow judgment sought to strip the arguments of the Eastern Cape courts of their constitutional color. (Conradie first acted as a judge

in 1984 and was appointed to the Supreme Court of Appeal in 2002. Harms was a member of the panel that decided the case.) This help from the Supreme Court of Appeal was eagerly seized upon by the provincial administration. See Froneman judgment in *Kate v. MEC for the Department of Welfare* (2005), where he also explicitly attempted to tie the Supreme Court of Appeal's judgment to its facts in order to rehabilitate its jurisprudence. A different bench of the Supreme Court of Appeal has largely vindicated the approach of the Eastern Cape courts in *MEC, Department of Welfare v Kate* (2006).

39. See Hutton (2007, 197), referring in note 8 to my essay in the memorial volume for Mureinik (Dyzenhaus 1998).

40. One troubling example of this tendency arose recently when the Democratic Alliance, the principal opposition party in the national legislature, managed to form an alliance with other opposition parties sufficient to form a majority in the municipality of Cape Town. The provincial government threatened to use legislation to change the municipal structure of Cape Town in a fashion that would secure an ANC-led coalition. For a time the national government not only refused to intervene but seemed to be in alliance with its provincial counterparts—see Joubert (2006a). Had the provincial government gone ahead, the matter would likely have ended up in the Constitutional Court, but eventually the national government did intervene and brokered a compromise.

41. Though see the very strong statement by Moseneke (2007) of the principle of judicial independence in his address at his installation as chancellor of the University of the Witwatersrand.

42. See "Serjeant at the Bar" (2007): "In our haste to use race as a shield against criticism, we stifle any chance of developing the framework that can achieve a nonracial, non sexist judiciary. African values must transform the core of our legal system, but these values surely cannot support allegations of lack of accountability, corruption and arrogance—if these are properly proved. Until the country as a whole and the judiciary in particular can develop an agreed set of standards to evaluate performance, we will only experience a further absence of proper public debate and, more important, an implosion of precious institutions. Make no mistake: whatever the achievements of the Constitutional Court, the judiciary still has a long way to travel."

BIBLIOGRAPHY

Abel, Richard L. 1995. *Politics by Other Means: Law in the Struggle against Apartheid, 1980–1994.* New York: Routledge.

African National Congress. 2005. "ANC Statement on Comments on Judiciary," 10 January. http://www.anc.org.za/ancdocs/pr/2005/pr0110.html (accessed 22 May 2009).

African National Congress, National Executive Committee. 2005. "Statement of the National Executive Committee of the African National Congress on the occa-

sion of Year 93 of the ANC." http://www.anc.org.za/ancdocs/pr/2005/pr0108
.html (accessed 22 May 2009).

"At Last, the Law Inscribed on Tablets." 2005. *Mail and Guardian Online,* 10 October.
http://www.mg.co.za/.

Bolin, Lynn. 2004. "Small SA Pharmacies "Will Soon be Extinct.'" *Mail and Guardian Online,* 21 October. http://www.mg.co.za/articlepage.aspx?area=/breaking
_news_national&articleid=140090 (accessed 22 May 2009).

Chaskalson, Arthur. 2006. "Background to the Judicial Bills." Presented at the
General Council of the Bar of South Africa, Human Rights Committee: Conference on the Justice Bills, Judicial Independence and the Restructuring of
the Courts, Johannesburg. 17 February. http://www.lrc.org.za/images/stories/
IssueConstitution/transcript.pdf (accessed 26 May 2009).

Constitution of the Republic of South Africa, No. 108 of 1996. http://www.info.gov
.za/documents/constitution/1996/a108–96.pdf (accessed 26 May 2009).

Corder, Hugh. 1984. *Judges at Work: The Role and Attitudes of the South African Appellate Judiciary, 1910–1950.* Cape Town: Jutta.

———. 2006. "Reviewing 'Executive Action.'" In *A Delicate Balance: The Place of the
Judiciary in a Constitutional Democracy. Proceedings of a Symposium to Mark the Retirement of Arthur Chaskalson, Former Chief Justice of South Africa,* ed. Jonathan
Klaaren, 73–78. Cape Town: Siber Ink.

Currie, Iain. 2006. "What Difference Does the Promotion of Administrative Justice
Act Make to Administrative Law." *Acta Juridica* 2006: 325–51.

"DA Calls for Hlophe Probe to Be Reopened." 2007. *Mail and Guardian Online,* February 2. http://www.mg.co.za/articlePage.aspx?articleid=297843&area=/breaking
_news/breaking_news_national/ (accessed 22 May 2009).

Davis, Dennis M. 2006. "To Defer and When? Administrative Law and Constitutional Democracy." *Acta Juridica* 2006: 23–41.

Dawes, Nic. 2004a. "A Drug Test for the Judiciary." *Mail and Guardian Online,* 23 December. http://www.mg.co.za/.

———. 2004b. "Traverso Drawn into Cape Judges Uproar." *Mail and Guardian Online,* 8 October. http://www.mg.co.za/.

Dawes, Nic, and Fikile-Ntsikelelo Moya. 2005. "ANC Divided on the Judiciary." *Mail
and Guardian Online,* 14 January. http://www.mg.co.za/.

De Ville, J. R. 2003. *Judicial Review of Administrative Action in South Africa.* Durban:
LexisNexis Butterworths.

Dyzenhaus, David. 1991. *Hard Cases in Wicked Legal Systems: South African Law in the
Perspective of Legal Philosophy.* Oxford: Oxford University Press.

———. 1998. "Law as Justification: Etienne Mureinik's Conception of Legal Culture." *South African Journal on Human Rights* 14: 11–37.

———. 2006. *The Constitution of Law: Legality in a Time of Emergency.* Cambridge:
Cambridge University Press.

Ellman, Stephen. 1992. *In a Time of Trouble: Law and Liberty in South Africa's State of
Emergency.* Oxford: Oxford University Press.

Forsyth, Christopher. 1985. *In Danger for Their Talents: A Study of the Supreme Court of South Africa, 1950–1980*. Cape Town: Jutta.

Fraenkel, Ernst. 1941. *The Dual State: A Contribution to the Theory of Dictatorship*. New York: Oxford University Press.

Hartley, Wyndham. 2007. "DA Welcomes Judicial Bill, Asks for More Time." *Business Day Online*, March 6. http://www.businessday.co.za/.

Haynie, Stacia L. 2003. *Judging in Black & White: Decision Making in the South African Appellate Division, 1950–1990*. New York: Peter Lang, 44–61.

Hoexter, Cora. 2004. "The Principle of Legality in South African Administrative Law." *Macquarie Law Journal* 4: 165–85.

———. 2006a. "'Administrative Action' in the Courts." *Acta Juridica* 2006: 303–24.

———. 2006b. "Standards of Review of Administrative Action: Review for reasonableness." In *A Delicate Balance: The Place of the Judiciary in a Constitutional Democracy. Proceedings of a Symposium to Mark the Retirement of Arthur Chaskalson, Former Chief Justice of South Africa*, ed. Jonathan Klaaren, 61–72. Cape Town: Siber Ink.

Hutton, Will. 2007. *The Writing on the Wall: China and the West in the 21st Century*. London: Little, Brown.

Joubert, Pearlie. 2006a. "ANC Top Dogs in the Loop." *Mail and Guardian Online*, 25 September. http://www.mg.co.za/articlePage.aspx?articleid=284876&area=insight/insight_national (accessed 22 May 2009).

———. 2006b. "Racial Split over Hlophe." *Mail and Guardian Online*, 15 December. http://www.mg.co.za/articlePage.aspx?articleid=293522&area=/insight/insight_national/ (accessed 22 May 2009).

"Judicial Bills on Hold 'for now.'" 2005. *Mercury*, 12 October. http://www.themercury.co.za/.

Khan, Tamar. 2005. "Bid for Healing Formula as Court Rules on Drug Pricing. *Business Day Online*, 3 October. http://www.businessday.co.za/.

———. 2006. "Cool Heads Prevail in Medicine Battle." *Business Day Online*, 16 May. http://www.businessday.co.za/.

Klaaren, Jonathan. 2006. "Five Models of Intensity of Review." In *A Delicate Balance: The Place of the Judiciary in a Constitutional Democracy. Proceedings of a Symposium to Mark the Retirement of Arthur Chaskalson, Former Chief Justice of South Africa*, ed. Jonathan Klaaren, 79–82. Cape Town: Siber Ink.

Klaaren, Jonathan, and Glen Penfold. 2002. "Just Administrative Action." In *Constitutional law of South Africa*, 2nd ed., ed. Matthew Chaskalson, Janet Kentridge, Jonathan Klaaren, Gilbert Marcus, Derek Spitz, Anthony Stein, and Stuart Woolman, 63-1–63-39. Cape Town: Juta.

Klare, Karl. 1998. "Legal Culture and Transformative Constitutionalism." *South African Journal on Human Rights* 14: 146–188.

Klug, Heinz. 2000. *Constituting Democracy: Law, Globalism and South Africa's Political Reconstruction*. Cambridge: Cambridge University Press.

Langa, Pius. 2006. "A Perspective from the Chief Justice." Presented at the General

Council of the Bar of South Africa, Human Rights Committee: Conference on the Justice Bills, Judicial Independence and the Restructuring of the Courts, Johannesburg. 17 February. http://www.lrc.org.za/images/stories/IssueConstitution/transcript.pdf (accessed 26 May 2009).

Lewis, Carole. 2005. "Reaching the Pinnacle: Principles, Policies and People for a Single Apex in South Africa." *South African Journal on Human Rights* 21: 509–24.

Lewis, Jonathan. 2005. "Executive-mindedness Reinvented?" *South African Journal on Human Rights* 21: 127–43.

Loveland, Ian. 1999. *Due Process of Law: Racial Discrimination and the Right to Vote in South Africa, 1855–1960.* Oxford: Hart Publishing.

Maclennan, Ben. 2005. "Judge Given Chance to Explain Racism Row. *Mail and Guardian Online,* 17 October. http://www.mg.co.za/articlepage.aspx?area=/breaking_news/breaking_news_national/&articleid=253843 (accessed 22 May 2009).

Medicines and Related Substances Control Act 101 of 1965 after amendment by the Medicines and Related Substances Control Amendment Act (Act 90 of 1997). http://www.pharmcouncil.co.za/documents/ACT%2090%20OF%201997.pdf (accessed 26 May 2009).

Michelman, Frank R. 2002. "The Rule of Law, Legality and the Supremacy of the Constitution." In *Constitutional law of South Africa,* 2nd ed., ed. Matthew Chaskalson, Janet Kentridge, Jonathan Klaaren, Gilbert Marcus, Derek Spitz, Anthony Stein, and Stuart Woolman, 11-1–11-42. Cape Town: Juta.

Moseneke, Dikgang J. 2007. Address delivered by Justice Dikgang Moseneke at his installation as chancellor of the University of Witwatersrand, Johannesburg, South Africa, 28 March. http://web.wits.ac.za/NR/rdonlyres/FF0006AB-2AF6-4DFB-94F4-33D25296DCF3/3895/ChancellorsSpeech270307.doc (accessed 22 May 2009).

Moya, Fikile-Ntsikelelo. 2006. "Judges to Talk Tough at Key Meeting." *Mail and Guardian Online,* 1 February. http://www.mg.co.za/article/2006-02-01-judges-to-talk-tough-at-key-meeting (accessed 22 May 2009).

Mureinik, Etienne. 1994. "A Bridge to Where? Introducing the Interim Bill of Rights." *South African Journal on Human Rights* 10: 31–48.

Musgrave, Amy. 2006. "Legal Challenge Again Stalls Drug-Price Rules." *Business Day Online,* December 22. http://www.businessday.co.za/.

"Publication of Judges' Bill during Holiday Lull 'Just a Coincidence.'" 2006. *Mail and Guardian Online,* 17 January. http://www.mg.co.za/.

Rickard, Carmel. 2007. "Judges Cannot Be Shielded from Scrutiny." *Business Day Online,* 10 February. http://www.businessday.co.za/.

Serjeant at the Bar [pseud.]. 2005. "Monster Judgment for Drug Pricing." *Mail and Guardian Online,* 17 October. http://www.mg.co.za/.

———. 2007. "Will the Judiciary Ever Catch Up?" *Mail and Guardian Online,* 27 February. http://www.mg.co.za/.

Spitz, Richard, and Matthew Chaskalson. 2000. "The Constitutional Court." In *The*

Politics of Transition: A Hidden History of South Africa's Negotiated Settlement, 191–210. Johannesburg: University of the Witwatersrand Press.

Temkin, Sanchia. 2006. "World Body Chides SA's Legal Plans." *Business Day Online*, 24 April. http://www.businessday.co.za/.

Tshabalala-Msimang, Manto. 2005. "We Will Not Compromise." *Mail and Guardian Online*, 1 February. http://www.mg.co.za/article/2005–02–01-we-will-not-com promise (accessed 22 May 2009).

LEGAL REFERENCES

Bato Star Fishing (Pty) Ltd. v. Minister of Environmental Affairs and Others, 2004 (4) SA 490 (CC).

Harris v. Minister of the Interior, 1952 (2) SA 428 (A).

Jayiya v. Member of the Executive Council for Welfare, Eastern Cape, 2004 (2) SA 611 (SCA).

Kate v. MEC for the Department of Welfare, Eastern Cape, 2005 (1) SA 141 (SE).

MEC, Department of Welfare, Eastern Cape v. Kate, 2006 (4) SA 478 (SCA).

Minister of Health and Another v. New Clicks South Africa (Pty) Ltd. and Others, 2006 (2) SA 311.

Minister of the Interior v. Harris, 1952 (4) SA 769 (A).

New Clicks South Africa (Pty) Ltd. v. Tshabalala-Msimang and Another NNO; Pharmaceutical Society of South Africa and Others v. Minister of Health and Others, 2005 (2) SA 530 (C).

Ngxusa v. Permanent Secretary, Department of Welfare, Eastern Cape, 2001 (2) SA 609 (E).

Pharmaceutical Manufacturers Association of SA: In re Ex Parte President of the Republic of South Africa, 2000 (2) SA 674 (CC).

Pharmaceutical Society of South Africa v. Tshabalala-Msimang and Another; New Clicks South Africa (Pty) Ltd. v. Minister of Health and Another, 2005 (3) SA 231 (C).

Pharmaceutical Society of South Africa v. Tshabalala-Msimang and Another NNO; New Clicks South Africa (Pty) Ltd. v. Minister of Health and Another, 2005 (3) SA 238 (SCA).

Vumazonke v. MEC For Social Development, Eastern Cape, 2005 (6) SA 229 (SE).

Anticorruption Reforms in Democratic South Africa

Marianne Camerer

Weeks before South Africa's fourth democratic election, acting National Prosecuting Authority (NPA) boss Mokotedi Mpshe announced on 6 April 2009 that all charges of corruption against African National Congress (ANC) president Jacob Zuma would be dropped: "I have come to the difficult conclusion that it is neither possible nor desirable for the NPA to continue with the prosecution."[1] While the timing may have raised some eyebrows, this "difficult conclusion" allowed South Africa's new president to take up the reins of office without the indignity of corruption charges hanging over his head.

The corruption charges against President Zuma stemmed from an investigation into his relationship with his financial adviser and Durban-based businessman, Schabir Shaik. A lengthy public trial finalized four years earlier, in June 2005, saw Shaik sentenced to fifteen years in prison. In terms of the charge sheet, the other party to the corruption and bribery charges for which Shaik was jailed was Jacob Zuma.

On 14 June 2005, in what many wrongly predicted as Zuma's political demise, Thabo Mbeki rather unceremoniously fired his deputy president, stating to a joint sitting of the National Assembly that "the court has made findings against the accused and at the same time pronounced on how these matters relate to our Deputy President, the Hon Jacob Zuma, raising questions of conduct that would be inconsistent with expectations that attend those who hold public office."[2] Interestingly, this act would signal Mbeki's own political death knell: he would be defeated in his quest to continue in office as ANC president at the ANC conference in Polokwane (December

2007) and in an unprecedented turn of events would be recalled by the ANC as president of South Africa in September 2008, six months before completing his second term of office.

On Tuesday, 3 March 2009, South Africans woke up to the news that convicted fraudster Schabir Shaik, after serving just over two years of the fifteen-year sentence, mostly in private hospitals, had walked free the night before on medical grounds.[3] (He has subsequently applied for a presidential pardon.) Shaik's release followed a controversial decision by the parole board, for in terms of the law, medical parole should be given only in terminally ill cases. On 22 October 2009 the *Mercury* reported that Shaik had been seen playing a round of golf on the Papwa Sewgolum Course in Reservoir Hills, Durban.[4]

Just over a month later, in April 2009, the charges against Zuma were dropped. Alleged political interference into the corruption investigation by overzealous NPA bosses loyal to former president Thabo Mbeki and alleged abuses involving power and political conspiracies were given as reasons for the charges being dropped. The information of political interference came to light in tapes made available to Zuma's defense team by seemingly sympathetic intelligence agencies. It is not clear at this stage whether the tapes were legally obtained.

Three years earlier Zuma, his defense lawyers, and supporters had argued that the charges brought against him by the NPA were part of a "political conspiracy." In a 2006 affidavit submitted to oppose a prosecution request for a postponement in his corruption trial, Zuma argued that the investigation was "designed solely or mainly to destroy my reputation and political role. . . . My conviction on any possible type of offence is being pursued at all costs. . . . I have been touted as a potential presidential candidate. . . . Just as there are . . . ANC members who have come out in support of me being the next president, so there are those in public and in government who are very much opposed to me being president and indeed some who wish me not to have a role to play in the politics of this country. . . . The charges against me have been initiated, and certainly fuelled, by a political conspiracy to remove me as a role player in the ANC."[5]

At Polokwane, where Zuma won his decisive victory to head the ANC, a decision was taken to disband the "Scorpions," the elite unit of prosecution-led investigators alleged to have been targeting Mbeki's political enemies. Widely regarded as South Africa's most effective anticorruption unit, the Directorate of Special Operations—the Scorpions—was set up by Mbeki ten years ago, in 1999, when he came to office on a "zero tolerance against corruption" campaign. Despite huge public outcry, in May 2009 a new Directorate for Priority Crime Investigation (DPCI) was set up within the South African Police Services, headed by Anwa Dramat, a former ANC underground operative.[6] This is now effectively a specialized police unit with no prosecution powers, known as "the Hawks."

The charges of political interference by the NPA involved the former head of the Scorpions, Leonard McCarthy, now vice president for integrity at the World Bank in Washington, and the first national director of the NPA, Bulelani Ngcuka. The tapes played to the NPA authorities and on which they based their decision not to pursue a case allegedly demonstrate how certain individuals such as McCarthy set out to get Zuma convicted on corruption charges at any cost. The content of these tapes has not been made public.

Law experts such as Wim Trengrove have strongly questioned the grounds on which the NPA's national director dropped the charges and suggested that this decision was both "wrong" and "indefensible."[7] The main opposition party, the Democratic Alliance, is appealing the decision by the NPA to drop the charges against Zuma. While there may indeed have been abuse of process by the prosecuting authority in conducting its investigation, the Democratic Alliance believes there is still a case of corruption that Zuma needs to answer for.[8] As things stand, it is unlikely that charges will be reinstituted, although Zuma has always said that the rule of law must take its course and he would be happy to have his day in court. Indeed, he has appeared many times in court in the course of defending his innocence in a corruption case that has cost taxpayers more than R100 million.[9]

On 19 October 2009 it was reported that acting prosecutions head Mokotedi Mpshe was opposed to a legal challenge by the Democratic Alliance to his decision to drop charges against Jacob Zuma, saying it would "lay bare" the president's highly sensitive personal records and should not be allowed to happen: "The disclosure of such a record would not only breach and undermine Mr Zuma's rights, it will be invidious. . . . If a decision is taken to reinstate charges against Mr Zuma, his fair trial in terms . . . of the constitution would quite evidently be infringed," he said.[10]

The effectiveness and leadership of both the NPA and the South African Police Services have been severely constrained in recent years; former NPA boss Vusi Pikoli was suspended by Thabo Mbeki in September 2007, allegedly on the basis of an irretrievable breakdown in the working relationship between the minister of justice and constitutional development and the NDPP.[11] However, Pikoli believes he was removed from office for issuing a warrant of arrest in the case of former police commissioner and Interpol boss, Jackie Selebi. Pikoli was accused of abusing his powers to pursue the case against Selebi, an Mbeki ally, shortly before the decisive ANC conference at Polokwane in December 2007, where Mbeki, seeking a third term in office, was ousted by ANC rank and file as president of the organization.[12] Pikoli is appealing his suspension. The former police commissioner, Jackie Selebi, has subsequently been suspended and is currently in court appealing charges of corruption and racketeering relating to organized crime. A new police commissioner, Bheki Cele, has recently been appointed.

It is not only the institutions of the criminal justice system that have been crippled by accusations of corruption and abuses of power. Corruption and maladministration in service delivery departments such as Home Affairs is rife. South Africans traveling to Britain now have to apply for a visa to enter the former colonial power.[13] In a post-9/11 world, the state of the Department of Home Affairs is such that the integrity of South African identity documents and passports can no longer be guaranteed. The cost of systemic corruption is starting to be felt even by the traveling classes.

What hope is there for the future? Under the Mbeki regime, Jacob Zuma headed the Moral Regeneration Movement. At the time, he not only faced corruption charges but was also on trial for an alleged rape, for which he was later acquitted.[14] In his inaugural address on 9 May 2009, President Zuma spoke of his administration's vision to achieve its goals: "We must hold ourselves to the highest standards of service, probity and integrity. Together we must build a society that prizes excellence and rewards effort, which shuns laziness and incompetence."[15] However, his cabinet, according to the *Mail and Guardian* newspaper, is potentially compromised in its quest to serve the public interest; over 40 percent of ministers have perceived or real conflicts of interest in terms of their involvement in private companies.[16] These interests will need to be fully disclosed and potential conflicts closely monitored if the public's trust in the Zuma cabinet is to be justified.

Shortly after he was appointed minister of transport, it was reported that S'bu Ndebele had accepted a gift of a luxury sedan worth R1.14 million and other gifts from a consortium of KwaZulu Natal contractors. The gift from Vukuzakhe, a development program established by Ndebele when he was still transport MEC in KwaZulu-Natal, was accepted at a public function and was to thank the minister for his previous role, in which he had created business opportunities for these contractors. It was only after a sustained public outcry that Ndebele decided to return the gifts, which could have created a potential conflict of interest in his new role. The presidency had apparently advised Ndebele that it was okay to keep the generous gifts and merely declare them in terms of the Executive Members Ethics Act.[17]

Some of Zuma's new cabinet ministers have benefited from black economic empowerment (BEE) deals, a system that brings its own corruption challenges. To address poverty and inequality, empowerment policies to democratize the economy through state interventions such as BEE are clearly important in overcoming the apartheid legacy. However, these policies have also opened up new opportunities for corruption and given rise to accusations that a small group of politically connected elite is benefiting from such interventions. The sense that it is "payback time" following the harsh deprivation of the struggle for liberation that many political leaders have endured must be factored into the self-deceptive calculations of those for whom public office is not about serving the public interest but rather about serving themselves. The infamous remark by former ANC spokesperson Smuts Ngonyama, "we did not struggle to remain poor," is telling. With the change of guard represented by Zuma coming into power, there are undoubtedly new players who will seek to benefit from access to power and state contracts.

Independent analyst Mamphele Ramphele, a former managing director of the World Bank in Washington, D.C., has warned of the culture of entitlement and rampant materialism that has taken root among South Africans as a further potential cause of corruption:

> The temptations of materialism are everywhere. Success is defined not by what one accomplishes, but by what one owns. Many young people know no other motivation for developing their talents than to be able to make money. The use of state resources to feed this materialism is worrying. The National Party government used 'state capture' to enrich their constituency at the expense of the rest of the population. Post-Apartheid South Africa cannot afford to allow 'state capture' by the new elites. It would undermine everything we yearn for in a free, democratic society.[18]

The effectiveness of the bulwarks in place to prevent "state capture" is precisely the rationale for assessing the anticorruption measures discussed in this essay.

ANTICORRUPTION REFORMS IN DEMOCRATIC SOUTH AFRICA

With some background and context now in place, my argument turns to corruption and its associated crimes—which unfortunately did not disappear with the largely peaceful transition to democratic rule—and how they have been dealt with in postapartheid South Africa over the past fifteen years. The discussion considers anticorruption reform efforts, with the following three questions framing the analysis:

- Does democratic South Africa have the systems in place to effectively address corruption?
- Are these anticorruption systems (laws, institutions, policies, strategies) working in practice?
- Does the necessary political will exist to address corruption wherever it occurs?

First, in a series of twelve statements, some initial hopes and aspirations that provide a vision for a South African state that is truly accountable are articulated. Second, the main anticorruption policy initiatives introduced since 1994 are identified. Third, the 2008 Global Integrity Index results are introduced to highlight certain deficiencies in South Africa's anticorruption arsenal. The index illuminates several "integrity challenges" that remain to be addressed (e.g., regulation around the funding of political parties) if the fight against corruption in South Africa is to be both credible and sustainable. I conclude with brief comments on how well the state administration is likely to overcome these weaknesses in its strategy.

WHAT WERE THE INITIAL HOPES AND ASPIRATIONS?

Corruption neither emerged nor disappeared overnight with South Africa's transition to democracy. By its very nature and operation, the apartheid state and its multiple systems of retaining power were corrupt. If corruption is defined as "the abuse of entrusted power for private gain," an abusive regime benefiting a minority at the expense of a majority was systematically corrupt.

While abuses of power are more likely to come to light in democracies because of institutions such as free media and values such as openness, accountability, and transparency, developed democracies are not entirely sheltered from corruption. Here, however, corruption manifests itself in more entrenched, subtle, and sophisticated ways to protect various special interests. It follows that the emergence of democracy in and of itself is a necessary but not a sufficient condition for preventing corruption.

The following twelve statements capture some of the initial hopes and aspirations for the "new" South Africa with respect to preventing abuses of power such as corruption:

1. That South Africa post-1994 would be a qualitatively different moral society compared to the venal values that characterized the apartheid regime and that the constitutional values of openness, transparency, and accountability would infuse all government institutions and interactions between citizens and their state.

2. That the ethical leadership characterizing the struggle against apartheid would continue to inspire those committed to the hard work of governing, and that South Africa would provide a leadership role, particularly in Africa, to fight corruption and promote good governance.

3. That South Africa, because of its special circumstances (e.g., its level of development), would not become a stereotypical postindependence African economy, largely dependent on the state, characterized by patronage and dominated by ethnic interests.

4. That systems set up by the apartheid state to further its illegitimate racist ends would be truly ruptured, and that under a new system of democratic governance all South Africans would tangibly experience the gains of the struggle for freedom and democracy, leading to true equality.

5. That race would not play a corrupting influence in both the state and the economy, and that whereas legitimate interventions to address inequality and "the legacy of apartheid" would be undertaken, these interventions would not occur at the expense of professionalism and efficiency.

6. That the new state would establish an impartial professional civil service committed to creating "a better life for all," and that the delivery of basic services such as security, housing, water, electricity, education, and infrastructure would not be undermined by maladministration, inefficiency, and corruption.

7. That there would be a multiparty democracy and a strong opposition that would be vigilant in demanding accountability from the ruling party, and that a strong distinction between the ruling party and the state would ensure that state resources would not be abused for political ends.

8. That Parliament would exercise effective oversight over the executive, particularly in relation to public funds, to ensure that the public interest was served by responsible and rational public expenditures.

9. That the media would be independent, fair, and vigilant, and that journalists would be safe and responsible in exposing corruption wherever it emerged.

10. That organizations in civil society would play an active role as a partner in holding the state accountable and facilitating access to information for citizens to exercise and uphold their rights.

11. That citizens would be equally protected before the law, and that those who spoke out against unfair or corrupt practices in the public or private sector would be protected and rewarded.

12. That where maladministration and corrupt practices were reported or exposed, appropriate measures would be taken by dedicated and specialized anticorruption resources to investigate, prosecute, and convict both corruptor and corruptee, and that the criminal justice system, in particular the judiciary and the NPA, would be independent, respected, and impervious to manipulation for political ends.

On what basis can these articulated hopes and aspirations be assessed in terms of whether or not they have been realized? What are the strengths and weaknesses of South Africa's national integrity system? Before considering these questions, in the following section I note the impressive range of anticorruption mechanisms, both laws and institutions, that South Africa has introduced after apartheid to demonstrate its intent to curb corruption and prevent abuses of power.

ANTICORRUPTION ON THE AGENDA

Since 1997, when the corruption issue was placed firmly on the table—not least because of a number of high-profile scandals that dominated the local media (e.g., *Sarafina,*[19] Motheo Housing[20]), but also the impetus of the international community in this regard, culminating in the United Nations Convention Against Corruption—numerous policy statements, laws, and institutions have been introduced in democratic South Africa to control corruption. Over several years a comprehensive national anticorruption strategy has been developed through a conscious partnership approach involving all sectors of society.

In many respects, the anticorruption reform policy process in democratic South Africa has been both systematic and sequenced, and has benefited from the global context that since the mid-1990s has strongly promoted good governance as the key to sustaining democratic reforms. Specific programs and policies have largely realized the three key policy objectives identified at the First National Anti-Corruption Summit in April 1999. These were:

1. *Combating corruption:* Programs included a review of anticorruption legislation; establishing a whistle-blower mechanism; enacting an access-to-information law; establishing special courts to adjudicate on corruption cases; and establishing sectoral coordinating structures and a national coordinating structure (the National Anti-Corruption Forum) to coordinate, monitor, and manage the national anticorruption program.
2. *Preventing corruption:* Programs included efforts to blacklist individual businesses and organizations involved in corruption; establishing an anticorruption hotline; establishing sectoral hotlines; taking disciplinary action against corrupt persons; putting in place systems to ensure consistent monitoring and reporting on corruption; and the promotion and implementation of sound ethical, financial, and related management practices.
3. *Building integrity and raising awareness:* Programs included the promotion and pursuance of social research, analysis, and advocacy to analyze the causes, effects, and growth of corruption; enforcement of a code of conduct and disciplinary codes; inspiring youth, workers, and employers toward intolerance for corruption; promotion of training and education in ethics; and a sustained media campaign to highlight aspects of the strategy.

In 2006 the African Peer Review Mechanism's (APRM) Country Self Assessment Report for South Africa noted the culmination of the government's anticorruption efforts in the 2002 adoption of the comprehensive Public Service Anti-Corruption Strategy, a strategy that "has served as a blueprint for consolidating and reinforcing the anti-corruption legislative and regulatory framework as well as strengthening the institutions mandated to monitor, investigate and prosecute corruption." A further cornerstone of South Africa's anticorruption effort noted in the APRM report is the development of key partnerships between the government, civil society, and the private sector in fighting corruption. Examples of such partnerships include the two National Anti-Corruption Summits (held in 1999 and 2005) and the launch of the tripartite National Anti-Corruption Forum (www.nacf.org.za) in 2001.

Additionally, the APRM report regards anticorruption legislative and regulatory measures adopted since 1994 as "strong and in keeping with international practices." The anticorruption laws include the Public Service Code of Conduct (1997); the Parliamentary Code of Ethics (1997); the Executive Members Ethics Act (no 83 of 1998) and the Codes of Ethics (2000); the Public Finance Management Act and Municipal Finance Management Act; the Promotion of Access to Information Act; the Protected Disclosures Act (no. 26 of 2000); the Financial Intelligence Center Act (no. 38 of 2001); and finally the Prevention and Combating of Corrupt Activities Act (no. 12 of 2004).

This last, state-of-the-art act focused on preventing and combating corruption came into force on 27 April 2004—significantly, on the tenth anniversary of South Africa's transition to democracy—and is a particularly comprehensive law that spells out more than twenty specific corruption offenses. It was crafted against the backdrop of the finalization of the United Nations' Convention Against Corruption and takes into account other regional anticorruption protocols such as those developed by the Organisation for Economic Co-operation and Development, the South African Development Community (SADC), and the African Union. In addition to these specific laws, South Africa's range of specialized anticorruption agencies include the NPA, the Directorate of Special Operations (the Scorpions—now defunct), the South African Police Services, the Special Investigating Unit, the Independent Complaints Directorate, the Public Protector, the Auditor General, the Public Service Commission, and various parliamentary committees.[21]

Indeed, South Africa's anticorruption arsenal, developed systematically since 1994, is impressive, and the country appears to have in place, at least at the national level, many of the key institutions and laws cited in the good governance and anticorruption literature as being important to expose and prevent abuses of power. I now turn to the question of the effectiveness of such measures.

THE 2008 GLOBAL INTEGRITY INDEX

The data in this section were generated by the international NGO Global Integrity (www.globalintegrity.org).

The Global Integrity Index, an international anticorruption rating, uses independent in-country analysts to assess 320 indicators that capture the existence (in law) and effectiveness (in practice) of mechanisms in place in a country to promote public integrity. It was developed to provide a more objective evaluation and critical assessment of anticorruption reforms at the national governance level and is regarded as complementary to perception-based opinion surveys, such as those of Transparency International or the World Bank Institute, that assess perceived levels of corruption.[22]

The index provides a useful snapshot of the national governance picture at a particular moment in time and can potentially be used to benchmark and monitor trends. The six dimensions and twenty-three subcategories of the index are:

1. *Civil Society, Media and Public Information:* civil society organizations; media; public access to information
2. *Elections:* voter and citizen participation; election integrity; political financing
3. *Government Accountability:* executive accountability; legislative accountability; judicial accountability; budget processes
4. *Administration and Civil Service;* civil service regulations; whistle-blowing measures; procurement; privatization
5. *Oversight and Regulation:* national ombudsman; supreme audit institution; taxes and customs; financial sector regulation; business licensing and regulation
6. *Anticorruption and the Rule of Law:* anticorruption law; anticorruption agency; rule of law; law enforcement

What does the 2008 Integrity Scorecard for South Africa tell us?

The index, it must be stressed, does not measure levels of corruption—which postapartheid South Africa continues to suffer from and which is perceived as a growing problem in terms of national priorities (after unemployment, housing, poverty, HIV/AIDS, and crime).[23] Rather, the index assesses the existence of systems to prevent abuses of power, their effectiveness, and citizens' access to these mechanisms. In this way it provides an *indication of political will* to enact accountability mechanisms that prevent abuses of power.

Unsurprisingly, given the impressive efforts undertaken by the ANC government to create a new society and institutions based on sound democratic principles, South Africa ranked "moderate" overall on the 2008 Global

Table 9.1   South Africa Integrity Scorecard 2008

Category I	Civil society, public information, and media	83	Strong
I-1	Civil society organizations	88	Strong
I-2	Media	92	Very strong
I-3	Public access to information	70	Weak
Category II	Elections	67	Weak
II-1	Voting and citizen participation	94	Very strong
II-2	Election integrity	100	Very strong
II-3	Political financing	8	Very weak
Category III	Government accountability	70	Weak
III-1	Executive accountability	77	Moderate
III-2	Legislative accountability	82	Strong
III-3	Judicial accountability	54	Very weak
III-4	Budget processes	67	Weak
Category IV	Administration and civil service	77	Moderate
IV-1	Civil service regulations	51	Very weak
IV-2	Whistle-blowing measures	77	Moderate
IV-3	Procurement	93	Very strong
IV-4	Privatization	87	Strong
Category V	Oversight and regulation	90	Very strong
V-1	National ombudsman	88	Strong
V-2	Supreme audit institution	92	Very strong
V-3	Taxes and customs	100	Very strong
V-4	State-owned enterprises	85	Strong
V-5	Business licensing and regulation	85	Strong
Category VI	Anticorruption and rule of law	84	Strong
VI-1	Anticorruption law	100	Very strong
VI-2	Anticorruption agency	78	Moderate
VI-3	Rule of law	83	Strong
VI-4	Law enforcement	75	Moderate

Source: Global Integrity (2008): *Country Report: South Africa,* http://report.globalintegrity.org/South%20Africa/2008.

Integrity Index, with certain weak areas that are discussed below. The Integrity Scorecard found that most of the laws and institutions are in place to prevent areas where abuses of power may occur. However, certain key regulations, such as a law regulating the sensitive interface between the public and private sector when it comes to post–public sector employment (IV-1) and a law regulating the disclosure of the private funding of political parties (II-3), are notably absent. Additionally, the index highlights that where laws are already in place, much work still needs to be done to ensure that statutes such as those dealing with corruption (VI-4), access to information (I-3), and whistle-blower protection (IV-2) actually work in practice.

INTEGRITY CHALLENGES

The weaknesses in South Africa's national integrity system that the Global Integrity Index highlights relate to the absence of certain key laws and regulations and the questionable effectiveness of certain laws, such as access to information and whistle-blower protection. While it is impossible to give a complete analysis and overview of the governance and accountability challenges that continue to confront South Africa, four key challenges stand out as we look to the future:

- The arms deal scandal that won't go away
- Opaqueness around money and politics
- Uneven implementation of existing laws
- Parliamentary oversight and integrity

THE ARMS DEAL SCANDAL THAT WON'T GO AWAY

We turn now to some key contentious areas informing a discussion of the credibility of the anticorruption agenda in South Africa. The first of these is the arms deal.

In April 2007, demonstrating global leadership in the fight against corruption, South Africa hosted Global Forum V, an intergovernmental forum on fighting corruption, attended by over a thousand delegates. The *Mail and Guardian* newspaper's editorial of that week was scathing. Titled "Corruption Doublespeak," it challenged the credibility gap separating President Thabo Mbeki's sincere commitment to fight corruption because it was a "barrier to the objective of liberating billions of human beings from the scourge of poverty," along with his call to crucially involve global cooperation in the fight against graft, and the fact that Mbeki's government had "ignored, frustrated and side-stepped crucial international investigations into the arms deal, aimed precisely at discovering who in Europe corrupted a new government in the developing world, and at punishing those who damaged its institutions and its poor."[24]

Curiously, there has been continuous and disingenuous denial of any corruption in the arms deal, with former president Thabo Mbeki reiterating this point at the World Economic Forum in Davos. However, for an observer of the criminal trials and convictions of both Tony Yengeni, former chief whip of the ANC, who was jailed for covering up his receipt of a large discount on a luxury vehicle from one of the bidders in the deal, and Schabir Shaik, financial adviser to Jacob Zuma, sentenced to fifteen years in jail for fraud and corruption related to the arms deal, ousted ANC MP Andrew Feinstein has pointed out that "it seems that these events blatantly belie this fact where it has now been proven in courts of law that there was indeed corruption in the arms deal."[25]

The comprehensive Joint Investigating Team's (JIT) investigation, which included three agencies, the NPA, the Auditor General, and the Public Prosecutor (but excluded the Special Investigating Unit, then headed by Judge Willem Heath), concluded in November 2001 that the government was exonerated from corruption with regard to the primary contracts. However, as ANC whistle-blower and former MP Andrew Feinstein points out, "Pressure on the companies bidding for the main contracts compelling them to appoint favored [BEE] sub-contractors before they would be awarded the main contracts was a crucial flaw in the procurement process."[26]

Information emerging in the public arena from German and British investigations into the deal, allegedly probing more than $200 million and up to $1 billion in bribes or "commissions" relating to the South African arms deal, is coming to light, with the government no longer controlling the flow of information on the arms procurement.

What is required is finality in terms of the arms deal investigation. As leading analysts at the Institute for Security Studies have stressed, South African anticorruption agencies must assert themselves and cast the net wider to achieve closure on a saga that has bruised almost all of South Africa's democratic institutions. Requests for mutual legal assistance by countries investigating the deal must be prioritized if South Africa is to credibly contribute to international efforts to deal with corruption in the arms industry.[27]

For now, calls for a full judicial commission of inquiry into the arms deal (and possibly amnesty for full disclosure) continue to echo across the political and NGO spectrum. The breakaway political party, the Congress of the People (COPE), led by, among others, former minister of defense Mosiuoa Lekoto, has called for a full inquiry into the arms deal.[28] Should this happen, former president Mbeki's role in the deal would come under increasing scrutiny—after all, he chaired the cabinet subcommittee that approved the deal. He is also alleged to have met several times with arms companies at crucial times in the procurement process, something he conveniently cannot recall.

Within the new ANC leadership structure, pressure is being put on Mbeki to come clean on his role in the arms deal, and a committee has been appointed to gather facts as part of an internal ANC fact-gathering process on the arms deal and allegations of corruption that, after almost ten years, have not gone away. While calls have been made for these findings to be made public, it remains to be seen whether the ANC will comply. With no public judicial commission of inquiry similar to the Scott Commission of Inquiry into UK arms dealing in sight, the South African public will continue to be in the dark about the R50 billion arms deal, whose rising cost has indirectly impacted the cost of power and electricity regeneration, literally ensuring that South Africans across the country are in the dark, as a result of the frequent load shedding and power cuts.

OPACITY AROUND MONEY AND POLITICS

The second locus of a credible anticorruption campaign concerns disclosure, transparency, and the funding of political parties.

When it comes to knowing who funds the political process in South Africa, the corrupting nexus between power and money, this remains a shocking lacuna in an otherwise impressive array of anticorruption mechanisms. And it is something that the ruling party (as well as other parties in Parliament) seemingly has no real interest in remedying. Allegations of corruption in the arms deal have continually harped on whether kickbacks from arms companies to secure lucrative contracts were possibly funneled into ANC party coffers rather than to purely individuals within the process who might have benefited from the deal.

South Africa does not have regulations governing private contributions to political parties, nor are there limits on individual or corporate donations to candidates or political parties or any limits on total political party expenditure. Most important, in law there are no requirements for the disclosure of donations to political parties or candidates, or any legal requirements for the independent auditing of political parties' finances and candidates in respect to private party financing. Since there are no regulations, these cannot be effectively implemented.

The public interest NGO, the Institute for Democracy in South Africa, made a legal attempt to gain access to financial records of political parties under the terms of the Promotion of Access to Information Act, which proved futile. The "conspiracy of silence" between political parties and private contributors is a major fault line that undermines anticorruption efforts. If corruption occurs where money and power intersect, then those serious about transparency and accountability need to push for disclosure about the money that flows into the political process. Money lubricates access to those with influence, and the quid pro quo that inevitably results from the exchange of it needs to be regulated and placed in the public domain so ordinary citizens can see who the paymasters of their democracy are. Only members of Parliament can put in place laws to regulate the funding contributions to political parties. So far it seems there is no will to do so.

Equally important is the fact that no concrete steps have been taken to place a stopper or "cooling-off period" in the revolving door between government employees entering private sector corporations, through the creation of postemployment restrictions. In order to serve the public interest, it is also necessary to have policies that regulate and sanction civil servants who don't disclose their assets and strictly regulate the almost fifty thousand civil servants who have business interests outside of government.[29]

UNEVEN IMPLEMENTATION OF EXISTING LAWS

The third blight on South Africa's anticorruption program has to do with the uneven implementation of existing good governance laws, such as those regarding access to information and whistle-blower protection.

It appears that while in many cases, the right laws are on the books, such as the access to information and whistle-blower protection laws, these laws are not working in practice. Rather than being a matter purely of the absence of the political will to institute reforms, the weakness here may touch on deeper realities, such as the extreme thinness of human capacity in the South African public sector in terms of skills and resources to apply and administer such laws.

In law and on paper, South Africa has a model Promotion of Access to Information Act with all the essential components, such as the right of appeal if a record is denied and an established institutional mechanism for citizen requests for government records. However, when one considers whether the right of access to information is effective or not, a very different story emerges.

As detailed in section 25 of the act, the information officer of a public body must respond in as reasonable a time as possible and within thirty days of the request being received must notify the requester of his or her decision either to grant or to refuse the requests for information. This rarely happens in practice. Results of the Open Society Justice Initiative comparative studies conducted by the Open Democracy Advice Center (in 2003 and 2004) show that public bodies responded to only thirteen of the one hundred requests submitted, and 62 percent of requests were simply ignored. The majority of internal appeals not responded to within the set time limit may ultimately end up in the higher courts, precipitating a lengthy process that requires the requestor to brief both an attorney and an advocate to assist in the appeal. This process can take as long as three to four years in different courts.

The improvements needed to effectively implement the access to information law may require training as well as technology (e-government), as well as political will on the part of the responsible civil servants. The emergence of national security considerations as a reason to deny the release of government records is an increasingly worrying trend both in South Africa and internationally. The Protection of Information Bill (or so-called "Secrecy" Bill) which has spawned the Right2Know Campaign (www.r2k.org .za) is a case in point.

In law, the Protected Disclosures Act of 2000 protects civil servants and private sector employees who report a criminal offense, a failure to comply with a legal obligation, a miscarriage of justice, the endangering of the health or safety of an individual, the damaging of the environment, or unfair discrimination. The act also states how these wrongdoings should be reported, preferably within the organization, and only outside the organization under certain circumstances. If the wrongdoing concerns one of the above and it is reported correctly, then the act protects the whistle-blower from victimization or dismissal. The employee who feels that he or she has been unfairly treated after blowing the whistle can institute legal action against his or her employer. The remedy for unfair treatment could be reinstatement, removal of the discrimination, or two years' salary as compensation.

There is; however, still widespread ignorance about the whistle-blower protection law. In practice, most civil servants who report financial wrongdoing suffer recrimination or negative consequences, and when allegations are made against very senior civil servants, the backlash is worse because of the power and influence those civil servants wield. Some government departments, such as the Department of Home Affairs, have established confidential hotlines, but it is too early to comment on their effectiveness. The Law Commission is currently considering deficiencies that have been identified in the law, such as the fact that the whistle-blower's confidentiality is not protected, the law does not deal with defamation charges that are brought against a whistle-blower, and the maximum compensation that can be claimed is twenty-four months' salary.

PARLIAMENTARY OVERSIGHT AND INTEGRITY

The fourth area that warrants illumination by the anticorruption spotlight is that of parliamentary oversight and integrity.

How does one make sense of the political interventions of the ANC executive in the operations of Parliament, as demonstrated so starkly in the case of the arms deal? In a dominant-party democracy, can parliament function to serve and protect the public interest? For example, aren't parliamentary committees such as the Standing Committee on Public Accounts (SCOPA) and the Ethics Committee almost superfluous to exercising oversight of the public purse when their proposed investigations are cast aside by an investigation (the JIT), admittedly ordered by Parliament but seemingly controlled by the executive and the ruling party?

While the constitution provides for the passing of legislation conferring budget amendment power on the legislature, such legislation has yet to be passed. A Draft Money Bill Amendment and Procedure and Related Matters Bill was published in 2008. The perception exists that parliamentary capacity to engage with the budget would have to be strengthened before assuming amendment powers. The absence until now of budget amendment legislation has generated a highly executive-driven budget process in which Parliament retains a primarily rubber-stamp function. Most parliamentarians lack the skills to deal substantively with the budget, and resources going to the parliamentary research office remain limited. The "approval" of the Strategic Defence Procurement Package, in other words the arms deal, by Parliament is a case in point. While Parliament may have approved the vision provided by the Defence Review process, executive—political—decisions determined the size and scale of the final defense package.

It appears that the damage done by the arms deal debacle where SCOPA was effectively undermined and sidelined by the ANC and the JIT from the investigation has left scars. In terms of capacity, SCOPA cannot follow up every possible financial irregularity, and so relies significantly on reports from the Auditor General. Concern was noted in the 2006 Global Integrity Report that SCOPA would be hesitant to initiate investigations that went expressly against the wishes of the executive. Clearly, the capacity of parliamentary committees more generally to play an oversight role needs to be bolstered.

Beyond the challenges to exercising its oversight function, the integrity of Parliament itself has been damaged enormously in the past few years by the Travelgate scandal, which involved the widespread abuse of travel vouchers by members of Parliament in collusion with travel agents. Four of the ANC MPs charged in Travelgate have survived to chair various parliamentary committees in the Zuma administration. The opposition has pointed out that since these chairpersons play a critical role in holding the executive to account, they must be beyond reproach, if MPs and the public are to have full confidence in their ability.[30]

As the main institution for representing the public interest, the importance of an effectively functioning Parliament cannot be stressed enough. It has been argued that the strength of the national legislature may be a—or even the—institutional key to democratization. As such, the focus for democrats should be on creating a powerful legislature, and in polities with weak legislatures, democrats should make constitutional reforms to strengthen the legislature a top priority. If politicians fail to establish a national legislature with far-reaching powers, citizens will still find themselves in a polity where their votes do not count (or are not counted properly) and their voices are not heard. On the other hand, if a powerful legislature is established, the people will probably gain and retain their freedom and a say in how they are ruled, even in countries that embark on regime change with inherited structural and historical advantages.[31]

"The price of freedom is eternal vigilance," Thomas Jefferson reminds us. In a society that is transitioning from both a struggle and lager mentality into an open, accountable, and transparent society, there are multiple interests and centers of power, including institutions to check and balance power. These institutions include an active and free press that cannot be suppressed, constantly reminding those in power that they are ultimately accountable to the citizens who entrust them with that power.

Today, South Africa has a dedicated anticorruption law as well as most of the institutional mechanisms in place to prevent corruption. South Africa's leadership on the African continent in purporting to fight corruption is impressive. However, whether the necessary political will exists in South Africa to address corruption wherever it occurs is still not clear.

It appears that cases of petty corruption—rife if one follows media reports—are mostly followed up on when they come to light either through the media, internal investigations, or audits. However, the government's sensitivity, defensiveness, and mishandling of high-profile allegations of "grand" corruption in cases such as the arms deal that involve enormous and often overlapping political and business interests and agendas prevents one from answering this question decisively.

Corruption scandals do not materialize out of nowhere. They are rooted in the absence of key regulatory mechanisms and their effective implementation. In a democracy, citizens have rights and well as responsibilities, one of these being to use democratic means to hold accountable those entrusted with the power to make decisions that affect their lives. As such, political will is not just the preserve of politicians. Citizens themselves need to demand more of their social and political space and ensure that the rules of the democratic game both exist and are followed. External peer pressure and international monitoring, be it through NEPAD and the Africa Peer Review Mechanism or governance scorecards conducted by international NGOs such as Global Integrity or Transparency International, provide an incentive for countries to keep democratic anticorruption reform efforts on track. South Africa's hosting of the 2010 soccer World Cup guaranteed ongoing international interest in these reforms.

Ironically, the arms deal scandal, from 1999 on, may not only have stimulated a bitter succession debate within the ANC tripartite alliance but also played a critical role in profiling anticorruption reforms. It certainly put Mbeki's presidency on the spot and fully engaged and tested, and in some cases severely bruised, the key institutions of democratic accountability, from the press to Parliament, from prosecuting authorities to the Auditor General. In another way, it kept the issue of corruption firmly on the policy agenda and may have stimulated specific reforms in areas such as the tightening of procurement regulations and the range of corruption offences stipulated in the new Prevention and Combating of Corrupt Activities Act. This act, however, has yet to be fully tested.

The hopes and aspirations expressed in the twelve aspirational statements provide an additional checklist for the kind of society South Africans deserve to live in. There are clearly aspects that are under threat, as demonstrated by the erosion of both integrity and independence in a criminal justice system tasked with upholding the law and fighting corruption. South Africa's constitution provides the foundational values for this vision. The best hope for fighting corruption lies with educating citizens about the laws, institutions, and structures that have been conceived in their best interests with the intention of preventing the abuses of power that characterized the worst excesses of apartheid, and with promoting systems of integrity that truly will provide "a better life for all."

APPENDIX: TIMELINE OF ANTICORRUPTION REFORMS AND CORRUPTION CASES

April 1994: The ANC wins a landslide victory in South Africa's first democratic election.

May 1996: Parliamentary Code of Conduct with regard to financial interests is passed.

March 1997: Special Investigating Units (SIUs) are authorized and the Special Tribunals Act becomes law.

June 1997: The Public Service Code of Conduct is passed.

December 1997: Thabo Mbeki is elected president of the ANC.

September 1998: Cabinet approves a National Campaign Against Corruption.

October 1998: Moral Summit takes place in Johannesburg.

November 1998: The Public Sector Anti-Corruption Conference is convened by Parliament.

April 1999: The First National Anti-Corruption Summit is convened.

June 1999: Thabo Mbeki becomes president of South Africa.

June 1999: Formation of the Directorate of Special Operations, a k a "the Scorpions," is announced.

September 1999: The Strategic Defence Procurement Package (SDPP) is announced.

September 1999: PAC MP Patricia de Lille blows the whistle on alleged arms deal corruption.

October 1999: South Africa hosts the Ninth International Anti-Corruption Conference.

March 2000: The Promotion of Access to Information Act becomes law.

July 2000: The Executive Members Ethics Code is passed.

September 2000: The Auditor General's special review of the SDPP finds irregularities.

October 2000: SCOPA releases its fourteenth report, calling for an investigation into the arms deal.

January 2001: President Mbeki announces the exclusion of the SIUs from the Joint Investigating Team.

February 2001: The Protected Disclosure Act becomes law.

June 2001: The National Anti-Corruption Forum (www.nacf.org.za) is launched.

August 2001: South Africa signs the SADC Protocol Against Corruption.

November 2001: The final JIT report on the arms deal is released to Parliament, exonerating the government from corruption in the arms deal.

January 2002: The cabinet adopts the Public Service Anti-Corruption Strategy.

August 2003: NPA boss Bulelani Ngcuka announces a prima facie case of corruption against Zuma, but Zuma will not be charged with Schabir Shaik.

March 2004: South Africa signs the AU Convention on Preventing and Combating of Corruption.

April 2004: The Prevention and Combating of Corrupt Activities Act 12 becomes law.

October 2004: Shaik pleads not guilty to charges of corruption and fraud.

November 2004: South Africa ratifies the UN Convention against Corruption.

March 2005: The Second National Anti-Corruption Summit is convened.

2 June 2005: Judge Hilary Squires finds Shaik guilty of corruption and fraud.

14 June 2005: President Thabo Mbeki sacks Zuma as deputy president.

20 June 2005: NPA boss Vusi Pikoli announces that Zuma will be charged with two counts of corruption.

29 June 2005: Zuma appears in the Durban magistrate's court.

August 2005: The offices of the French arms company Thint, the office of Zuma's attorney, Michael Hulley, and Zuma's homes and former offices are raided.

May 2006: Zuma is acquitted of rape.

September 2006: Judge Herbert Msimang strikes Zuma's case off the roll after the prosecution said it was not ready to proceed.

November 2006: The Supreme Court of Appeal rejects Shaik's bid to appeal.

March 2007: South Africa hosts the Africa Forum on Fighting Corruption.

April 2007: South Africa hosts the Global Forum V on Fighting Corruption.

September 2007: Mbeki suspends NPA director Vusi Pikoli

October 2007: The Constitutional Court rejects Shaik's bid to appeal his conviction and fifteen-year sentence.

November 2007: The Supreme Court of Appeal rules in favor of the NPA in the case relating to various search and seizure raids in the Zuma case.

19 December 2007: Jacob Zuma is elected president of the ANC at the Polokwane Conference.

28 December 2007: The Directorate of Special Operations, a k a the Scorpions, serves Zuma with papers to stand trial in the high court on various counts of racketeering, money laundering, corruption, and fraud.

March 2008: Zuma and Thint appeal to the Constitutional Court against the Supreme Court of Appeal ruling in favor of the NPA.

April 2008: The Constitutional Court dismisses Shaik's appeal against the validity of a confiscation order regarding R33 million of Shaik's and his companies' assets.

July 2008: The Constitutional Court rules in favor of the NPA in the Zuma-Thint appeal

12 September 2008: Judge Chris Nicholson rules that Zuma was entitled to make representations before the National Director of Public Prosecutions (NDPP) decided to recharge him, effectively halting his prosecution. He also said he could not exclude the possibility of political interference in the decision to recharge Zuma.

20 September 2008: Drawing on the Nicholson judgment, the ANC announces that Mbeki will be recalled from office.

22 September 2008: Mbeki, after nine and a half years in office, announces his resignation.

23 September 2008: Mbeki applies for leave to appeal the Nicholson ruling in the Constitutional Court.

11 November 2008: The Constitutional Court dismisses Mbeki's application, saying it would not be in the interest of justice to hear the case because the NDPP was already in the process of appealing the Nicholson ruling.

28 November 2008: The Supreme Court of Appeal hears the NDPP appeal against the Nicholson ruling.

12 January 2009: The Supreme Court of Appeal upholds the NDPP appeal but dismisses Mbeki's application to intervene, and dismisses the application to have Nicholson's "political meddling" findings struck out

March 2009: Schabir Shaik is released from prison on medical grounds after serving just over two years of a fifteen-year sentence.

6 April 2009: NPA acting director Mokotedi Mpshe, after receiving representations from Zuma's lawyers, announces that charges against him will be dropped.

22 April 2009: South Africa holds its fourth democratic elections.

May 2009: President Zuma takes up office vowing to stamp out corruption.

May 2009: The Directorate for Priority Crime Investigation (DPCI) is set up within the South African Police Services to replace the Scorpions.[32]

NOTES

1. "Statement by the National Director of Public Prosecutions on the Matter S v Zuma and Others," http://www.mg.co.za/uploads/2009/04/06/statement.pdf.

2. "Statement of the President of South Africa, Thabo Mbeki, at the Joint Sitting of Parliament on the Release of Hon. Jacob Zuma from His Responsibilities as Deputy President" (Pretoria: Government Communication and Information System, 14 June 2005).

3. SAPA, "Shaik Released on Medical Parole," 3 March 2009, http://www.news24.com/News24/South_Africa/News/0,,2-7-1442_2478896,00.html.

4. "Schabir Shaik Keeps Head Down on Durban Golf Course," *Mercury,* 22 October 2009.

5. "Twist in Tale of Victims and Villains," Zuma Corruption Trial, *Sunday Times,* 6 August 2006.

6. "I Won't Make 'Scorpions' a Spy Outfit," *Mail and Guardian,* 23 May 2009.

7. See the website http://www.podcart.co.za/audio/UCT/wim.mp3.

8. The Democratic Alliance's founding affidavit in the Zuma review application is at http://www.politicsweb.co.za/politicsweb/view/politicsweb/en/page71654?oid=124514&sn=Detail.

9. See the appendix to this essay, "Timeline of Anticorruption Reforms and Corruption Cases."

10. "NPA Head Defends Zuma", *Mercury,* 19 October 2009.

11. "Mbeki Suspends NDPP's Vusi Pikoli," *SAPA,* 24 September 2007.

12. "The Desperate Bid to Shield Selebi," *Mail and Guardian,* 5 October 2007.

13. "Compulsory Visas for South Africans," *Times,* 9 February 2009.

14. "SA's Zuma Cleared of Rape," *BBC Online,* 8 May 2006, http://news.bbc.co .uk/2/hi/4750731.stm.

15. J. Zuma, "Address by His Excellency Mr. Jacob Zuma on the Occasion of his Inauguration as Fourth President of the Republic of South Africa," 9 May 2009, www.info.gov.za/speeches/2009/09050912051001.html.

16. "Zuma's Cabinet Inc.," *Mail and Guardian,* 15 May 2009.

17. "S'bu Ndebele Decides to Return the Merc," *SAPA,* 19 May 2009, Politics Web.co.za, http://www.politicsweb.co.za/politicsweb/view/politicsweb/en//page 71627?oid=129699&sn=Detail.

18. Mamphele Ramphele, *Laying Ghosts to Rest: Dilemmas of the Transformation in South Africa* (Cape Town: Tafelberg, 2008).

19. The health minister at the time, Nkosazana Dlamini-Zuma, was accused of misleading Parliament about the use of EU funds in the awarding of a contract of R14.2 million to produce an AIDS awareness musical, *Sarafina Two.* An Auditor General report found that bidding procedures were violated, and an inquiry by the Office of the Public Protector found donor money was allocated through improper tender and awarding procedures, with a litany of irregularities. The EU ambassador to South Africa stressed categorically there had been no prior authorization, and regarded the diversion of funds as a serious misuse of EU support. While no evidence or implication of the abuse of official position for personal gain was found, this was a clear case of diversion of aid in a manner bordering on mismanagement and a lack of both transparency and public parliamentary accountability.

20. The Motheo Housing scandal involved an unknown company run by a close friend of then housing minister, Sankie Mthembi-Mahanyele, that was awarded a R198 million contract to build more than ten thousand houses. The director general in the Ministry of Housing, Billy Cobbett, blew the whistle on the deal and was fired. The commission of inquiry looking into the matter found no proof of outright corruption, but criticized the Mpumalanga government's irresponsible handling of housing funds.

21. *Country Self Assessment Report,* African Peer Review Mechanism, 9 June 2006, www.aprm.org.za.

22. See M. Camerer, "Measuring Public Integrity," *Journal of Democracy* 17, no. 1 (2006).

23. "The Public Agenda: Change and Stability in South Africans' Ratings of National Priorities," Afrobarometer briefings no. 45, June 2006, www.afrobarometer .org/abbriefing.htm.

24. "Corruption Doublespeak," *Mail and Guardian,* 4 April 2007.

25. Andrew Feinstein, "Arms Deal Returns to Haunt ANC," *Mail and Guardian,* 11 February 2007.

26. Ibid.

27. Hennie Van Vuuren, "Priorities for South Africa's Anti-corruption Agenda in 2007" (Cape Town: Institute for Security Studies, February 2007).

28. "COPE Promises Arms Deal Justice," *Business Day,* 26 March 2009.

29. Van Vuuren, "Priorities for South Africa's Anti-corruption Agenda."

30. Donwald Pressly, "Rise of Travelgate Survivors Harms Democracy," *Business Report,* 24 May 2009.

31. Steven Fish, "Stronger Legislatures, Stronger Democracies," *Journal of Democracy* 17, no. 1 (January 2006).

32. This timeline draws on the "Timeline of Zuma Events: News 24," 6 April 2009, file:///Users/admin/Desktop/Timeline%20of%20Zuma%20events:%20News 24:%20SouthAfrica:%20News.webarchive.

The Land Question

Exploring Obstacles to Land Redistribution in South Africa

Lungisile Ntsebeza

The gradual conversion of a large number of the indigenous people of present-day South Africa into wage laborers, particularly after the discovery of minerals in the latter part of the nineteenth century (see Bundy 1988; Mafeje 1988), has led to a peculiar situation in which the land question in South Africa has been marginalized. Yet, compared with the situation in other countries on the African continent, the extent of land plunder in South Africa was extraordinary. The Natives Land Act of 1913 was the first major legislative attempt on the part of colonialists to grab a substantial amount of the land. This act confined the indigenous people to about 7 percent of the land in areas that were designated reserves. They were thus not legally allowed to own land outside the reserves. The area of land available to indigenous peoples in the reserves was increased in terms of the Land Laws of 1936 to 13 percent of the landscape. However, this hardly made a dent in the chronic shortage of land in these reserves, a development that forced many African producers to sell their labor, with some becoming migrant workers and others fully fledged workers in the cities. From the late 1960s, however, the concerns of the liberation movement focused on urban issues to the neglect of the countryside.

A key problem currently facing South Africa is black poverty, the roots of which cannot be dissociated from colonial conquest and land dispossession. It is hard to imagine how a permanent solution to black poverty and the legacy of colonialism and apartheid in South Africa can be achieved without some resolution of the land question. Indeed, land remains at the heart of the struggle not only for livelihoods, but for citizenship as well. Consequently, resolving the land question is crucial to what it means to be a citizen in South Africa.

Against the background outlined above, this essay surveys the land question in South Africa and attempts by the African National Congress (ANC)–led government to deal with it since the advent of democracy in South Africa. I show that the land reform program in South Africa, which has very limited objectives, given the ravages of colonialism and land plunder, has not gone far toward resolving the land question. The entrenchment of the property clause in the constitution, coupled with weak civil society organizations focused on the land question, presents a major obstacle to achieving even the limited objectives of the land reform program. Recent pronouncements in the 2009 ANC election manifesto and government's recently renewed commitment to rural development and land reform do not change the picture.

This essay is not about what blacks will do or should do with their land once it has been returned to them, or they have claimed it back. These are important questions, but they should be addressed separately and not confused with the need to address historical injustices—the thrust of this essay.

THE LAND QUESTION AND ITS RESOLUTION IN THE POLITICAL NEGOTIATION PROCESSES

Archie Mafeje's and Colin Bundy's work is representative of a considerable scholarship that has addressed the issue of colonial conquest and land dispossession, and how this resulted in the proletarianization of the indigenous people of present-day South Africa. I agree with this characterization and do not repeat it here. However, notable in this narrative is that, unlike in Zimbabwe and Mozambique, for example, the liberation struggle in South Africa was not overtly fought around the land question. This was particularly the case when popular resistance against apartheid rekindled in the late 1960s and early 1970s, following the massive political clampdown against resistance in the early 1960s. Prior to this, there was limited involvement by the All African Convention (AAC) and the ANC in rural struggles against government policies that sought to limit the quantity of land and stock. Both organizations adopted clauses on the land question in their political programs—the ten-point program of the Non-European Unity Movement (which emerged from the AAC), adopted in 1943, and the Freedom Charter of the ANC, which was adopted in 1955. But the land question was peripheral to the activities of these organizations. An organization that promised to put the land question high on its agenda, the Pan Africanist Organisation (PAC), which was formed in 1959, unfortunately never managed to move beyond the slogan and devise a program of action.

Although the land question was pushed to the periphery during the liberation struggles, particularly from the late 1960s and during the debates of the 1980s, it came up for discussion during the political negotiations of the early 1990s, this time in the context of discussing the issue of property rights. The ANC, the leading liberation organization involved in the political negotiations, had indicated in its Freedom Charter that land would be shared by those who worked it. However, during the negotiations, the ANC shifted from this earlier position to an acceptance of the property clause in the interim constitution of 1993, and later the final constitution of 1996.[1] The issue of property rights is dealt with in section 28 of the interim constitution. It is widely accepted that this section represented a compromise between the ANC and the National Party (NP) (which led the former apartheid government) positions. Subsection 1 clearly protects existing property rights and those who have the resources to "acquire" and therefore buy property, while subsection 3 opens a loophole for the expropriation of land by the government with compensation. This, in my opinion, gives rise to a fundamental tension between, on the one hand, the protection of existing property rights, and on the other a commitment to expropriate land "for public purpose."

At the time, analysts such as Chaskalson were optimistic that in a democratic South Africa, the tension would be resolved in favor of the historically disadvantaged by the courts. Although agreeing that the wording of section 28 "is not always clear," he imagined that the courts "would do well to adopt a purposive approach" in interpreting this section, bearing "in mind the compromise which the section" sought to achieve. Drawing on comparative legal history, Chaskalson concluded that if courts were "overzealous in their protection of property rights . . . the potential for constitutional conflict between court and state will be substantial" (1994, 139). However, current indications suggest that the South African courts have been, and will be, inclined to protect property rights.

As with the interim constitution, the property clause was entrenched in the final constitution. The final version of the constitution essentially reinforced and refined what was already contained in the interim constitution: protection of existing property rights of landowners, the vast majority of whom are white, while at the same time making a commitment to redistributing land to the dispossessed majority. The main difference seems to be that whereas the interim constitution allowed for expropriation only for public purposes, the final constitution expanded this language to include public interest. The issue of expropriating land only for public purposes raises the question of how to classify land expropriated for land reform purposes. It can be argued that land expropriated for land reform purposes is not for public purposes, given that it is transferred to the historically dispossessed. On this point, Chaskalson correctly argues that, insofar as "any substantial land reform programme is likely to depend on expropriation . . . land reform could be rendered 'constitutionally impossible'" (1994, 136–37). By expanding expropriation to public interest, the constitution opened the way for expropriating land for redistribution purposes.

LAND REFORM IN A DEMOCRATIC SOUTH AFRICA: A BRIEF SURVEY

The land reform program in South Africa has not made notable inroads in resolving the land question. The facts and figures of land ownership are by now very familiar. Of the 30 percent of agricultural land that was supposed to be redistributed in the first five years of democracy in South Africa, barely 5 percent has been distributed after seventeen years of democracy. I do not propose to develop a full critique of the land reform program in this essay but to point out the key features of the South African land reform program that have not been realized.[2] The program is based on market principles, according to which the ANC-led government would undertake to buy land from white commercial farmers to facilitate the redistribution of land. In 1997, the Department of Land Affairs adopted a white paper on land policy that, among other things, endorsed the principle of "willing seller, willing buyer." The initial target proposed by the World Bank was the transfer of 30 percent of agricultural land from white farmers to blacks within the first five years of South Africa's democracy. This target was not achieved, and it is doubtful that it will be achieved under current conditions.

OBSTACLES TO LAND REDISTRIBUTION IN SOUTH AFRICA

As I indicated earlier, this essay focuses on two key issues (out of many) as obstacles to land redistribution in South Africa, even in the limited form of the transference of 30 percent of white-claimed agricultural land to blacks: the entrenchment of the property clause in the constitution and the weakness of civil society organizations. Let me elaborate on these issues.

Debate over Current Policies with Specific Reference to the Property Clause

Various explanations have been offered to account for the slow delivery of land reform. Until recently, there were those who argued that the policy fundamentals are in place, and that what is missing is a commitment from the government to ensure that the policies are implemented. This argument was often couched in terms of the lack of political will on the part of the ANC-led government and lack of capacity on the part of government officials.[3] As I have argued (Ntsebeza 2007), scholars such as Ruth Hall do not query the fact that section 25(1) protects existing property rights (2004, 5). Her point is that although the land reform policy is based on a "willing seller, willing buyer" condition, the state can expropriate land. She argues that far-reaching land reform is possible within the existing constitutional framework. Hall's overall argument is that expropriation powers "have been largely unused," having been applied in only two restitution cases so far. This leads her to conclude that there is "room for manoeuvre" and that the call for legal and constitutional amendment "seems misplaced. Constitutional amendment is not the immediate challenge since the constraint is a political rather than legal one" (2004, 7).

Radical analysts, on the other hand, do not consider current policies adequate and argue for policies that will facilitate a radical land redistribution program that goes beyond the meager 30 percent target. These critics consider the entrenchment of the property clause in the constitution, as well as the endorsement in policy of the willing seller, willing buyer principle, as major obstacles to implementing even the limited land redistribution program of government. Hendricks and Ntsebeza (2000), Hendricks (2004), and Ntsebeza (2007) have argued that the provisions of section 25 of the constitution are contradictory in the sense that they protect existing property rights while at the same time making a commitment to redistribute land to the dispossessed majority. The two objectives, these scholars argue, cannot be achieved at the same time, simply because the bulk of land outside the former Bantustans, or black "homelands," is under private ownership and consequently safeguarded by the constitution. In this regard, a declaration that land will be made available to blacks is rendered void for the simple reason that whites privately own most land. As commentators like Mafeje (2002) might put it, the declaration eschews the land question and in so doing confirms the pre-1994 situation. With this in mind, Hendricks (2004) asked, Does the South African constitution justify colonial land theft?

What about the issue of expropriation? It is important to remember that because expropriation is accompanied by compensation, a second question arises of how compensation is determined. Subsection (3) of section (25) of the constitution is supposed to guide the determination of compensation. However, this subsection is extremely vague. It merely states that "the amount of compensation and the time and manner of payment must be just and equitable." But what precisely counts as a just and equitable dispensation is not clearly spelled out, other than a further statement that the compensation should reflect "an equitable balance between the public interest and the interests of those affected." In this respect, "all relevant circumstances" would include the history of the acquisition and use of the property, the market value of the property, and the extent of direct state investment and subsidy in the acquisition and beneficial capital improvement of the property.

To my knowledge, the only clarity on the issue of compensation emanates from the so-called Geldenhuys formula. Justice Geldenhuys is a land claims court judge who worked out a formula for determining compensation in cases involving expropriation for restitution. In essence, the formula takes into account two of the five circumstances mentioned in section 25(3) of the constitution: the market value of the property and the extent of direct state investment and subsidy in the acquisition and beneficial capital improvement of the property. Circumstances that the formula is silent on are the current use of the property, the history of the acquisition and use of the property, and the purpose of the expropriation. These are important factors that may have an effect on the price. In a nutshell, the amount of compensation is the market value of the property minus the present value of past subsidies. Although this formula was applied in a land restitution case, I argue that it could also be used as a guide in cases of land redistribution.

The pertinent question is whether the possibility of expropriation undermines the argument that the property clause in the constitution is a hindrance to fundamental land redistribution. I contend that the expropriation clause does not affect my core conclusion about the property clause. First and foremost, government has shown great reluctance to invoke the expropriation clause (for an elaboration on this argument, see Ntsebeza 2007). Of note here, in 2008 the ANC-led government was forced to withdraw an expropriation bill largely because of pressure from organized white commercial farmers and their capitalist allies. The issue of the constitutionality of expropriation became the main bone of contention.

Second, even if the government were to pursue expropriation, there is still the question of compensation and how the price is determined. Gelden-huys ruled that the price of land should be determined by the market. Al-though the Geldenhuys formula takes into account the critical issue of sub-sidies, which should be deducted from the market price, the fact that com-pensation is based on the market price makes it almost impossible for the government to budget for land reform, for the simple reason that the role of the state in determining the price is very limited, if it exists at all. This seems to pour cold water on the optimistic view expressed by Chaskalson about the role of courts in resolving the land question. Indeed, virtually all the director generals of the former Department of Land Affairs complained that white commercial farmers were inclined to inflate their prices. Despite her posi-tion, Hall also concedes that in practice, white farmers "determine when, where and at what price land will be made available" (2004, 6).

Most recently, the issue of the inflated prices charged by white farm-ers and implications for land reform was raised by the minister of the newly established Department of Rural Development and Land Reform, Gugile Nkwinti.[4] He accused some white commercial farmers of trying to sabotage the land reform program by inflating the prices of land. In this regard, he made the following remark: "The department will have to investigate less costly alternative methods of land acquisition, by engaging with all stake-holders within the sector."[5] The minister also indicated that the willing seller, willing buyer policy would have to be reconsidered. These remarks are viewed by the biggest farmers union, AGRISA, as a threat. Its president, Jo-hannes Moller, produced this telling response: "If government really does go ahead and scrap the willing-buyer, willing-seller principle and not replace it with a system based on market value, we will see it as an infringement on property rights and a violation of the constitution." He went on to say that "South Africa cannot afford losing investor confidence in agriculture, in property, and in the country and economy in general . . . we cannot af-ford it."

It was remarks of this kind that arguably compelled the ANC-led govern-ment to withdraw the expropriation bill in 2008. It is also clear that white commercial farmers and their allies have only one reading of the constitu-tion: that it must protect their property rights and, where land has been expropriated, that they must be paid market-related prices for their land, with limited involvement of government in the establishment of the prices. White farmers use the protection of property in the constitution as their de-fense. However, their interpretation does not take into account the legiti-macy of the claims of Africans whose land was violently taken from them.

As Mafeje would say, tedious as it is, the land question in South Africa and its consequences cannot be resolved without taking into account colonial conquest and land dispossession. The attitude of white farmers in many ways strengthens my contention that the property clause is a major obstacle to resolving the land question in South Africa. Contrary to Hall's argument, the issue of existing property rights and the possibility of expropriation is not merely a political issue, it has legal implications too. The Geldenhuys judgment provides a clue to how courts may rule in these cases.

It is intriguing that the history of how colonialists acquired land in the first instance has not received prominence in the determination of compensation. Insofar as reference is made to history, the suggestion is that this refers to the history of land acquisition by the affected landowner. But it is rather the history of colonial conquest and land dispossession that lies at the heart of the land question in South Africa. It is hard to imagine how any process of land redistribution that submerges this history can hope to gain legitimacy, particularly in the eyes of those who were robbed of their land. Closely linked to this is that the naked exploitation of black labor, which was central to the success of white commercial farming in South Africa, is also interestingly not considered to be one of the crucial factors that must to be taken into account when the amount of compensation is calculated.

While the issue of the property clause is critical in discussions about obstacles to a successful land redistribution program, equally important is the question of agency, to which I now turn.

Civil Society Organization on the Land Question

Agency around the land question has been weak in South Africa. This is particularly the case since the reemergence of urban-based civil society movements, including trade unions and rights struggles since the early 1970s. Yet an organized campaign around the land issue, with clear objectives and strategy and involving those who are directly affected, is a necessity for successful land redistribution. Such a structure becomes all the more necessary given the organized nature of commercial farmers and the alliances they enjoy with other formations of capital in South Africa.

Land and agrarian movements in South Africa have dealt with the land question in different ways, but for the most part these movements have been weak. Why? Two interlinked issues seem to be operant. First, the land question tends to be defined as a rural phenomenon, with an almost exclusive focus on agriculture. This view endorses a very narrow and limited way of thinking about the land question. Not only does it exclude urban struggles related to the land question, including housing and the possibility of urban agriculture, it also tends to push the mining industry out of the discussion. This leads us to the second issue, which has to do with the nature of land and agrarian movements and questions of strategy. Defining the land question as rural and concerned with agriculture shapes the nature and strategy of land and agrarian movements in negative ways, and it raises hurdles to the possibility of striking up alliances with urban-based movements involved in land struggles (though not necessarily for agricultural land) as well as movements involved in struggles in the mining industry. With these shaping phenomena in mind, let us turn to land and agrarian movements in South Africa.

The organized voice from below in the land sector at the advent of democracy in 1994 was a group of NGOs that established a network referred to as the National Land Committee (NLC). These organizations had emerged during the apartheid period, mainly in the 1980s, as a response to the forced removal of millions of black Africans from white-designated areas. Thus, land and agrarian movements were led by NGOs that acted for and on behalf of land-seeking black victims of segregation and apartheid in South Africa. The composition of land movements since the 1980s differed tremendously from the rural land lobby of the 1940s, 1950s, and early 1960s. The earlier movements were led by those directly affected by the policies of those times. In the majority of cases, there was no direct involvement of formal political organizations, and NGOs hardly existed (Matoti and Ntsebeza 2004). The best-known of these movements is the one that organized the Mpondo revolt of the early 1960s that Govan Mbeki (1984) writes about. But there were others, for example in the former Xhalanga district in Western Thembuland (Ntsebeza 2006). However, these movements were ruthlessly suppressed in the early 1960s as part of the mopping-up campaign of the NP. While the fact that these struggles were led by the rural residents themselves, with hardly any involvement by political organizations, meant that the struggles were led and controlled by those affected, the downside was that the struggles became isolated and thus were relatively easily suppressed.

When resistance reemerged after the clampdown of the early 1960s, the focus was on urban areas, particularly those connected to trade unions. The attention to urban land struggles intensified after the student uprising of 1976 and the establishment of the United Democratic Front (UDF) in 1983. It is in this context that NGOs, which were urban-based, emerged, with some affiliates of the NLC, to address forced removals. This form of organization was different from earlier forms, as NGOs took the lead in pursuing issues on behalf of rural residents. In the 1980s, most of the affiliates of the NLC cast their lot with the broad liberation movement under the auspices of the UDF. In the early 1990s, during the political negotiations, the NLC became part of the land lobby identifying with the ANC. Although some affiliates were not happy with the adoption of the property clause in the constitution, they nonetheless remained loyal to the ANC.

The ANC went on to adopt a market-led approach to land reform, but when it came to power, many thought that the ANC government was seriously committed to redressing historical injustices and would somehow do so within the limits of neoliberal capitalism. The government, for its part, had in 1994 followed a World Bank recommendation that 30 percent of white-claimed agricultural land be transferred during the first five years of democracy. As a result, some members resigned from their organizations and joined the Department of Land Affairs (DLA) as government officials. Those remaining in the NGOs took it upon themselves to support the DLA. The presumption was, "this is our government," and the room to maneuver seemed quite wide.

The embarrassing and frustratingly slow pace of land delivery, however, gave rise to discontent, which fed into the formation of the Landless People's Movement (LPM) in 2001. The NLC played a crucial role in the establishment of the LPM. Events in Zimbabwe also helped to propel the formation of the LPM, as did connections with the Brazilian Landless Workers' Movement (MST) and Vía Campesina.

The growth of a discontented landless people supported by the NLC was rather short-lived. By the end of 2003, the NLC and LPM were in disarray. Long-standing disputes within the NLC over support for the LPM intensified in the period following the World Summit on Sustainable Development in 2002. By 2004 the NLC had formally disbanded as a network, although its affiliates continued to exist, with some establishing an informal network. After the demise of the NLC, barely two years after the world summit, there came into existence an alliance of various movements under the acronym ALARM (Alliance of Land and Agrarian Reform Movements). The formation of ALARM was a direct response to a call for a land summit by the DLA. The summit was eventually held in July 2005. To bridge the gap that appeared when the NLC became defunct, various organizations came together to form ALARM. However, as with the LPM, ALARM's lease on life appears to be threatened. Interviews with activists who come from the membership of ALARM suggest deep divisions, with some, mainly the former affiliates of the NLC, correctly claiming that ALARM was established as a response to the land summit organized by the former DLA. For these activists, there is no life for ALARM after the land summit.

Activists of the Trust for Community Outreach and Education (TCOE), on the other hand, were strongly in favor of the continued existence of ALARM. TCOE's roots are in the black consciousness movement after the death of Steve Biko, and in liberation theology. At a time when the NLC and LPM were garnering most of the publicity and attention, TCOE and its affiliates were quietly involved in low-profile rural organization. Their initial programs were in response to the education crisis following the students' protests and boycotts against "gutter education" in the 1970s and early 1980s. Since 2000 the focus of TCOE has been on issues of land, local government, and basic needs. To mark its twentieth anniversary, TCOE organized a people's tribunal on landlessness in Port Elizabeth, Eastern Cape Province, in December 2003. For them, it seems, the issue with ALARM has to do with the importance of and the need for a national structure, especially given the demise of the NLC. But even within TCOE there are subtle differences. Part of the problem with TCOE is that while advocating for the continued existence of ALARM, the organization is at the same time in the process of organizing what its leaders consider to be a rural people's movement made up of those directly affected by landlessness and problems surrounding land use and production. In this new situation, TCOE sees itself in a supportive and facilitative role.

In a nutshell, most of the above is still in an embryonic phase. Current indications suggest that struggles connected to the land question and the problems of the rural poor are weak. Whether things will remain as they are remains to be seen.

In closing, I want to reflect on two related issues: why the state has not, does not, and seems very reluctant to act in a manner that may antagonize white commercial farmers, and the relevance of the land question in contemporary South Africa. Regarding the former, a standard response from some analysts, as in the case of Hall, cited earlier, suggests that the state does not have the political will to use its expropriation powers. Others, such as Marais (1998), point to the defeat of the Left in the tripartite alliance (of the ANC, SACP, and Congress of South African Trade Unions, or COsatu) in the mid-1990s when there was a shift from the Reconstruction and Development Programme (RDP) to Growth, Employment and Redistribution (GEAR).[6] This only begs the question, though, of why the Left lost the battle.

A more substantial explanation cannot afford to ignore the global political and economic order that emerged after the collapse of Soviet communism beginning in the late 1980s and how this affected the balance of forces. The transition to democracy in South Africa in the early 1990s took place at a critical moment (Burawoy 2004). The international climate clearly favored neoliberal capitalism, thus making it almost impossible to imagine the emergence of a left radical agenda in a marginal country such as South Africa. Thus, when the ANC announced its election manifesto, the RDP, in 1994, there was a fundamental reversal of the Freedom Charter's call for the nationalization of land. Although the RDP had redistributive elements, the document equally committed the ANC, though cautiously, to a market-led land reform program. The adoption of GEAR, though, suggested that the neoliberal tendencies took the upper hand. In many ways the land reform program, and the property clause in particular, are good examples of how the ANC tried to deal with the dilemma of the reality of the dominance of neoliberal capitalism, on the one hand, and the pressure toward redress and equity on the other. Gillian Hart brilliantly captures this dilemma: "GEAR sits uneasily astride the emancipatory promises of the liberation struggle, as well as the material hopes, aspirations, and rights of the large majority of South Africans" (2002, 7).

There seems little doubt that the ANC-led government is under tremendous pressure from both local and international capital to pursue a neoliberal capitalist agenda in South Africa. For example, the land summit in July 2005 passed radical resolutions regarding land reform in South Africa. But, as my discussion above of the response of AGRISA to the remarks by Minister Nkwinti in June 2009 shows, it will be difficult for the ANC-led government to deal with the resolutions of the land summit without a possible legal and political challenge by white commercial farmers and their allies. Their strength currently is that they are organized in themselves as farmers. Not only this, they also have the backing of fellow capitalists, both here and abroad. In a sense, white commercial farmers in South Africa, despite being a minority, are aware of their strength arising out of the support they get or may get from global capitalism.

Be that as it may, there is a land question in South Africa that cannot be denied and is in need of urgent attention. The current global economic and financial crisis, which exploded openly in 2008, and the resultant massive unemployment call for creative solutions, which will have to include the role of land in combating poverty. The ANC, and indeed all political parties in South Africa, seemed to realize this point in the run-up to the national and provincial elections in 2009. Virtually all the South African political parties' manifestos said something about the importance of land to the issue of deepening poverty and unemployment. Quite possibly for the first time since the advent of democracy, rural development and the land question rank among the top five priorities of the ANC. Even in the best of times, South African capitalism has never managed to adequately employ its growing urban population. This statement applies particularly to blacks. The situation has been made even bleaker by the global economic and financial meltdown of 2009. Thus, the consideration of land as part of the solution is critical.

Further, the claims of the dispossessed and poor South Africans are legitimate. There is no doubt that the market-led approach to land reform, the inclusion of the protection of property rights in the constitution, and the willing buyer, willing seller approach to land reform are insufficient to redress years of colonial and apartheid dispossession. In this regard, it may be appropriate to recall the words of Judge Didcott in 1988 when reflecting on a bill of rights for a democratic South Africa:

> What a Bill of Rights cannot afford to do here . . . is to protect private property with such zeal that it entrenches privilege. A major problem which any future South African government is bound to face will be the problem of poverty, of its alleviation and of the need for the country's wealth to be shared more equitably. . . .
>
> Should a bill of rights obstruct the government of the day when that direction is taken, should it make the urgent task of social or economic reform impossible or difficult to undertake, we shall have on our hands a crisis of the first order. (quoted in Chaskalson 1993, 73–74)

In conclusion, there is a need to open up debate and discussion on the issue of property rights. The starting point in that debate should be whether a comprehensive land redistribution program in South Africa can take place if it ignores colonial conquest, land dispossession, and the triumph of commercial farming through the naked exploitation of black labor. Above all, the debate would have to address the entrenchment of the property clause in the constitution. Current initiatives by the ANC administration, laudable as they are, have not dealt with these hard realities. Yet it is difficult to imagine how rural development and land reform could be sustainable under current policies, which were crafted within a broadly neoliberal framework. Finally, for these debates to be meaningful, it is of utmost importance that those who suffered these injustices, the indigenous people of South Africa, play a leading role. Those who sympathize with them, including the state and NGOs, should assume a supportive rather than a leading role.

NOTES

A version of this chapter was published in 2007 by HSRC Press; see Ntsebeza (2007).

1. For a detailed treatment of the property clause, see Chaskalson (1993, 1994, 1995) and Ntsebeza (2007).

2. For a comprehensive attempt to assess the land reform program in South Africa, see Ntsebeza and Hall (2007).

3. See Ntsebeza (2007) for an elaboration of this line of thinking.

4. When the new ANC administration under President Jacob Zuma came to power in 2009, the former Departments of Agriculture and Land Affairs, which were under one minister, were reorganized into the Department of Rural Development and Land Affairs, with its own minister, and the Department of Agriculture, Forestry and Fisheries, also having its own minister.

5. See the website http://af.reuters.com/article/topNews/idAFJOE5510FJ2009 0619?sp=true (last accessed 21 June 2009).

6. See the next paragraph for an elaboration of the differences between the two.

BIBLIOGRAPHY

Burawoy, M. 2004. "From Liberation to Reconstruction: Theory and Practice in the Life of Harold Wolpe." Harold Wolpe Memorial Lecture, Cape Town, 29 July.

Bundy, C. 1988. *The Rise and Fall of the South African Peasantry.* Cape Town: David Philip.

Chaskalson, M. 1993. "Should There Be a Property Clause: Implications of the Constitutional Protection of Property in the United States and the Commonwealth." In *Land, Property Rights and the New Constitution,* ed. Minnie Venter and Minna Anderson. Belleville, SA: University of the Western Cape.

———. 1994. "The Property Clause: Section 28 of the Constitution." *South African Journal on Human Rights* 131:131–39.

———. 1995. "Stumbling Towards Section 28: Negotiations over the Protection of Property Rights in the Interim Constitution." *South African Journal on Human Rights* 11:222–40.

Hart, G. 2002. *Disabling Globalization: Places of Power in Post-aparteid South Africa.* Pietermatzburg: University of Natal Press.

Hall, R. 2004. "Restitution and the Politics of Land Reform: Stepping Outside the Box." Paper presented at a conference, "Ten Years of Democracy in Southern Africa," Queens University, Kingston, ON, 2–5 May.

Hendricks, F. 2004 "Does the South African Constitution Legitimise Colonial Land

Alienation?" Paper presented at the Sociology Department seminar series, Rand Afrikaans University, 5 March.

Hendricks, F., and Ntsebeza, L. 2000. "The Paradox of South Africa's Land Reform Policy." Paper presented at SARIPS Annual Colloquium, Harare, Zimbabwe.

Mafeje, A. 1988. "The Agrarian Question and Food Production in Southern Africa." In *Food Security Issues in Southern Africa: Selected Proceedings of the Conference on Food Security Issues in Southern Africa. Maseru 12–14 January 1987,* ed. Kwesi K. Prah. Southern Africa Studies Series no. 4, Institute of Southern African Studies, National University of Lesotho.

———. 2002. "The Land and the Agrarian Question in Southern Africa." Seminar paper presented to the Sociology and Industrial Sociology Department, Rhodes University, Grahamstown, 8 October.

Marais, H. 1998. *South Africa, Limits to Change: The Political Economy of Transformation.* London: Zed Books.

Matoti, S., and L. Ntsebeza. 2004. "Rural Resistance in Mpondoland and Themluland 1960–1963." In *The Road to Democracy in South Africa,* vol. 4 (1960–1970), ed. T. Sadet, 177–208. Cape Town: Libra Press.

Mbeki, G. 1984. *South Africa: The Peasants' Revolt.* London: International Relief and Aid Fund.

Ntsebeza, L. 2006. *Democracy Compromised: Chiefs and the Politics of Land in South Africa. The Challenge of Transformation and Redistribution.* Cape Town: HSRC Press.

———. 2007. "Land Redistribution in South Africa: The Property Clause Revisited." In Ntsebeza and Hall, *The Land Question in South Africa,* 107–31.

Ntsebeza, L., and Hall, R., eds. 2007. *The Land Question in South Africa: The Challenge of Transformation and Redistribution.* Cape Town: HSRC Press.

PART IV

Language and Media

After Apartheid

The Language Question

Neville Alexander

In their book, *Writing Science: Literacy and Discursive Power,* Halliday and Martin (1993, 10) state what ought to be obvious, but for the fact that most of us never think about language as an issue in our societies. They write, "The history of humanity is not only a history of socio-economic activity. It is also a history of semiotic activity."

In South Africa, where race has been the main ideological prism through which people have perceived their realities, this insight has tended to be ignored even by intellectuals working in the social sciences. However, although the racial fault line was the most prominent feature of the South African sociopolitical landscape for most of the twentieth century, there were occasions when the language issue erupted with volcanic menace to remind the world that South Africa cannot be viewed in simple black-and-white terms. On occasion, the apparently antagonistic contradictions in the language domain became manifest with respect to the status and use of Afrikaans, especially as a language of teaching in the educational sphere.[1] During the rule of Lord Milner (1901–5) and of Verwoerd and Vorster (1958–79), social conflict was articulated, among other ways, in the use and recognition of Afrikaans in the schools that catered to Afrikaans-speaking white children and Bantu-speaking black children.[2] It was the Soweto uprising of 1976 that set off the series of tremors that eventually caused the implosion of the apartheid state.

In broad historical terms, the issues remained the same throughout the twentieth century. The dominance of English in the modern sector of the economy, the challenge to its consequent hegemonic status that came from the rising Afrikaans-speaking elite, and the passive but powerful support of most black people for the continued dominance of English as one of the ways in which they could demonstrate their rejection of the racial order— one of the insignia of which was precisely Afrikaans, "the language of the oppressor"—influenced and characterized, in part, the interactions between the contending elites. For reasons that reach far back into the history of co- lonial conquest, slavery, and the role of the missionaries, in the course of the nineteenth century, English rather than Afrikaans became the language of aspiration and eventually the language of national unity and of liberation for the black elites. The pro-English sentiments of the black leadership were never more clearly enunciated than in the well-known words of Dr. Abdur- rahman in 1912:

> The question naturally arises which is to be the national language. Shall it be the degraded forms of a literary language,[3] a vulgar patois: or shall it be that language which Macaulay says is "In force, in richness, in ap- titude for all the highest purposes of the poet, the philosopher, and the orator inferior to the tongue of Greece alone?" Shall it be the language of the "Kombuis" [kitchen] or the language of Tennyson? That is, shall it be the Taal [Afrikaans] or English? (cited in Alexander 1989, 29)

In what follows, I show briefly how vested interests and ignorance about and the consequent neglect of the significance of language policy and language use on the part of the new rulers of South Africa have resulted in missed op- portunities to deepen and broaden the liberal democratic dispensation that was the issue of the negotiations between African and Afrikaner national- isms during the early 1990s.

"LEAVE YOUR LANGUAGES ALONE": THE FALLACY OF COMMON SENSE

In his *Planning Language, Planning Inequality,* James Tollefson writes, "[Language] is built into the economic and social structure of society so deeply that its fundamental importance seems only natural. For this reason, language policies are often seen as expressions of natural, common-sense as- sumptions about language in society" (1991, 2). The purpose of his book is to rebut this all-pervasive notion and to demonstrate by way of many signifi- cant historical and contemporary examples that language policies are governmental strategies designed, mostly consciously, to promote the interests of specific classes and other social groups.

It should be stated clearly, therefore, that it is not true that languages simply develop "naturally," as it were. They are formed and manipulated within definite limits to suit the interests of different groups of people. Such social formation is very clear in the case of so-called standard languages as opposed to nonstandard regional or social varieties (dialects, sociolects). The former are invariably the preferred varieties of the ruling class or ruling strata in any given society. They prevail as the norm because of the economic, political-military, or cultural-symbolic power of the rulers, not because they are "natural" in any meaning of the term. The importance of this proposition derives from the fact that it validates the claim that languages, like cities or families, can be planned. Indeed, in any modern state, whether or not it is explicitly acknowledged by governments, languages are always planned, in that legislation prescribes, often in great detail, where and how one or more languages are to be used. This is universal practice, and it has important consequences in critical social domains such as education. This is why Weinstein writes, "[If] it is possible to show that language is the subject of policy decisions as well as a possession conferring advantages, a case can be made for the study of language as one of the variables pushing open or closed the door to power, wealth, and prestige within societies" (1983, 3).

In regard to postapartheid South Africa, it remains to be said that the principle—as well as the practice—of language planning is accepted, however reluctantly. Not surprisingly, however, lack of implementation, planning, and thus of delivery tends to negate the principle and to reduce it to mere lip service. This observation points to a definite political orientation or stance toward the language question on the part of the ruling strata.

THE POWER OF LANGUAGE AND THE LANGUAGE OF POWER

There are two fundamental sources from which language derives its power, the ability of the relevant individuals or groups to realize their intentions (will) by means of language (empowerment) and, conversely, the ability of individuals or groups to impose their agendas on others (disempowerment of the latter). For human beings to produce the means of subsistence they have to cooperate, and to do so they have to communicate. Language is the main instrument of communication at the disposal of human beings; consequently, the specific languages in which the production processes take place become the languages of power. To put it differently, if one does not have the requisite command of the language of production, one is automatically restricted in one's options as regards access to employment and all that that implies in a state where employment opportunities are hierarchically structured and differentially rewarded. At this point, the relationship between language policy, class, and power ought to become intuitively obvious. Rather than take for granted the automatic recognition of this relationship, however, I spell out some of the implications of this particular insight for modern industrial societies, with special reference to South Africa.[4]

For reasons connected with the colonial history of southern Africa, the language of power in postapartheid South Africa is undoubtedly English. Afrikaans continues to play an ancillary role in the processes of economic production in the so-called formal economy, even though there are determined attempts to reduce its presence in this domain as well, as in other high-status domains. The question that I consider presently is whether this fact in and of itself implies, as is often said and universally assumed, that "English is enough," and what the implications of this belief are for democracy and development.

Before I deal with these issues, however, I refer briefly to the other source of the power of language, namely, its function as a mechanism for transmitting "culture," or, more popularly, its role in the formation of individual and social identities. I do not address this matter further here, even though it is implicated in the general discussion of the broader topic of language, class power, and democracy. Suffice it to say that being able to use the language one has the best command of in any situation is an empowering factor, and conversely, not being able to do so is necessarily disempowering. The self-esteem, self-confidence, potential creativity, and spontaneity that come with being able to use the language (one or more) that has shaped one from early childhood (one's "mother tongue") is the foundation of all democratic polities and institutions. To be denied the use of this language is the very meaning of oppression. In the words of Vladimir Ilyich Lenin, "A democratic state is bound to grant *complete freedom* for the native languages and annul all privileges for any one language. A democratic state will not permit the oppression or the overriding of any one nationality by another, either in any particular region or in any branch of public affairs" (1983, 138; emphasis in the original). It is this aspect of the language question that has fueled and often justified ethnonationalist and separatist movements during the last three centuries, including that which eventually led to the Anglo-Boer War of 1899–1902.

ENGLISH IS ENOUGH: THE CLASS CHARACTER OF THE MONOLINGUAL HABITUS

Later in *Planning Language, Planning Inequality,* Tollefson goes on to write that

> The hegemony of English, or of other languages, is not merely tolerated in the "developing" world; it is considered a legitimate model for society. In many newly independent states, a tiny English-speaking elite controls state policy-making organs while the masses of the people remain excluded. . . . A world system that is more just and equitable depends upon an understanding of how people can gain control of their own institutions. A key issue is the role of language in organizing and reproducing those institutions. (1991, 201)

Twenty years earlier, Pierre Alexandre (1972, 86) had shown clearly how in postcolonial Africa, proficiency in the language of the former colonial power (English, French, or Portuguese) constituted "cultural capital" and was an index to the class location of the individual, since this ability almost automatically elevated the speaker into the ruling elite. This insight derives primarily from the meticulous theoretical and practical studies of Pierre Bourdieu and his associates with respect to the evolution of linguistic markets. For present purposes, however, I simply draw attention to the immediately relevant propositions as they apply to the South African context.[5] The hierarchical relations between different varieties of a language or between different languages are a reflection of the historically evolved relations of domination and subjugation between and among the speakers of the relevant varieties or languages. In the South African case, Dutch, English, and, later, Afrikaans came to be the "legitimate languages" in different periods of the country's history. This legitimacy was and is the result of colonial conquest in the first instance, but as the structural transformations that accompanied that historic event became commonsense routine, dominance was complemented and reinforced by hegemony. That is to say, consent of the victims of colonial subjugation became the major factor in the maintenance of English and, until roughly 1994, of Afrikaans as the legitimate languages.

In South Africa, unlike in most other African countries in the British sphere of influence, the presence of a relatively large group of first-language speakers of English reduced the potential "profits of distinction" that came with proficiency in the legitimate language, although the rate of profit remains relatively high. For, according to Bourdieu, the smaller the number of people who are proficient in the legitimate variety and the more widespread the perception of the value of that variety in the relevant population, the greater the profits of distinction. This is, incidentally, the objective economic reason for the phenomenon of "elite closure" referred to below. I make the point here simply to stress the fact that there is a material reason for the maintenance of a particular language policy in any given period.

While it remains the case that proficiency in the dominant languages of European origin co-determines one's class location in most countries on the continent of Africa, this does not tell us anything about the class consciousness or the class position of individual members of the elite. What has to be established in any given case, therefore, is the degree of consciousness of the ruling strata of the de facto policy of "elite closure,"[6] or exclusion of the masses by means of language policy.[7] To do so is no easy task, since the levels of mystification and, more problematically, the veils of ignorance that delude policymakers and other power brokers into believing that their understandings are "scientific" defy the logic of mere argument and historical experience.

The relevant essential proposition is simple enough. It states that in a multilingual society, it is in everyone's interest to learn the dominant language (of power), since this will help provide equal opportunities in the labor market as well as in other markets. In postcolonial Africa, this proposition has led to the almost complete marginalization of the local languages of the people and the valorization of English, French, and Portuguese in the relevant African states. Indeed, in most other African states, the distinction between "official," that is, European, and "national" (African) languages ironically highlights in an unintended manner the social distance between the elite and the masses of the people. Because of the role model status of the middle class in most societies, the monolingual habitus becomes generalized in such a manner that the vast majority of the people come to believe that all that matters is knowledge of English in so-called anglophone Africa.[8] This utterly disempowering disposition assumes the character of a social pathology, one that I have called the "static maintenance syndrome."[9]

To add insult to injury, as it were, Tollefson's paradox notes that in modern societies,

> while vast resources are directed toward language teaching and bilingualism, especially involving English, more people than ever are unable

to acquire the language skills they need in order to enter and succeed in school, obtain satisfactory employment, and participate politically and socially in the life of their communities. . . . The great linguistic paradox of our time is that societies which dedicate enormous resources to language teaching and learning have been unable—or unwilling—to remove the powerful linguistic barriers to full participation in the major institutions of modern society. (Tollefson 1991, 7)

Tollefson arrives at the conclusion that inadequate competence is not mainly the result of poor books and other texts, inadequate pedagogy or lack of motivation, or other similar suggested deficiencies. Instead, "language competence remains a barrier to employment, education, and economic well being due to political forces of our own making. For while modern social and economic systems require certain kinds of language competence, they simultaneously create conditions which ensure that vast numbers of people will be unable to acquire that competence. A central mechanism by which this process occurs is language policy" (Tollefson 1991, 7).

Postapartheid South Africa is, despite numerous improvements on its predecessor, a textbook example of this paradox. While it is understandable, given the colonial and racist history of South Africa, that before 1973 the ruling class was fundamentally concerned with maintaining the limited markets in raw materials and semiprocessed commodities that South Africa, because of its place in the international division of labor, had to provide to the transnational corporations and other imperialist entities, the implicit continuation of such policies in postapartheid South Africa is something of an anomaly. For, whereas in apartheid South Africa, the rulers could afford to, and did, approach African languages as though they had no economic or cultural value, in the new South Africa this attitude is clearly self-limiting and self-defeating, if not self-destructive. Unless we are prepared to grant that, we are simply trotting along the same footpaths as those pioneered by the neocolonial states after 1960, where the indigenous languages of Africa were seen not as resources but as problems. In this connection, it is germane to our focus to point out that Africa, including South Africa, is today subject to the intensified pressures of globalization and that the pressure to adopt English, which is incontestably *the* global language, as the only legitimate language is exceptionally strong in anglophone territories.[10] One of the most serious strategic errors in this respect has been the failure to introduce mother tongue–based education.

ONE STEP FORWARD, TWO STEPS BACK

The history of language policy and planning in postapartheid South Africa is one of exhilarating potential and great expectations being squashed at regular intervals. By the time the formal negotiations process began in earnest, in about 1991, with respect to the language dispensation in the new South Africa, the situation might be described in broad brush strokes as follows. On the side of the white minority, specifically the Afrikaner nationalists represented in the main by the National Party, there was a clear commitment to the retention of the formal constitutional equality of Afrikaans and English. The white nationalists had little doubt that Afrikaans would continue to be one of the dominant languages in the new republic. On the side of the liberation forces, represented in the main by the African National Congress, the predominant instinct was to press for English as the only official language on economic as well as political grounds. These two positions reflected in woodcut simplicity the historical experience and aspirations of the two divergent nationalist movements. The Afrikaner nationalists had gained political power by mobilizing the votes of the Afrikaans-speaking white population during the decades of the pigmentocracy known as the Union of South Africa, and the elite had used the language to entrench its economic power, based initially on agriculture but increasingly also on mining and, much later, on manufacturing industry. The African nationalists, on the other hand, had experienced exactly the same developments that established and augmented the sectionalist power of the Afrikaners as a process of dispossession and disenfranchisement as well as racial and class disempowerment in the same Union of South Africa, which for them was a brutal pigmentatorship. For reasons that have been discussed in detail elsewhere,[11] it was high proficiency in the English language that appeared to the black elite to hold out the promise of liberation, unification, and empowerment. The antiapartheid leadership would have followed unerringly in the footsteps of their anticolonial predecessors by opting for the officialization of English only. Indeed, in 1990, at the very time they began their historic dialogue with the "racist Pretoria regime," the leadership of SWAPO—the Southwest Africa People's Organization—had declared English to be the only official language of free Namibia.

That this did not happen in South Africa eventually had two main reasons, both of which had very little, if anything, to do with the strategic vision or theoretical clarity of the leadership of the negotiators on either side. To begin with, there was the simple political fact that if the representatives of the black majority conceded equality of status to Afrikaans and English, they could not justify not doing the same for all the indigenous African languages. Had they done so, they would have been seen as adopting a neo-apartheid language policy that it would have been impossible to sell to their constituency. The ironic consequence of the Afrikaner nationalist demand, therefore, was the wholly unplanned-for and unexpected officialization of eleven South African languages.[12]

This decision was facilitated by the availability to the liberation movement of a comprehensive theory of language planning as an integral aspect of the program for the liberation and democratization of South African society.[13] This theory was derived from a body of both international and domestic research on language use in many domains of life. It postulated, among other things, that language is a resource, not a problem; that multilingualism is the global norm today; and that individual multilingualism,[14] together with the proliferation of link languages, is one of the keys to intercultural communication and social cohesion. This latter insight is important, since it provides the answer to one of the persistent fallacies of postcolonial African states, namely, that the officialization of indigenous languages would inevitably lead to ethnic rivalry and separatist movements.

With this theoretical life jacket at its disposal, the liberation movement took the plunge, and in so doing made history, or appeared to. To gauge to what extent history was made, we have to consider what was actually done between 1995 and 2007. To begin with the new constitution: the negotiations of the early 1990s, for reasons I have intimated above, resulted in one of the most progressive sets of constitutional provisions on language use in the world. Section 6 of the constitution (Act 108 of 1996) reads as follows:

(1) The official languages of the Republic are Sepedi, Sesotho, Setswana, siSwati, Tshivenda, Xitsonga, Afrikaans, English, isiNdebele, isiXhosa and isiZulu.

(2) Recognising the historically diminished use and status of the indigenous languages of our people, the state must take practical and positive measures to elevate the status and advance the use of these languages.

(3) (a) The national government and provincial governments may use any particular official languages for the purposes of government, taking into account usage, practicality, expense, regional circumstances and the balance of the needs and preferences of the population as a whole or

in the province concerned; but the national government and each provincial government must use at least two official languages.

    (b) Municipalities must take into account the language usage and preferences of their residents.

(4) The national government and provincial governments, by legislative and other measures, must regulate and monitor their use of official languages. Without detracting from the provisions of subsection (2), all official languages must enjoy parity of esteem and must be treated equitably.

(5) A Pan South African Language Board established by national legislation must:

    (a) promote, and create conditions for, the development and use of:
        (i)   all official languages;
        (ii) the Khoi, Nama and San languages; and
        (iii) Sign language; and
    (b) promote and ensure respect for:
        all languages commonly used by communities in South Africa, including German, Greek, Gujarati, Hindi, Portuguese, Tamil, Telegu and Urdu; and Arabic, Hebrew, Sanskrit and other languages used for religious purposes in South Africa.

Other significant sections of the constitution refer to rights in the domains of education—(29)(2); culture—(30), (31), (185), and (186); and the judiciary—(35)(3)(k) and (35)(4). All of these protect and promote the right of the individual or the relevant "linguistic community" to use their mother tongue or other official language of their choice in all interactions among and between themselves and between themselves and the state.

    Because of the pro-English attitudes that prevail among most of the middle-class elites and other formally educated South Africans, with the significant exception of a majority of Afrikaans-speaking citizens in these categories, the realization of these provisions in daily practice is beset with serious problems. The shaping of a consistently democratic multilingual language policy and practice reflecting the values and the aspirations of the constitution will require decades, perhaps even generations, of see-saw progress.

ACHIEVEMENTS

    In the twelve years since democratization, the beginnings of the requisite language infrastructure have been put in place.

- The Pan South African Language Board (PanSALB), representative of all the official languages as well as South African Sign Language, has been created.[15]
- Nine Provincial Language Committees have formed. Their main task is to represent PanSALB and to watch over the implementation of official language policy at provincial level.
- Fourteen National Language Bodies have formed whose main task is to see to the corpus development of their respective language.
- Eleven Lexicographic Units now exist, each of which ultimately must create and maintain a comprehensive monolingual explanatory dictionary as well as promote and publish other dictionaries for the respective language.

Although it has constitutional autonomy as a statutory body, administratively, PanSALB falls under the Department of Arts and Culture, which has responsibility for managing language matters in the new South Africa. Since the National Language Service (NLS), which originally was no more than the translation and terminology service to government, also falls under this department, overlapping concerns and conflicts of interest inevitably occur, and in fact, in recent years there have been numerous, sometimes paralyzing, tensions between the two entities. It should also be noted that important departments of state, among others Education and Defence, have tended to make policy independently, with only nominal consultation with PanSALB.

Notable among PanSALB's successes have been the successful piloting and inauguration of the Telephonic Interpreting Service of South Africa (TISSA); the commissioning of the vital survey, *Language Use and Language Interaction in South Africa. A National Sociolinguistic Survey* (2000); and the institution of the structures referred to above. In general, however, it has not been a prominent force and has been obstructed by the hegemonic national and global forces that shape the asymmetrical power relations of all multilingual states. Except for the South African Broadcasting Corporation, which has an improving record as far as the use of indigenous languages is concerned, most media, the public service, and the vital tertiary education sector have tended to join the slide toward a unilingual public policy delivery, even though this disposition favors the English-knowing elite and thus deepens the asymmetry of power relations in South Africa. Since each province has its own official languages, the Provincial Language Committees potentially play a decisive role with respect to developments on the ground.

In practice, however, few of them have the necessary skills and resources at present, and the de facto language policy in most provinces is a laissez-faire English-mainly policy. As long as mother tongue–based multilingual education does not become the default approach to language-medium policy in the schools of South Africa, these divisive and ultimately oppressive practices will continue to ensure economic and cultural constraint and stagnation.

Two other important language policy initiatives should be noted. The National Language Policy Framework,[16] approved by the cabinet in 2002, was shaped by a dedicated task team that reported directly to the minister of arts, culture, science and technology. The same team formulated the South African Languages Bill, which has not yet been placed before the National Assembly, even though it was similarly approved by cabinet. The Language Policy for Higher Education (2004) also resulted from the work of a special committee appointed by the minister of education.

CHALLENGE AND RESPONSE

By way of demonstrating the complexity of the problems faced by the new South Africa with respect to the practical realization of a consistently democratic language policy, in this section I consider briefly the challenges posed in the central domain of education.

Bourdieu stresses the social reproductive role of education. Through compulsory education, individuals are forced—*and also want*—to learn the legitimate language, mainly because of its pivotal role in the production processes and the social status that proficiency in it confers on its speakers. An array of certificates, diplomas, and degrees constitutes a market, regardless of the real levels of proficiency and competence, and these items are traded like any other commodity. They take on the character of "cultural capital" (assets) and can be translated into economic assets via enhanced salaries, wages, bonuses, and other rewards. Linguistic capital is necessarily the most important component of this cultural capital.

The legacy of apartheid education in South Africa exacerbates the static maintenance syndrome,[17] since most black people continue to equate mother tongue–based education with the ravages of Bantu education. Without analyzing the matter further, I maintain that this tendency, even though there are currently the hesitant beginnings of some countervailing tendencies, will continue to undermine South Africa's ability to expand and consolidate democracy, and at the same time represents a built-in constraint on economic development, the magnitude of which remains to be established by means of carefully designed research in all branches of the economy.

The following studies show how we unnecessarily restrict the capabilities of our workforce and the efficiency of economic production, besides the not unimportant factors of inadequate job satisfaction and a reduced work ethic. It should be noted, however, that not much detailed research has as yet been done in this area. The numbers quoted here are indicative and do not reflect the real magnitude of the phenomena, which in all probability will be found to be much greater than our statistics indicate at present.

A University of Cape Town thesis titled *Medium of Instruction and Its Effect on Matriculation Examination Results in 2000 in Western Cape Secondary Schools* hypothesized that African language speaking learners in the Western Cape will tend to do badly in the matriculation examination largely because the medium of instruction and assessment is not the mother tongue, but a second or third language (October 2002, 5). The dissertation, among other things, compares the performance of Afrikaans L1 and English L1 students with that of Xhosa L1 students in key subjects and confirms the hypothesis. The actual statistics are, in the context of the "new" South Africa, ironic and extremely disturbing because they demonstrate all too clearly some of the avoidable continuities between apartheid and postapartheid education. Probably the most significant finding of this study is that the only "learning area" in which all the matriculation candidates performed at comparable levels was the First Language (Higher Grade) subject, that is, English, Afrikaans, and isiXhosa. This was for the Xhosa L1 speakers the only subject in which they were taught and assessed in their mother tongue.[18]

These findings have been reinforced by a recent survey of matriculation results by Simkins and Patterson (2005). Although the point of departure for their inquiry in *Learner Performance in South Africa* is, pedagogically speaking, somewhat conservative, since its preferred model appears to be a transitional bilingual one, they none the less arrive at the conclusion in respect of the causal significance of the language of teaching (medium of instruction) factor that

> social and economic variables at the individual household level do not play an enormous role in determining performance, with the exception of the language variables. Pupils whose home language is an African language are at a considerable disadvantage in the language of instruction [read: English] by the time they reach Grade 11 if the language of instruction is never spoken at home. This can be offset somewhat if the

language of instruction is spoken sometimes at home and it can be off-set considerably if the language of instruction is spoken often at home. (Simkins and Patterson 2005, 33)

They also claim that competence in the language of instruction is crucial for performance in mathematics. "Every extra per cent earned in the language test is associated with an addition of one-sixth of a per cent in the mathematics test in Grade 9 and one-third of a percent in Grade 11" (ibid., 34).[19] Their study, although limited and preliminary in many respects, has advanced the argument for mother tongue–based education from postulating a correlative to demonstrating a causal relationship between educational success and language medium.[20]

At a quantitative level, our project calculated a few years ago that, on the assumption that in a properly functioning educational system, a 90 percent pass rate would be reasonable, we have been wasting approximately R3 billion annually on paying the salaries of the teachers employed in grades ten to twelve who produce the average 50 percent failure rate we have experienced in the matriculation examination in the period 1987–2002. If these impressions do nothing else, they ought to demonstrate the need for in-depth educational research, in which the language issue, specifically the language-medium policy and practice, should feature centrally. The recent Human Rights Commission hearings appear, after initial silence on the language factor, to have realized its significance as a valid, indeed a crucial, research question. A major revision of policy in respect to languages of learning and teaching has in fact been initiated. Thus, for example, in the commission's report on its public hearing, *The Right to Basic Education,* one of the recommendations reads as follows:

Given the recognised importance of mother-tongue learning, the Department [of Education] must re-evaluate the decision of granting SGBs [School Governing Bodies] the power to determine language policy. Possible amendment to SASA [South African Schools Act] should be considered. Affected parties need to approach the issue based on what is in the best interests of the child. (Human Rights Commission 2006, 43)

SHIFTING PERSPECTIVES?

We can only hope that evidence such as that presented above will lead to a shift in the perceptions of political and cultural leaders, who, it should be noted, have in recent months begun to speak more openly and frequently in public about the virtues and benefits of mother tongue–based education.

One of South Africa's most prominent education analysts and researchers, who until recently was at best skeptical about the demand for and practicality of mother tongue education, remarked recently in response to a question about fundamental changes between apartheid and postapartheid education that

> we haven't made much progress in realising the potential of poor children in terms of giving them quality schooling. . . . The legacy of apartheid-era education is seen in the poor education of black teachers who, generally, teach black children. The [Joint Education] trust's research shows that the average mark a sample of grade three teachers in 24 rural schools in SA achieved on a grade six test in their subject was 55%. Teachers are shaky in terms of the subject they are teaching, and this is exacerbated by the language problem. They are not teaching in their own tongue. He praises Education Minister Naledi Pandor for her promotion of mother tongue education, at least in the earlier years of school. (Blaine 2005, 17)

In the Western Cape Province, the government is firmly committed to the implementation of mother tongue–based bilingual education for a minimum of seven years of primary schooling and will be investigating the financial and training implications of extending the system into the secondary school.

However, unless African languages are given market value—unless their instrumentality for the processes of production, exchange, and distribution is enhanced—no amount of policy change at the school level can guarantee their use in high-status functions and, thus, eventual escape from the dominance and the hegemony of English. We have understood for many years that the previous and current language-medium policy causes cognitive impoverishment and, consequently, necessitates investment in compensatory on-the-job training by the private sector to enhance the "trainability" of the just-from-school recruits. This wastefulness would be completely avoided if a national development plan existed that more effectively integrated reform of education and economic development planning. This would mean that fundamental changes in the language-medium policy would be directly related to the increased use of the African mother tongues, where relevant, in the public service and in the formal economy. An articulated program of job creation and employment on the basis of language proficiencies would, in the South African context, also serve as an organic affirmative action program, one that would not have the unintended consequence of perpetuating and entrenching divisive racial identities inherited from the apartheid past.

More generally, we have to move rapidly beyond mere posturing and gesturing in the direction of implementing a consistently democratic language policy in South Africa. We have to do so not only to improve and consolidate the democratic political culture that has been initiated here but also to expand the potential of national economic development that will become possible because of a higher level of general education of the workforce and a deeper substratum of ordinary South Africans attuned to the needs and dynamics of modern science and technology that will have been mediated through local languages as well as English. To achieve this goal, we will have to review and refurbish the impressive but underfunded and bureaucratized language infrastructure established since 1995. It is, in my view, of the utmost importance that the original independent statutory character of PanSALB be restored and reinforced so that real progress, as opposed to the uneven achievements hitherto, can be made and accelerated.

LANGUAGE POLICY AS A CLASS PROJECT

This new phase of the development and use of African languages in high-status functions should be approached and understood against the background of the strategies, activities, and programs of the African Academy of Languages (ACALAN), viewed as an instrument of the African renaissance and of the cultural revolution on the continent during this, the "African century," both of which were so hopefully proclaimed by President Mbeki at the end of the twentieth century. As a specialized bureau of the African Union, ACALAN is beginning to influence decisively the direction and modalities of language policies on the continent.[21] South Africa, because of its own recent history and its human and material resources, is bound to play an important role on this new road, and clarity about our own positions on and commitment to a democratic language dispensation is therefore fundamental. The success of ACALAN will have direct and enduring consequences for all African countries, not only the Republic of South Africa.

It is clear that the future direction of language policy in South Africa will be influenced as much by exogenous as by endogenous factors. If mother tongue–based multilingual education proves to be a success, the pressure to expand the system and related practices will become irresistible. The key challenges to be addressed at the beginning of the twenty-first century are the increasing hegemony of English, the need to raise literacy levels through the successful implementation of appropriate language-medium policies in the schools and universities, and, closely related, the need to demonstrate the positive relationship between functional multilingualism and economic efficiency and productivity. The inculcation and nurturing of a culture of reading in African languages is the key to all of these issues.

It is necessary that we "return to the source" and pose once again a question first suggested by Amilcar Cabral with respect to the continent as a whole: Will South Africa's middle class find the courage, does it have the imagination, to commit class suicide by moving away decisively from the current English-mainly and often English-only language policy, with all its negative consequences for a democratic polity? My answer to this apparently rhetorical question is simple but, I suspect, only too true. The middle class can move away from English language dominance if we can demonstrate the economic value of the African languages. Efforts in this direction are now increasingly evident, although they are still offset by negative attitudes toward African languages.[22] My colleague Michellé October, among others, has begun researching this area. Preliminarily, she has discerned a definite move on the part of major economic players such as the banking sector, parastatal and privately owned communications firms, and the public service administration toward the increased use of African languages in the workplace, in their administrative functions, and especially at the interface with customers. One of the country's biggest banks, for example, has made available on its autobank screens instructions in isiZulu and Sesotho, and not only in English and Afrikaans, as was the case in the past. According to the bank's latest data, just under 30 percent of its customers use the two indigenous African languages. The bank intends to make this faculty available in all eleven official languages of the country.[23] The parastatal South African Broadcasting Corporation found that during the fiscal year 2003–4, it saw a jump in revenue because of the increased provision of local content programs in African languages.[24] If this trend continues in all the different economic sectors and large institutions, including especially the educational system, the market potential of the languages will be enhanced in ways that cannot now be anticipated.

The challenge, however, is not only to the political, business, and cultural leadership of the country. It is a challenge also to applied language scholars and language practitioners of southern Africa. The intelligentsia must begin to move out of its comfort zone and accept that language policy, class, and power are tightly interwoven, and that unless we devise our own agendas in the interest of our people as a whole, we are willy-nilly carrying out others' possibly nefarious agendas.

NOTES

1. During Milner's tenure, it was the Dutch language that was nominally at issue. In fact, however, "Dutch"-speaking people used Afrikaans except in formal writing.

2. See Giliomee (2003) for a sensitive account of the social conflict around the school language of Afrikaans-speaking white children and for numerous references. See Hirson (1979), Kane-Berman (1979), and Lodge (1984), among others, for the social conflict around the school language of Bantu-speaking black children.

3. This refers to the "Dutch" that was actually spoken by the Afrikaans-speaking population. See note 1.

4. In doing so, I base my analysis and comments on the insights derived from the many historical and sociological studies informed by the approach of Pierre Bourdieu.

5. An excellent summary of Bourdieu's theory as it pertains to the language question is Niedrig (2000, 21–27). The classic English exposition of the relevant theory is Bourdieu (1991).

6. The concept of elite closure is described by its author as "a tactic of boundary maintenance. It involves institutionalizing the linguistic patterns of the elite, either through official policy or informally established usage norms in order to limit access to socioeconomic mobility and political power to people who possess the requisite linguistic patterns" (Meyers-Scotton 1990, 27). Myers-Scotton also makes it clear that in sub-Saharan Africa, we are invariably dealing with cases of "strong elite closure," where the social gap between the elites and the masses is deepened by the dominant position of foreign—that is, European—languages in which more than half of the population do not have adequate proficiency (ibid., 27–28).

7. Ayo Bamgbose, emeritus professor of linguistics and African languages at the University of Ibadan, Nigeria, published an elegant study of the many ways in which elite closure has operated in postcolonial Africa. His justified optimism about the evolving language policy in the new South Africa at the time remains to be realized in practice (see Bamgbose 2000).

8. Ingrid Gogolin (1994), drawing on Bourdieu's work, coined the term "monolingual habitus" to describe the ironical phenomenon of colonially oppressed peoples "voluntarily" denying that their indigenous languages have any value and valorizing only the former colonial languages. In metropolitan European states, this valorization is manifest in the standard variety of the relevant language.

9. This means simply that most African people are willing to maintain their first languages in the primary contexts of family, community, elementary school, and religious practice but do not believe these languages have the capacity to develop into languages of power. Their consciousness reflects the reality of the linguistic market, and they have become victims of a monolingual habitus, even though most African people are proficient in two or more languages. My use of the term was inspired by the analysis of Colin Baker (1996).

10. For a more detailed discussion of this aspect of the issue, see Alexander (2005a).

11. See, among others, Alexandre (1972), Herbert (1990), and Bamgbose (2000).

12. The eleven languages were those that had enjoyed national or regional official status under the previous regime.

13. For an account of how this position evolved in South Africa, see Alexander and Heugh (1999).

14. In the Council of Europe's usage, this aspect of multilingualism is now referred to as "plurilingualism."

15. See the PanSALB website, www.pansalb.co.za, for details.

16. The NLPF is an important interim provision, since all departments of state and provincial governments can and do use it as a set of guidelines for the formulation and implementation of language policy. As such, it constitutes an important guarantee for the practical realization of a democratic policy of multilingualism and language equality in the longer term.

17. See my earlier discussion under "The Power of Language and the Language of Power," this essay.

18. See October (2002, 76–77).

19. However dubious such number crunching might be, the authors have grappled with a large measure of success with the issue of relative weighting of causal factors, which October (2002, 77) had been forced to leave in abeyance. Their statistical methods for weighting the effects of different relevant variables are explained in chapter 3 of the study.

20. Other important variables, such as a good meal once a day and a favorable home literacy environment, are essential, of course, but for the first time in post-apartheid South Africa, the language-medium issue has been demonstrated to be a central cause of success or failure.

21. An introduction to ACALAN is Alexander (2005b).

22. This is largely a function of the fact that proficiency in African languages continues to be inadequately remunerated except at the highest levels of translation and interpreting.

23. By the end of 2006, isiXhosa and SeTswana had been added to the menu of language options.

24. Michellé October, personal communication.

BIBLIOGRAPHY

Alexander, N. 1989. *Language Policy and National Unity in South Africa/Azania.* Cape Town: Buchu Books.

———. 2002. "Linguistic Rights, Language Planning and Democracy in Post-apartheid South Africa." In *Language Policy: Lessons from Global Models,* ed. S. Baker, 116–29. Monterey, CA: Monterey Institute of International Studies.

———. 2005a. "The Impact of the Hegemony of English on Access to and Quality of Education: With Special Reference to South Africa." Lecture delivered at the Language and Poverty Conference, Cornell University, Ithaca, NY, 14 October.

———, ed. 2005b. *The Intellectualisation of African Languages.* Cape Town: Praesa/University of Cape Town.

Alexander, N., and Heugh, K. 1999. "Language Policy in the New South Africa." In *Cultural Change and Development in South Africa,* ed. A. Zegeye and R. Kriger (special issue, *Culturelink,* 1998–99). Zagreb: Institute for International Relations.

Alexandre, P. 1972. *An Introduction to Languages and Language in Africa.* London: Heinemann.

Baker, C. 1996. *Foundations of Bilingual Education and Bilingualism.* Clevedon, UK: Multilingual Matters.

Bamgbose, A. 2000. *Language and Exclusion.* Hamburg: LIT-Verlag.

Blaine, S. 2005. "Losing the Legacy of Apartheid Education." *Business Day* (20 Years Anniversary Edition Supplement), 23 August, 17.

Bourdieu, P. 1991. *Language and Symbolic Power.* Edited and with an introduction by John B. Thompson; trans. Gino Raymond and Matthew Adamson. Cambridge: Polity Press.

Giliomee, H. 2003. *The Afrikaners. Biography of a People.* Charlottesville: University of Virginia Press.

Gogolin, I. 1994. *Der monolinguale Habitus der multilingualen Schule.* Münster, Germany: Waxmann.

Halliday, M., and J. Martin. 1993. *Writing Science: Literacy and Discursive Power.* London: Falmer Press.

Herbert, R., ed. 1990. *Language and Society in Africa: The Theory and Practice of Sociolinguistics.* Johannesburg: Witwatersrand University Press.

Hirson, B. 1979. *Year of Fire, Year of Ash.* London: Zed Press.

Human Rights Commission. 2006. *Report of the Public Hearing on the Right to Basic Education.* Pretoria: South African Human Rights Commission.

Kane-Berman, J. 1979. *Soweto. Black Revolt, White Reaction.* Johannesburg: Ravan Press.

Lenin, V. 1983. *Lenin on Language.* Moscow: Raduga Publishers.

Lodge, T. 1984. *Black Politics in South Africa since 1945.* London: Longman.

Mesthrie, R., ed. 2002. *Language in South Africa.* Cambridge: Cambridge University Press.

Myers-Scotton, C. 1990. "Elite Closure as Boundary Maintenance: The Case of Africa." In *Language Policy and Political Development,* ed. B. Weinstein, 25–42. Norwood, NJ: Ablex.

Niedrig, H. 2000. *Sprache, Macht, Kultur: Multilinguale Erziehung in Post-Apartheid Südafrika.* Münster, Germany: Waxmann.

October, M. 2002. *Medium of Instruction and Its Effect on Matriculation Examination Results for 2000 in Western Cape Secondary Schools.* Praesa Occasional Papers no. 11. Cape Town: Praesa.

Republic of South Africa. 1996. *The Constitution of the Republic of South Africa.* Act no. 108 of 1996. Pretoria: Republic of South Africa.

Simkins, C., and A. Patterson. 2005. *Learner Performance in South Africa: Social and Economic Determinants of Success in Language and Mathematics.* Cape Town: HSRC Press.

Tollefson, J. 1991. *Planning Language, Planning Inequality. Language Policy in the Community.* London: Longman.

Weinstein, B. 1983. *The Civic Tongue.* Norwood, NJ: Ablex.

Wilson, M., and L. Thompson. 1969. *The Oxford History of South Africa,* vol. 1. Oxford: Oxford University Press.

Contested Media Environments in South Africa
The Making of Communications Policy since 1994

Guy Berger

The democratic transition in South Africa has seen complex developments over who controls communications. Unlike the apartheid era of racist state control, aspirations for a nonracial and pluralistic landscape have largely been fulfilled. However, during the democratic period, there has been increased involvement by government in communications policymaking, and a decline in participatory opportunities and processes. This situation reflects the government's desire to steer communications for reasons that are professedly "transformational," in the sense of deepening nonracialism, democracy, or development (even if in effect not always such), and also sometimes politically self-serving.

In overview, the postapartheid government's commitment to a mixed economy has entailed the inherently contradictory approach of "managed liberalization" in the communications arena. This approach in turn has given both space and cause for (mainly) elite interests to contest the government's handling of a range of policy matters. The institutions of Parliament and the communications regulatory authority have been sites of this contestation. Government has also had to temper its managerial inclinations owing to changing technologies that complicate attempts at regulation, and the inexorable marketization of the arena as a result of liberalization. The contemporary reality is one of elite pluralism, with a vibrant diversity of actors, even if civil society is far from having the influence it anticipated having at the dawn of democracy.

These developments are especially evident in public broadcasting, where the South African Broadcasting Corporation (SABC) has been challenged on its political independence, transformational role, editorial policies, business model, and license conditions. There has also been major contestation around policy and law concerning the independence and authority of the regulator, the power of the minister, and communications convergence. Technological and market dynamics in all this flux presage a future of continuing, even intensified, elite contestation, with the role of government ultimately being diminished—for both better and worse.

STATE-MEDIA RELATIONS IN PERSPECTIVE

Racial politics dominated media under apartheid; less color-conscious economics came to the fore after South Africa's first decade of democracy (see Netshitenzhe 2004; Wasserman 2004; Fourie n.d.). This does not mean an absence of policy and politics: the intense commercialization of the country's media, and especially broadcasting, is a function of specific policies and law, their practical effect, and contestation around these. That the market increasingly rules in South African media does not mean the absence of political choices and disagreements. Further, the market dispensation has not excluded state attempts to control or co-opt media and the regulator. However, overall, the configuration of the communications landscape has diminished the power of the state in this space. Such a situation perpetuates elite pluralism rather than allowing for control of communications by a consolidated ruling bloc.

The postapartheid communications environment, insofar as media and to a lesser extent telecommunications are concerned, has its origins in "negotiated liberalisation" (Horwitz 2001a, 2001b). Democratic South Africa evolved from a "progressive" policy environment with participatory and deliberative stakeholder politics to a top-down, state-directed liberalization applied mainly in the interests of industry, which increasingly means that the market, not the state, dominates the communications environment.

This evolution to a market-driven media policy has been assessed in liberal terms, as in the following quotation:

Every few years, it seems, the mandarins of communication make a bid to take power away from the broadcasting regulator, Icasa [the Independent Communications Authority of South Africa]. The pattern has been regular: they table a new Bill that lessens Icasa's independence, every industry player goes to parliament and unanimously and unequivocally warns that this is unconstitutional, damaging to our broadcasting in-

dustry and against everything we are preaching to the region, the continent and the world about the need for independent regulation. (Harber 2006)

To caricature this perspective slightly, it reads postapartheid history as ev-
idencing the existence of a power-hungry state held at bay by a communications industry seeking freedom. In this view, government reluctantly
concedes to liberalization because it is pressured to, although it would really prefer a command model in relation to communications, and this motive frequently comes to the fore. Such a perspective is overly simplistic. It
entails the a priori assumption of a control-seeking government (i.e., anti-
democratic) that inexorably moves toward suppression of an independent
media (pro-democratic).

An alternative interpretation could be a "social democratic" position
that would read the state as merely seeking to do its duty through intervening to ensure "transformation" of the legacy inequities of apartheid. A
third (Marxist) account sees transition as exhibiting a captured state and corrupted African National Congress (ANC) increasingly acting in corporatist
alliance with capital to promote a pro-profit market landscape for the benefit
of a multiracial middle class.

There are insights to be had from each of the three perspectives, but perhaps a fourth view—a liberal pluralist assessment—most aptly encapsulates
the dynamics at play. This approach recognizes that government strategy
both embraces liberalization and at the same time seeks to control the process, and notes that this contradiction accounts for the substantial (elite)
disputation that has occurred. The prediction is that with liberalization,
the scope of government interventions will narrow, whether these are for
pure political self-interest, to promote capitalist interests, or to deliver on
the promise of transformation.

This essay begins by sketching the situation just prior to 1994 and goes
on to assess the changes since then, largely through a periodization linked to
different ministers of communication. The political and legislative media environment in general is examined, with special attention to various important moments of conflict and changes of direction. Four phases are identified.
The first was characterized a government hands-off approach, in which the
regulator ruled pretty much autonomously; the second saw the state gaining strong control over telecommunications and also insisting on a policymaking role with regard to broadcasting. The third phase was characterized
by increased governmental intervention (although checked by various forces

and institutions), for a variety of reasons, some narrowly political and related to promoting government self-interest, others more related to transforming race and class inequalities. The fourth, contemporary phase is characterized by market forces playing an ever greater role, with the influence of both state and civil society diminishing into the future. This scenario does not fully meet the interests and aspirations of any single interest group, whether government, Parliament, regulator, business, civil society, citizens, or consumers, but it is a reality likely to endure. Market relations, with all their pros and cons, will become ever more central to the communications landscape over the next five to ten years.

THE APARTHEID MEDIA LANDSCAPE

The foundations for the future environment were already in place in the years preceding the first democratic elections in 1994. In legal terms, the strict controls of the 1970s and especially of the State of Emergency years of the 1980s had mainly come to an end. As regards economics, the vast majority of the media were commercialized, with the SABC also financed largely through advertising. These aspects have persisted in the media environment, and have been the subject of ongoing debate. Telecommunications in 1994 were a separate field of regulation from media but had seen two private cellular companies licensed, and this development was soon followed by the partial privatization of the fixed-line operator, Telkom (see Horwitz 1997).

The ANC in 1992 did not give much attention to telecommunications policy, but it did draw up a media policy that included a dose of neoliberalism that coexisted uneasily with a control-oriented tendency within the organization. However, in the wake of the collapse of East European socialism, it was generally conceded that a degree of private pluralism was essential to democracy. A state-commandist media landscape was discredited. Neoliberalism also meant that the principle of public funding for public-service media was off the ANC's agenda, as was any substantial commitment to helping the fringe "alternative press" emerge as the new mainstream. However, reflecting ANC populism plus civil society input, the policy also included some participatory policy thrusts, such as access for all to media and access to information. It further specified that media freedom needed to be complemented by conscious efforts to ensure that its benefit was not limited to debates among elites. These policy positions were to inform much actual practice of the ANC-dominated government in the years after 1994.

FIRST PHASE: GOVERNMENT'S HANDS-OFF POLICY

After the ANC came to power, it had priorities other than communications. For example, it took six years to legislate on access to information policy (and thereby actualize the constitutional right to freedom of information), with the Promotion of Access to Information Act (2000). The terrain of corporate print media escaped major attention altogether, in part because of the immunity of a constitutionally enshrined right to freedom of the media and in part owing to the wider balance of forces. However, broadcasting, having been largely a state monopoly under apartheid, was a clear candidate for early changes, although even here government would play little role in the early years.

As Horwitz (2001a, 2001b) has shown, the broadcast landscape that emerged after apartheid had its roots in conflicts that began several years earlier (see also Minnie 2000; Tleane and Duncan 2003). A historic compromise in 1993, also reflecting the balance of power at the time, took broadcasting out of the party political power stakes, at least temporarily. Thus, the National Party agreed to relinquish control of the SABC ahead of the election in return for the ANC committing to the same after the poll. Civil society was not just an equal partner in this negotiated resolution, it also brokered the deal and drafted the legislation. A year before the elections the SABC was restructured so that its board was appointed by the president on the recommendation of Parliament after public interviews with potential candidates. What also emerged as a guarantor of the compromise was the vestment of substantial power in the hands of a broadcast regulator, whose independence was enshrined in the 1993 interim democratic constitution and retained in the final 1996 constitution. This arrangement was given practical effect in 1993 in the form of the Independent Broadcasting Authority (IBA) Act.

In the postelection period, the then minister of the newly created Department of Communications (DoC), Pallo Jordan, adopted a hands-off approach, and the early development of policy was, in effect, decentralized to the IBA. The IBA thus became the key player in communications policy in the early postapartheid period.[1]

Significantly, the IBA Act had called for an inquiry into the viability of public broadcasting, cross-media ownership rules, and local content provisions, the findings of which would guide licensing policy and practice. Once constituted, the IBA accordingly proceeded with what became known as the Triple Inquiry. An indication of the participatory nature of this policy development stage was that 105 written and 35 oral submissions were made to the regulator (IBA 1995).

The IBA Act and the Triple Inquiry report (IBA 1996) put into effect a policy of a three-sector broadcast landscape characterized by three kinds of licensing—public, private, and community. The philosophy was that the three would be complementary, but the reality turned out to be more sector competitive in terms of audiences and advertising, and it was also less distinctive in regard to content. One especially significant policy element in the Triple Inquiry report was its assessment that broadcast pluralism would benefit from privatizing the SABC's more commercially run television and radio stations. It also identified some areas of SABC programming that would require public subsidy. The broadcaster itself responded by arguing for a lesser privatization, and at the beginning of 1996, the ANC-dominated Parliament came into the arena as a policy player and decided in favor of the SABC's position, so that ultimately a third of its radio stations, though none of its TV channels, would be sold off (see Barnett 1999).

The development reflected a disjuncture in that the IBA made policy, but Parliament had the final say. Further, government as a third factor retained the power to dispose of assets as it saw fit. Thus, the sales revenue from the privatization went to the central fiscus rather than back to the corporation—to the SABC's chagrin. Further, whatever the IBA said about government grants for the public broadcaster, it was toothless in regard to actually mobilizing funds in any direction. A split power situation pertained, and however healthy this may be in terms of democracy, its potential dysfunctionality and instability invited government attempts to reengineer the equilibrium into a different and more workable balance.

The sell-off of SABC stations did work to the benefit of an embryonic fraction of the business community that gained from the black empowerment preferencing in the sale. The subsequent opening up of the airwaves more broadly by the IBA, with the authority also licensing seven new stations in March 1997 to broad-based black-controlled consortia, was evidence that liberalization could work for a degree of racial and even class transformation. Although this disappointed big (white) business, it was hard for any forces to reject policy measures for black ownership in the context of South African history. A similar situation applied with the IBA Act's constraints on cross-ownership by the (white) newspaper industry of broadcast assets, and the limits it placed on concentration of radio ownership and the extent of foreign ownership.

Where resistance did arise was from would-be private broadcasters when the IBA decided to prioritize the licensing of community rather than commercial radio stations. While this delay frustrated the (white) business sector, it also reflected the strength of opinion emanating from civil society groups, as well as a government orientation, if short-lived, toward the RDP— the populist-oriented Reconstruction and Development Programme. The IBA's prioritizing of community radio corresponded with the 1992 ANC policy provision about enhancing access to media, although it did not emanate from government. Indeed, it reflected the way in which the new-born regulator was unwilling to play second fiddle to external forces, be they business or government.[2]

In summing up this period, one can point to the involvement in the design of the media landscape by a range of distinct players: civil society, various business groups, the IBA, Parliament, and to a relatively limited extent government. Telecommunications were not a major issue in this period.

SECOND PHASE: GOVERNMENT STEPS IN

A situation in which government stayed on the policy sidelines was unlikely to last. As outlined by Horwitz (2001a, 2001b), various developments signaled a more interventionist stance, especially with regard to telecommunications, the IBA, and the SABC. Minister Pallo Jordan was replaced in 1996 by Jay Naidoo, who was quick to promote a stronger role for government.

Under the new minister, the government set up a special regulator for telecommunications in 1996—the South Africa Telecommunications Regulatory Authority (SATRA). But in a departure from the 1993 compromise that had taken broadcasting out of the political arena, this new body was far less independent than the IBA. Thus, while the IBA's councilors were nominated by public parliamentary process and appointed by the president, whose only power was to veto recommended candidates, SATRA's members were appointed directly by the DoC minister. Further, while the IBA had full authority over whom to license in broadcasting, the minister retained the right to decide in regard to telecommunications. SATRA's role was to license and oversee new telecommunications players (preferably black), and it also levied licensees for contributions to a body called the Universal Service Agency. Aimed at compensating for market failure by promoting community Internet access centers and rural telephony, this agency (renamed in 2005 as the Universal Service and Access Agency of South Africa) is generally agreed to have been a failure since its inception (see Open Society Foundation—South Africa 2007).

Naidoo also turned government attention to the IBA. Taking advantage of accountability problems, where IBA councilors were accused of abusing institutional credit cards, he moved to clip the wings of the organization. The government's argument was that the regulator's role was to regulate and implement policy, not to make policy. The contention was that government was elected precisely to give direction and transform society, and it should not neglect this responsibility. Accordingly, instead of leaving policymaking to the IBA, Naidoo took the initiative, although not complete control. Under his leadership, a green paper process, drawing in stakeholders such as academics and the broadcasting industry, commenced in 1997. The final green paper was released for comment in November 1997. The government then produced its policy decisions in a white paper published in June 1998, and a draft broadcasting bill came out a mere two months later. This rapid sequence generated doubts about whether government had taken seriously responses to the white paper (Berger 1998). The participative tradition out of which the IBA was born, and which had continued in the early years of democracy, was beginning to decline.

It is important to note that the green paper had posed as a question the issue of which body should make policy. An unpublished DoC discussion paper in 1998 proposed that "policy making is a shared responsibility of . . . Parliament, Government and the Regulating Authority." But who was entitled to the greatest share? In the end, disputes in various forums, involving opposition parties, the media, and civil society, produced a compromise. The 1999 Broadcasting Act specified policymaking as the prerogative of the minister, but with conditions: policy had to be in the form of broad directives that also had to be transparent (published in the *Government Gazette*) and open to public response. The minister would also have to consult the IBA and Parliament in the process. These provisions in the law were an indication of the role of Parliament as a check on ministerial quests for unfettered authority. This conflict over authority would remain an issue in subsequent years.

As regards public broadcasting, the white paper proposed that the SABC be guided by a public service charter (akin to the BBC's) and a corporatized business model (unlike the BBC) whereby the SABC would have a commercial arm that would cross-subsidize a public service arm. These positions were also enunciated in the 1999 Broadcasting Act. Tleane and Duncan (2003, 71) warned that the act's charter for the SABC did not bind the commercial arm, noting, "The SABC has been forced into financial self-sufficiency, leading to an ever-increasing dependency on advertising revenue, a source of funding that has in-built biases towards historically privileged audiences."

The legacy of this policy decision, based ultimately on neoliberal premises that ruled out subsidization through public funds, has been major ongoing repercussions. One was the Broadcasting Amendment Act of 2002, which required a formal relicensing of SABC owing to the corporatization of the broadcaster and its expected division into commercial broadcasting services (CBS) and public broadcasting services (PBS). The relicensing commenced in 2004, with the SABC arguing that all that was needed was for the regulatory authority to formalize which SABC stations fell into which division. The delineation of anything more specific (such as quantified public service obligations such as language or drama) would threaten the financial viability of the institution as a whole. This argument was strongly opposed by the majority of private broadcasters, which wanted to see the SABC more restricted in its commercial activities and behaving less like a law unto itself in interpreting its public obligations. From civil society, the Freedom of Expression Institute (FXI), among others, said the SABC had taken as a given its business model (and therefore accepted the underpinning governmental policy), and that it was seeking the lightest-touch relicensing to avoid watertight commitments that could cost money or reduce advertising earning potential (Freedom of Expression Institute 2004).

As it turned out, the relicensing process culminated in the regulator issuing detailed and costly public service requirements for most SABC stations (although even the public service arm remained authorized to carry substantial advertising) (ICASA 2005a, 2005b). For the SABC, this meant the broadcaster has since been required to be even more commercial, so as to make even more money, to pay for a now measurable public service—and yet to do so without compromising that service in the process. This imperative pulls in different directions, but government (at least until the time of writing, early 2011) has kept up its refusal to fund the institution, arguing that it has other priorities to meet. There is also a policy irony in the SABC selling off the lucrative stations in one period and in a later period being required to draw revenue from its remaining, less profitable enterprises. At heart, the government stance has been to regard the SABC as a strategic tool for at least the transformative public service obligations outlined in policy and legislation, but required to self-finance through activities that contradict this very orientation. The position reflects, in a nutshell, government's ongoing dilemma vis-à-vis the broader communications field.

An earlier, politically oriented intervention during Naidoo's tenure was in regard to the sector's regulator. In 2000, the IBA and SATRA were merged into a single body, ICASA, as per the 1998 white paper (see Burns 2001). The key question in this merger was which dispensation would prevail—the autonomous one of the IBA (as per the 1999 Broadcasting Act) or the government-dependent one of SATRA, which was favored by the DoC. In the end, after civil society and industry made representations to Parliament, a compromise came into being: despite there being a single regulator, the body would operate a dual administration. Thus, ICASA would be subject only to broad policy from government as regards broadcasting decisions but would be subject to specific government approval in respect to telecommunications. As convergence subsequently evolved, this dichotomy would become increasingly unsustainable. At the time, however, the merger signaled, once more, a control-oriented initiative coming from the top, meeting with resistance, and then being changed.

By the time Naidoo left office, government was much more involved in the design of the broadcast and telecommunications landscapes than it had been at the start of his tenure. The government's motivation in this period appeared to be mainly to want to steer developments in a direction that would avoid an uncontrolled market situation. This was especially evident in the decision to partially privatize Telkom and give it a five-year monopoly on fixed-line services on condition that it rolled out two million lines to underserved communities—a developmental intervention that failed in practice (see Gillwald 2004). But, as indicated above, in addition to seeking to promote this kind of "transformation," aspects of Naidoo's interventions also appear to have sought to strengthen government political authority more narrowly.

THIRD PHASE: INTENSIFIED CONTROL AND CONTESTATION

Naidoo's 1999 successor, Ivy Matsepe Casaburri, came to symbolize a third era in which government policy strove to get similar levels of control over broadcasting as existed over telecommunications. Naidoo had entered a terrain that had previously been forfeited in the 1993 negotiations, and he had staked out government's claims. Casaburri now wanted formalized and greater government authority in this realm. Casaburri's initiatives sought to build on Naidoo's legacy to give government a greater say for purely political reasons in addition to interventions that were also aimed at promoting transformation issues more broadly, with the two interrelated rationales being often difficult to entirely separate.

The SABC's role in particular was a troubling policy issue during Casaburri's term of office. However, notable in the early part of this period was the appointment by Parliament of a new SABC board that in turn concentrated on the SABC making money, in line with government's opposition to public funding (see Tleane and Duncan 2003).

For a time, it was hard for government to fault the intensified commercial approach at the SABC. After all, the alternative to neoliberal economic policies would have required public funding from the fiscus.[3] Indeed, the 1999 Broadcasting Act was followed by the 2002 Amendment Act, which explicitly corporatized the SABC. This meant that not only would the institution run as a company, with the state as shareholder, it would also pay tax to the state.

The market-driven dimension of the SABC's activities, the direct result of governmental policy on broadcasting, elicited much disagreement from civil society. Trade union federation COSATU (Congress of South African Trade Unions) and the FXI pressure group complained about the corporation's pursuit of middle-class and English-fluent urban audiences, which derived from the quest to attract advertisers (see Tleane and Duncan 2003, 165–66; Msomi 2004). Others, such as the then chair of the Portfolio Committee on Communications and the Pan South African Language Board, also condemned SABC for marginalizing African languages. The broadcaster itself recognized the problem, saying it was "onerous" to have to manage the contradiction between chasing revenues and delivering public service broadcasting (SABC 2004). In 2006 the CEO called for the model to be reviewed (Mpofu 2006).

Even within the ANC, although at a party level rather than governing level, there was unhappiness. In a 2002 discussion document, the party argued, "There is a need to develop a publicly-funded model in order for the public and community media to serve as vehicles to articulate the needs of the poor, rural people, women, labour and other marginalised constituencies" (ANC 2002a). The party's conference at the end of 2002 called for a publicly funded public broadcaster by 2012 (ANC 2002b). Despite the ANC being the ruling party, however, the ANC party position had no visible impact on government policy and practice.[4]

Although there was no action on the funding model, government did not sit back. Indeed, Casaburri had herself expressed unhappiness with, inter alia, the SABC's neglect of African languages, and her response was twofold. First, she sought to remedy the situation (and deal with other matters of political concern to government) by requiring the corporation to develop editorial policies. Second, the DoC came up with a proposal for two new TV stations to provide indigenous language services, and this became part of the 2002 Broadcasting Amendment Act. For Tleane and Duncan (2003), the latter initiative showed DoC's distrust of the SABC's ability to meet its language obligations. At any rate, the new station plan also begged the questions of control and funding. Government's initial bid was to propose the new ventures as being outside the SABC and directly reporting to the minister. This politically self-serving thrust was later changed by Parliament after representations from various NGOs and the SABC itself, and the two stations were legislated to become part of the public broadcaster's portfolio.

What this meant was that a big SABC was about to become bigger—to the concerns of private broadcasters. But at least the new channels would be subject to the checks and balances for public broadcasting as applied to the SABC, as distinct from being directly government-controlled outlets. However, this also meant the two new stations would face the same problems the SABC already had in regard to financing expensive language delivery. In 2005, ICASA authorized the SABC to run the two new stations, envisaging them as being funded mainly through advertising. The SABC, however, had long maintained that this was not workable, and in 2006 it stated that it was negotiating with the government on funding for the two outlets. For these reasons, and because of impending technology change for digital broadcasting, the new channels still had not come on-stream by early 2011. Inasmuch as the government's original policy for the initiative was based on transformation reasons, it was also undercut by the same actor's wider neoliberal policy on funding. A combination of financial crises and SABC deficits makes the launch of these new channels a very distant prospect.

Once again, the issue reveals a pluralistic picture in terms of diverse role-players shaping the media environment for public broadcasting. And again, the pattern is one in which the government's proposals were a mix of political control and transformation-oriented service delivery, and these aspirations were reduced as a result of challenges and the inherent limits of government's overall policy approach.

The government also put forward a policy and legislative requirement that the SABC have editorial policies. This is another specific issue around which disagreement arose, and one that reveals in microcosm some of the particularities of the period and its contrast to communications policymaking in the earlier phases.

THE EDITORIAL POLICIES PROPOSAL

According to Tleane and Duncan (2003), "the crisis of accountability" faced by the SABC reached "boiling point" in 2002. According to the 2002 Broadcasting Amendment Bill, the SABC needed to have editorial policies and a code of conduct in order to be more accountable for its public service obligations. Enormous controversy arose. Motivations for the editorial policies by the minister of communications were that the SABC's content was imbalanced in terms of language, as well as irrelevant, and that the SABC was guilty of ignoring government leaders' opinions. The bill (Republic of South Africa [RSA] 2002a) specified that the corporation's board should prepare the policies, subject to ministerial approval.

A related aspect in the bill was the scrapping of a clause in the 1999 Broadcasting Act whereby the SABC's governing charter provided the corporation with freedom of expression and journalistic, creative, and programming independence. This was to be replaced with terminology that required "accurate, accountable and fair reporting." Other sections in the bill included the words "responsible reporting," and added "national interest" to the existing "public interest" among the various objectives to be served by the SABC. As a package, therefore, the draft law envisaged that the policies would be the mechanism whereby such objectives could be elaborated and enforced.

These provisions led various stakeholders to accuse the minister of seeking increased governmental rather than public accountability of the corporation (Holomisa 2002; Tleane and Duncan 2003, 170). And though government may have hoped to see the bill passed in its initial form, the Parliamentary Portfolio Committee on Communications decided to call for public comment and scheduled public hearings. In the representations that followed, among the critics were the regulator ICASA, and indeed the SABC itself (see ICASA 2002; South African Press Association 2002). The issues they disputed included the notion of "national interest," the proposed deletion of the freedom of expression clause, and the proposed ministerial powers over editorial policy. A host of civil society groups added additional criticisms (Holomisa 2002; COSATU 2002a, 2002b; FXI 2002, 2003; South African National Editors' Forum 2003; Tleane and Duncan 2003;)

In response, the parliamentary committee rewrote the bill (see RSA 2002b). While retaining the formulation of the SABC board needing to prepare and submit policies, it said the policies should then go to ICASA (i.e., not to the minister). This preserved the SABC's independence. It also went further by adopting proposals by COSATU (2002a, 2002b), among others, that the board adopt a public participatory approach in the development of the policies. Parliament's ruling thereby privileged a participative over a power approach to policy formulation.

Significantly, the parliamentary committee also reversed the original bill's attempt to scrap the clause that guaranteed the SABC freedom of expression and independence. Also dropped were the provisions about "the best interests of the Corporation," as well as the phrase "responsible reporting." However, despite the representations, the bill's original inclusion of advancing the "national interest" alongside the public one remained.

After the 2002 Broadcasting Act was gazetted (RSA 2003), the SABC drafted editorial policies and put them out for public comment in printed form in many languages, through public meetings, and though promotion of the opportunity on its broadcast platforms. At the end of the consultation process, the SABC said there had been 920 written submissions, 847 of which were from individuals and 73 from organizations (Hassen 2004, 11).[5]

To summarize the significance of the whole exercise, the result was a law that spelled out in more depth that the SABC needed to strive for a better balance between its divergent imperatives of commercial operations and public service.[6] The policy-formulation experience made it appear as if South Africa had returned to the participative traditions of the transitional period. However, the DoC's basic thrust, to increase control of the electronic communications environment, was not changed by the "setbacks" experienced by the minister on the editorial policy initiative.

PHASE 4: GOVERNMENT WINS SOME, BUT CONTESTATION AND ITS STRATEGIC LOGIC ULTIMATELY GIVE MARKET FORCES MUCH OF THE PLAY

The trend up till 2002 had seen government moving away from participative policy development, and it was Parliament that, responding to lobbying, blocked the minister on a number of issues. In 2003, government showed even less inclination toward lengthy consultative processes—a politics that with the convergence bill would ironically lead to an even greater role being played by Parliament, civil society, and the state president as well.

Thus, in contrast to the situation in 1993, the ANC in government ten years later no longer seemed to see civil society as allies and advisers for "transformation"; it believed it knew best. In the end, government would have more power in some respects—but also less in many others.

The convergence bill arose from a colloquium in July 2003 convened by the DoC. Despite references to the need for a new policy, the director-general Andile Ngcaba put the focus on drawing up an actual draft law, with a proclaimed timetable of one month. In attendance were representatives from the opposition parties, plus the broadcasting, telecommunications, and Internet industries. Civil society, apart from a trade union representative, was mainly absent. There was no green or white paper process—even though convergence is not something that can be regulated by simple amalgamation of the previous separate policies for broadcasting and telecoms. When Ngcaba turned down appeals from business to do policy work before rushing into law, the industry took a second-best option: it jumped aboard by volunteering legal experts for a Convergence Policy Committee that would draft a new law. Draft legislative proposals were then produced as a self-acknowledged "incomplete end-product" by mid-September 2003. In December, a draft convergence bill was published—to a barrage of criticism.

Notwithstanding its name, the bill retained the provisions of the Broadcasting Act regarding the conditions for licensing traditional broadcasting (including local content quotas and political impartiality). But one change was to the previous system of vertical oligopolistic bundles whereby, for example, a broadcast license had covered use of frequency as well as dissemination of content on it. Now this would be disaggregated into separate horizontal services, each with a different license, where telecommunications players could enter the audiovisual industry. In addition, telecommunications operators were enabled to do business in terms of services offered (e.g., voice, data, audio-video), and no longer in terms of the technology utilized (e.g., cellular, land line). The licensees would thus be able to utilize whatever technology became available, for example voice-over-Internet protocol, if they wished to sell voice telephony services. Broadcasting and Internet service provision could be delivered over numerous technologies. The expressed rationale was to promote competition in the interests of expanded and cheaper services in the communications arena. However, the government also sought to increase its political control as part of the process.

The problems of trying to leapfrog or bypass policy and going straight to law on such a complex issue caught up with the whole process. Hence, what should have been a primarily legal process inevitably turned into one that dealt with policy and law simultaneously rather than sequentially. The messy situation led to a lengthy and hotly contested situation, with several versions of the bill proposed, and ultimately the splitting of the initiative into two laws, neither of which kept the original term "convergence." These complications are some reasons why the 2004 bill attracted sixty-five critical submissions and much adverse media coverage. In 2005, more than forty critiques reached Parliament about the bill's second version. Almost thirty direct representations were also made to the parliamentary committee dealing with the law.[7] The result was that the second version of the bill underwent so many amendments that it effectively became a third edition (Berger 2005a).

The new law finally took effect, as the Electronic Communications Act (ECA), three years after the process was initiated. Retained in the law is the original characteristic of a persistent dualism between telecommunications and broadcasting services. In a tortuous distinction, however, not all transmission of audiovisual content counts as "broadcasting"; only that which is "unilinear" transmission will need such a license. Yet unilinear transmission could apply to some dissemination methods (e.g., via cell phones and website streams) but not others, no matter whether the actual content is identical in all cases.

Prior to its final passage, this legislation contained a provision, eventually dropped by Parliament after lobbying, which would have watered down the 1999 Broadcasting Amendment Act requirement for the minister to consult on policy directives. The obligatory consultation was reinstated in the final law, and there was also a provision that expressly forbade the minister from deciding on licensing as such. Earlier versions of the bill had also stipulated that the minister's approval was needed for granting licenses for broadcast, communications services, and communications network services. This would have extended the old SATRA model to all licensing (see Berger 2005b). The eventual act—responsive to protests—limited government power to the minister deciding if and when anyone could apply for a network services (i.e., infrastructure) license on a substantial scale. The apparent reason for this was so that government could shield its own enterprises in this area (Telkom and Sentech). Critics argued that this provision contradicted the wider pro-competition objectives of the law and kept telecommunications costs unnecessarily high. Government's own rationale was that these entities were strategic levers for "transformation" that therefore warranted protection.

The ICASA Amendment Bill emerged in October 2005 from the former convergence bill as a sister piece of legislation to the Electronic Communications Act. The idea was to redefine the functions and powers of the authority in light of the new licensing regime.

Echoing the thrust of the original convergence bill, which would have subjected all services to government approval and have had ICASA function as an administrative arm of government, the proposed amendments to the ICASA Act dropped the word "independent" from the title of the regulator. It also entailed an attempt to take Parliament and the president out of the business of appointing and dismissing councilors, and it sought to manage the appointees through performance appraisal of them by the minister. Last, it specified a funding mechanism that maintained government, rather than ICASA, in charge of the budget of the agency. The bill was changed by the National Assembly to keep ICASA's name intact and give the minister less control, but this second version was then changed in its turn by the House of Provinces back toward much of the minister's original vision. Finally, the approved law on this model went to the president, who, after being lobbied extensively, sent it back to Parliament as potentially unconstitutional.

The eventual outcome was a third version that reinstated Parliament in the ICASA council appointments, though in a lesser role than previously. The president, however, remained entirely removed from the equation. This is one less check and balance than had previously been there—and that had proved decisive in terms of the actual progress of the legislation itself.[8] Performance appraisal remains, but Parliament must be consulted.

Overall, the DoC's attempts to drive convergence interventions in the communications arena were tempered by the mediation of other state institutions (in this case Parliament and the president) and through the mobilization of interest groups. These groups included state-linked players, such as Telkom, Sentech, the SABC, and ICASA itself. Most active lobbying came from businesses affected by the Electronic Communications Act, and civil society drove most of the changes over the ICASA Amendment Act.

The outcome of the whole package meant that while government became more powerful than previously in regard to ICASA councilors, the regulator itself became a less powerful body than it formerly was, not only in regard to the minister but also vis-à-vis industry interests in the marketplace. The Electronic Communications Act requires the regulator to ensure that no previous licensee (including, but not limited to, Telkom, the SABC, and Sentech) is deprived of previous rights. This requirement limits the regulator's ability to promote competition. In addition, ICASA is now required to give decisions to applicants for a local class license within sixty days, and if this time limit is not met, the license may be taken as given. "It means curtailing Icasa's ability to independently decide strategic priorities" (Berger 2006). The ultimate irony of all this, therefore, is that state control is also reduced in terms of the market.[9]

GOVERNANCE AND THE SABC

Notwithstanding its leading role in initiating the editorial policies proposal, the DoC found itself caught up in a number of contradictions relating to governance of the SABC.

In 2008, exploiting the corporatized status of the SABC, the minister used her power as representative of "the shareholder" to thwart the appointment of an internal SABC candidate to the post of chief operating officer at the broadcaster. But when the board in 2009 (after several botched attempts) fired the chief executive officer, there was a surprising silence from the minister. Indeed, in court papers during the CEO's appeals, the Ministry claimed not to be involved in hiring or firing at this level of appointment. The shambles involved in the incident, and the emergence of a subsequent huge deficit at the SABC, further diminished the standing of the department vis-à-vis the broadcaster.

The DoC also found itself sidelined by political shifts in the ruling party in 2007–8. The locus of this was the SABC board. The process began with the ANC undermining the integrity of the parliamentary system of interviewing candidates for the board and submitting a slate to the president for his signature. In late 2007, after the requisite public interviews, the ruling party MPs voluntarily sent their list to ANC headquarters—which then ordered changes so as to include three interviewees who were deemed to be more aligned with the then dominant Thabo Mbeki party faction. The amended list then went to Mbeki, who, despite subsequently losing control of the party in the interim to the Jacob Zuma camp, soon went on to appoint the individuals on the revised list. Months later he was toppled as head of state. But before he was ousted, the very ANC parliamentarians who had accepted the party line over their own judgment decided they no longer wanted the board, despite having recommended it. After several heated meetings with the board, the Portfolio Committee on Communications thus engineered a legislative amendment designed to empower Parliament to force the president to dismiss the board.

During the height of the controversy, Minister of Communications Cassaburi remained in cabinet (despite the dismissal of Mbeki) and futilely attempted to propose a more wide-ranging and time-consuming review of the entire SABC governance system. The impatient MPs, now seemingly pro-Zuma in orientation, would have none of this, and proceeded in haste with their attempt to change the law so as to change the board before national elections. Mbeki's subsequent ousting as president made redundant the need to compel the new president to act. But Mbeki's successor, Kgalema Motlanthe, also showed he would not be a simple tool of Parliament. In the face of civil society representations about unconstitutionality, he sent back the law for further amendment (to ensure due process in deciding whether a board should be fired). The law was later passed, but the election period then intervened and delayed its implementation. By July 2009 the previous board was out of office and replaced by an interim structure with a six-month term of office. But in terms of the amended law, the members of this interim board were appointed by Parliament without any public nominations or hearings.

Politics, it seemed, was getting back into command—and "managed liberalization" temporarily took a back seat. This trend was intensified not only by the politics of the Mbeki-appointed board but also by its notable failures in corporate governance. The lengthy dispute it had with the CEO contributed to a collapse in management, which in turn saw the public broadcaster in mid-2009 unable to pay bills or honor previous wage settlements. As with the experience of the former IBA's flaws, this case provided legitimacy for government involvement in the affairs of the broadcaster. In June 2009 the broadcaster was reported to be begging government for almost $200 million to bail it out of its financial crises. Without safeguards put in place, any such support could reduce the autonomy of the SABC that is needed for it to play a public service role.

It was likely, however, that it would be back to mixed business as usual as a new administration settled into the Ministry.

THE BOUNDARIES OF POLICY

Communications policymaking in postapartheid South Africa has generally been located in the DoC. Between 1994 and 2008, only one initiative emerged outside the department, in the form of the Government Communication and Information Services set up under the presidency. This sector of the executive then championed the birth in 2002 of the Media Development and Diversity Agency (MDDA), which provides (on a small scale) finance and training to grassroots media. It draws on contributions from the mainstream media industries, and from government grants. On balance, however, the MDDA is a minor factor in the broader communications landscape, and its character does not much alter the status of the DoC as the locus of state communications policy.[10]

In 2006, however, two new developments arose that reflected the interests of other state agencies in the communications field, and seemed to reflect government's reservations about the liberal dimension as manifested in part of the DoC's "managed liberalization" strategy. The first was an initiative by the Department of Home Affairs to rewrite the Film and Publications Act to include the mainstream media in its system of prepublication screening (which up to then had applied only to pornographic titles and cinematic materials). This step was immediately condemned by the industry and civil society groups on the basis that it undermined the constitutionally enshrined jurisdiction of the regulator, ICASA, over broadcasting content. The media industry also highlighted its self-regulation under ICASA (in the case of broadcasting) and the press ombudsman (in the case of newspapers). The bill was amended in 2007 to continue the standing exemption for mainstream media from its purview. Had it passed, however, it would have reduced the indirect influence that the DoC had over broadcast content via its broad policy directives to ICASA, but would have greatly extended governmental say over all media.

The second area of interventions on the turf of the DoC was signaled in the announcement by the Ministry of Public Enterprises, also in 2006, that it would create a semi-state broadband infrastructure company in the wholesale market, to be called Infraco. This initiative trod squarely on the toes of the DoC, under which falls the partly privatized Telkom (which co-owns the undersea broadband cable, SAT3), Sentech (a signals and—shortlived—wireless Internet provider), and the EASSy broadband cable being built up the east coast of Africa. The Infraco initiative was widely interpreted as a response to the inability of the DoC to ensure a steep reduction in telecommunications costs in South Africa. This inability was painted as not just an issue of constraints on the levers available to DoC but also of managerial competence in the department—else Infraco could as easily have been sited within the DoC's portfolio of state-linked communications enterprises. The divide continued into late 2009, when a DoC draft policy on broadband made no mention of Infraco (which entity still had not yet been licensed by ICASA).

In another case of government perceiving that direct intervention was needed, the migration of analogue to digital TV broadcasting highlighted the limits of managed liberalization. Government has given enormous sums to the SABC and Sentech and is also planning a major subsidy of set-top boxes (see Stones 2007). Without these interventions, the market would likely leave the totality of transformation till the last minute.

However, what these steps represent is, arguably, a consequence of the contradictions besetting the role of the state in the communications arena, rather than the character of the DoC specifically. While the DoC has been tied to managed liberalization—that is, tied ultimately to a market-centered emphasis—the notion of government being a player, and not just a controlling referee or facilitator, seems to have informed the Home Affairs, Public Enterprises, and digital migration initiatives. In each case, state bodies other than the DoC were presented as giving government the necessary control to resolve what it saw as social and delivery problems. Seen holistically, these initiatives reflect a new perception that a market-oriented trajectory will not alone produce the social and economic engineering sought by government. This change of perspective paralleled a growing lobby within the ruling party from 2007 for a "development state." The new government that took office in May 2009 did indeed expand its ministries related to the economy, although the DoC was not included in the cluster. The Ministry was given to Siphiwe Nyanda, who, while being a senior member of the party, did not have specific background in the sector. However, it seemed likely that the new authorities would put more stress on the control side of the managed liberalization equation. This appeared to be the case with the SABC in late 2009. Despite the corporation getting a new interim board, and then a permanent board, Nyanda's office warned that much tighter financial controls on the SABC would henceforth be implemented directly by government.

While Horwitz and other writers used the term "negotiated liberalisation" in regard to the 1990s, in the subsequent decade, the DoC—in the Electronic Communications Act in particular—came to tout the phrase "managed liberalisation." The difference is telling, and indeed, as outlined in much of this essay, the DoC has over the period sought much greater ministerial powers in the communications arena. For opposition parliamentarian Dene Smuts, this has reflected a political tactic to introduce "shock measures that reverse the negotiated order," and then, "having created a panic, to retreat in a show of reason, namely to compromise a position which becomes the new norm or point of departure" (Smuts 2002). A similar point of view is expressed by the FXI (2006). Such assessments, however, locate government actions in power-play tactics in the DoC. While they are not without some relevance to understanding policy development after apartheid, the matter goes deeper.

What underpins this history more fundamentally is managed liberalization, which has explicit roots in 2001 in the state discourse about the telecommunications field in the face of liberalization (Gillwald 2004; Gillwald and Esselaar 2004). Indeed, several other government departments—for instance, in transport and energy—deployed the rhetoric at the same time (see Dobson 2002; Cassim and Jackson 2004; Eberhard 2004). There are two components to this orientation: allowing new competitors into a less regulated market, and at the same time protecting state-linked assets from unfettered competition. The latter is predicated on the position that state-linked assets are an essential tool for achieving government objectives, for example, to achieve universal service or African languages services. The extent to which this stance has blurred into political control motives varies over case and time.

One recent instance of all these dynamics took place in May 2009 when ANC alliance partner the trade union federation COSATU lobbied ICASA to mount last-minute public hearings into the sale of shares by semi-state-owned Telkom in the cellular phone operator Vodacom to the UK's Vodafone. While COSATU said it was concerned about potential job losses, press reports argued there was also major ANC interest in blocking a deal in which supporters of former president Mbeki stood to gain huge amounts. In the end, a court case blocked ICASA from implementing the hearings, and the sale went ahead. The incident showed the complications of liberalizing a sector while trying to control it, at the same time that self-serving actions by ruling party interests are taking place. It further revealed the complications of liberalizing for foreign investors while also providing for public participation.

The underlying complication in all this is that managed liberalization embodies an intrinsic contradiction: management implies control, liberalization implies autonomy (see Van den Broek 2006). Together, this means the government seeks to do two things simultaneously: unleash market forces, but steer them in the interests of "transformation" and political self-interest. Complete control is not an option when liberalization is officially embraced. But liberalization itself is a target of intervention so that it can be controlled for a variety of reasons. Erroneously referred to as a "policy" by the DoC, managed liberalization gives no clear guidance about where or why there is to be "management" (i.e., control) or "liberalization." It certainly does not equate with a policy that would coherently and explicitly seek to address the contradictory tendencies of promoting commercialization, on the one hand (including within state assets), and trying to channel the character and impact of the process on the other. What it is, instead, is a strategic direction entailing contradictory dimensions. Industry is favored, but the limits of managed liberalization are also evident in the developments in 2006, as noted in the case of Infraco, Home Affairs, and digital migration.

In regard to making sense of all this, a classic liberal paradigm would assume a notion of "power corrupts" and of "despots" in government seeking control for control's sake. But such a view overlooks the positive and often necessary roles of the state in regard to communications development and democratic transformation in the interests of the wider public. A Marxist analysis tends to underplay contradictions between state and business and among and between statutory and parastatal entities. The social democratic position minimizes the play of self-interest and abuses by both governmental and market power. What perhaps better captures the character of the situation, however, is an approach that takes cognizance of all three approaches and dynamics—one that acknowledges the pluralism. A liberal pluralist paradigm recognizes contradictions and spaces that are created by a managerialist-inclined government that also pays allegiance to the "liberalization" part of managed liberalization, and which outcomes in turn allow for, and stimulate, the representation of elite interests to mobilize against the "managed" part of the process.

Meanwhile, the management aspect of managed liberalization lends itself to control for purposes of political self-interest, as evidenced in many of the initial government interventions. Thus, government has indeed increased pursuit of political control over the organizing agencies of the landscape (for a mix of control for political as an end in itself, and control for reasons of transformation), and this has been in direct proportion to its loss of control of that landscape as brought about by liberalization and deregulation. However, the strength of postapartheid South Africa is vested in the aggregation of interests and wisdoms that check government self-interested designs and make for a far better final product. This is shown, perversely, in the changes that have usually come about as a result of participation by actors other than government in regard to key issues over the period.

The character of postapartheid period in communications policy since 1994 is not quite mass participation, but it is also far from being a dying democracy or on the road to a Zimbabwe-style commandism over communications. It is a continuously contested terrain, not least because managed liberalization leads to a strengthening of the market vis-à-vis the state. The resistance around this dynamic suggests an elite democracy. That is not quite what many democrats had initially hoped for, but it is also a major advance on the monopolistic control of communications that characterized apartheid.

NOTES

1. The only real policy initiative from the new government in its early years was outside the DoC and took the form of a commission, which included civil society media representatives, to review (and reinvent) the government communications services. It is known as the Task Group on Government Communications, or Comtask, and its report, completed in 1996, is online at www.gcis.gov.za.

2. More than most other interventions, this prioritization resulted in nonracial pluralism in broadcasting—by 2006 an estimated ninety of some licensed 122 radio stations were community stations. The SABC then had three commercial radio stations and fifteen supposedly public service ones (although they also carry advertisements). The SABC also had three TV channels in operation, competing with one private national TV channel, etv (see OMD 2005; BBC World Service Trust 2007). Figures published in 2009 and attributed to ICASA specified 126 community radio licenses, of which eighty-seven were on air, constituting 4.6 percent of the total radio audience, with the sector paralleled by fourteen privately owned commercial radio stations, making up 16.5 percent of total radio audience (Media Development and Diversity Agency 2009).

3. In South African conditions, increasing license fees from the public to requisite levels was not and is not a viable option.

4. Tleane and Duncan (2003) suggest that the DoC had sought public funding for SABC, and that it was the Treasury and general governmental policy which blocked this.

5. Regarding internal consultations within the corporation itself, it is not clear how far the participatory paradigm extended in this regard. The importance of this consideration lies in how the policies are regarded, and even known about, by the people who are, at the end of the day, the subjects who should be using the guidelines in their daily practice. Some evidence since then (see Sisulu and Marcus 2006) suggests there have been problems in disseminating knowledge, and also in the impartiality of interpretation, of these guidelines.

6. This orientation was later laid down in compulsory and more measurable license conditions when it came to the SABC's relicensing process (see ICASA 2005b).

7. Criticisms came from IT companies, telecommunications companies, communications equipment manufacturers, communications service providers, value-added network services, the Post Office, the Universal Service Agency, law firms, signal distributors, a private schools' association, broadcasters from all three sectors (public, private, and community), the regulator, political parties, and NGOs.

8. The history of the ICASA Amendment Act shows how different criteria are brought to bear by the two offices even when minister and president hail from the same party.

9. In fact, ICASA was already leaning in the direction of serving business interests when it opened bidding in 2006 for subscription television licenses. Community and provincial free-to-air television licensing were thereby delayed. This is a reversal of the situation in 1995 when community radio licensing was prioritized above the commercial.

10. The DoC for many years provided its own direct subsidy to community radio, independently of the MDDA (which has more checks and balances to prevent political bias in funding). In 2008, it agreed to begin channeling this support via the MDDA.

BIBLIOGRAPHY

African National Congress. 2002a. "Media in a Democratic South Africa." http://www.anc.org.za/ancdocs/pubs/umrabulo/umrabulo16/media.html (accessed 30 May 2009).

———. 2002b. "Resolutions Adopted by the 51st National Conference of the African National Congress, Stellenbosch, 2002." http://www.anc.org.za/ancdocs/history/conf/conference51/resolutions.html (accessed 30 May 2009).

Barnett, C. 1999. "The Limits of Media Democratization in South Africa: Politics, Privatization and Regulation." *Media, Culture and Society* 21:649–71.

BBC World Service Trust. 2007. *South Africa: Research Findings and Conclusion.* Africa Media Development Initiative, *BBCWorldServiceTrust.org.* www.bbcworldservice trust.org/amdi (accessed 7 February 2007).

Berger, G. 1998. "The Role of Broadcasting in the Future: Principles and Policy." Presentation to the Broadcasting Policy Colloquium, Benoni, March.

———. 2005a. Comments on draft licence conditions for SABC's sound and television broadcasting services, 14 March. http://journ.ru.ac.za/staff/guy/fulltext/sabclicensing.doc (accessed 30 May 2009).

———. 2005b. "Convergence: Two Steps Forward, One step Back." *Mail and Guardian Online,* 30 March. http://www.mg.co.za/articlePage.aspx?articleid=200525&area=/insight/insight_converse/ (accessed 30 May 2009).

———. 2006. "Three Steps Backwards in Communications." *Mail and Guardian Online,* 16 August 2006. http://www.mg.co.za/articlePage.aspx?articleid=280940&area=/insight/insight_converse/ (accessed 30 May 2009).

Burns, Y. 2001. *Communications Law.* Johannesburg: Butterworth.

Cassim, R., and W. Jackson, eds. 2004. *Sustainable Development: The Case of Energy in South Africa.* Trade Knowledge Network. International Institute for Sustainable Development. http://www.tradeknowledgenetwork.net/publication.aspx?id=616 (accessed 30 May 2009).

Congress of South African Trade Unions. 2002a. COSATU Submission on the Broadcasting Amendment Bill to the Portfolio Committee on Communications, 18 September. http://www.cosatu.org.za/docs/2002/broadsub.htm#removal; (accessed 30 May 2009).

———. 2002b. Clarification on Submission on the Broadcasting Amendment Bill. Submitted to the Communications Portfolio Committee, 16 October 2002. www.cosatu.org.za/submiss2002.htm (accessed 30 May 2009).

Dobson, W. 2002. "A Guide to the Microeconomic Reform Strategy." Discussion paper, dti of South Africa, May. http://www.naci.org.za/Innovation_gateway/downloads/microeconomicreform.pdf (accessed 30 May 2009).

Eberhard, A. 2004. "The Political Economy of Power Sector Reform in South Africa." Working Paper WP-06, Program on Energy and Sustainable Development, Stanford University, April. http://www.gsb.uct.ac.za/gsbwebb/mir/documents/StanfordPSREberhardSep2004final.pdf (accessed 30 May 2009).

Fourie, P. n.d. "Leapfrogging into the Market Approach: The Loss of Public Service Broadcasting for Development and Nation Building." http://www.pucrs.br/famecos/iamcr/textos/fourie.pdf (accessed 30 May 2009).

Freedom of Expression Institute. 2002. Comments on Broadcasting Amendment Bill. Freedom of Expression Institute, Public hearings: Portfolio Committee on Communications, 17 September. http://66.249.93.104/search?q=cache:jZXWtZTAZYwJ:fxi.org.za/archives/amendment_bill_comments.html+site:fxi.org.za+sabc+editorial+policies&hl=en&gl=za&ct=clnk&cd=8&client=firefox-a (accessed 30 May 2009).

———. 2003. "SABC Editorial Policies." Submission by the Freedom of Expression Institute, 13 June. http://66.249.93.104/search?q=cache:IstHNZcIvAsJ:fxi.org.za/comm_regul/sabc_editorial_policies.doc+site:fxi.org.za+sabc+editorial+policies&hl=en&gl=za&ct=clnk&cd=1&client=firefox-a (accessed 30 May 2009).

———. 2004. Freedom of Expression Institute. Submission on the South African Broadcasting Corporation's Application for Licence Amendments, Submitted to the Independent Communications Authority of South Africa, 9 June. fxi.org.za/pdf/Submission%20to%20Icasa%20on%20the%20SABC's%20license%20application.pdf (accessed 30 May 2009).

———. 2006. "FXI: Call for Government to Stop Drafting 'Unconstitutional' Legislation," 21 April. http://www.sangonet.org.za/portal/index.php?option=com_content&task=view&id=3757&Itemid=211 (accessed 30 May 2009).

Gillwald, A. 2004. "Transforming Telecom Reform: Lessons from Africa." Presented at a meeting of the International Telecommunications Union (ITU), "Africa Telecom 2004," Cairo, Plenary Session 1: Policy Visions, 4–7 May.

Gillwald, A., and S. Esselaar. 2004. *South African 2004 ICT Sector Performance Review*. LINK Centre Public Policy Research Paper no. 7, University of the Witwatersrand.

Harber, A. 2006. "Hold That Pen, Mr President." http://www.big.co.za/wordpress/2006/02/28/hold-that-pen-mr-president/ (accessed 30 May 2009).

Hassen, F. 2004. "Presentation on Final Editorial Policies." Lecture, Rhodes University, August 2004. http://journ.ru.ac.za/staff/guy/Teaching/Policy/policy04/policies_rhodes_august 2004.ppt (accessed 30 May 2009).

Holomisa, B. 2002. "Broadcasting Bill Threatens Public Interest." *Sowetan,* 18 September. http://www.udm.org.za/statements_dir2002/assocs/broadcasting_am mendment_bill_recipe_for_disaster.htm (accessed 30 May 2009).

Horwitz, R. 2001a. "'Negotiated Liberalization': Stakeholder Politics and Communication Sector Reform in South Africa." http://arxiv.org/abs/cs/0109097 (accessed 30 May 2009).

———. 2001b. *Communication and Democratic Reform in South Africa.* Cambridge: Cambridge University Press.

Horwitz, R. B. 1997. "Telecommunications Policy in the New South Africa: Participatory Politics and Sectoral Reform." *Media, Culture and Society* 9:553.

Independent Broadcasting Authority. 1995. List of submissions received for the Triple Inquiry into Public Broadcasting, Local Content and Cross Media Control. http://www.Icasa.org.za/Default.aspx?page=1271&moduledata=577 (accessed 30 May 2009).

———. 1996. *Triple Inquiry into Cross Media Ownership, Local Content and South African Music and the Protections and Viability of Public Broadcasting Services.* www .icasa.org.za (accessed 30 May 2009).

Independent Communications Authority of South Africa. 2002. Submission on Broadcasting Amendment Bill Final, 18 September. http://www.Icasa.org.za/Default.aspx?page=1537&moduledata=972 (accessed 30 May 2009).

———. 2005a. "Decision on the Application by the South African Broadcasting Corporation Limited for the Amendment of Its Broadcasting Licences in Terms of Section 22 of the Broadcasting Act, Act 4 of 1999 2 February 2005." http://guyberger.ru.ac.za/Teaching/Policy/2006.htm (accessed May 30, 2009).

——— 2005b. "Licence Conditions." http://guyberger.ru.ac.za/Teaching/Policy/sabc1/SABCLicences2005.pdf (accessed 30 May 2009).

Media Development and Diversity Agency. 2009. "Trends of Ownership and Control of Media in South Africa." Unpublished report for the Media Development and Diversity Agency, Johannesburg.

Minnie, J. 2000. "The Growth of Independent Broadcasting in South Africa: Lessons for Africa." In *African Broadcast Cultures: Radio in Transition, ed. R. Fardon and G. Furniss,* 174–79. London: James Currey.

Msomi, S. 2004. "SABC Still Favours Rich, Urban Viewers." *Sunday Times,* 19 September. http://www.sundaytimes.co.za/Articles/TarkArticle.aspx?ID1253534 (accessed 30 May 2009).

Mpofu, D. 2006. "SABC Unveils New Strategic Outlook and Executive Structure." SABC Corporate Communications, 1 May. http://www.sabc.co.za/portal/binary/com.epicentric.contentmanagement.connectors.cda.CDADisplay Servlet?connectorID=cda&moid=43397b9d6c8ba010VgnVCM10000030d4 ea9bRCRD (accessed 30 May 2009).

Netshitenzhe, J. 2004. "Media Ethics, Politics and Social Transformation: Gujrat,

Commissions and Weapons of Mass Destruction." Speech to the SANEF/Multi-Choice Ten-Year Media Review Seminar by Joel Netshitenzhe, GCIS CEO, 13 August 2004.

OMD. 2005. *South African Media Facts.* Johannesburg: OMD Media.

Open Society Foundation—South Africa. 2007. *Meeting Their Mandates? A Critical Analysis of South African Media Statutory Bodies.* Cape Town: Media Programme of Open Society Foundation for South Africa. www.osf.org.za/File_Uploads/docs/MeetigtheirMandates.pdf (accessed 15 June 2009).

Republic of South Africa. 2002a. Broadcasting Amendment Bill, 2002. http://www.info.gov.za/gazette/bills/2002/23745.pdf (accessed 30 May 2009).

———. 2002b. Broadcasting Amendment Bill. B-34d-2002. http://www.info.gov.za/gazette/bills/2002/b34d-02.pdf (accessed 30 May 2009).

———. 2003. Broadcasting Amendment Act, 2002. *Government Gazette,* 4 February, no. 24340. http://www.info.gov.za.

Sisulu, G., and G. Marcus. 2006. *South African Broadcasting Corporation Commission of Enquiry into Blacklisting and Related Matters Report.* http://www.fxi.org.za/pages/<edia%20n%20ICTs/SABCComplaint/SABCBLACKLISTREPORT.pdf (accessed 19 July 2010).

Smuts, D. 2002. "Broadcasting Requires Neutral Regulator." *Business Day,* 28 October.

South African Broadcasting Corporation. 2004. Application for Amendment of SABC Licences in terms of Section 22 of the Broadcasting Act Number 4 of 1999. 31 March 2004 http://guyberger.ru.ac.za/Teaching/Policy/2006.htm (accessed 30 May 2009).

South African National Editors' Forum. 2003. "SANEF Comment on SABC Editorial Policies." http://guyberger.ru.ac.za/fulltext/SanefonABCpolicies.doc (accessed 19 July 2010).

South African Press Association. 2002. "SABC 'Will Not Be a Propaganda Tool.'" *Herald Online.* http://www.theherald.co.za/herald/2002/09/17/news/n16_1709 2002.htm (accessed 16 June 2009).

Stones, L. 2007. "Broadcast Digital Upgrade Will Boost Jobs and Skills." *Business Day,* 1 February.

Tleane, C., and J. Duncan. 2003. *Public Broadcasting in the Era of Cost Recovery: A Critique of the South African Broadcasting Corporation's Crisis of Accountability.* Johannesburg: Freedom of Expression Institute.

Van den Broek, E. 2006. "Sex, Drugs and the Dutch Social Model." In *Beyond the European Social Model. OpenEurope.org.* http://www.openeurope.org.uk/research/6broek.pdf (accessed 30 May 2009).

Wasserman, H. 2004. "The Last Word: All the News That Is Fit to Sell? Media Freedom, Commercialism and a Decade of Democracy." *Communicare* 23, no. 2: 139–48.

Contributors

Neville Alexander is Director of the Project for the Study of Alternative Education in South Africa (PRAESA).

Janine Aron is a research officer in the Department of Economics, Oxford University.

Guy Berger is Professor of Journalism and Media Studies at Rhodes University, South Africa.

Anthony Butler is Professor of Political Studies at the University of the Witwatersrand, South Africa.

Marianne Camerer, a 2005 Yale World Fellow, is co-founder and International Director of Global Integrity (www.globalintegrity.org).

David Dyzenhaus is Professor of Law and Philosophy at the University of Toronto.

Theuns Eloff is Vice-chancellor at North-West University, Potchefstroom, South Africa.

Courtney Jung is Professor of Political Science at the University of Toronto.

Robert Mattes is Professor in the Department of Political Studies and Director of the Centre for Social Science Research at the University of Cape Town, South Africa.

Nicoli Nattrass is Professor of Economics at the University of Cape Town, South Africa.

Lungisile Ntsebeza is Professor and Incumbent of the NRF Research Chair, Land Reform and Democracy in South Africa, Department of Sociology, at the University of Cape Town, South Africa.

Lauren Paremoer is a doctoral candidate at the New School for Social Research, New York.

Jeremy Seekings is Professor of Political Studies and Sociology at the University of Cape Town, South Africa.

Ian Shapiro is Sterling Professor of Political Science at Yale University, New Haven, and Henry R. Luce Director of the Macmillan Center for International and Area Studies.

Kahreen Tebeau is a doctoral candidate at Yale University, New Haven.

Index

Italicized page numbers indicate figures and tables.